A Special Kind of Courage

Chris Ryder is an author, journalist and broadcaster. He was formerly Northern Ireland Correspondent for the *Sunday Times* and *Daily Telegraph*. He also broadcasts frequently on radio and television. His previous books include *Drumcree: The Orange Order's Last Stand*, *Inside the Maze: The Untold Story of the Northern Ireland Prison Service, The RUC: A Force Under Fire* and *The Fateful Split: Catholics and the Royal Ulster Constabulary*.

Also by Chris Ryder
available from Methuen

Inside the Maze: The Untold Story of the Northern Ireland Prison Service

The Fateful Split: Catholics and the Royal Ulster Constabulary

With Vincent Kearney
Drumcree: The Orange Order's Last Stand

A SPECIAL KIND OF COURAGE

321 EOD Squadron – Battling the Bombers

Chris Ryder

Methuen

Published by Methuen 2006

10 9 8 7 6 5 4 3 2 1

First published in hardcover 2005
Revised edition with a new Postscript first published in paperback 2006

Methuen Publishing Ltd
11–12 Buckingham Gate, London SW1E 6LB
www.methuen.co.uk

Copyright © Chris Ryder 2005, 2006

The right of Chris Ryder to be identified as author of this work has been asserted
by him in accordance with the Copyrights, Designs and Patents Act 1988

A CIP catalogue record for this book is available from the British Library

Methuen Publishing Limited Reg. No. 3543167

ISBN 10: 0-413-77567-4
ISBN 13: 978-0-413-77567-2

Typeset by SX Composing DTP, Rayleigh, Essex
Printed and bound in Great Britain by Bookmarque Ltd, Croydon, Surrey

Contents

For Harry and Liz Castles

Foreword

I first encountered at first hand the skills, bravery and panache of the Army's bomb-disposal teams in East Belfast in 1971. My platoon was billeted in St Matthew's Church Hall on the Newtonards Road. One evening someone threw a home-made grenade at the building. It hit the wall beside the door and bounced into the alley. We called for ATO (the Ammunition Technical Officer, affectionately known as Felix). It was a time of many explosions in the city and so it was many minutes before he arrived. He dismounted from his vehicle, took one look at the grenade and said rather disparagingly: 'Oh, it's another of *them* – they don't work.' With that he picked it up, pulled it apart and departed to the next task, urging me on no account to have a go myself if I came across another one.

As you will discover from this remarkable book, the bomb-disposal men at the start of the campaign were long on courage, resourcefulness and skill, but they were short on technical equipment. Much of their dangerous work had to be done in very close contact with the devices they were attempting to make safe. But with the help of the scientific and research communities, the ATOs became the best equipped, best trained and most skilled bomb-disposal officers in the world. The world-famous Wheelbarrow was perhaps the most decisive element in their toolkit, because it allowed many of the most hazardous operations to be carried out remotely.

But as the equipment improved, so too did the skill and ingenuity of the terrorist. Over the next thirty or so years terrorist and ATO each tried to be one step ahead of the other. The terrorist's aim was the destruction of life and property; the ATO's was to protect life and property, and the ATO had to try to beat the bomber every time. In this history you will read of the successes and failures, and of the tragedies too. Because no matter how good the equipment and skills, there were always those occasions when time or luck ran out.

The British Army's Ammunition Technical community has suffered disproportionately large numbers of casualties over the years in Northern

Ireland. It has also very deservedly attracted disproportionately large numbers of gallantry awards. No matter how well equipped the ATO might be, there always came the moment when the heavy protective suit had to be donned, the device approached at very close quarters, and there in the most lonely of positions, the final act of making the device safe. Thus ended the 'long walk' and the ATO without fuss would bring the incident to an end as if he had done nothing at all out of the ordinary. Those of us who were privileged to watch them at their work have no doubt at all that their long list of distinguished gallantry awards is the very least they deserved.

But I know that the ATOs themselves would be disappointed if I did not also mention the men and women without whom they could not have operated. They needed drivers, close protection, and a variety of technical specialist assistants. These were closely knit teams that would respond in seconds to a call for assistance; they lived together and took on the terrorist together. Sometimes there would be so many calls that there would hardly be enough time to eat, let alone sleep. At other times there would be long periods of boredom, waiting for the call that never came. It was a life living on the edge for all of them.

The bomb-disposal teams have over the years made an incalculable contribution to the creation of a more peaceful Northern Ireland. The people of the Province owe them an enormous debt, a debt repaid in considerable measure by this remarkable and stirring record of their exploits and courage. During the course of numerous tours of duty in Northern Ireland I have had very many ATOs and their teams under my command. It has been a privilege and I am delighted that this book stands testimony to an inspirational record of public service.

Lieutenant-General Sir Alistair Irwin KCB CBE
General Officer Commanding Northern Ireland 2000–3

Author's Note

For most people, the Special Forces are the ultimate example of bravery and daring-do against impossible odds. Usually outnumbered and operating behind enemy lines, they track and lethally confront their targets or storm an Embassy or aircraft and free hundreds of hostages from the deadly grip of hijackers or suicide bombers. But there is another elite cadre among the armed forces whose exceptional bravery is not so widely acknowledged. Because of their professionalism in detecting terrorist bombs and rendering them safe before they can kill or maim, bomb-disposal officers are relatively unsung heroes.

This book tells their story, tracing the development of rudimentary bomb disposal from the end of the Second World War to the age of IEDD (Improvised Explosive Device Disposal), as the experts call it. The principal focus is on the personal courage and sacrifice of the members of 321 Explosives Ordnance Disposal Squadron, Royal Logistics Corps. Whatever the sophistication of modern equipment, such as the 'Pigstick' disrupter and the 'Wheelbarrow' robot, the 'Mark One human eyeball' remains the most reliable guarantee that a bomb has been neutralised.

Mere words are inadequate to record the special kind of courage demonstrated by the 1,000 or so soldiers who have served in the ranks of 321 EOD in Northern Ireland since 1969, when the longest ever continuous campaign in the history of the British Army began. It would be impractical to describe or even list the 54,000 bomb incidents they have attended over the years and impossible to record all the exploits of the individuals involved. In any case, many of them are as modest as they are brave. So in writing this book, I have attempted to give a representative account of the devices and dangers the EOD teams encountered and the skill and bravery with which they handled them. Inevitably the ATOs, who make 'the long walk' to deal with bombs at close quarters, are the centrepiece of the story but they would be unable to function without the support of the other members of their teams and the back-up drivers and escorts, technicians and mechanics, search teams and others who ensure that everything they require is in place and in order.

I am in awe of the courage of the EOD experts I have met and privileged to write this account of their battle with the bombers. I must express my sincere thanks and gratitude to a number of people whose co-operation and frankness enabled me to compile the raw material and made the book possible: Lieutenant-General Sir Alistair Irwin KCB CBE, General Officer Commanding Northern Ireland 2000–3, encouraged the idea and contributed a fitting foreword; Colonel Steve Smith, Principal Ammunition Technical Officer, Lieutenant-Colonel Alex Boyd and Major Jim Convery smoothed the way for me to gain access to vital records and individuals to tell the story; WO2 Jon Dixon and Staff Sergeant Eddie Cochrane produced the material and answered every query; Major Martin Pope and Captain Colin Whitworth at 321 EOD Headquarters provided information and introductions of inestimable value; Majors Jane Brown and John Hipkins and Corporal Tony Hitchman of the Royal Military Police also facilitated my research.

My gratitude is also due to Mervyn Wynne Jones, Major Tim David and the staff at the Defence Press Office in Northern Ireland, and Captain Paul Snape. I must also acknowledge the assistance of Dr Anthony Morton and the staff at the RLC Museum, Camberley, the National Archives at Kew, the Public Record Office, Northern Ireland, Andrea Frazer of Soldier magazine and Walter Macauley, the Belfast Telegraph's unsurpassable librarian.

Mick Coldrick, Mike Dolamore, John Gaff, Sarah Gatheridge, Chris and Victoria Henson, Aminul Islam, Ivor Wynne Jones, Mike Knox, Shirley Lyle, Malcolm Mackenzie-Orr, Ian Magee, Hugh McCormack, Alan McQuillan, Rev. Mick Micklethwaite, Peter Miller, Paul Myring, Seamus O'Brien, Margaret Pattinson, Rod Roberts, Jean Sheard, George Styles, Alan Swindley, Andy Wallace and Michael Walsh and family as well as the officers at SO13 in the Metropolitan Police all assisted me in different ways for which I thank them. Sir Ronnie Flanagan GBE and his officers at the WERU provided me with valuable data for which I am also most grateful. Peter Birchall's *The Longest Walk* (Arms and Armour Press, 1997) was a most useful source of reference.

Above all I must express my deep appreciation to Major Ian Jones for his towering assistance, introductions and advice as well as for reading the draft manuscript. I am indebted on an equally elevated scale to Lieutenant-Colonel Mark Wickham for sharing his own experiences, facilitating research and, from the jaws of the deadly conflict in Iraq, taking the time to read and communicate his views on the draft manuscript.

Inevitably I have not been able to incorporate everything into the book so I apologise for the omissions and stress that, much as I appreciate the help of all my sources, the conclusions I draw about events are, of course, mine.

I must thank my agents, Anthony Goff and Georgia Glover at David Higham Associates, Max Eilenberg at Methuen, for commissioning the book, Eleanor Rees, who edited the text with her customary incisive skill, speed and insight, and the staff at Methuen, who produced it.

Finally, I must not forget to acknowledge the enduring tolerance and support of my wife, Genny, who continues to cheerfully accept my preoccupations with 'the book' and lets me get on with it. Michelle, Paul, Declan and Edward are, as ever, interested in progress, and the bon mots of Ciara and Erin, my beloved granddaughters, provide welcome distraction.

Chris Ryder
March 2005

Acknowledgements

The author and publisher acknowledge with thanks the permissions granted to use the text extracts and illustrations included within this publication. Every effort has been made to trace copyright owners, and permission has been obtained from: the Defence Press Office Northern Ireland; The National Archives, London; Hastings Hotels; Lieutenant-Colonel Eric Wakeling (ret'd); Royal Engineers Bomb Disposal Club; and HarperCollins Publishers.

Introduction

The Grim Reaper Calls

Improvised explosive devices (IEDs) are devices placed or fabricated in an improvised manner incorporating destructive, lethal, noxious, pyrotechnic or incendiary chemicals, designed to kill, destroy, disfigure, distract or harass.

British Army definition of a terrorist bomb

Explosive Ordnance Disposal (EOD) operators are reminded that all Improvised Explosive Devices (IEDs) are the product of terrorist ingenuity and although, outwardly, a device may resemble a well-tried or proven model, internal changes such as anti-handling devices, collapsing circuits and other modifications may be encountered. Familiarity with the external appearance should not produce the automatic response that the device is unchanged internally.

Extract from training notes for British Army bomb disposal teams

We do not ask who planted the bomb or why. We simply put ourselves between the device and the public and get on with the job.

A senior bomb disposal officer

One evening in September 1982, Sergeant Paul Myring was settling into new quarters at Hereford in the English Midlands when the telephone rang. On the line from the British Army's operational headquarters at Wilton, near Salisbury, was the 'Grim Reaper', so called because he plotted the postings of bomb-disposal officers throughout the organisation. 'I was told there was an unscheduled vacancy in Northern Ireland, it needed to be filled urgently and I was going over for six months.'

The summons came as a complete surprise. After completing a two-year posting in Germany, Myring had been advised he would not be asked to undertake what was always a demanding and hazardous tour of duty there for at least a couple of years. 'I had been married in 1978 and now that we were back in England for a time, we had intended to start a family,' he recalls. But, well used to the exigencies of military life after seven years' service, he promptly put his personal affairs in order, said goodbye to his wife and, a couple of days later, reported to the Army School of Ammunition at Kineton in Warwickshire.

Myring was already a fully qualified and experienced Ammunition Technician (AT), whose job it was to ensure the safe storage and handling of all ammunition and explosives used by the British Army from bullets to guided missiles. ATs are also responsible for disposing of explosives and for counter-terrorist bomb disposal and it was this line of work that was taking him to Northern Ireland. Even so, before beginning his emergency assignment, he had to complete the standard, preoperational course updating and testing his knowledge of the latest terrorist bombs, intelligence and sharpening his wits for the life-threatening trials that lay ahead. This was done at the Felix Centre in Kineton, where bomb-disposal officers from all over the world are trained to deal with ever more complex terrorist weapons and tactics, such as those used by Republican and Loyalist terrorists in Northern Ireland, where conflict had been raging for almost fifteen years.

Three busy weeks later, in the late morning of 6 October, Myring flew from Birmingham to Aldergrove airport, a dozen miles from Belfast, where he was discreetly picked up by a driver in plain clothes and taken to his new base, a heavily fortified barracks at Magherafelt, County Londonderry. There the detachment of 321 Explosive Ordnance Disposal Unit, Royal Army Ordnance Corps shared accommodation with another British Army formation, a battalion of the locally recruited Ulster Defence Regiment.

On his arrival, Myring was taken directly to the Magherafelt base operations room to meet the people he would be working with and the other members of the four-strong bomb-disposal team he would command. In the role of 'Number One', he would be primarily responsible for leading them safely through the complexities of any clearance operation to which they were tasked. His right-hand man, the 'Number Two', would assist him in deploying equipment when dealing with suspect devices. The third team member, the 'Bleep', was from the Royal Signals. He would operate the top-secret electronic countermeasures equipment to protect them all from the state-of-the-art radio-controlled devices periodically deployed against them by the outlawed Irish Republican Army. The fourth member of the team was an armed infantryman whose job it was to provide them with armed protection when travelling to and from call-outs and while deployed on the ground in the vicinity of a suspect bomb. In practice, they were also further protected at incident scenes by a support force of infantry, search specialists and, usually, the police.

About the same time as Myring was travelling to the barracks from the airport, at about 2.15 p.m., a couple of miles away a farmer started to pull open a sliding door on one of the outbuildings at his Lime Hill farm near Pomeroy. He had good reason to be cautious moving about his smallholding, for as a part-time private in the Ulster Defence Regiment, giving up several nights a week and regular weekends to go out on patrol as part of the Army's unrelenting effort to deter or capture terrorists, he was a prime IRA target. Thus, when he spotted a strand of fishing wire extending in front of him as he slid open the barn door, the man was immediately suspicious and ran inside his house nearby to raise the alarm.

A short time later, at 3.20 p.m., the direct-line 'tasking telephone' rang in Magherafelt barracks. Myring, welcoming cup of coffee still in hand, dressed in civilian clothing and his suitcases not yet unpacked, reached for the handset. It was the watch-keeper in the 8 Brigade operations room at Ebrington Barracks in Londonderry. Myring looked at his watch. 'I had been in post for precisely twenty-five minutes,' he recalls, claiming the record for what he says is still the fastest 'flash to bang' in the history of 321.

Myring abandoned the remains of his coffee, changed into his combats and clambered into the first of the two heavily-armoured Transit EOD vehicles drawn up outside. Ten minutes later, with blue emergency lights flashing, the convoy pulled out of the base into the gathering darkness and miserable uncertainty of a bleak, drizzly Northern Ireland afternoon. As they travelled, he turned over in his mind all that he had recently been reminded about the need for caution approaching the area, the risk of gunmen lying in wait to ambush the vehicles, the possibility of a secondary bomb having been placed underneath the road and the odds on successfully defusing any bomb and coming away with his life and limbs intact. Although he had earlier served in Northern Ireland, this was his first tour as a Number One with ultimate responsibility for his own safety and that of his team members and escorts. He reflected on their families and his own, safely back at home in England, far away from the sectarian tension and political division in Northern Ireland, the ruthless gunmen and bombers and the fiery politicians who seemed unable to agree on anything despite the endless funerals and the daily destruction.

Once at the scene, after nearly an hour's journey, such thoughts were banished. The emphasis now had to be concentration on the task in hand, checking if the main device was merely a come-on to lure him into the path of another cunningly concealed bomb nearby, or if it incorporated a booby-trap designed to kill or maim him once he thought it had been safely neutralised.

From his preliminary reconnaissance, Myring had already decided the gap in the shed between the open door and wall was too narrow to send in the remotely controlled 'Wheelbarrow' which would have allowed him to inspect the device through its closed-circuit television, diagnose its type, size and construction and attack it from a safe distance. Instead, he would be obliged to make a 'manual approach' to the bomb, exposing himself to the danger of it going off, or of setting off a tripwire or detonating it accidentally while working to neutralise the circuitry. He put on the heavy EOD (Explosive Ordnance Disposal) suit, a garment made of Kevlar with glass-reinforced plastic plates to protect the front and rear of the torso, and a toughened helmet, clicking down the clear visor to shield his face. His Number Two checked that all the pieces were in place and fastened the leggings. Bomb-disposal operators joke that the suit is really intended to keep them in one piece for burial if a bomb detonates, but, despite its weight and bulk, the way it restricts their movements and their body heat steams up the visor, they endure the discomfort for it is the only protection available.

Around him he next gathered the working equipment he would need: his personal electronic countermeasures box, the radio through which he would give a commentary to his colleagues, a mini 'Pigstick' disruptor, designed to fracture the timing and firing mechanism of a bomb before it could detonate the explosive, and a few basic tools including a hook and line. When he could not find a spare finger to clasp a torch, the Number Two said he had an idea and speedily produced a roll of heavy-duty adhesive tape with which he lashed the torch to one of his Number One's forearms.

At that point Myring set out on what the bomb disposal officers call 'the long walk', the lonely approach to a bomb through a sterile security zone along a cleared street or a sealed country lane or, in this case, across a deserted farmyard into a dark barn where all sorts of unseen dangers could have been created. It was a lonely task, for a strict 'one-man risk' rule had been introduced after earlier incidents when more than one ATO inspecting a device had been caught in an explosion.

The first part of the journey was uneventful and he stopped at the door to inspect the ground immediately ahead by torchlight. He could clearly see the thin length of fishing line glinting in the gloom as it snaked across the ground to a green twenty-five-litre oil drum placed at the back of the sliding door, a metre from the wall. He recognised at once the sort of device it was. As the door was slid open, the fishing line attached to it was designed to tighten and pull a small piece of rounded wooden dowel from the jaws of a spring-loaded clothes peg, completing an electronic circuit. The resulting surge through the timer-power unit would have set off a detonator embedded in explosive inside the drum, killing or injuring anyone close by.

Myring shone the torch around the building looking for another bomb or wire that might indicate further danger. Having satisfied himself that there was nothing obviously present, he was preparing to approach the bomb cautiously when the torch slid from his forearm and tumbled across the ground, the beam of light shining directly into his eyes. Unable to see anything, including the lethal length of fishing line, he carefully retrieved the torch and entered the building, taking great care not to disturb the dangling cord as he stepped over it. He again inspected the interior by torchlight and gingerly set down his equipment before commencing a closer examination of the oil drum. All the time, working from the cramped desk in his vehicle parked close by, the Bleep was scanning the radio frequency spectrum for any warning signs that bombers were active in the area, preserving a protective electronic bubble against any incoming radio signal which could detonate the bomb.

Terrorist bombs are known as improvised explosive devices (IEDs) within the bomb-disposal profession to distinguish them from ordnance and munitions rigorously manufactured to consistent factory standards. Over the years, ATOs have developed about 150 designated actions which make up their 'render-safe procedure', each action numbered for recording on the report form completed after every incident. Procedures are constantly reviewed and updated to take account of every move the terrorists make in laying their ambushes and every modification they incorporate in their bombs.

In this case, having again checked for anything untoward and scanned the immediate area with his personal electronic countermeasures pack, Myring first turned his attention to the timer-power unit attached to the oil drum. If it could be successfully neutralised, the entire bomb could probably be prevented from exploding. The mini-Pigstick was the piece of equipment specifically designed for this – it would aim a pressurised water slug at the heart of the device. Myring set it up and withdrew to a safe distance. Standard operating procedure required that he did not approach the bomb again for thirty minutes to ensure that no secondary device had been set running. After this pause, he made another approach and inspection. With the timer-power unit well and truly shattered, he X-rayed the drum and after completing a range of other technical and visual checks, he turned his attention to clearing it.

Although the disruption of the timer-power unit had theoretically rendered the device safe, Myring knew all too well that there was still a great potential for danger. An anti-handling device could have been installed to set off the explosive in the drum if it was moved. The explosive could be unstable. There could even be a secondary booby-trap device, triggered by the disruption of the first, waiting for the unwary ATO. Having encountered these scenarios in ever-changing combinations before, military scientists had developed another piece of equipment to help. This one was called Flatsword and it was capable of cleanly severing metal oil drums, milk churns, gas cylinders, beer kegs and other containers favoured by the terrorists as containers for explosives. So Myring set up the blade and retired to operate it, again from a safe distance. Half an hour later he returned to inspect the results and found the drum neatly severed and the white explosive spilled out across the floor. The successful ATO never takes anything for granted, so, yet again, Myring X-rayed the debris, carried out the electronic countermeasures routines and, using his torch, conducted one final visual check before giving the all clear.

The whole operation took just over four hours. When it was completed, Myring was able to tell the fortunate part-time soldier that if he had pulled the fishing line by just another eighth of an inch, it would have snapped the dowel out of the clothes peg and triggered the explosive: 20 lb. of home-made explosive with a 5 lb. booster charge and five metres of detonating cord. The timer-power unit comprised an electric detonator of Republic of Ireland origin, a modified Memopark timer (designed to remind motorists when their parking meter would expire) and two batteries.

As his assistants helped Myring strip off his heavy protective suit, the Number Two asked how his idea of strapping the torch to his arm had worked. 'It didn't,' grinned Myring. 'It fell off. From now on you keep your bloody ideas to yourself.' The successful clearance at Lime Hill Farm was one of 1,135 similar operations conducted by members of 321 EOD Unit, Royal Army Ordnance Corps in 1982 and counts among the 54,000 bomb-disposal call-outs answered between 1970 and the present day, the equivalent of one every six hours. In some cases, the terrorists gave no warning and all the bomb-disposal officers could do was declare an area safe for the recovery of bodies, but in many more instances lives were protected and property saved because of the formidable bravery and heroic professionalism of the men, and nowadays women, who selflessly pit their wits and their personal safety against the terrorists. On many occasions they have had to deal with false alarms, alerts caused by someone innocently leaving a parcel behind on a bus or in a pub, but there have been equally many malicious hoaxes intended to instil fear, cause disruption and force a bomb-disposal officer to make the long walk, for, of course, all such devices have to be treated as live until proved otherwise.

The people of Northern Ireland have suffered a considerable toll of death, injury and destruction at the hands of the bombers over the thirty-five years of the 'Troubles'. In that time there have been nearly 19,000 explosions and incendiary attacks, an average of one every seventeen hours, and some fifty tons of explosive have been detonated or neutralised in another 6,300 incidents. The human and financial cost would have been compounded manyfold without the exceptional courage and skill of the thousand or so people who have served in the ranks of 321 over the last three decades. Notwithstanding its size – there have never been more than one hundred personnel on the ground at any given time – it is by far the most decorated unit in the British Army because of its unyielding commitment to preserve lives and protect property. In so doing, twenty brave bomb-disposal officers have been murdered.

This is the story of how the men and women of what is presently called 321 EOD Squadron, Royal Logistics Corps display a special kind of courage in carrying out their exceptional role in combating the conflict in Northern Ireland. In this, the longest continuous campaign ever conducted by the British Army, 655 soldiers and 302 police officers have died as a result of terrorist activity since 1969.

Chapter One

Sooners or Laters

Around the year 1250 Roger Bacon, an English-born Franciscan friar, philosopher and scientist, worked out that a fusion of potassium nitrate, charcoal and sulphur created a powerful propellant explosive. Although there is evidence that the Chinese contemporaneously developed similar compounds, Bacon is generally credited with the invention of what became known as gunpowder. The breakthrough transformed the nature of military conflict for it enabled enemies to engage more lethally from a distance but, as it was such a highly volatile substance, it required careful handling by experts. Another six hundred years passed before the Swedish chemist Alfred Nobel perfected a means of stabilising the ingredients and producing an even more powerful explosive, which he called 'dynamite'. A few years later, in 1875, he produced another explosive, a water-resistant and virtually fume free combination of nitro-glycerine, ethylene glycol dinitrate, nitrocellulose and either sodium nitrate or ammonium nitrate, which Nobel designated 'gelignite'. Although it was relatively safe to handle by earlier standards, great care and expertise was still required in its use, handling and storage.

As far back as 1414, because of the inherent volatility of its gunpowder-based armaments, the Crown had appointed a Master (later Master-General) of Ordnance, based at the Tower of London. According to Brigadier AH Fernyhough's *Short History of the RAOC* (1980), one of his tasks was to transport and deploy gunpowder-based weapons and ammunition safely and securely. Much later, as Nobel's products were harnessed to producing ever more powerful hardware, responsibility for the supply and safety of military weapons, ammunition and explosives fell to the Army Ordnance Department, established in 1896. At the end of the First World War, when the potential of explosives was more fully exploited in conflict than ever before, this department amalgamated with the Army Ordnance Corps to form the Royal Army Ordnance Corps (RAOC), which went on to develop and enforce high standards for the storage and handling of munitions throughout the British Empire. The

RAOC was also responsible for disposal of unexploded shells and mortar bombs and, with the development of military aviation, neutralising enemy aircraft bombs which failed to detonate.

The Second World War brought even more significant advances in the size and complexity of lethal explosive devices and a rapid expansion in the volume of unexploded ordnance. Early in the conflict, German ships laid large quantities of mines in the waters around Britain and, from the autumn of 1940 onwards, they exploited their then overwhelming air-power with waves of saturation bombing raids on British cities designed to dishearten the civilian population and destroy the infrastructure of government vital to defending the island from invasion. With unexploded mines washing up on beaches, the introduction of time-delay bomb firing mechanisms and a 10 per cent failure rate in the fuses of devices dropped during the early stages of the Blitz, there were soon large numbers of unexploded bombs all over the country. Thus there developed an urgent need on a daunting scale for an entirely new and hazardous military skill: bomb disposal.

In the late 1930s, there had been some tentative discussion about the need for civil defence measures such as the issue of gas masks and the provision of air-raid shelters. According to Lieutenant-Colonel Eric Wakeling's *A Short History of Royal Engineer Bomb Disposal,* the problem had been entirely underestimated. There was, at first, no realisation of the probable need to deal with unexploded bombs and when the issue was raised, it was suggested that teams of specially trained Air Raid Precautions Wardens could be formed to collect and take them to the Army for disposal. When the folly of this was pointed out, it was simply proposed to blow the devices up where they had fallen. After experts explained this would cause damage on a scale as great as the enemy had intended, the decision was finally taken to ask the three armed services to develop specialised bomb-disposal teams. The Royal Navy was charged with keeping strategic sea lanes clear of mines and making safe those that had come ashore below the high-water mark, while the Royal Air Force had to deal with unexploded devices at its rapidly growing number of airfields.

The overwhelming burden of the new task fell on the Army but as the demands were well beyond the existing skills and capability of the Ordnance Corps alone, the Royal Engineers were ordered to gear up for it. In many ways they were ideally suited for the role with their engineering and construction knowledge, expertise in the applied use of explosives for demolition, facility with heavy equipment and ability to shore trenches. By May 1940, a Royal Engineers Bomb Disposal Unit was in command of twenty-five sixteen-man bomb-disposal sections, but as the inadequacy of this deployment became apparent, the establishment rapidly expanded and by July there were 220 teams. There was no specialised bomb-disposal equipment. Each was merely kitted out with picks and shovels, hammers and chisels, blocks and tackles, balls of string and a small quantity of explosive.

Under the operational pressures of war, effective expertise, techniques and some rudimentary equipment were developed to assist the operators but, as the public quickly came to realise and applaud, bomb disposal was a formidably risky occupation. The bomb-disposal operator became a heroic figure risking his life against the unpredictability of a potentially lethal device. At the peak of the Luftwaffe campaign, over a 287-day period between 21 September 1940 and 5 July 1941, 24,108 bombs were made safe but such was the intensity of the attacks that at times up to four thousand live bombs were waiting to be dealt with. By the end of the war, the Royal Engineers, according to Wakeling, had dealt with 45,441 bombs and another 6,983 'butterfly' anti-personnel bombs. In the process 490 members of their bomb-disposal units were killed and another 209 injured. Thirteen George Crosses, 111 George Medals and fourteen MBEs were awarded for outstanding bravery in completing bomb-disposal tasks.

The RAOC played an essential part in the Second World War. Starting with a nucleus of a few hundred officers and a few thousand men of the Regular and Territorial Army, within four years it expanded to an organisation of 8,000 officers and 130,000 men. Commanded by the Ordnance Directorate in the War Office, the corps operated supply bases in the United Kingdom for the provision of stores and services, vehicles of every type, ammunition and explosives to forward distribution points in the theatres of conflict around the world. Close to combat lines, the corps organised Ordnance Field Parks, ammunition and stores depots and maintenance and even mobile laundry and bath units. They also provided units to run ports and railways and provide industrial gas although when the corps of Royal Electrical and Mechanical Engineers (REME) was created in 1942, responsibility for the repair, recovery and manufacture of a large range of equipment was transferred.

The end of the global conflict in 1945 brought little respite for the practitioners of bomb disposal. As much of the swollen wartime Army was demobbed, their former barracks and vast storage and training areas had to be cleared of unexploded ordnance before being handed back for civilian use. Clearing the rubble and debris from urban bomb sites frequently exposed high-explosive relics of the war and rebuilding had to be halted until they could be made safe. The work sometimes took days and required the evacuation of surrounding areas for safety reasons, attracting interest from newspapers which regaled their readers with dramatic accounts of the battle of nerves between the lonely bomb-disposal operators and the highly unstable devices they were now having to deal with.

As the Second World War had progressed, effective bomb-disposal techniques and rudimentary equipment had been developed. In the summer of 1949, the War Office established a joint-service committee to oversee the standardisation of procedures and the development of new equipment. Among the items on the shopping list were a purpose-designed electrical stethoscope and a carbon monoxide indicator. There was also a requirement to redesign or improve items hastily produced during the war. For instance, operators badly wanted a proper submersible pump to drain water away as they excavated buried bombs and improved means of field photography so that they could carefully examine devices' inner workings before going up close to defuse them. It was suggested that the new technology of television might be of some use.

By 1953, much remained to be done. One shortcoming was the lack of intelligence about the sort of bombs likely to be encountered in any future conflict. The prospect of dealing with unexploded nuclear missiles, from either enemy action or accident, had also begun to figure in deliberations, but in 1956 the joint chiefs of staff ruled that nuclear bomb disposal was far too sensitive and specialised to be entrusted to anyone other than the people who had designed the devices. The topic did not remain closed, however, and there were those who continued to campaign for the bomb-disposal role to be widened to include the entire range of weapons. Discussing the relative dangers for an operator between defusing a conventional bomb or a nuclear missile, a paper prepared in October 1957 for the Under-Secretary of State for War said that 'to the individual', apart from the hazard of primary radiation peculiar to nuclear weapons, 'it is no more dangerous to risk a big bang than a little one.' In 1961, the Executive Committee of the Army Board commissioned another review of bomb disposal, including how it would be organised in any future war. They argued that as much of the 'Atomic Secret' classification had since been removed, sufficient 'Secret' details could now be made available to enable the nuclear disposal task to be undertaken by existing bomb-disposal officers.

During the post-war deliberations, the Royal Engineers had jealously defended their lead role in bomb disposal. They headed the Joint Service Bomb Disposal Organisation and training school at Broadbridge Heath in Sussex and maintained a sixty-six-strong Bomb Disposal Unit which was responsible for clearing the regular ongoing finds of wartime devices. Meanwhile, the RAOC had 125 ammunition personnel in the UK dedicated to the day-to-day task of ensuring the safety of the Army's ammunition and responsible for the disposal of 'stray' ammunition, aircraft cannon shells and any rogue guided weapons.

The rivalry between the two corps was not confined to home soil. After the war, internal disorder erupted in several British colonies, such as Malaya, Cyprus, Borneo and Aden, and the government in London deployed troops to put down uprisings and combat guerrilla warfare very much on the pattern established by the IRA in Ireland during the War of Independence, 1919–21. The RAOC argued strongly that disposing of terrorist booby-traps and explosive devices was for their specially trained Inspecting Ordnance Officers and Ammunition Examiners rather than the Royal Engineers: 'RE personnel are not specially trained to dismantle complicated explosive devices and normally they clear the devices in situ having cleared the area and taken precautions to minimise the effect of the explosion. The resultant damage must be accepted in the interests of safety.' They stressed the need to render devices safe, recover evidence and work in close co-operation with the civil police, but in a tart response on 27 April 1960, a lieutenant-colonel responded: 'The facts are that RE by virtue of their general knowledge of the use of explosives and demolitions are called upon from time to time to deal with explosive devices.'

The RAOC's claim to the job was heavily staked on their record during the Greek–Turkish confrontation in Cyprus from 1955 to 1959, 'the first emergency in which EOD or bomb disposal was a widespread and continuous problem', according to Fernyhough. During the period, EOKA (the National Association of Greek Cypriot Fighters), headed by the elusive Colonel George Grivas, made good use of sabotage methods widely disseminated during the Second World War and waged a widespread guerrilla campaign in support of their demand for *Enosis*, complete unity with Greece against the wishes of the Turkish Cypriot minority. One priority for the bomb-disposal operators during the Cyprus campaign was to dismantle devices so that evidence could be gleaned to identify the bombers and assist the police in bringing them to justice. Over four years, RAOC Inspecting Ordnance Officers and Ammunition

Examiners, administratively seconded to the Cyprus government and police, investigated 4,300 explosions, dealt with 4,688 unexploded devices, including landmines and pipe bombs, and handled explosives captured in some 3,000 raids and searches. They were led by the legendary Major Harry Harrison, better known as 'Bomber', who once responded to 150 call-outs over a six-week period. He described bombs as 'sooners', those he got to before they went off, or 'laters', those he didn't get to in time.

Among the most spine-tingling of Harrison's many exploits was the removal of an explosive device from under the governor's bed in his official residence in Nicosia, the island's capital, in April 1956. One version of the episode has it that the bomb had been fitted with a trembler switch designed to set it off once the lofty Sir John Harding got into bed and stretched out his legs. However, a more authoritative account is contained in a despatch from Harding to the Colonial Office on 21 May in which he says the bomb did not function because the room heat failed to drop sufficiently to set off a temperature-sensitive firing mechanism. Harrison managed to manoeuvre the bomb on to a shovel and carry it outside where it was made safe and dismantled in a bid to unmask the EOKA sympathiser with access to the governor's quarters. It was a daring action that clinched the award of both an MBE and a George Medal for Harrison. Altogether two RAOC bomb-disposal personnel were killed and two injured doing their dangerous job in Cyprus and the team were awarded three more George Medals, two British Empire Medals and seven mentions in dispatches, one of which was posthumous.

Back in London, the turf war continued between the Royal Engineers and the Ordnance Corps over the delineation of responsibilities for the disposal of ammunition, explosives, aircraft bombs and missiles in the UK and a meeting was convened on 11 August 1961 to discuss the matter. A couple of days beforehand, a highly partisan briefing document was prepared at Broadbridge Heath Camp and forwarded to a colonel at the War Office so that he could make the RE case. Listing in detail its wide-ranging capability to clear enemy bombs, beach mines, blind anti-aircraft shells, pipe mines, training areas and guided missiles, the document concluded:

> The RAOC cannot do all these things. They have not the training, the men, nor the equipment. RE can take on anything, RAOC can not. The important point is that the police and public will get a better service

than if one arm of the service keeps passing the baby to another arm, which all leads to delay and frustration. Our case is that we can do it more quickly and more efficiently, using most of the same personnel, without troubling the RAOC, and also we can effect manpower savings. This will be a benefit to the public.

The meeting failed to end the rivalry. One key element of disagreement was who should be responsible for disposing of explosive devices in internal security operations, clearly the growth area now that post-war clearances were becoming less frequent. The Engineers were far from impressed by the RAOC's operations in Cyprus, claimed they were attributable to special circumstances and insisted they should not become the explosive ordnance blueprint for future emergencies. In support, they cited the War Office Code on Field Engineering and Mine Warfare which stated that the responsibility for the detection and clearance of traps rests primarily with the Engineers and infantry assault pioneers. 'It would be quite wrong to depart from this principle in internal security operations,' said an official minute dated 7 September 1961.

A full-scale summit to settle the issue was convened in the War Office on 29 September 1961. Opening the meeting, the chairman, the Principal Ammunition Technical Officer, RAOC, said the aim was to examine in detail the division of responsibilities between RE and RAOC for the disposal of British, allied and enemy ammunition, explosives, aircraft bombs and non-nuclear missiles. The meeting was told that in the previous two years there had been 8,965 reported incidents of which 8,582 had been dealt with by the RAOC. The RE had dealt with 1,239 incidents and passed another 182 to the RAOC. There was good progress in settling demarcation lines. The RAOC would continue to deal with 'stray' enemy ammunition while the RE, as they had been doing since 1940, would tackle aircraft bombs. There was also agreement about some key aspects of joint training and exchanging information about guided missiles, but the disagreement about the clearance of terrorist devices and booby-traps during internal security and emergency operations continued. The RAOC again staked a large claim to the task, since it was then conducting internal security operations in Northern Ireland, Kenya and the Caribbean. Its team stressed their capability and success in working with local civil police to gather evidence, give expert testimony in court and secure the conviction of subversives. They also pointed to 'Keeping the Peace', a draft War Office policy pamphlet in which RAOC responsibility was affirmed, with the RE to assist in event of a major emergency. This document, which dated back to 1957 and laid down the principles of internal security operations, was being extensively updated following the recent emergencies in Kenya, Malaya and Cyprus. Nevertheless the Engineers laid such strenuous claim to the task that the disagreement was referred to another meeting at which a policy on bomb-disposal could be agreed.

The encounter took place on 7 December 1961 and the two sides submitted their now familiar arguments in competing drafts. The Engineers said they had no desire to usurp RAOC functions in identifying, dismantling or making safe 'fancy explosive devices' but wanted to be sure that no restrictions would be applied to RE and infantry responsibilities for clearing these devices to allow security forces to get on with their jobs. The chairman suggested that the senior man on the spot should be given the responsibility for deciding whether operational considerations necessitated the quickest possible removal or whether the need to identify and use bomb components as evidence was overriding. This accommodation was accepted.

Around this time, the Defence Operations Staff ruled that, in line with revised NATO policy, the term 'bomb disposal' should be replaced by 'Explosive Ordnance Disposal' or EOD. In a related change, a few years later, the traditional titles of Inspecting Ordnance Officer and Ammunition Examiner were abolished in favour of Ammunition Technical Officer (ATO) and Ammunition Technician (AT), the former a commissioned officer, the latter not.

During the early 1960s, as more and more colonies gained independence and rival factions clashed for control of emerging new states, British troops were constantly required to deal with civil disorder and frequently associated bomb attacks, although the devices encountered were crude and low-powered by later terrorist standards. For the RAOC's EOD personnel, the next major intervention after Cyprus came in Aden in 1964. Britain had first colonised Aden, at the southern end of the Red Sea, in the nineteenth century and by 1961 a considerable Middle East Command was located there, as the area remained an important staging post and regional base to support British military operations in the ever volatile Middle East. Three years later, after growing violence by insurgents infiltrating the Aden Protectorate from Yemen to the north, a major land operation was required to put down the trouble but on 1 September 1965 the assassination of the Speaker of the Aden Legislative Assembly provoked fresh conflict. Harold Wilson's government in London swiftly announced British withdrawal by the end of 1967 but the deadline aggravated antiBritish feeling and service families were all evacuated in the summer, leaving the remaining forces to fight their way out.

The RAOC's role in Aden before the emergency had been its traditional one of providing supplies. But once the trouble started, so, inevitably, did the bombing. According to Brigadier LTH Phelps, Major JP Elliott, the Senior Ammunition Technical Officer, personally investigated 189 incidents between November 1964 and December 1965. Most devices were rudimentary and home-made, containing decomposed and volatile explosives, but, reflecting the insurgents' Eastern Bloc training, many included crude but effective antilifting mechanisms. In all Elliott dismantled 309 potentially lethal objects of which 154 proved to contain explosives, and was awarded the George Medal in April 1966. Major GC Brownlee, who remained until the withdrawal, was also awarded the George Medal. In some fourteen months under the threat of direct terrorist attack, he answered over 170 calls. The most notable of his accomplishments was the neutralising of a bomb in a village well. The safest option would have been to blow the device in the well, denying the villagers their water supply. However, Brownlee valiantly lowered himself into the dark, narrow shaft and dismantled the device.

The RAOC were called to British Honduras during tensions in 1967 and 1968. Again, most of the bombs they encountered were crude and relatively easily disposed of, but trouble in Hong Kong, which began in 1967, resulted in a more sustained EOD commitment. Chinese communists, aiming to make the colony ungovernable, had been strewing explosive devices and booby-traps in large quantities which peaked at 150 in one day. Two-thirds of these – placed in doors, lamp-posts and traffic lights, hanging from fences, on tram lines, in ferries, even under flagpoles on hilltops – were merely hoaxes intended to disrupt traffic and stretch the EOD resources in the densely populated, built-up area. When opened many were found to contain such unattractive contents as dead rats and human excrement. The live bombs mainly consisted of milk tins filled with black powder which produced no significant blast effect when exploded but could injure or kill bystanders. The danger was emphasised when a bomb-disposal officer lost two fingers and the tips of three others while working on such a device. More dangerous, though, were grenades thrown at operators working at devices.

Occasional gelignite devices were encountered, the explosive stolen from local quarries, but with the bombers sensitive to the hostile reaction that would follow from the killing of any Chinese people or damage to their property, the concentration was primarily on 'nuisance' bombs causing disruption, mainly to the colony's bustling traffic. Nevertheless, anti-handling booby-traps, commonly made by inserting an additional electrical circuit to detonate the bomb, were frequently used. In one notorious case such a device was attached to the body of a dead baby.

The operation was co-ordinated by an RAOC/EOD cell located in the Colonial Police headquarters who tasked teams usually consisting of an ATO or an AT with an escort/recorder and a party of police. Operators worked twelve hours' duty, then twelve at one-hour standby followed by twelve at four-hour standby and then twelve hours' rest. At busy times, they worked twelve hours on and twelve off. The operator generally travelled in a standard military Land Rover towing a trailer carrying his equipment. While working at a device he wore earplugs, a commercial helmet and visor, with some adaptations, and the standard military 'body fragmentation protective jacket' augmented by leg, arm and hand protectors, designed to withstand the blast from one pound of gunpowder or penetration by two-inch steel nails. The nylon-based kit was hastily designed and despatched to Hong Kong after the emergency started. The operator had a miner's headlamp for night work, a fire extinguisher, camera and flash, first-aid kit and morphine, a rope and fish hook and a collection of basic carpentry and electrical tools.

The main disposal tactic was to detonate the device on the spot and as most consisted of gunpowder, there was generally limited blast and little damage. In some cases they tried to pick up devices with a 'mechanical hand', a pole and hook manipulated like a fishing rod through the observation hatch of an armoured car. This technique was even used to dangle a detonator close to a device to set it off. In time, after some hasty development work back in the UK, a new approach was conceived. This involved the use of an armoured shield on wheels with an armoured-glass window and several holes through which poles could be manipulated with a variety of attachments including a scoop, hook, lasso, wire-cutters and claw-tongs.

The operators faced a considerable workload, averaging sixty-six alerts a day: twenty false, thirty-five hoax and eleven live. Over one fifteen-day period 100 devices were investigated and during another four-day spell the teams were called out 200 times. After an exhausted RAOC officer was wounded dealing with his sixtieth device, extra ATOs and ATs were drafted in from Singapore and the 233 EOD trained officers serving in the British Army of the Rhine. The Royal Engineers were watching the campaign in Hong Kong with deep misgivings and in December 1967, after Headquarters Land Forces in Hong Kong rejected an offer of personnel, Brigadier Richard Clutterbuck, the Engineer-in-Chief, accused the RAOC of 'hogging' the task and said scornfully that the devices were 'not really "bombs" at all but booby-traps'. He continued: 'There is no doubt that the RAOC are doing all they can to build up a case for taking over this responsibility completely, worldwide. This is clearly impracticable . . . nevertheless I think we would lose some sympathy if we were to emulate their intrigues and try to deprive a non-operational Corps of their only "ewe lamb" of danger.'

The rival Whitehall warriors were out in force for a meeting in London on 5 December 1967 to discuss the bomb-disposal situation in the colony, supposedly breaking down 'because insufficient technical assistance was being received from the United Kingdom'. The alarm had been raised by Dr HM Wilson, the Army's chief scientist, who reported that during a recent visit he had been formally briefed by General Beckett, Chief of Staff, and other senior officers in Far East Land Forces (FARELF). Colonel SE Dutton, as the Chief Inspector Land Service Ammunition (CILSA), the ultimate commander of the teams, admitted that the daily frequency of incidents was high but said the situation was under control, although it could deteriorate if, as expected, 'the terrorists intensified their activities and used more sophisticated devices'. There was a particular fear, he added, that they might introduce remotely-initiated weapons.

After some discussion, the meeting agreed to a series of urgent actions to improve equipment. Twenty-three sets of arms and leg protectors were to be urgently produced and shipped and new foot and ankle protection was to be developed. There were also to be experiments with shaped nylon 'biscuits' to create a blast-proof blanket to smother devices. Other innovations were an evaluation of a portable x-ray kit with the capacity to develop photographs on the spot using new Polaroid technology, new stethoscopes to replace existing models which had been designed to listen to the workings of large aircraft-borne bombs, and improved equipment, such as gas-powered torches, to cut and enter devices. There was also to be research on combating remote-controlled devices, a task which was rapidly justified only four days after the London meeting when, on 9 December, terrorists remotely detonated two devices filled with high explosive on a road often used by cars carrying VIPs.

The RAOC came out of the episode well. A minute to Colonel Dutton from the War Office on 11 December noted: 'It seems RAOC require no assistance at present either in the form of equipment or know how.'

Following an inquest into what had been said over the gin and tonics in Beckett's house in Hong Kong, it was concluded, according to a widely circulated letter, that Dr Wilson 'inadvertently got the wires crossed in an overenthusiastic effort to be helpful. Whatever may be the intrigues in London, the men on the ground have done a very good job.' There were good grounds for the RAOC's indignation, since they had tackled nine thousand incidents, 1,441 involving real devices, and sustained only thirteen casualties, of which one was fatal. Sergeant CC Workman died on 28 August 1967 while dealing with a device planted on Lion Rock overlooking the Kowloon district.

The RAOC circulated a situation report on the Hong Kong emergency at the end of 1967, giving an account of EOD activity over the previous six months which, Brigadier Phelps said, 'makes it plain that ATOs and ATs have dealt with a very exacting situation speedily and successfully. The [need for] EOD activity broke suddenly without warning from intelligence sources and was entirely unexpected.' He added that the terrorist saturation technique they encountered was unique in the history of the British Army and that 'it reflects great credit on those concerned that the threat has been successfully contained'. Among this appreciative audience, as Peter Birchall recalls in *The Longest Walk*, were sixteen young Chinese female practitioners in a house of ill-repute, who offered an AT the hospitality of the establishment after he successfully defused a device left on the premises. With extreme devotion to duty, it is recorded, he declined.

Meantime, the Engineers, who had been confined to a peripheral role, were actively critical of the RAOC's conduct of the campaign. They took great pleasure that the trial of an experimental 'blast container' vehicle, designed to move a suspect device to an area where it could be safely detonated, had failed miserably during a tryout. 'The shock wave put the vehicle entirely out of commission,' reported the Engineers gleefully, dismissing the initiative as 'a crazy idea. The box must have an open top with strong sides to guide the blast safely upwards,' they said. There was also criticism of the project to develop more effective body armour: 'ATOs are too much inclined to go and investigate instead of destroying with as little personal exposure as possible. Dismantling devices for intelligence purposes rarely justified the risk.' In June 1968, the sniping continued in a letter from the RE detachment at Hong Kong Land Forces Command to the Chief Engineer at the Royal School of Military Engineering at Chatham in Kent:

It is clear that we must be capable of carrying out the clearance of booby-traps and terrorist devices wherever and whenever they occur and we definitely have this task in Hong Kong at present. Local co-operation with RAOC is reasonable but clearly they want to take over this task *in toto* and are giving it a degree of priority that, with our present resources and other responsibilities, we may find it difficult to match. We are concerned that the Corps may not be giving this subject the attention and priority it deserves in training, in pamphlet cover, and in the development of techniques and equipment. If we do not treat the subject as it deserves, we will lose the responsibility (and very rightly) to RAOC who are keen to have it and perhaps be unable to meet our commitments here or elsewhere should there be another, and better organised, terrorist campaign.

While the 1960s had been years of protest in several colonies, the bomb-disposal and associated forensic skills honed there were also called into action on the home front. Early in 1963, plans to flood the Tryweryn Valley to augment the water supply for Liverpool infuriated Welsh nationalists and prompted the mobilisation of the self-styled Mudiad Amddiffyn Cymru (Movement for the Defence of Wales). On 10 February they bombed an electricity transformer in an unsuccessful bid to disrupt work on the project. Over the next few years, there were periodic attacks with explosives on water and electricity supply installations, statues and monuments, government buildings in Cardiff, an RAF base and a Cardiff police station. They were far from simple nuisance bombs. One attack with a demolition charge at West Hagley in Worcestershire fractured the main water pipe from the Elan Valley to Birmingham.

Early in 1968, once Queen Elizabeth decided that Prince Charles, the heir to the throne, should spend a term studying at the University College of Wales in Aberystwyth prior to his investiture as Prince of Wales the following year, the need to prevent the sabotage attacks in Wales and adjoining English counties from overshadowing the ceremony became paramount. Apart from ensuring the safety of the many who would be attending, there was also a need to protect the four thousand troops, two thousand police and staff from the royal household, all with the full ceremonial panoply of horses and carriages, who were being accommodated in specially constructed tented camps at the former RAF base at Llandwrog near Caernarfon. Providing sufficient EOD cover was at the very heart of the security operation, so by the time the young prince arrived in to commence his studies in April 1969, an EOD team was installed in a caravan in the yard of Aberystwyth police station, ready to screen anything sent to him by post and to attend any incidents involving suspected explosives. When term ended in June, they had dealt with eighteen incidents, the majority being hoaxes or false alarms. One suspect package sent to the prince turned out to be nothing more lethal than a leg of succulent Welsh lamb.

There was very good reason for the intensive security. In February Special Branch officers had discovered a 'Free Wales Army' cell making plans to disrupt the investiture by using 'elite volunteers' to attack the castle and 'other key positions held in the town by the enemy'. Several incidents in the immediate run-up to the investiture contradicted any notion that they were merely fantasists. A week before the event, police captured three men with a crude incendiary device in a holdall. In a related episode, a 6 lb. gelignite bomb was neutralised on Holyhead Pier. The most serious incident occurred in the early hours of investiture day itself, 1 July, when two men were killed in a premature explosion in the town of Abergele while transporting a device supposedly to be placed in the path of the royal train. The Queen, Prince Charles and other senior members of the royal family were already installed at Vaynol as the guests of Sir Michael Duff. In other incidents a bomb blew a three-foot hole in the wall of a postal sorting office in Cardiff, another went off in the garden of the chief constable's Caernarfon home and a child lost a leg after coming across a hidden bomb in a backyard at Bangor Street.

By this time a major deployment of the RAOC's EOD assets had taken place around Caernarfon and as the prince set out on an extensive 'progress' through Wales, teams fanned out to help clear his route and sweep up subsequent alerts. Unusually, officers worked singly to spread the cover as widely as possible but there were plans to speed back-up to any location where it became necessary. They were not kept fully occupied. At Betws-y-Coed, shortly before the prince passed, an operator blew up a suspicious biscuit-tin bomb and nipped suspicious wires in a manhole. The immediate threat to peace in Wales afterwards subsided as many of the extremists were traced, prosecuted and imprisoned.

During this same period, principally in and around London, RAOC bomb-disposal teams were involved in dealing with a cadre of anarchists who styled themselves 'The Angry Brigade'. The first incident attributable to them is the planting of a high-explosive device at the new Paddington Green police station in west London on 22 May 1970 but they and anarchist associates appear to have launched a wave of bombings in

Britain well over a year earlier, some co-ordinated with like-minded activists in other European capitals. The most symbolic was the attack on the Post Office Tower in London, causing the closure of its rotating restaurant and access for the public. Other targets were a trendy Kensington boutique and a BBC Outside Broadcast vehicle, bombed at the Royal Albert Hall during the Miss World contest, but the most serious attacks were those on leading Conservative figures such as Duncan Sandys MP, the attorney-general, Sir Peter Rawlinson, Robert Carr, minister of employment, and John Davies, the trade and industry secretary. Court, police and military establishments in several parts of the country were also hit, some of the latter in protest at events in Northern Ireland where urban terrorism was already gathering force. One of the most provocative attacks was on the home of the Metropolitan Police Commissioner, Sir John Waldron, whose newly formed 'Bomb Squad' was at the forefront of the hunt for the bombers which led to the imprisonment of its core members in December 1972. The attacks, especially on political leaders, were the first of their type in modern political history and exploited what was still a comparatively relaxed security environment.

The RAOC had foreseen the development and taken steps to deal with it. In his annual report for 1968 from Vauxhall Barracks at Didcot, Brigadier Phelps had correctly forecast that, in addition to customary overseas EOD commitments, the surge in terrorist activity in the British Isles would probably continue and impose an even greater call for the services of the fourteen RAOC EOD teams. During that year, with this commitment in mind, the corps formed 321 EOD Unit as a 'shadow asset' for use by the Army worldwide or in Britain. In the event of a crisis, the unit would be staffed by ATs from various depots and instructors from the Army School of Ammunition.

The ten-strong team was formed up for the first time at Bramley in June 1968 for what the *RAOC Gazette* later described as two weeks of 'strenuous revision'. They were lectured about EOD operations in Hong Kong, events in British Honduras earlier in the year and the trials and tribulations of dealing with 'the Viet Taff' of Western Command – the 'Free Wales' bombers. Over the weekend the group, drawn from the Ammunition Inspectorate at Southern Command and the Central Ammunition Depots at Bramley, Kineton and Longtown, went on exercise to Larkhill ranges where the programme included 'an energetic loading exercise' and voice procedure training.

The unit's first live deployment followed in March 1969 when an EOD section travelled with elements of the Parachute Regiment to the British dependency of Anguilla in the Caribbean after disturbances. The operation was uneventful and the section returned within weeks. They did not know where, when or even if they would be deployed next.

Chapter Two
Clothes Pegs and Blue Touch-paper

During the twilight years of empire after the Second World War, when RAOC officers had been providing bomb-disposal services in Cyprus, Aden, Hong Kong and elsewhere, some had also been briefly in action nearer home, in Northern Ireland. Following the partitioning of the island in the early 1920s after the War of Independence, hardcore elements of the Irish Republican Army remained committed to ending British rule in the six northern counties. Their periodic attempts to do so by force were devoid of any significant public support and were easily suppressed by the governments in Dublin and Belfast, largely by rounding up the activists and interning them without trial. The Republicans were not completely subdued, however, and there were five bomb attacks on RUC stations in Belfast during 1950. In June 1951 they managed to steal a considerable quantity of arms and ammunition from the Royal Navy's Sea Eagle base in Londonderry. Two years later small bombs were detonated at several cinemas showing newsreels of the coronation of Queen Elizabeth but an attempt to obtain a further large consignment of arms and ammunition from the Officers' Training Corps armoury at Felsted School, Essex, was foiled and the raiders captured.

A more serious sign of IRA preparation for hostilities came on 12 June 1954 when fifteen men entered a British army base in Armagh in a cattle lorry, overpowered the guards and escaped with seven hundred weapons. Later in the year, on Sunday 18 October, the IRA tried in vain to repeat their success. At 3.15 a.m., a large group of armed men stormed Omagh military barracks but were engaged by the guard force who sustained five casualties. Some of the attackers fled in a waiting lorry but eight were rounded up by the police and ultimately sentenced to long terms of imprisonment.

On 2 July 1955 another IRA operation went wrong. A bomber attempting to blow up the telephone exchange at Belmont Road, Belfast, to sever the lines serving the nearby Parliament Buildings at Stormont and other government offices, was killed when the device exploded prematurely. Some six weeks later, there was a further arms raid at a military installation, this time an armoury at Aborfield, Berkshire, from which a hundred weapons and over 30,000 rounds of ammunition were removed but the three raiders were captured and their haul recovered. Everything pointed to a new IRA offensive but before they could act, a breakaway group called Saor Uladh (Free Ulster) attacked a police station on the border and a number of customs posts, losing one member shot dead by the RUC.

The main IRA offensive, 'Operation Harvest', was launched soon afterwards on 11 December 1956. That night ten attacks throughout Northern Ireland included the bombing of a BBC transmitter at Londonderry, the burning of the courthouse at Magherafelt, the firing of a B Special drill hut in Newry and an explosion at an Army barracks in Enniskillen. Elsewhere bridges were severed. The next night two police stations at Lisnaskea and Derrylin, both in County Fermanagh, endured gun and bomb attacks. On 30 December the attackers returned to Derrylin, opening fire from across the border and shooting dead a policeman.

In Belfast, the prime minister, Lord Brookeborough, asserted his determination to crush the campaign and the RUC Reserve Force was quickly loaned seventy military vehicles from the War Office, including armoured half-track personnel carriers, Scout cars and Land Rovers. The 150-strong force, armed with heavy automatic weapons, deployed along the border and was later backed up by some British troops and 200 Special Constables. Sentry posts with sandbags and barbed-wire entanglements were thrown up at RUC stations throughout Northern Ireland and several unapproved border roads were either spiked or cratered. Internment was again introduced and before long nearly 200 people had been taken into custody. At night, especially in the border areas, there were widespread road checks and the part-time B Specials were deployed to guard vital installations. These were usually attacked with gelignite bombs ignited by the bombers before they ran away. In some cases they used gunpowder accumulated from fireworks to make explosive devices capable of causing minor damage or serious injury.

The RUC faced the brunt of the violence and successfully defended its fortified stations against a number of frontal bomb and gun attacks. This caused the IRA to change tactics to try and lure RUC patrols into the path of booby-trapped bombs along the border and in the countryside. In one incident, at 2 a.m. on 4 July 1957, a member of the Reserve Force sitting in a patrol vehicle about two hundred yards from the border was fatally wounded when gunmen opened fire after a landmine had failed to detonate under the vehicle. The bombs used in such attacks were of straightforward construction, consisting of variable quantities of stolen commercial gelignite, a detonator, a power unit, customarily a small battery, and a timing mechanism, commonly an alarm clock. Such devices were of course unstable (four IRA bomb-makers died in a premature explosion on the southern side of the border in November 1957) and would have killed anyone within range when they detonated but they were all the more dangerous when booby-trapped and concealed. At 11.25 p.m. on 17 August, a sergeant led a party of police and soldiers to an empty house near Coalisland, County Tyrone, to check out an anonymous report that a man was acting suspiciously at the premises. The party saw a candle burning in the kitchen and surrounded the house but when the sergeant kicked open the kitchen door he set off a booby-trapped bomb and died instantly.

While RAOC experts were available as part of the Army support for the RUC, all too often the untrained police chose to carry out their own bomb disposal in a fashion that veered between foolhardiness and bravery. One such incident took place on 16 October 1957 after an anonymous telephone call was made overnight to the police station at Stewartstown, County Tyrone, stating that there was an obstruction on a road in the area. For fear of ambush, a patrol was not sent out to investigate until daybreak, when it was discovered two trees had been felled to block the road. In between them, sitting on the road in the middle of Doon Bridge, was a wooden butter box with what appeared to be the remains of a burnt-out fuse jutting from it. Mindful of the recent death of their colleague in the Coalisland booby-trap, the police officers, a district inspector and sergeant, approached the device and after attaching a rope, retired to a distance and toppled it sideways without causing an explosion. They then carried the box into a nearby field where they took cover and threw rocks to break it open. Inside they found twenty-five sticks of gelignite and an elaborate antihandling circuit which had failed to operate. Afterwards one officer received the MBE, the other the BEM.

Ten days later, the police station at nearby Coalisland received a similar warning call in the evening, this time reporting men acting suspiciously at a derelict house in Mousetown. Again it was decided not to respond to the call until daylight and by the time the police arrived at the location the next morning a local farmer had spotted a length of white string stretched across the lane leading to the house. Nearby were a bucket and the battery of a flash lamp and earth had been recently disturbed. According to a contemporary police report, the device was 'rendered harmless' by the local sergeant, John Hermon. The string tripwire was intended to detonate 118 sticks of gelignite buried in the hole. Had it gone off, the young officer would have perished instantly. Instead he survived to become Chief Constable of the RUC some twenty years later and led the force for a turbulent decade after that.

There were many other actions where it was impossible to distinguish between rashness and courage. After beating off terrorists who opened fire on his station with heavy automatic weapons, a head constable sent his colleagues to pursue them while he defused two unexploded gelignite devices they had left behind; in Londonderry a woman sergeant was awarded the BEM and her constable colleague the George Medal for pulling the lighted fuse from a gelignite bomb planted in the docks. Another sergeant was given the BEM for clearing his station and removing a 62 lb. suitcase bomb to waste ground. The George Medal was awarded to Major (later Brigadier) Harry Baxter for an unorthodox act of military bomb disposal. About 1.45 p.m. on 5 September 1957, a patrolling sentry discovered a time bomb in a zipped bag concealed in sandbags around an explosive store close to the armoury in Gough Barracks, Armagh. It was a typical IRA device consisting of 4 lb. of gelignite, 10 lb. of home-made guncotton and three electric detonators connected to a battery and alarm clock. Baxter immediately removed the bag and placed it on the back of a truck. As his colleague started the engine one of the detonators went off but the explosives did not detonate, so they set off through the streets of the town for some waste ground on the outskirts where the bomb was safely dismantled. Two soldiers training at the barracks, who came from the Irish Republic, subsequently failed to return from leave and one of them, who had been on guard duty the night before the incident, was later found to have IRA connections.

RAOC officers also played a vital part in dealing with explosives during this campaign. Undoubtedly the most distinguished was Captain George Prosser, a Scotsman with seventeen years' Army service, including in Malaya, who was awarded the George Medal in July 1957. He had arrived at Lisburn only the previous November, two weeks before the IRA attacks began, and over the succeeding months he attended twenty-six incidents, some of which, according to his citation, were 'hazardous in the extreme, requiring courage of the highest order, great technical skill and outstanding devotion to duty'. Among the bombs he tackled was a suspicious 'ticking' suitcase found by police officers in Belfast docks on 13 December 1956. By the time Prosser got there the ticking had stopped, but despite the possibility that it could go off at any moment, he opened the case and disconnected the fuse from what turned out to be 54 lb. of high explosive. The following February, he was called to a deserted house near Newry where a complex booby-trap had been discovered. According to the citation, 'after ten minutes of the most hazardous investigation during which one slip might have meant instant destruction the dangerous contraption, which contained 28 lb. of gelignite, was duly dismantled.' The citation concluded that Captain Prosser had been 'subjected to the most extreme physical and mental strain being called upon at all hours of the night to carry out work far outside the normal call of duty. By his specialist training, he must have been constantly aware of the risk he was taking but he has never hesitated to carry out his dangerous duties.'

The high explosive used in these attacks was mainly gelignite. Its importance to the IRA was underlined on the first night of the campaign when 250 lb. was stolen from two explosives stores. The RUC posted armed guards on the two commercial explosive magazines and the premises of two distributors until electronic security systems could be fitted and thereafter, with the help of the Army, provided escorts for explosives being used in quarrying and for other purposes. These restrictions prevented the IRA obtaining any explosives locally, so their future supplies came from the south of Ireland or various parts of the British mainland where controls were not so rigorous. Consignments were dispatched to Ireland by post or through one of the commercial freight services and police in both Belfast and Dublin made repeated interceptions of parcels and packages, usually addressed to unsuspecting individuals or companies who were not party to the smuggling plot. As with firearms, the government infrastructure also proved porous. A bomb intended to demolish a telephone exchange in Northern Ireland was found to consist of Tonite, originally an underwater demolition explosive used in the manufacture of fog signals for Trinity House, the organisation responsible for the safety of shipping and seafarers around the British coast.

There was another unsuccessful arms raid at a military facility in Blandford, Dorset, in February 1958, the year 'Operation Harvest' peaked. From that point, the number of incidents steadily dwindled and the campaign was unilaterally called off on 26 February 1962. The IRA had been humiliated that the Catholic population had not risen in support and embarrassed by criticism from both the leaders of the Catholic Church and prominent political figures in Dublin. Even the traditional sectarian hotbeds in Belfast had remained dormant. In all there had been 605 outrages since 1956, leaving sixteen people dead – six RUC and ten IRA – and thirty-two wounded, while 160 had been interned. Security operations had cost some £3 million, while damage had exceeded £1 million.

An assessment of the IRA, prepared in the War Office in June 1958, said the organisation 'is made up of groups of young men, all of whom are fanatics in their fight for "the cause" who would use any means they can to get their object'. It concluded:

> It is not wise to underestimate the IRA in their cunning and ruthlessness which has been proved on countless occasions. There is no doubt that the IRA will continue to carry out hostile acts against this country and incidents must be expected as long as there is a Northern Ireland Government and there are British troops in Ulster. The IRA will be satisfied with nothing less than a United Ireland (32 counties) governed by Sinn Fein.

This assumption was entirely in line with the views of the Ulster Unionist administration in Belfast which, in its propaganda, never underestimated the IRA's penchant for plotting or its capacity for causing trouble. So, despite the 1962 ceasefire declaration, the fearful Belfast government maintained the semimilitary RUC Reserve Force at full strength. The military authorities in Northern Ireland also maintained prudent precautions against the possibility of repeated attacks or arms raids. The fiftieth anniversary of the Easter Rising in Dublin in 1966 raised security fears sufficiently for a secret, state-of-the-art 'contraption' to be manufactured to deal with sophisticated explosive devices 'believed to be under development by the IRA'. The trailer and equipment, which included radioactive gamma-ray containers and cost £5,600, was then assigned to the Army's Northern Ireland Command in 1966.

At that point, there was a considerable armed forces garrison in Northern Ireland: 5,420 Army, 400 Royal Navy and 1,600 Royal Air Force. Together with 4,650 dependents and 5,070 locally employed civilians they occupied forty-five locations. The RAOC's commitment was to supply the garrison with stores from its depots at Kinnegar and Lisburn, vehicles from its workshop at the wartime airfield at Long Kesh and ammunition, which was stored at Ballykinler on the County Down coast. In line with standard practice, a captain and a warrant officer were attached to the garrison headquarters in Lisburn to inspect the supply and storage of ammunition and explosives. Their standing responsibilities included dealing with bombs if requested by the police, but, at that time, military inspection and safety tasks were their routine concerns.

After the collapse of the 1956–62 campaign, although some diehards remained within its ranks, the IRA had largely forsaken violence and become engaged in all-Ireland social agitation. The policy adjustment reflected the changing nationalist mood in Northern Ireland in the late 1960s which was influenced by events of historical significance elsewhere: the Russian invasion of Czechoslovakia; the assassinations of Martin Luther King and Robert Kennedy; the student riots in Paris and the worldwide protests against the United States' involvement in the Vietnam war. But the greatest inspiration for Catholics in Northern Ireland, strongly wedded as they were to the concepts of struggle and martyrdom, was undoubtedly provided by the civil-rights campaign in the United States. By early 1968 a Northern Ireland civil-rights movement was campaigning for peaceful reform within the Partition set-up. It contained a broad church of Republicans, liberals, socialists, Catholics, Protestants, Unionists, Nationalists and even a prominent Communist. Although the newer IRA activists infiltrated this group and others, traditional Republicans, discredited by the failure of the recent border campaign, were forced to take a back seat as the civil-rights movement took to the streets. Its first major venture was a march in Londonderry on 5 October 1968, the venue pointedly chosen because the city manifested many social and political injustices between Protestants and Catholics. The unyielding Unionist government in Belfast prohibited the march and when the RUC moved in with batons drawn and water cannon, violent rioting erupted which continued for many hours. The Troubles had begun.

Over the next few months, with only 3,000 officers, the under-strength and ill-equipped RUC was overwhelmed by sustained street disorder and the political institutions were shaken to their foundations. Under pressure from the British government to push through reforms and smother the worsening disorder, the moderate Unionist prime minister, Captain Terence O'Neill, called an 'Ulster at the crossroads' general election for 24 February 1969 in a bid to outflank the opponents of reform within his party. The gamble failed but O'Neill pledged to fight on. On 31 March, however, the Ulster Unionist Council seriously undermined what little authority he had left when it passed a vote of confidence in him by only seventy-five votes: 338 to 263.

Behind the scenes more sinister elements, inflamed by what they saw as unreasonable concessions, were already at work to ensure O'Neill's political demise. In the early hours of that morning there was an explosion which caused £500,000 worth of damage to a vital electricity transformer at Castlereagh in south-east Belfast. The bombers removed a section of perimeter railing and placed four linked explosive charges at various points inside the complex. The RUC Special Branch blamed the IRA, a view conveyed verbally to O'Neill and Robert Porter, the new home affairs minister, when they visited the scene to inspect the extensive damage. 'Oh, I don't think so,' replied O'Neill shrewdly. 'I think this is some of my own people trying to tell me to go.'

The Belfast government immediately announced that 1,000 B Specials were to be mobilised to guard similar vital installations. Despite this precaution, bombers caused two explosions on the night of Saturday 19 April. Four charges at the cross-border electricity interconnector at Kilmore, County Armagh, were inexpertly placed and failed to knock out the supply, but the pylon was blown two feet off its concrete plinth and one of its thirteen high-tension electricity cables was brought down. The second bomb, at the Silent Valley reservoir in County Down, was more expertly positioned adjacent to vital control valves and distribution pipes and caused serious restrictions of supply to Belfast.

That Sunday morning, as an air of crisis gathered, the new Security Committee of ministers, officials, police commanders and senior soldiers formed to manage the emergency decided that soldiers should help guard sixteen key utility installations – VPs (Vital Points) in military parlance. A simultaneous signal from Army headquarters at Lisburn to the Chief of the Defence Staff pointed out the lack of any independent intelligence information but, citing 'relations with the RUC of the finest', said that in their view the weekend sabotage had been carried out by 'skilled operators' led by a man who had recently broken away from the main-stream IRA. The information was completely inaccurate and O'Neill's suspicions proved to be well-founded. In the meantime, though, London agreed to provide 120 troops.

With the faltering O'Neill government plagued by yet another internal dispute, this time over the 'One man, one vote' reform of the electoral franchise, there was yet another explosion near Dunadry on 24 April, completely severing the northern water main from Lough Neagh to Belfast and denying the city another 4,500,000 gallons of water a day when the authorities were still struggling to maintain adequate supplies after the Silent Valley sabotage. Barely twenty-four hours later another critical link in the water infrastructure was attacked near Annalong, County Down. Later that day the government announced two military helicopters would join the security operation to maintain surveillance on water and electricity mains and, for the first time, British troop reinforcements were requested. Despite the growing political and military concern in London about becoming embroiled in civil conflict in Northern Ireland, a 500-strong battalion was flown to Belfast, bringing the military guard force to a total of 850 soldiers all tasked to guard 48 VPs in remote rural areas. O'Neill, however, announced his resignation on 28 April.

At the end of June, Porter, the home affairs minister, advised the Stormont parliament that nobody had been made amenable for any of a series of bombings, save for one person committed to a mental institution. Austin Currie, a Catholic MP, replied: 'I would have thought others might have been committed to a mental hospital as well.' The other targets listed by Porter included a memorial to an Irish Republican leader, a customs post, a Catholic church, a Plymouth Brethren hall, two Belfast Corporation buses, two Special Constabulary drill halls and ten post offices: a grim variety of destruction that would be repeated with greater frequency and intensity for years. From the targets chosen and the types of explosive devices planted, the disposition of the bombers was not clear and there was as yet no evidence of central organisation behind the attacks. (Curiously, the list disclosed to MPs was far from complete. There was no mention of an incident at the RUC station in Saintfield on 27 April, nor of earlier attacks at a garage, a public house, four shops, a taxi depot and premises occupied by the Presbyterian Church.)

Responsibility for the series of blasts at water and electricity installations eventually became clear in October 1969, after Thomas McDowell, a forty-five-year-old quarry foreman from Kilkeel, County Down, with links to the outlawed UVF and the Reverend Ian Paisley's Free Presbyterian Church, was found fatally injured at a power station in Ballyshannon, County Donegal. He had suffered severe burns in a premature explosion while priming a bomb. RUC follow-up investigations confirmed extremist Protestant culpability for the earlier attacks, vindicating O'Neill's opinion that the explosions 'quite literally blew me out of office'. Expert evidence later presented to the Scarman Tribunal (the judicial investigation into the origins and early events of the Northern Ireland disturbances) concluded that the sabotage campaign had been the work of people whose knowledge of the use of explosives was limited to quarrying.

O'Neill's departure failed to halt the slide to anarchy. As the situation steadily deteriorated, with the police outnumbered and overpowered by the scale of the disorder, British troops were requested to come to their aid on 14 August 1969. They were first deployed in Londonderry and then, next day, in Belfast. Over the course of a week, the Northern Ireland garrison soared by 6,000. The sudden influx instantly doubled the RAOC's workload and they struggled to find accommodation and issue stores to the reinforcements. The situation was summed up in a dispatch to the *RAOC Gazette* that November: 'At last the proverbial crunch has come. Headquarters has put away its fishing rods, cricket bats and exercise kit and taken out respirators, DMS boots, Biros and shillelaghs to become operational at the sharp end. The staff have been somewhat in a daze at the whirlwind of events in the past few weeks.'

Within days of their first deployment, as the troops were still trying to calm the worst sectarian clashes for some fifty years, there came the first real fear that the hitherto dormant IRA might once again become a factor in the situation. At 9 p.m. on Sunday 17 August a car was driven into the garden in front of the police station at Crossmaglen, close to the border in south Armagh. When the station sergeant noticed one of the two occupants was carrying a Sterling sub-machine gun, he fired a shot. As he did so a grenade was thrown at the station and the raiders ran off towards the nearby village square. There another car pulled up. Three more armed men emerged and ordered local people to clear the area. Back at the station, the police found 50 lb. of explosives in a plastic container inside the abandoned car. The bombers had been prevented from lighting the two-and-a-half minute fuse when the sergeant fired, causing them to flee. In retrospect, this incident can be seen as marking the start of the IRA's new campaign. Over the next couple of months, traditionalists in the organisation, sceptical about the value of social and political agitation in bringing about a united Ireland, broke away to form the 'Provisional IRA' while the original core became known as the 'Officials'. The split would have profound security, economic and political implications for years ahead.

The Crossmaglen attack had fuelled hysteria among some government ministers and senior police officers in Belfast about an IRA uprising and the station had been sandbagged after the thwarted bombing incident. The police asked the Army to start patrolling the border area as they had done during the previous IRA campaign but the threat of all-out gun and bomb attacks was considered remote by the more detached and cool-headed military commanders, whose priority was to quell the disturbances on the streets and provide reassurance to the community that there was not going to be the bloody civil war many feared. Any EOD workload was judged still to be well within the capability of Captain Bob Willcox and WO Glover, his sole assistant at Headquarters Northern Ireland, so the shadow 321 EOD Unit was stood down before it physically mustered. It would be only a brief reprieve. In the meantime, Willcox and Glover were reinforced by personnel from the Ballykinler depot when their bomb-disposal burden increased. Corporal Colin Goodson, then serving as an AT, remembers being reassigned to the Lisburn detachment. 'We went around in Land Rovers with blue lights and the "red wings" sign on them and our main task was to go in after a night's rioting and pick up the remains of blast bombs and the like. We often worked at first light, early in the morning and for a time we were everybody's friend. But eventually they started to throw bricks at us.'

By the end of 1969, according to Army records, there had been nine explosions, one device defused and about half a ton of explosives captured, but the blasts continued with increasing frequency into 1970. On 15 January, a twenty-one-year-old employee at a hairdressing salon in Ardoyne, Belfast, found a parcel addressed to 'The Manager' when he turned up to open for business. He took the package inside but when he untied the string he saw wires and batteries and it started to fizz. As he turned to run it exploded, scorching his face and stomach. Willcox reported: 'This was a deliberately constructed explosive device capable of killing someone alongside it. It was made from readily available everyday materials which were probably innocently retailed.' Not long afterwards, on the cold, windy Saturday evening of 31 January, the Brown Square police barracks, now shared with a company from 2 Queens Regiment, was bombed. About 9.15 p.m. a sentry spotted a car cruising slowly along Peter's Hill in front of the base. It stopped briefly and an object was thrown into a ventilator. This then exploded, blowing a substantial hole in the wall of the building but causing no injuries.

On 3 February, offices at Botanic Avenue, occupied by the moderate New Ulster Movement, were the target but a bakery on the ground floor of the building suffered the real impact of the blast. Another political moderate was singled out for attack on 8 February when the Belfast home of Sheelagh Murnaghan, a prominent barrister and the only Liberal MP ever to sit in the Northern Ireland parliament, was bombed. The Crumlin Road prison in Belfast was rocked by another explosion on 10 February, for which the UVF acknowledged responsibility a few days later. There was an even more intimidating occurrence on 18 February when a small device went off in a corridor of the nearby Courthouse close to the climax of the trial of five men charged in connection with the earlier water and electricity explosions. Several hours later, after almost five hours' deliberation, the jury acquitted the accused.

The majority of these incidents were attributable to Loyalists but the thirteenth explosion of the year on 1 March was clearly the work of elements sympathetic to the Republican cause. At about 3 a.m. a taxi driver passing through Carlisle Circus on the northern fringe of Belfast city centre spotted three youths jumping from the plinth of a statue in the centre of the roundabout. He went round again for a closer look and saw a polythene-wrapped bundle wedged at the feet of the ten-foot cast bronze statue of the Reverend Hugh 'Roaring' Hanna, a nineteenth-century Presbyterian preacher whose anti-Catholic ranting frequently provoked sectarian disorder. The taximan reported the situation and, after a reconnaissance by soldiers in the area, the watch keepers at Lisburn called Willcox and his driver from their beds. By the time they reached Belfast the device had exploded but the only casualty was Hanna's statue, intact but for a gaping hole in his metal crotch. From what they were told by soldiers who had inspected the device, and from his own examination of the debris, Willcox concluded the blast had been caused by between 3 and 5 lb. of Quarrex gelignite ignited by a timer-power unit in a Regal cigarette packet taped to the polythene wrapping. 'A home-made device set to fire quarrying explosives to demolish the statue of the Rev Hugh Hanna, an exercise which was disappointingly successful,' he wrote on the official report.

The incident and the escalating EOD workload prompted high-level discussion in Lisburn. Some felt that the time had come to base an EOD officer in Belfast, where most of the devices were being planted. Even at dead of night, with little civilian traffic on the move, it was taking Willcox and his colleagues call-out time plus twenty or twenty-five minutes to cover the ten miles from Thiepval Barracks to the scene of an incident. Colin Goodson says: 'By the time we were called out and reached the scene, the bombs had gone off and there was not a lot we could do by then except look in the wrecked buildings for things of forensic interest.' (After a bomb went off close to the flat where Goodson was living at Ormeau Road in south Belfast, he was quickly moved to the more secure confines of Thiepval Barracks.)

At this point, Willcox, who was within days of the end of a two-year tour in Northern Ireland, decided to review the growing EOD require-ment. Priorities had changed drastically and all the prevailing signs were that demands would continue to soar. So, soon after he departed in March a couple of bomb-disposal officers were posted in to provide extra cover for six months. If anyone had dared predict that there would be an indefinite need for a major EOD deployment more than thirty years later, they would have been laughed at. Shortly before this deployment, however, clashes had taken place at the sprawling Ballymurphy housing estate in west Belfast over Easter 1970, which would prove to be a critical turning point. Late on the Tuesday evening, as one of the last Orange marches of the weekend returned to an obscure Orange Hall adjacent to the predominantly Catholic area, Catholic youths stoned the Orangemen in a premeditated attack. Members of the Royal Scots Regiment moved in to separate the two sides and the disturbances quickly materialised into a direct confrontation between the Catholics and the military, which seems to have been the rioters' primary intention.

Over the next five hours, as vehicles were hijacked and set alight to block roads, the soldiers came under sustained attack from petrol bombs and other missiles. Similar orchestrated trouble continued for two more nights and was only brought to a distinctly uneasy end by what was later described to London as 'very firm military action' on the night of 2/3 April when a large quantity of CS gas was fired. That night, the ongoing trouble was aggravated by mobs of Protestants who gathered in the nearby Woodvale area and threatened to invade the Catholic suburb. The clashes were a dangerous turning point in that, for the first time, well prepared, stone-throwing, teenage male Catholic rioters formed elusive gangs and aggressively attacked soldiers. It quickly became clear that the trouble had been carefully stage-managed to mark the violent debut of the Provisional IRA.

Chapter Three
A Savage Twist

There was no honeymoon period for the additional bomb-disposal operators. The number of explosions rapidly multiplied and the bombers were reckless in their choice of targets and ruthless in their methods. Reinforcements in the form of a cadre from the 321 EOD shadow unit arrived short-term for the marching season and had 'a quiet stay', according to a note in the *RAOC Gazette*. By then a no-warning bombing at the Northern Bank in High Street, Belfast on 16 July 1970 had provided a depressing foretaste of the unprecedented callousness to come. The device, between five and eight pounds of commercial blasting explosive, was wrapped in a bundle of clothing and abandoned under a flight of stairs in the busy foyer of the building. When it suddenly exploded at 2.20 p.m., thirty passers-by were caught in the blast. Light fittings crashed to the floor, doors flew off their hinges and panels from walls and ceilings collapsed as a cloud of churning dust and debris swept through the building. It was surprising that nobody was killed or that more people were not grievously injured by the shards of flying glass from the many broken windows. The force of the explosion so badly distorted the heavy metal door of the walk-in bank vault that it could not be closed afterwards.

According to the comprehensive EOD incident reports now being filed after each call-out, some of the attacks were being carried out by competent bombers. After an explosion caused serious structural damage to an electricity installation serving the Gallaher tobacco factory in Belfast on 8 August 1970, the report stated: 'This was an efficient sabotage job in which the explosive device was placed well inside the sub-station where it could be expected to do the most damage to the equipment.' But there were still many incidents where less expert bombers endangered themselves and anyone in their path. The British Legion Hall at Stewartstown on the western suburbs of Belfast was the scene of a failed attack on 13 July. When the bomb-disposal officer arrived he found a cluster of six unexploded eight-ounce sticks of gelignite attached to a bunch of burned-out match-heads. He concluded: 'This was a desperate attempt by an amateur with no knowledge of explosives and no hope of success.'

Events took a far more serious turn in August when two police officers perished as they opened the door of a stolen car which had been booby-trapped with 20 lb. of gelignite and abandoned on the roadside near Cullaville in south Armagh. This was plainly not the work of amateurs. The following month, the growing danger to the security forces was underlined again when, at nearby Forkhill, a concealed secondary device was found at the site of an explosion. The green box, packed with explosive and old nuts and bolts, was discovered before it could go off and kill or injure those turning up to investigate the first incident. According to the Army's official spokesman, with this incident the bombing campaign had taken 'a savage twist'.

The number of attacks rose, with fourteen in June, twenty in July and twenty in August. Targets included the warehouse of a business operated by William Morgan, one-time health minister at Stormont, a social club, a bookmaker's shop, the home of barrister Richard Ferguson, a former Unionist MP, numerous private dwellings, hotels and public houses, a Belfast department store, customs posts, telephone exchanges, banks, a bus depot, the *Irish Independent* newspaper office, the Aer Lingus office in Belfast, council headquarters, water mains, an income tax office, several police and Army posts and the Army recruiting office in Belfast. A major disaster was narrowly averted in July when a Belfast–Dublin passenger train jumped a twelve-inch gap blown in the line but was not derailed.

By the end of the year there had been 170 bombings, up from ten in 1969, and the haul of explosives captured had increased from 0.4 to 2.6 tons. Of the twenty-five deaths attributable to the security situation in 1970, nine were linked to the bombing campaign. Apart from the two police officers murdered in south Armagh, the other seven were all terrorists killed as the result of premature explosions, 'own goals' as they came to be described in the macabre humour that developed to mask the trauma and tragedy steadily engulfing Northern Ireland. Five people died in the first of these incidents after an explosion in the kitchen of a house in Londonderry's Creggan estate shortly after midnight on 26 June. Fire officers found two men burned to death on the kitchen floor and two girls, aged four and nine, asphyxiated by fumes in their bedroom upstairs. One was dead on arrival at hospital and the other died soon afterwards, as did a third man eleven days later. The three dead men, one of them the father of the two girls, had long connections with the IRA and forensic evidence established they had been working in the kitchen with a volatile substance which had exploded. The next victim, also associated with the IRA, died on 4 September while setting a bomb at an electricity installation in south Belfast. On 6 November, another young man, with no known IRA connection, was fatally burned while trying to set fire to an Orange Hall near Carrickfergus, County Antrim. These episodes demonstrate why the Army describe terrorist 'bombs' as Improvised Explosive Devices (IEDs).

In fact, terrorist explosive technology had evolved little from the dynamite and gunpowder devices first used by nineteenth-century Irish Republican 'dynamite bombers'. Over a two-year period from 1883 they set off 'infernal machines' at the offices of *The Times*, on the London Underground, at mainline stations, the House of Commons, the Tower of London and even Scotland Yard before they were apprehended. An alert policeman saved Nelson's Column by spotting a bag containing sixteen sticks of gelignite. The advent of batteries led to modifications but the 'bombs' were still IEDs, in many shapes and sizes from a simple petrol or nail bomb, containing a few ounces of high explosive, to a vehicle containing hundreds of pounds with sophisticated electric initiation and anti-handling mechanisms. The ready availability of chemicals and other everyday components meant that in a free and open society it was virtually impossible to prevent insurgents from making powerful bombs and the threat they posed was truly terrifying.

At the end of 1970, the Northern Ireland government put a bold face on the growing crisis, saying that while there had been a monthly average of fifteen explosions, for every seven sticks of gelignite detonated the security forces had recovered six. Meanwhile the Army had again been required to enhance its bomb-disposal capability. In September 1970, RAOC Major George Styles, who had first arrived in Lisburn a year earlier on a routine posting as Deputy Assistant Director of Ordnance Services, was appointed Senior Ammunition Technical Officer (SATO). He welcomed the responsibility of a real job for he had spent his time trapped between two under-employed RAOC lieutenant-colonels vying for control of resources. Up to this point most officers sent to Northern Ireland contented themselves with the quality hunting, shooting and fishing to be had while coasting to retirement in a posting which required little actual soldiering. They had, furthermore, little interest in or appreciation of the local political climate. As Styles confessed in his later memoir, 'I formed the belief then – and I hold it today – that the troubles in Northern Ireland were planned and fomented by international Communism in the guise of the IRA. Everywhere I looked I could see evidence of a hidden hand pulling the strings. I could see Reds under the bed.' A Sussex man, married with three children, and with a wry sense of humour, Styles would say 'I am careful – like a cat', when asked how he was going to tackle the growing number of bombs. Sir Ian Freeland, the General Officer Commanding who appointed him, merely said: 'You'll be busy.'

The first job recorded in 321 EOD's 1971 log was a request from Armagh Council on 2 January to check out an abandoned black Austin A55 car. The bombings had made people nervous of unidentified objects and bomb-disposal teams were being routinely called to anything suspicious. During that week, teams were also called to a suspect parcel in Belfast which turned out to be a dead rabbit and to another which proved to be nothing more lethal than waste paper. On 7 January, after a robbery at Peter's Hill Post Office, Belfast, they were called to remove two ounces of unexploded gelignite so that business could resume.

One successful defusing that month was not attributable to an RAOC operator. On 18 January, Sergeant John Green of 32 Heavy Regiment, Royal Artillery detached an alarm-clock timer from a 48 lb. bomb at a BBC transmitter near Newry, County Down. When he had finished he noticed the timer had just three seconds left to run.

The launch of a concerted arson campaign using small incendiary devices presented the most serious problem for the EOD teams. Overnight on 23 January eight premises in Belfast were attacked, leaving a trail of destruction at a building supplier, an auction room, an upholstery factory, an electrical wholesaler and a textile warehouse. A few weeks later the Army passed what would be the first of many grim milestones when Gunner Robert Curtis was shot dead in Belfast, the first fatal casualty since the troops had gone on to the streets over eighteen months earlier. Over the following violent weekend, bomb-disposal officers were at one point dealing with an incident every hour. On the morning of 9 February came the major bombing tragedy that everyone feared. A BBC Land Rover passing along a rough track leading to the TV transmitter at Brougher Mountain, County Tyrone, snapped a knee-high tripwire stretched across the path and triggered a huge explosion, instantly killing the five engineers on board. The trap was probably intended for the Army patrol which regularly used the same route.

By now the bomb-disposal officers were encountering ever more complicated and sophisticated devices. Their caution was justified by what Captain Murray Stewart found when he was called to a cement works near Cookstown, County Tyrone, just after 7 a.m. on 9 August. There, concealed in machinery, was a total of 53 lb. of Greencast explosive and 500 feet of Cordtex detonating cord, divided into six charges each encased in twelve-inch sections of steel pipe. The timer was set to detonate at 00.30 but the clock had stopped at 23.45 so the device failed to fire. 'A professional attempt at what would have been a hundred per cent successful demolition prevented only by mechanical failure,' Captain Stewart commented on the incident report. What he did not dwell on was the fact that the bomb was fitted with a complex anti-handling device, not encountered before, which would have caused it to detonate if he had not recognised and broken the secondary electrical circuit. The captain's concentration and courage during the four-hour clearance operation was later recognised by the award of the MBE.

The 1970 escalation of violence was as nothing to that which occurred as 1971 progressed. The three EOD operators in Northern Ireland answered 1,000 calls over one four-month period. In an unprecedented onslaught on the social and economic infrastructure of the community, the terrorists imposed carnage and destruction on a previously unthinkable scale. Among a series of spectacular fires set off by explosions was a huge blaze at the Esso petroleum depot at Belfast harbour triggered by a 15 lb. bomb placed inside a cluster of distribution pipes.

The Provisional IRA was responsible for most of the bombings, not all of which were publicly acknowledged, but a considerable number were carried out by the disparate factions of extreme Protestants that had sprung up to 'defend' Northern Ireland. As the terrorists became steadily more indiscriminate, neither side seemed to care if friend or foe was affected. There was no guarantee that a bomb planted in a shop, an office or a pub would not injure or even kill somebody from the same community as the bomber. One Army intelligence officer in north Belfast heard that an intrepid 'IRA Volunteer' got a good thrashing from his mother after she narrowly missed being injured by the bomb he boasted of exploding in the city centre. In Belfast, fourteen newborn babies and their mothers were showered with glass when a bomb went off outside the Mater Hospital. People drinking in pubs and clubs, out shopping, or in their workplaces were having to flee bomb scares. Often there was no or an inadequate warning and people were injured: six in a crowded social club; five at an estate agent's; six on a city centre street; nineteen in a suburban pub. In one of the most brutal attacks, in the early evening of 25 May a suitcase containing a 30 lb. gelignite bomb was thrown into the crowded front office of the Springfield Road station in Belfast. As the device landed on the floor, Sergeant Michael Willets of the Parachute Regiment pushed two young children into a corner and crouched over them to protect them from the blast. They survived but he died some hours later in hospital. For sacrificing his life, the sergeant was post-humously awarded the George Cross, the highest award for bravery in peacetime.

In a bid to get on top of the deteriorating situation, the Northern Ireland government increased to £50,000 a standing reward for information leading to the conviction of any of the people responsible for the out-rages. A publicity campaign was launched to stimulate public vigilance. Police distributed thousands of copies of a poster showing images of a cigarette packet, a padded envelope and a shopping bag. 'They may look harmless but they could be firebombs. Report anything suspicious,' it stated. Crime prevention officers toured town centres urging the business community to search their premises, especially after closing for the night. Firebombs were sometimes being planted by female bombers late in the afternoon so that they would go off once staff had departed. Shop staff were particularly advised to check the pockets of clothing on display, furniture and inflammable material such as paint tins. On the first weekend of May there were forty-two overnight firebomb attacks in Belfast city-centre stores. Fourteen ignited before the alarm was raised. Prompt reaction by bomb-disposal teams and firefighters foiled what would otherwise have been a conflagration, gutting the city's largest shops.

The seriousness of the situation caused the beleaguered prime minister, Brian Faulkner, to give a personal warning of the need for vigilance to combat the attacks. 'They are the work of rats on the run,' he said, but by then the total number of explosions had risen inexorably since January to 136, with as many as eight or twelve incidents some nights. The bombers were even attacking guarded targets, like police stations, in daylight hours. Only nine people had been convicted after well over 300 explosions and the chances of getting conclusive evidence against others was severely inhibited when the already inadequate forensic science laboratory in the Markets area of Belfast, which was mainly geared to analysing drink-drive specimens and matching car paint samples in hit-and-run cases, suffered extensive structural damage in a triple bomb blast on 27 April. As intended by the terrorists, it knocked out the little specialist equipment the laboratory had and destroyed vital evidence gathered from the scenes of earlier explosions.

Nevertheless, the security forces were having some success. Roadblock checks and search operations found in excess of 1,000 lb. of gelignite, while controls on the storage, movement and use of explosives were reinstated. Quarry operators were fined between £10 and £100 for breaches of the new regulations and a man whose hoax call caused Telephone House in Belfast to be evacuated and searched was fined the then considerable sum of £40.

Because incidents were now occurring all over Northern Ireland, in April Styles had for the first time assigned an EOD detachment to each of the three Brigade areas: 8 Infantry Brigade in Londonderry, 19 Airportable Brigade at Lurgan and 39 Brigade at Lisburn. Although the members were all nominally posted to the shadow 321 EOD unit, he recalls that in those frantic days nobody ever mentioned the 'magic numbers' and the military administration had not yet got round to creating the paperwork to formalise its existence. Instead he was caught up in an internal feud with the newly arrived Chief of Staff, Brigadier Marston Tickell, a career Sapper who was seeking to secure prime responsibility for the growing EOD task for his parent corps. With the RAOC's territory to be defended against the dreaded Sappers, one of the vying lieutenant-colonels, 'Digger' Faralay, took up the cause. 'Digger and I would have welcomed a takeover for all the thanks we got but the guidelines had been long drawn and we were too proud to relinquish our claim to disaster,' recalls a cynical Styles. 'The fight back worked and it gave Digger the clout to get more officers from senior ranks to deploy in EOD units to deal with the calls that were now streaming in.' It also brought a halt to the uphill struggle Styles was encountering in getting vehicles and equipment for his growing number of teams.

> I used to get calls asking me why I needed more than one driver per Land Rover. I replied that although, with some persuasion, the vehicle could be driven for twenty-four hours constantly, I was unable to make the driver do the same. At the most inopportune moment, Digger was sent on a retirement bricks-and-mortar course instead of being promoted. His replacement was less than dynamic and despite the fact that we were regularly handling twenty-four bomb calls in twenty-four hours, he insisted on trying to put the bomb-disposal officers on normal duty rosters.

However, David Bayley-Pike, scientific adviser to the GOC, was an influential ally. 'With his help, small things and great things became possible,' says Styles, who soon had a suite of offices instead of the 'cupboard' in which he had originally been confined and a flow of vital kit. 'RAOC ammunition regulations permitted only bronze tools but we got the Wilkinson secateurs we wanted through local purchase. We preferred them to the other type because they had overlap blades.'

Whatever the odds and with minimum regard for their own safety, the bomb-disposal officers continued to race from incident to incident in an often futile bid to beat the bombers. From time to time they were helped by intrepid members of the public. A 'Mr X' who was arriving at the Store Bar near Templepatrick, County Antrim, after midnight on 23 June 1971 saw a package with a burning fuse being lobbed into the premises by a man who was quickly driven away. Without hesitation he grabbed the device and threw it into an adjacent field where the fuse went out. A bomb-disposal officer discovered that a detached detonator had prevented the 10 lb. of gelignite from exploding.

Geoffrey Johnston-Smith, the Under-Secretary of State for Defence, who visited troops soon after this incident, said the operation in Northern Ireland was one of the most difficult that had ever been undertaken by the Army, 'but we are getting on top of it'. Yet he must have been aware that the Belfast administration was at that very point trying to persuade Prime Minister Edward Heath to introduce internment without trial. The Army was already secretly building accommodation at Long Kesh, a disused Second World War airfield ten miles from Belfast, and helping the police to draw up 'wanted' lists. It was an article of faith for Northern Ireland's Unionists that internment was the one weapon which would beat the IRA. By mid-1971, after all that had happened, even people of moderate views believed the time had come for a round-up but the GOC, Sir Harry Tuzo, his military superiors in London and his closest advisers in Lisburn remained adamantly opposed to it. They believed there were still plenty of military options to be tried.

Street violence and bombings continued to surge. About 8.30 p.m. on 30 July, an attendant discovered a box in the ladies' section of an ornate underground Victorian public toilet at the front of Belfast's City Hall. Fortunately she did not interfere with the device, for while a bomb-disposal officer was dismantling it in the confined space of a toilet cubicle he found not one but two anti-handling mechanisms: a signal that the terrorists were now actively trying to kill bomb-disposal officers.

With seventy-eight explosions in July and more over the first few days of August, including the destruction of the *Daily Mirror* printing plant,

Heath bowed to Faulkner's wishes, overruled the wary soldiers and ordered arrest swoops. Just as the security forces were gearing up, on 8 August 1971 there was a three-bomb assault on an electricity power station near Larne, by far the most damaging incident of the campaign to date. A saboteur climbed to a lofty catwalk and planted high-explosive devices against each of the three main oil-fired boilers, knocking out a quarter of Northern Ireland's generating capacity. (Only emergency repairs prevented widespread power cuts during the approaching winter.)

By breakfast time on 9 August, the morning of the swoops, a head count showed that 354 of the 452 suspects on the 'wanted' list had been detained but any hopes that internment would inhibit the violence were quickly dispelled. Within a week twenty-four people had been killed, including three soldiers. Catholics were appalled that only alleged Republicans had been arrested and even those with no sympathy for the IRA shared the anger. Furthermore, those in the most troubled areas already knew that the wrong people had been arrested in what turned out to be an abysmal failure of police and military intelligence-gathering. As clouds of smoke from burning buildings and vehicles hung permanently in the summer air over parts of Belfast, Londonderry, Newry and other towns, the security forces were under constant attack and the booming of explosions became as regular as the chiming of the clocks. The death toll could easily have been worse. On 10 August an attempt was made to float a bomb under an Army post at Flax Street Mill in Belfast, occupied by 330 men of the Light Infantry, but the 50 lb. of gelignite went down the wrong sewer pipe and exploded under a local drinking club, fortunately empty at the time.

About 11 a.m. on 25 August, a switchboard operator at the Electricity Board for Northern Ireland headquarters at Danesfort in south Belfast answered what was far from a routine call. 'There's a bomb in the building,' said a woman curtly before ringing off. Six hundred employees began to evacuate the three-storey block, but two minutes later a bomb concealed in a locker alongside one of the main exit routes suddenly exploded, bringing down an adjacent stairway packed with people trying to leave the building. One man was killed and thirty-five people injured. Even more might have perished if a second bomb nearby had also exploded, but its timer-power unit was disrupted by the first blast. Two days later the badly rattled Northern Ireland government placed full-page advertisements in local newspapers, addressed 'to the occupiers of business and other premises':

It is vital you help to BEAT THE BOMB. Search your premises
regularly! Watch for anyone acting suspiciously! Check all goods
entering your premises! Ring 999 (Police) immediately if you are at all
suspicious.

When August ended there had been 120 explosions amidst a dreadful
upsurge of violence and death which showed no sign of dissipating. The
Army had brought in substantial reinforcements, among them further
RAOC experts to help tackle the bombs. One model incorporated a
hidden micro-switch in the base designed to trigger the bomb after the
more obvious clothes-peg switch had been made safe but wet weather
rendered the first one harmless before the EOD team tackled it. An even
more sophisticated bomb appeared within days. Captain David
Stewardson, aged twenty-nine, who had only arrived in Northern Ireland
ten days earlier, was with Styles in Lisburn on 9 September when a
request came through for an ATO to examine a suspicious box left at
the door of an Orange Order hall at Castlerobin, County Antrim. The
captain and his team arrived at the scene at 10 a.m. where a small crowd
of onlookers had gathered. One of them, an experienced quarryman,
warned that what appeared to be a length of fuse was protruding from
the box.

Captain Stewardson climbed over the wall at the front of the hall and
examined the device before starting to cut at one of the corners with a
hacksaw. He paused for twenty or thirty seconds, then started sawing
again but almost at once there was a bright orange flash and puffs of
white smoke which temporarily blinded one of the policemen, followed
by a loud explosion. The captain was killed instantly, his body blown
twenty feet on to the road by the explosion of an estimated 10 lb. of
quarry gelignite. Later in the day the Provisional IRA acknowledged
responsibility.

A few days after the murder, Major Styles stood alongside Captain
Stewardson's colleagues who had survived the blast, as local clergymen
conducted a memorial service for the dead officer. A piper, standing on
the spot where the bomb had been placed, played the haunting lament
'Flowers of the Forest'. As a further mark of sympathy, the local
community donated £250 for the Stewardson family, and there was a tide
of condemnation and sympathy throughout Northern Ireland. Paying
tribute to the 'men of courage' in the bomb disposal teams, the *Belfast
Telegraph* said:

These men would not wish to be regarded as heroes. To them the danger is part of the job. But they possess a kind of courage that most people could not match. They are a marked contrast to the men who plant the bomb and claim to be heroes for carrying out their murderous actions with stealth and cowardice.

Apart from mourning the loss of a respected colleague and sympathising with his wife and two young daughters in Edinburgh, the most urgent necessity for his colleagues was to work out precisely what had caused his death. From an examination of the debris they were quickly able to establish that the bomb was of a type never seen before. They called it the 'Castlerobin' and circulated a hand-drawn diagram to all operators, showing details of its antiopening and antilifting micro-switches.

Operators' growing vulnerability to bombs of rapidly developing complexity was repeatedly made clear. Among other incidents, an old tyre with wires leading from it was found lying at a street junction in the Ardoyne area of north Belfast on 17 September. Just after 8 a.m., as an ATO was walking back along the cleared street after inspecting the device, a number of shots rang out. Lance-Corporal Peter Herrington, a member of a Green Howards patrol giving cover to the bomb-disposal team, was shot dead. Two other soldiers were wounded in the sniper fire and a civilian narrowly missed being hit as bullets ripped through his caravan nearby. It is probable that the 22 lb. device had been placed to draw a bomb-disposal team into the area for the sniper to attack them.

There was another Castlerobin-type incident at an electricity sub-station in Lisburn on 2 October, but this time the bomber himself died when the sensitive anti-handling device triggered after a cat ran out and startled him as he was planting it. Next day the Army managed to defuse a similar bomb outside a shop on Belfast's Antrim Road with a controlled explosion. The fuse had been partly burned, but closer examination by portable x-ray revealed this was merely a ruse to deceive the operator. Inside the device was yet another Castlerobin antilifting mechanism. The EOD team then had a lucky break when five unexploded Castlerobins were captured in a bomb factory, rendered safe and taken away for examination. Thanks to this opportunity, the construction of the bombs was now fully understood and within days two more were successfully neutralised.

Not long afterwards, however, a second operator lost his life. At 6.35 p.m. on 24 November, WO2 Colin 'Taffy' Davies, based with the Lurgan detachment, was sent to investigate reports of a bomb planted in a furniture store. When he got there, he found William Street already cordoned off and police still evacuating the nearby buildings. Just two days earlier in the same town, a twenty-one-year-old man had perished and several customers were injured when a bomb he was planting at a public house exploded prematurely.

Warrant Officer Davies and Lance-Corporal Hall headed towards an office at the rear of the premises, where there was a medium-sized box from which, according to the lance-corporal, came a distinct ticking sound. Davies indicated that he was going to let the device 'soak' – the term used by bomb-disposal officers to describe the intervals they build into their operating procedures as a safety measure – for an hour, but as they turned to leave the building, the timer expired and the 20 lb. of gelignite detonated. Hall was uninjured apart from shock and facial cuts, but Davies was buried under tons of debris as the roof and walls of the building collapsed. Rescue efforts were obstructed by a second explosion and fire in which two soldiers were injured. At first this blast was thought to be the result of another bomb but it was later established that a butane gas cylinder had ignited. When Davies was located by rescuers, he was dead. His body was removed to the mortuary in Belfast where Major Bernard Calladene, who had just arrived to command the bomb-disposal teams, formally identified the dead soldier, whom he had known for nine years. Thirty-seven-year-old Davies, who had already safely dismantled a number of devices during three months in Northern Ireland, was from Glamorgan in south Wales, and left a wife and four young children.

In his autobiography, Styles states his belief that it wasn't the bomb, but the collapsing building, which caused Davies's death. 'The Welshman had done everything "by the book" but he'd been very unlucky. [His death] brought home to us once again how narrow a tightrope we were walking on. You can train a man to the nth degree, you can give him courage and skill and caution but you can't give him good luck.'

Meanwhile Styles himself was involved in two major operations which demonstrated just how far the Provisional IRA was stretching the frontiers of urban guerrilla terrorism. The target was the recently opened Europa Hotel, a prestigious twelve-storey, 200-bedroom building on Great Victoria Street. In the late afternoon of 20 October, after an anonymous telephone call, staff found a box in a corner telephone booth in the Whip and Saddle bar on the ground floor. The eighty-four guests, including many journalists and television crews who had made the new hotel their headquarters for covering the Troubles, were evacuated as

Captain Roger Mendham and the Belfast bomb-disposal team were called to the scene. After a preliminary look they called for radiography equipment to get a closer look at the box's innards. It was a measure of the lack of proper equipment at the time that bomb-disposal teams on the ground had to use the public telephone system to communicate with EOD Headquarters at Lisburn. Styles ordered Captain Alan Clouter to head for the hotel with the X-ray kit, but because of the symbolic status of the target he decided to go along himself. As he was being driven the ten miles down the M1 from Lisburn, he vowed, as he later recalled in his memoir, 'it was going to be a belt, braces, safety pin and string operation. No chances whatsoever.' Equally, he decided, there would be no hasty action. The clearance would take as long as it would take.

Because the box was tight against the wall of the building with a lot of metal panelling around it, the team's first problem was to move it to get a clear X-ray. From the previous Castlerobin incidents, they knew the device probably contained two sensitive micro-switches, one to set it off if the lid was removed from the box, the other to detonate it if lifted. Moving it was therefore a highly hazardous proposition but they inched it forward on the carpet until it was sufficiently clear of the walls to be X-rayed. The portable reading equipment did not give enough clarity, so, at the suggestion of a police officer, the plates were taken half a mile to the Royal Victoria Hospital X-ray unit. The experts immediately recognised the handiwork of the unknown bomb-maker they had called Mr X. Back at the hotel, they set about rendering the device safe by separating the firing mechanisms from the 15 lb. of explosive.

Having made the bomb dormant, as Styles called it, the next step was to dismantle it. Rather than risk the building, the team decided to pull the bomb out of the hotel altogether and take it apart in a sandbag beehive, three feet thick and four feet high, which a team of Royal Engineers had been constructing on the hotel forecourt. Since the bomb might still have contained an anti-disruption circuit, a rope was looped around the box to pull it gingerly through the bar, then through the hotel entrance and along a path of sand to the dismantling bay. It was a slow and cumbersome operation. Styles and his team broke cover every few feet to check that the box had not tilted over, begun ticking or shown any other signs of going off. He wrote in his memoir:

I had every reason to believe the bomb was now harmless but you couldn't avoid the feeling of menace each time you walked towards it. Inside that box, secured by pulling line, was enough energy to blow your head from your shoulders, your arms and legs from your trunk, and your trunk straight through the plate windows of the Europa Hotel and into the Hamill Hotel across the road. Your combat jacket, flak jacket, would just about keep your trunk in one piece.

When Styles and his men had got the box into the beehive, they took a short break for coffee and fried-egg sandwiches laid on by the hotel, then started on the final stage of the operation. It took two controlled explosions to expose the device and finally separate the components. The operation ended in triumph at about 11 p.m. with the hotel undamaged and all the bomb-disposal operators safe. A large crowd had gathered outside the hotel as the evening progressed and there was still a considerable audience at the end. Television camera crews and photographers had watched every stage of the drama, especially when it moved outside within range of their telescopic lens, and there was widespread acclamation for the achievement next day. As the *Belfast Telegraph* noted that evening:

> There are degrees of danger in Belfast and other parts of Northern Ireland. There is danger to civilians, particularly in the cities. There is danger to troops and policemen as they try to carry out their duties. But it is a special kind of danger requiring a special kind of courage when men are faced with a bomb which could kill or maim them at any time. The bomb experts carry out their work with quiet courage. There is no bravado. They talk about the danger in a matter-of-fact way. There is no public adulation befitting heroes. To them the defusing of a bomb is merely part of a job. But the gratitude and the thoughts of every decent person goes out to them as they face their lonely, difficult and dangerous work.

No doubt provoked by all the favourable publicity for the Army, the bombers returned to the hotel two days later. In mid-afternoon three masked men entered the hotel by the main door and held staff at gunpoint while a fourth staggered in with a large, heavy box which he left close to the lifts, in front of the reception desk. Before he left, a witness said, he 'twiddled' with it.

Styles was alerted at his office in Lisburn where he was clearing his desk before taking his wife and a visiting colleague for dinner. That arrangement was hastily cancelled while Captains Clouter and Mendham were sent to the Europa again and Styles set off to join them. Before leaving Lisburn, Styles also alerted the Royal Engineers that he would again need their help with sand and railway sleepers. When he reached the evacuated hotel, he saw the bomb in a box eighteen inches square and two feet deep, with the message 'IRA – Tee-hee, Hee-hee, Ho-ho, Ha-ha' scrawled on it. Styles had no doubt that 'Mr X' had sent him a larger and more complex bomb this time, a suspicion confirmed by X-rays which revealed more than double the amount of high explosive and a maze of wires and micro-switches obviously designed to confuse. Having identified the key components, as Styles put it, 'we stunned the brute,' but it still had to be dismantled to remove all danger.

Styles decided to build a sandbag corridor around the bomb along which it would be pulled outside. Mendham discovered a piece of Formica in the hotel basement and the box, encircled with a length of fishing line, was carefully inched on to it. The pull was a slow, constantly interrupted business but in the end the bomb was manoeuvred into another sandbag beehive outside and carefully dismantled. The entire operation took nine hours and when the all clear was given at 1 a.m., Harper Brown, the steely hotel manager, threw an impromptu champagne party at which Styles and his team were the lavishly toasted guests of honour.

Again the operation was reported in detail, caught the public imagination and earned wide praise. The feelings of the large majority of the population were well expressed by Brian Faulkner in a letter to the GOC Northern Ireland on 5 November 1971:

> Nothing impresses me more than the cool, calculated, professional skill and courage of those who render safe or destroy the explosive devices which would otherwise have damaged or killed innocent people whilst also destroying property. I wish therefore to express my admiration and thanks to Major Styles and the officers and men of the EOD Unit, with special reference to those who were engaged on the Europa Hotel incident. Theirs and their colleagues' is a very special type of courage.

Soon afterwards Styles was awarded the George Cross for his impressive improvisation and exceptional courage. He thus emerged from the usual anonymity of the EOD constituency to become virtually the best known bomb disposal officer in the world, but he modestly insisted the prized medal was not for himself but for his small team: 'They have to find some idiot to hang it on.' His real view was that they should 'hang a medal on every ATO the minute he comes off the boat'.

But once again there was little respite for the EOD experts. The next target was the Celebrity Club, above the C&A clothing store in Donegall Place. Late on the evening of Sunday 24 October, four terrorists pushed through the queue of customers, held up the door staff, placed a large box in the entrance hall and shouted a bomb warning. As the raiders ran out of the club, two plain-clothes police officers opened fire on them, killing one man and wounding his woman companion. Another man was captured nearby. Soon afterwards, Captain Mendham arrived, followed in turn by Clouter and Styles. As they prepared to X-ray the square chipboard box, laying out hooks and lines, Styles went to see if the police had gleaned any information from the captured bomber. As he was walking back to rejoin his team, a huge explosion shook the ground and set off a sequence of ringing alarms, breaking glass and falling debris. Styles was most relieved to find all members of his team alive and uninjured. Mendham had left the building seconds earlier. The bomb-maker, they later concluded, had incorporated a two-hour timer to ensure that it would go off while the team was dealing with it. As Styles returned to Lisburn in the early hours he thought to himself: 'We're at the end of the plank.'

Captain Mendham narrowly survived again within a week when a bomb exploded while he was examining it. He was also involved in another epic clearance operation on 4 November 1971. The Regency Hotel, on Botanic Avenue in Belfast, sustained heavy damage when a bomb went off twenty minutes after being laid, but another at the York Hotel a few doors away failed to go off. From his recent experience, Mendham suspected that the timing device had been set before the bomb was screwed inside the container, protected by both anti-lift and anti-opening switches, and so he allowed it to soak for two hours while a sandbag blast wall was built ten yards away. Polaroid X-rays showed a simple time-delay mechanism with a standard travel alarm clock connected to a 4.5 volt battery, an electric detonator and 10 lb. of explosive. More detailed medical X-ray plates then revealed that the clock terminals had either closed and misfired or had several hours still to run, although no ticking could be detected. Ninety minutes later the position of the hands was unchanged and Mendham decided to extract the bomb from the hotel and dismantle it in a sandbag beehive. The team planned to lift the nylon bag containing the bomb with a pole and hook and lower it onto the sledge they had improvised from a litter bin. It proved easier said than done. In line with the 'one-man risk' rule, Captain Mendham, protected by a full armour suit, fished for the device, taking directions from a team of observers with binoculars. It was not possible to work in the cumbersome suit for more than five minutes without resting and clearing the sweat from the visor and the operator's eyes. In his autobiography, Styles recalls that while Mendham had the bomb hooked on his pole and line, a kitten suddenly appeared and began trying to play with the dangling object. Styles considered throwing an ashtray to scare it away but, fearful of hitting the bomb, instead began barking like a dog, which did the trick.

In the end the device was patiently pulled through the front door of the hotel, manoeuvred into the bucket of an armoured bulldozer and then carefully deposited in the beehive, where the bag was opened with a small explosive charge and the device disrupted. The whole operation had taken a painstaking nine hours, but Captain Mendham's tribulations were not yet over. Only days later, on 13 November, a bomb exploded just as he was withdrawing after his initial reconnaissance, yet he attended a further six incidents that day without displaying any qualms. On 25 November, another marathon day, he personally dismantled four devices and attended six further incidents. In fact during his tour of duty in Belfast, which began on 1 October 1971, immediately after his very close friend Captain David Stewardson was killed at Castlerobin, and ended on 2 February 1972, Captain Mendham answered 235 calls whilst the small team under his command dealt with no fewer than 936 requests for their services. His citation for the George Medal records that on several occasions he missed death by seconds.

> Such activity inevitably imposed great strain upon all concerned and it is to Captain Mendham's lasting credit, and due to his constant display of courage, leadership and technical proficiency, that nobody succumbed to the tension but rather grew in stature because of it. For one so young, this concentration of experience and ready acceptance of responsibility brought forth a response of the highest order well worthy of formal recognition.

Four other equally hard-earned George Medals were awarded to bomb-disposal officers the same year: Captains Alan Clouter and D Markham, WO2 T Green and Sergeant A Dedman. The workload endured by all the teams reflected the tide of terrorism they were now trying to hold back. Explosions had increased again to 175 incidents totalling 2,200 lb. of explosive in September. A military appreciation of the security situation sent to Downing Street in October 1971 concluded: 'The IRA has the initiative and is causing disruption out of all proportion to the relatively small numbers engaged. This is not to credit the IRA with any unusual skill; it is the normal pattern of urban guerrilla activity when the guerrillas are not opposed by a ruthless and authoritarian governmental machine.' The Army was increasingly frustrated that despite the commitment of fourteen full infantry battalions, two armoured reconnaissance regiments and a large detachment of support units, it was failing to halt the violence. The principal weakness, according to the Chief of the General Staff who visited Northern Ireland soon afterwards, was in intelligence-gathering.

Everyday life in Northern Ireland was now being disrupted on a grand scale. Worshippers had to flee their Belfast church when a bomb went off without warning in an office block next door. A ten-year-old boy and his piano teacher were showered with glass when a bomb devastated a neighbouring library and health centre. Old people, many bedridden, had to be evacuated from a home when bombs were planted nearby. A man was trapped inside his vehicle in a car park for twenty minutes after an explosion engulfed it in smoke and debris. A policeman risked his life going back into a hotel to rescue a comatose drinker moments before a bomb went off. Being evicted from buses at gunpoint became commonplace as masked men planted bombs on the vehicles. Traffic was regularly disrupted and workplaces were destroyed by blasts and fires. Apart from the enduring heroism of the bomb-disposal men, there were countless episodes of exceptional bravery on the part of fire, ambulance and police officers, rescuing the endangered, treating the injured and recovering the dead. Every scare and alert had to be treated as real until a bomb-disposal officer established otherwise. Derek Pickford, who was based at Ballykinler at this time, remembers one day when he cleared thirteen cars with suspect gas cylinders aboard.

Increasingly windows were criss-crossed with adhesive tape to cut down on flying glass once a bomb went off. Shops and offices introduced security measures, putting searchers at the entrances, issuing staff with identity passes and checking vehicles and deliveries. Such precautions were well justified as the bombers became ever more devious. On one occasion in Belfast a tin of paint was bought on approval and returned the next day. Shortly afterwards a bomb warning was telephoned to the shop and the returned tin was found to contain 8 oz. of gelignite and a delayed-action fuse. As the destruction multiplied, a new breed of entrepreneur sprung up. The 'hardboard millionaires' earned their wealth by turning out, day or night, after explosions to board up shattered windows and weatherproof buildings until proper repairs could be made. A more bizarre money-making practice also took root at this time. Police and soldiers were amazed to see people running into danger zones after explosions and lying down. Their aim was to be ferried to hospital where, in the absence of any visible injury, they would be recorded as suffering from shock and entitled to claim £300 compensation.

Apart from the urban terrorist campaign, security forces were facing an onslaught in rural areas. One morning eight customs posts in three border counties were devastated by explosions. Ambushes were laid to be initiated by command wire or radio control from over the border, where gunmen and bombers enjoyed virtual immunity from arrest. Indeed, the Irish courts upheld the defence, in the few cases brought before them, that such offences were 'political' and thus protected by the Irish constitution.

The government and Army continued to make optimistic predictions about the demise of the IRA but the Christmas season of 1971 provided no corollary for the claims. At the end of November there were twenty explosions in thirty hours. On the night of Saturday 4 December, fifteen people died when a no-warning bomb planted by Loyalists tore through McGurk's Bar in Belfast. Troops, police and other rescue workers clawed through the rubble with their bare hands to free casualties and retrieve bodies. Two days later a five-storey factory in Dublin Road, Belfast, was destroyed after armed men left a bomb in a shop on the ground floor. A member of the Salvation Army was killed when one of its walls collapsed on top of the Citadel next door during the twenty-hour firefighting operation.

On 20 December there was yet another blitz with ten attacks. A 3,500-gallon petrol tanker with a bomb on board was abandoned in the centre of Lisburn and other targets were a suburban railway station, an antique shop, a supermarket, an insurance office, a café and a large secluded hotel on the southern outskirts of Belfast. In one case a woman shop assistant carried a 10 lb. bomb into the road where it exploded minutes later. It was the fifth such attack on the premises. The very next day, John Lavery, a publican, was killed while trying to carry a bomb from his bar at Lisburn Road, Belfast. A few days earlier he had carried a similar device to the middle of the main road, but this time the bomb was fitted with an anti-handling device.

Christmas did not deter the bombers; 300 children were evacuated from a cinema moments before a bomb ripped through the building, and at the Ulster Hall 200 carol singers continued their concert on the street outside after a bomb warning. On Christmas Eve massive devastation was averted when a man drove a booby-trapped petrol tanker away from the centre of Dunmurry village. Soldiers fired shots to dislodge the explosive device before an ATO moved in to make it completely safe.

During this period, the bomb teams were encountering devices more lethal than the 'Castlerobin'. More and more were being specifically designed to defeat EOD action and a new layer of danger was realised after a light-sensitive device was found in a darkened room and failed to operate. With the safety of operators at increasing risk and a fear that a truly sophisticated bomb-maker was at large in Belfast setting devices to explode when an ATO would just be approaching, it was decided to reverse the standing policy that EOD teams would try to defuse every device. Henceforth, unless life was endangered, they would allow bombs to 'soak' or 'cook' for up to two hours and ten minutes. The time was calculated from the maximum period for which the various timers then in use could be set. Watches and clocks were used to give a thirty-minute delay while kitchen and parking-meter reminder timers could be set for two hours. Furthermore the soak period enabled searchers to check for secondary devices operated by, for instance, a pressure plate or tripwire.

This new procedure came as a relief to the hard-pressed operators. Until then, following close questioning of witnesses, they had had a 'window' to run in and try to sever the detonator lead with a scalpel or secateurs. For ease of movement they usually wore only their beret and flak jacket. 'The quicker you were in and out, the least you were exposed to danger,' remembers Mike Coldrick, who was later awarded the George Medal and MBE for bravery. However, the new policy did not meet with universal approval among the hard-pressed citizens of Belfast and or members of the security forces. Coldrick recalls:

> On two occasions, not long afterwards, I was accused point blank of cowardice. The first time was by an officer in the Devon and Dorsets who could see I was hanging around at the incident control point talking about the bomb to my partner and not going forward. But had I gone forward, I would have been breaking the standard operating procedure laid down by my own masters and been back on the next boat to the UK. Another time an irate fella came up and said 'Get in there and do your effin' job,' and that sort of thing, which was very frustrating for us.

Another ATO recalls turning up at Divis Flats in Belfast where an Army patrol was facing great difficulty containing a crowd near to a suspect bomb. When the ATO anounced he was going to let the device soak, he was confronted by an irate major who insisted it was only a hoax. 'Well, if you're that sure, you go down and clear it,' said the ATO.

Coldrick further recalls:

> At that time there was a lot of talk about finding some remote way to get at the bombs more safely and one day, when I saw some of the RUC guys carrying Browning shotguns, I came up with the idea of using a 12-bore as a remote attack method for many of the devices were in our line of sight. This worked very well for a time and I never had one device go off after it had been hit with the shotgun. The shot usually stopped the timer or severed the circuitry and after leaving it to soak for a time, I could usually cut it with the secateurs and make it completely safe. But there was one day in the Ardoyne when I approached a fertiliser bag packed with explosive with a timer on top and found that it was still ticking away. I must have got a bit cocky by then but I managed to cut into it and make it safe.

By the end of 1971, it was clear that internment had not deterred the terrorists but instead spurred them on. From January until early August, the number of explosions had slightly exceeded 250. After internment they increased steadily to a year-end total of 1,022. Before internment twenty-seven people had lost their lives that year; in the remaining five months of 1971 the death toll soared to 173. An Army end-of-year assessment of the situation noted that 'the "nerves" of the population can be measured by the incidence of false alarms and, in general, these increased as the bombings increased.' In fact the number of false alarms increased from 276 to 939, and hoaxes, which had numbered fifty-one in 1970–1, soared to 658 in 1971–2. The chief constable, Graham Shillington, described the problem in his annual report for 1971:

> Bomb hoaxes, averaging some twenty each day in the city of Belfast were a dreadful menace and added to the problems of the security forces and the trading and shopping public. Each hoax necessitated evacuation of buildings and diversion of traffic and considering that several areas of the city might be affected at any one time it can readily be appreciated the large number of police required daily for this work.

The bomb-disposal incident reports record this trail of fear: a suitcase abandoned on a bus; a parcel left outside a house; an unexpected delivery to a business. Most suspicions were misplaced. On one occasion the railway station at Great Victoria Street was evacuated after a brown-paper parcel was left in the ladies' lavatory. After EOD action, it was revealed to be a large box of Milk Tray chocolates. Other suspicious objects proved to be nothing more sinister than rolled newspapers, soiled nappies, sticks of seaside rock, a Christmas pudding, a loaf of bread and a handbag 'full of women's paraphernalia', as the EOD operator recorded it. After a call to a neatly tied box of potato crisps at the door of an office building in downtown Belfast, the operator reported: 'The tidy garbage packer strikes again.'

Shillington's report also referred to the countless incendiary devices deposited in department stores and other places and paid tribute to the high work-rate and incredible courage of the ATOs whose achievements were further recognised by more honours. Three operators were awarded the British Empire Medal. Sergeant Islay Carrier, aged thirty-one, tackled 120 bombs in three months and, says the citation, 'braved great danger to obtain valuable information about new bombs with ultra-sensitive anti-handling devices'. Sergeant Robert Lockwood, twenty-four, dealt with 148 bombs in four months, fourteen of them on a single day. He also faced mobs and was hit by stones. 'At all times he displayed great personal courage and never hesitated to tackle bombs he knew could explode at any time,' says his citation. Warrant Officer Terence Clark, thirty-two, who was called to 100 bombs in four months, found a firebomb in an Army vehicle and lifted it clear. According to his citation: 'His brave and timely action prevented severe injuries, possibly loss of life.'

During this busy period, the GOC, Lieutenant-General Sir Harry Tuzo, had become concerned about EOD resources. George Styles, who had endured more than his share of the burden, was being relieved, and, as the surviving records show, the shadow 321 EOD Unit was formally created as 321 Company RAOC on 9 November 1971 by amalgamating the disparate EOD resources up to then deployed in Northern Ireland. Because there were none of the usual records, rolls or inventories before that, Styles believes this marks the official starting point of the unit's history. Lieutenant-Colonel Paul Crosby would soon arrive on promotion as Chief Ammunition Technical Officer attached to Headquarters Northern Ireland, while Major Bernard Calladene, a thirty-nine-year-old Yorkshireman with some twenty years' ordnance disposal experience, who was already at Lisburn, assumed command of the new company.

Chapter Four
The Year of the Car Bomb

The new year of 1972 got off to a violent start in Belfast with seven explosions in forty-five minutes at a police station, supermarket, filling station, tobacconist, post office premises and a textile printing works, where there was a double blast. On 3 January there could easily have been mass murder in the centre of Belfast when a bomb concealed on a brewery lorry exploded without warning. Nearly fifty people were injured as hundreds of glass beer bottles splintered, aggravating the effect of the breaking windows in shops and offices nearby. In all 986 lb. of explosive – half of it gelignite – was detonated that week, the second largest weekly expenditure of the campaign according to a report submitted to the government security committee at Stormont.

Despite such a discouraging start, an Army spokesman issued an optimistic New Year statement declaring the IRA was on the run. Although there were further explosions in the interim, the Headquarters Northern Ireland Intelligence Summary for the middle week of January reported a reduction in terrorist activity and a further decrease in explosive attacks. In Belfast, the document noted, 'the quality of bombs and bombers has further declined: there are signs that the IRA are short of explosives and detonators and the attacks are being carried out by unenthusiastic and unskilled terrorists'. The optimism and the flawed military analysis heralded a false dawn, for the coming year would turn out to be the most destructive of the entire Troubles.

Contradicting the picture of declining IRA activity painted by intelligence analysts, 387 incidents concerning explosives had been logged by the end of January. In one case, with the help of a soldier who was related to a member of the IRA leadership in Belfast, terrorists penetrated the base of the 1st Battalion Parachute Regiment at Palace Barracks near Belfast and placed two bombs. Styles, whose family had already returned home and who was due to leave himself within days, arrived at the scene as one device went off, damaging several armoured vehicles. After a second device was spotted beside the officers' mess,

Styles called for a sniper and asked him to put four bullets in the package. Then he went forward and cut the internal wires to neutralise the device. At that point he noticed four bullet strikes on the mess wall and realised the sniper had missed the bomb. Styles roundly condemned himself for 'the sort of reckless carelessness that could get a bomb-disposal man killed'. A few days later he was back in England.

Meanwhile, according to the Special Branch's January assessment, 'Targets for explosive attacks have again been haphazardly chosen from commercial and unprotected public utilities.' Eight rural exchanges and a larger telephone installation in Belfast were severely damaged. A policeman had a leg amputated after being caught in a blast while he was trying to evacuate a department store in the centre of Belfast. In Newry there were thirty-five arson attacks. At Forkhill, on 27 January, in one of many engagements along the border, a three-hour exchange of fire between soldiers and gunmen was only brought to an end when the Irish Army arrived and arrested the seven IRA men. In a follow-up operation, a milk churn packed with 100 lb. of explosive was uncovered at the roadside and the British Army concluded the gunfire had been initiated to draw them towards the bomb.

Another border incident had far-reaching implications. On 19 January, at Aughnacloy, two men left an oil can at the customs post. An ATO found it to contain a harmless mixture of oil and sawdust, but while checking out an abandoned car nearby he made a far more disturbing discovery: 30 lb. of high explosive and a firing pack connected to the car aerial which incorporated a Staveley Tone Lock, which would have enabled a bomber to detonate the device by radio control. It was the first time a radio-controlled device had been used in this way and the development prompted a major row. On 10 February, Colonel KD Bangham, for the Chief Inspector Land Services Ammunition (CILSA), wrote a stiff minute to the members of the Joint Intelligence Committee's Working Party on Terrorist Devices complaining that essential intelligence information 'had been withheld and it is fortunate that the result was not fatal'. The colonel was referring to an apparent attempt by the IRA to recently obtain Staveley Tone Lock transmitters and receivers from a supplier in Manchester. This approach was reported to Government Communications Headquarters (GCHQ) at Cheltenham, who fed the information on to the Security Service and the Manchester police but not to CILSA. 'If this information had been disseminated with the utmost speed, as it should have been, the EOD operators would have been warned in time,' said the minute.

It is probable that a similar radio-controlled device had already been used to kill a soldier. Two days after the incident at Aughnacloy, a few miles away at Derrynoose, near Keady, three linked landmines detonated close to the border where a patrol from the Devon and Dorset Regiment was operating. Eighteen-year-old Private Charles Stentiford from Exeter, who had only arrived in Northern Ireland days earlier, was killed in the blast, which gouged craters three feet deep and eight feet in diameter. During the follow-up examination no sign of any command wire was found and it was concluded that the device had been detonated by radio control from across the border.

The two incidents, confirming earlier reports that the IRA had acquired a quantity of model aircraft control equipment, gave new impetus to secret work already going on to counter the threat. From May 1972 onwards members of the Royal Signals, known as the Bleeps, would become an integral part of every EOD operation with their 'Lilliput' electronic countermeasures equipment. Three teams and a reserve Lilliput were sent to Northern Ireland and a fourth crew was on twenty-four-hour notice at their base in England. (Eventually there would be one Bleep with every EOD team.)

Meanwhile the bombing campaign was intensifying, with 9,500 lb. of explosive being used, captured or neutralised in February and March. The dilemma now facing the security forces was summed up in a memorandum submitted to the government joint security committee at Stormont at the beginning of March:

> The basic weapon of the terrorist in Northern Ireland has traditionally been, and still is, the bomb. It has caused much of the loss of life, most of the injury, and practically all the damage to property which has occurred in the present campaign. The bomber, in spite of all the current protection afforded by police and Army, has a relative freedom to choose any target from hundreds in a variety of areas and at his own selected opportune time. This freedom develops mainly from the fact that by far the majority of citizens are pursuing their normal legitimate everyday life. In that environment there is a conflict between maintaining normality and constraining the terrorist. Furthermore the presence of people on the streets provides a cover for the terrorist and a limitation on reaction by security forces, especially so in areas where passive or active support is forthcoming from the general public.

In Belfast that March, 300 soldiers had a narrow escape when a 500-

gallon petrol tanker was crashed without warning at Albert Street Mill. Although a bomb in the cab exploded, it failed to ignite the fuel. Customers at the downtown Abercorn Restaurant on the Saturday afternoon of 4 March were not so lucky. Towards 4.30 p.m., two women abandoned a hold-all bomb and slipped out into the streets. Another woman noticed they had forgotten their bag but thought nothing of it and went on to catch her bus. Moments later, as she waited at the stop, she heard a loud explosion. Inside the restaurant, the bomb had gone off without warning, ripping through the café and the cabaret lounge upstairs. Ann Owens, a twenty-two-year-old comptometer operator who had been injured in a previous no-warning bomb attack at the Electricity Board Headquarters, died instantly along with her friend Janet Bereen, aged twenty-one, a radiographer at the Royal Victoria Hospital. Several members of Janet's family were in the medical profession, including her father, a senior anaesthetist, who helped treat the injured unaware that his daughter's body was lying in the hospital mortuary. Altogether 130 were hurt by the no-warning bomb. Many were maimed and scarred for life, among them two sisters, one helping the other choose a dress and other items for her wedding. She lost both legs, an arm and an eye and both her sister's legs were blown off. The coroner described what had happened as 'pathological murder of the most depraved kind'. It later emerged that almost simultaneously with the explosion, at 4.28 p.m., police had received a vague warning that a bomb would go off in Castle Lane in five minutes. No precise location was specified.

In many cases there was nothing the indefatigable EOD teams could do to halt the destruction. Many bombs went off without warning. When calls were made, devices frequently exploded before the time given, or the locations were so imprecise that police and soldiers had the almost impossible task of checking out every vehicle and building. The possibility of a booby-trap was a constant factor. Mike Coldrick remembers being sent to a derelict farm at Coalisland to search for arms after a tip-off:

> The worry was that the information was a leak to draw us in and injure or kill members of the security forces but after a careful search of the barn I found the bomb hidden halfway up the pile of hay bales, wedged under two bales. It was too deep to reach by hand so I pulled the bales off with a line and as I did so, the device exploded.

Both malicious hoaxes and genuine false alarms caused disruption. Two boys who absented themselves from school for the day prompted a major security alert when they hid their bags in bushes at Belfast City Hall. A suspect package on a bus in Belfast city centre one afternoon led to gridlock for over an hour while an ATO checked it out. In this case, a nervous bride had left her wedding dress behind. On many occasions people returned to find their cars blown open by the ATOs because of suspicious contents or thoughtless parking.

The burden of these operations was not exclusively borne by the bomb-disposal teams. Soldiers and police officers were engaged in clearing areas and evacuating buildings and being blown off their feet or suffering temporary deafness became an everyday hazard. A soldier and a policeman prevented the destruction of a bar at Beragh, County Tyrone, when they put a rope round a 20 lb. bomb and dragged it into the street where the soldier detonated it by firing rifle shots. His commanding officer reproached him for breaching Army regulations but admitted lives would have been lost, including their own, if the device had gone off. A police officer defended the 'foolhardy but very brave' pair: 'It's very difficult for people trained to protect life and property to stand by and watch a building blown to pieces before your eyes.' Despite the dangers, some impulsive citizens continued to do their own bomb disposal, removing devices from homes, pubs and workplaces.

At this time, the EOD team in central Belfast was led by Staff Sergeant Christopher Cracknell, aged twenty-nine, from Leamington Spa, and Sergeant Anthony Butcher, twenty-four, from Wilton. Since arriving in Belfast on 18 February Cracknell had attended forty-four bomb calls, while Butcher, who had been on duty since December 1971, had carried out well over 100 EOD tasks. Three days after the Abercorn blast, they were sent to the Belfast Co-Operative Society's department store at York Street after armed men held up the night staff and apparently placed bombs at several points in the building. By the time the EOD team arrived at 03.45 a.m., firemen had extinguished a fire on the second floor and Cracknell decided to let the other devices soak for twelve hours before beginning the daunting task of searching the four storeys. In due course, they made safe a 100 lb. device, saving the store.

Despite such regular successes there were constant setbacks. On the night of 14/15 March a 200 lb. bomb on the back of a hijacked lorry detonated at Great Victoria Street and two further explosions took place in the Belfast suburbs. Later in the morning, there were no injuries when a 15 lb. device seriously damaged Rea's Garage on the Ormeau Road. In the late afternoon, Major Simon Firth of the Gloucestershire Regiment, who was leading a patrol in the Grosvenor Road area, was asked to investigate a Ford Corsair abandoned at the junction of Willow street and the main road. A policeman told them its driver had been immediately picked up by another car. The soldiers quickly cordoned off the area as Cracknell and Butcher were summoned from nearby Albert Street Mill, but when they arrived at 5.05pm, they decided to let the car soak while they investigated yet another suspect car at the Whiterock Community Centre, a couple of miles away. Having carried out a controlled explosion and declared it clear, they returned to Willow Street and at around 7.30 p.m. Cracknell walked to the car, noted a cardboard package on the back seat and fitted a Cordtex charge to blow open the boot, which proved to contain only an empty box.

Now convinced that there was a bomb in the other box on the back seat of the car, Cracknell and Butcher made several unsuccessful attempts to radio-detonate any bomb with their own equipment, and then decided, along with another sergeant, to use a hook and line to pull open the rear door of the car. This operation was completed by Butcher, and the next move was to attach a line to the box to pull it free of the car. Cracknell remarked to Major Firth: 'This is a sophisticated bomb. I'll bring it back and show you.' They were the last words of his life. As he and Butcher reached the car, Butcher leaned in to the back window and almost immediately there was a whirlwind of fire and shrapnel as the bomb went off, killing them both instantly. Even before the smoke and debris had settled, gunmen in positions overlooking the scene fired several shots at the remaining police and soldiers but none was injured.

Cracknell was survived by a wife and son aged just over six; Butcher's wife had given birth to their daughter only eight months earlier. Lord Grey, the Governor of Northern Ireland, wrote a letter of condolence to both widows:

> Northern Ireland's people, so sorely afflicted in these days of civil disorder, owe so much – in some cases life itself – to the brave and skilful ATOs who, daily and nightly, must face daunting danger on behalf of others. Pride cannot take away the sting of sorrow but we hope that the knowledge your husband died for others will bring a proper pride at this sad time.

In a message of sympathy to Major-General LTH Phelps, the Army's Director of Ordnance Services, the Chief of the General Staff, General Sir Michael Carver, said:

The death of a member of the small body of experts in explosive ordnance disposal is especially distressing. The whole Army knows that these men – and they are a small and very devoted band – risk their lives every day – often more than once a day – for the sake of their fellow citizens; not just for their comrades in arms. The public know when an explosion takes place. They do not know so clearly how many explosions have not taken place or have taken place harmlessly because of the devotion to duty, skill and courage of these men.

Perhaps the most poignant and emotional tribute came from a sergeant in the RUC. In a letter to the 321 EOD headquarters at Lisburn, he wrote, 'I have been on duty with these teams and don't mind admitting that I was scared. I never cease to admire their tremendous courage. As long as the Army has men of this calibre, we will eventually beat the terrorists. May God bless them in their future work.'

The most important lesson from the tragedy was that never again should two operators expose themselves to risk by approaching a device together. From that point on a 'one-man risk' rule became rigid practice.

Within five days there was more murder on the streets of Belfast. This time the bomber, aware that the timer on his device was rapidly expiring, simply abandoned the car in busy Donegall Street and ran away. At the same time, police officers acting on contradictory telephone warnings about a device in the area were running from door to door alerting people and trying to clear the street. In the midst of this frantic activity, the 200 lb. of explosive went off.

Eyewitnesses said the street was like a battlefield when the smoke had cleared, with people strewn along the pavements, their clothes stripped away and blood pouring from their wounds. There was the sound of alarm bells ringing and sirens as the emergency services rushed helpers to the scene, punctuated by the regular crash of falling glass and the crunch of feet on rubble. People brought clothing and rugs from nearby buildings to cover the dead and towels from a hairdressing salon were distributed to help bind up the wounded. A lasting image of the incident is that of a soldier from the Parachute Regiment holding a towel against the bleeding stump of a victim who had lost a leg. When the casualties were counted, seven people had died and 150 suffered injury. Some of them had been moved from the path of a supposed bomb into the range of a real one. Two of the dead were police officers, killed while trying to save lives, and five were civilians, including three of the crew of a refuse lorry who were emptying dustbins in the street where the bomb went off.

Every day brought similar atrocities somewhere in Northern Ireland and the police and Army were stretched to the absolute limit. Since the introduction of internment the previous August, bombers had killed sixty-three people and injured 1,264, 111 seriously. Commenting on the blitz on 9 March, the *Belfast Telegraph* said: 'The tunnel is dark. It is hard to see even a chink of light.'

It was against this unpromising background, on 24 March, that the British government brought to an end almost exactly fifty years of unbroken governance by the Ulster Unionists with the promise of political reform under direct rule from London. The IRA, unwavering in its demand for British withdrawal and a united Ireland, ignored the potential gain from this fundamental redefinition of the Northern Ireland state. A few days later, in another act of ruthlessness, two men were killed in Limavady, County Londonderry, after bombers abandoned an explosive-laden vehicle outside the town's police station.

Another institution of the rule of law in Northern Ireland came under threat on 29 March when a stolen lorry loaded with scrap metal – 'Belfast confetti', as soldiers had come to call it – was parked in Chichester Street, Belfast, between the Royal Courts of Justice Building and the Magistrates' Court and Fire Brigade headquarters. The area was evacuated after an anonymous ten-minute warning. A second anonymous call identified the lorry as the location of the bomb. Major Calladene quickly arrived and confirmed the presence of an estimated 150 lb. of gelignite beneath the scrap. Using a Maxi-candle, he ignited the explosive in a bid to burn it off, but the device partly exploded, damaging nearby buildings and parked cars and starting a small fire at the Magistrates' Court. The destruction was a fraction of what would have resulted if the entire bomb had gone off and all three buildings were in operation again within hours.

About ten o'clock that evening, a white Austin 1800 car, stolen a day earlier, was abandoned in a narrow street by the side of Belfast's City Hall. At the same time an anonymous caller dialled 100 and issued a ten-minute warning to a telephone operator. An Army patrol in the city centre quickly spotted the car while the now well-practised call-out procedures swung into action. An EOD team, led by WO2 Peter Dandy and Staff Sergeant Hammond, reached the scene at 10.40 p.m. and saw a cardboard box with wires protruding from it on the back seat of the car. Concluding that it probably contained a device similar to that which had so recently killed their colleagues, they let it soak while they contacted Major Calladene, who had expressed a wish to inspect one. He arrived about an hour later and, after conferring with the team, walked forward alone into the dark side street. Dandy asked the driver of a Pig – the Army's name for their one-ton armoured Humbers – to shine his headlights towards the suspect car. As they watched, Calladene inspected the back of the car and then moved around it, shining his torch into the back seat.

Suddenly, without any warning, the 10 lb. device detonated, fragmenting the car and blowing Calladene right across the street where his body landed in a shattered shop window. His watch, pipe and tobacco box landed beside him among the tumbling debris and shards of glass. Suffering from multiple injuries, he was rushed to the Royal Victoria Hospital, where he died at 1.25 a.m. His body was formally identified by Captain Charles Cooke, a friend and close colleague for seven years.

Calladene left a widow and three children. At his funeral in York on 5 April, the Reverend RL Parsonage, an Army chaplain, expressed the feelings of many ordinary people in Northern Ireland when he said: 'People will rightly wonder – even marvel – that bravery of the sort that is before us can really be, whereby a man seems so willingly and unceremoniously to walk literally in the valley of the shadow of death doing simply what his job and duty requires of him.'

The death of their commanding officer, so soon after the murders of Cracknell and Butcher, came as a profound shock to 321 EOD Unit, who had lost five colleagues in action in seven months. In the following month there were another 258 incidents involving 4,336 lb. of explosive. The 321 log records one twenty-four-hour period when there were eighteen explosions, including one episode which WO2 Dandy, who dealt with it, described in his report as a 'supreme obscenity'. It began on the afternoon of 17 April, when James Elliott, a married man with three children from Rathfriland, County Down, who was a part-time corporal in the Ulster Defence Regiment, was abducted by the IRA. His main job as a lorry driver entailed frequent cross-border trips to the Irish Republic and it was while returning from one such journey that he was held up by armed men just north of the Killeen border crossing. His body was found in a field at Altnamackan, on the border near Newtownhamilton, County Armagh, thirty-six hours later. Access was along a narrow lane and the body, partly covered by a red tarpaulin, was booby-trapped, but nobody imagined the complexity of the macabre ambush that had been put in place.

As the hedgerow where the body had been dumped was yards from the border and overlooked by several ideal firing points, the recovery operation was frozen until Irish police and troops moved in. Meanwhile helicopters photographed the entire area. Armed with the pictures, the ATO set out on a circuitous route around the body, wading in a stream by the border. There he encountered Irish police officers who disclosed they had arrested 'two suspicious characters' and warned him that red and black wires were running from the body to a firing position about a mile away across the border. The ATO continued along the stream until he found the wires, cut them and traced them back along the hedge and under a culvert where they were attached to a milk churn and a length of Cordtex. Over the next two hours, he discovered six more churns, each containing 100 lb. of gelignite, concealed in the culvert.

The painstaking, day-long operation, which involved checking every inch of ground for a considerable area, uncovered four 10 lb. Claymore mines dug into the laneside. These were intended for the survivors of the first blast and those coming to their aid. All the devices had carefully concealed command wires leading to the cross-border firing point. In the final stage of the operation, the ATO used a hook and line to pull the tarpaulin clear of Elliott's body, lying on its right side. A medical officer estimated the corporal had been dead for between twelve and sixteen hours. Dandy then cut the ropes binding the body and used the hook and line to move it five yards and ensure there were no further booby-traps. It was then removed by a stretcher party. Shortly afterwards Dandy safely detonated the recovered explosives. He was later commended for 'the most efficient manner' in which he dealt with the difficult operation, but he recorded his horror in his incident report: 'They are nothing but animals using a body to lure troops on top of a command-type bomb.'

The Belfast Co-Operative store, saved by the gallant work of Cracknell and Butcher before their deaths, came under attack again on 10 May when bombers planted a high-explosive device on the third floor. Twenty people were injured when the device went off and there was collateral destruction over a 200-yard radius. Fire raged uncontrolled for a time as fears of secondary devices prevented firefighters from tackling it. 'This was a well-planned attack which was unfortunately also very successful,' the ATO wrote in his report, estimating the damage at £10 million. The store was closed for business, affecting 750 jobs. It was the most spectacular act of economic destruction to date and confirmed the IRA's growing reliance on home-made explosive (HME). For the previous nine months, they had been smuggling and exploding about 1,000 lb. of commercially produced explosive a month, most of it stolen in the Irish Republic.

The first sign of the use of ammonium nitrate came in March when traces were detected in defused bombs. It was already well known that ANFO – ammonium nitrate combined with fuel oil – had considerable explosive properties, especially when used with a primer or booster charge of commercial gelignite. The disadvantage for the terrorist was that it had to be mixed properly. Another easily prepared explosive compound, sodium chlorate and nitro-benzene, was afterwards referred to as 'Co-op mix' because of its first use in the destruction of the store. Although HME was inferior to the explosive power of gelignite by a factor of four to seven, the large quantities used, between 200 and 400 lb. a time, more than compensated.

The deadly effect was repeatedly underlined by similarly devastating bombings in May and June. On 24 June, the hundredth soldier to be murdered in Northern Ireland was one of three killed by two milk-churn bombs each containing 120 lb. of explosive when their convoy was ambushed at the Glenshane Pass on the Belfast–Londonderry road. At the half-year point, there had been 570 explosions and 107 deaths but the security forces had captured four tons of explosive before it could be used. Speaking at an inquest into the deaths of two men and two children in a no-warning explosion at a furniture shop, the Deputy Coroner for Belfast remarked that the perpetrators of the outrages should be taken to the city mortuary to see for themselves the mutilated bodies of those they had killed.

The first flicker of hope emerged at the end of June. Ever since direct rule had been introduced the previous March, William Whitelaw, Secretary of State for Northern Ireland, and his political advisers had been working to bring together the divided politicians and paramilitaries from both sides. The IRA responded favourably to the approaches and, as a preparation for further talks, called a ceasefire from midnight on 26 June. Within days, in conditions of the greatest secrecy, the RAF flew the entire leadership of the organisation to London for face-to-face talks with Whitelaw. However, the IRA's unrealistic political demands, predicated on Britain unilaterally setting a date for withdrawal, caused the talks to founder and hostilities resumed after the Army was drawn into a manufactured clash about housing allocation at Lenadoon in west Belfast on 9 July.

Another bomb-disposal operator was an early casualty of the renewed violence. At 6.45 a.m. on 15 July, an Army patrol operating in the countryside near Silverbridge, County Armagh, spotted a milk churn at the roadside with a double strand of wire stretching across the road and disappearing into a field. Captain John Young, a twenty-seven-year-old married man from Clanfield, Hampshire, arrived at the scene with his team from their base at Lurgan at 11.20. Captain Young pulled the churn out of the ditch using a rope attached to a Land Rover but was unable to lift the lid. He asked his driver to get him a hammer and returned, having advised the team members to get back fifty yards. According to one of those watching, he struck the lid upwards with the hammer seven times. At that moment the churn erupted in intense fire and smoke, killing him instantly. The force and heat of the explosion was such that it incinerated all trace of the dead officer's 9 mm. Browning.

The resumption of violence brought further casualties, but in scale and impact there was no parallel for the terror inflicted on the people of Belfast on 21 July, the day forever remembered as 'Bloody Friday'. By the anarchic standards of Belfast at the time, it started off unremarkably at 2.10 p.m. with an explosion in a car left in the yard at Smithfield bus station, causing extensive damage to buses and houses in nearby Samuel Street. Six minutes later a second blast wrecked the Brookvale Hotel on Antrim Road after three men armed with a sub-machine gun planted a suitcase bomb. At 2.23 pm the roof of the railway station at York Road was brought down by a bomb left in a suitcase on the platform. At 2.45 the Star Taxis depot at Crumlin Road was destroyed and the homes of warders at the nearby prison damaged by a car bomb. The repetitive thuds of the explosions were being heard all over the city and thick columns of black smoke could be seen steadily darkening the summer afternoon. At 2.48 a car bomb exploded without warning in Oxford Street bus station, killing six and injuring nearly forty. At precisely the same time, a blast from an abandoned Bedford van loaded with explosives, rocked the bus yard at the Great Northern Railway Station. Four buses were completely wrecked and forty-four damaged.

By now the city centre was in a state of panic and confusion. People ran from shop to shop or pub to pub seeking sanctuary, only to be evacuated again. At 2.50 p.m. a hijacked car exploded at the corner of suburban Limestone Road, injuring several people and wrecking a branch of the Ulster Bank and adjacent houses and cars. Simultaneously a commandeered bread van was blown to pieces at the York Hotel, damaging twenty cars and surrounding property. At 2.55, a Ford car exploded on the Queen Elizabeth Bridge which links east and west Belfast across the Lagan, creating further chaos and closing an escape route for the thousands of people desperately trying to flee the city. Two minutes later a car bomb went off between the Liverpool Bar and the ferry terminal and another exploded outside the Belfast Corporation Gas Department's ornate Victorian offices at Ormeau Avenue at 2.57. Two minutes later, a bomb planted by armed men devastated the premises of John Irwin, seed merchant, at Garmoyle Street in the docks area. Five minutes after that, a bridge spanning the M2 motorway at the Bellevue Arms, Antrim Road was undamaged when explosives in a car caught fire but failed to detonate.

At 3.05 Creighton's Garage on Lisburn Road was demolished by a car bomb, setting petrol pumps ablaze, and simultaneously an electricity sub-station at the junction of Salisbury Avenue and Hughenden Avenue was destroyed by a van bomb, while the railway bridge at Finaghy Road North, over the Belfast–Dublin line, sustained only minor damage from a bomb in a hijacked lorry. Four minutes later, further along the line, an explosion on the footbridge at Windsor Park Football Ground blew concrete sleepers onto the railway and broke windows in nearby houses. At 3.12 a Ford car exploded in Eastwood's Garage, Donegall Street, injuring many people and wrecking the premises. The final explosion of the day, the twenty-first in a horrific fifty-five minutes, took place at the Cavehill Road Shopping Centre where a 50 lb. device in a hijacked Ford Cortina, killed three people and damaged shops and houses over a seventy-yard radius. The ATO who attended this incident wrote in his report: 'A cowardly and murderous attack. Two, possibly four dead. Total number of injured unknown. No warning whatsoever.'

After nearly a year of escalating terrorism, people had become accustomed to regular detonations. Many had learned to distinguish the sharp crack of gelignite from the slower, flatter, rolling thud of HME. After a bang, they phoned around to discover where the blast was or eavesdropped on the emergency-service radio networks. No previous incident had reached the heights of panic, fear and then revulsion that united the city that terrible Friday afternoon and, albeit temporarily, swept aside its sectarian rivalries. People would never forget the television pictures of firemen putting human remains into plastic bags at Oxford Street bus station. It was the worst onslaught of the Troubles to date and the most intensive bomb attack on the city since the Nazi blitz in 1941. The IRA brazenly insisted it had given warnings of the various explosions, a claim heavily disputed by the authorities, but even if it had done so, the scale and spread of the attacks was such that the emergency services would have had no chance of reaching and evacuating all the affected areas.

Bloody Friday is significant in that it marked the most extensive use to date of the most lethal development of the IRA campaign, the car bomb.

Vehicle-borne explosive devices had, of course, been used before; one of the earliest recorded was in 1920 when anarchists detonated a cartload of explosives in New York's Wall Street. In 1970, car bombs were used by Quebec nationalists in Canada and an anarchist in Wisconsin, USA, but after six incidents involving IRA bombs in cars in late 1971, their use and the size of the explosive charge they contained was progressively increased. A report by the RUC Special Branch noted that from January 1972 onwards, a high proportion of bomb attacks, particularly in Belfast, 'consisted of charges placed in cars which were abandoned in busy streets, usually at times of peak hour traffic. This form of attack is easy to make as well as causing maximum inconvenience to the public and good material for television.' EOD analysts think the first car bomb deliberately placed to destroy the surrounding area was at the Killeen customs post on the main Belfast–Dublin road south of Newry, at the beginning of March 1972. An ATO examining an abandoned car set off what he anticipated would be a controlled explosion to blow open the boot. Instead 300 lb. of explosive, the largest bomb of the campaign to date, completely demolished a filling station and garage and caused blast damage over a wide area.

The car bomb had many advantages for the terrorist. The smallest car could carry a far heavier explosive load than could be ferried into a building by even several men. The available space in a car made it simpler to arrange the firing mechanism and both the device and the vehicle could be booby-trapped. Planting a car bomb was infinitely more simple than a bomb in a bag or box, which usually needed an armed escort. All a single driver had to do was park and walk nonchalantly away. Even when a warning was given it still took time to distinguish the car from others parked nearby.

The development of the car bomb was not, as has been speculated, a conscious innovation or tactical masterstroke by the IRA. It was the logical outcome of their earlier introduction of fertiliser-based bombs to augment dwindling stocks of gelignite. Because of their greater weight, these bombs required a vehicular rather than a human delivery platform. The IRA quickly realised that the exploding vehicle enhanced the effect of the HME. It was the ideal weapon for terrorists bent on causing economic destruction and disruption and so the use of larger and larger vehicle bombs became routine. Cars were parked in narrow streets between tall buildings, or in underground car parks, to contain the blast and further increase the damage.

*

After Bloody Friday, the principal security focus switched to Londonderry, where the police had been driven from the Catholic Bogside and Creggan areas at the outbreak of the Troubles. The Army managed to maintain a presence in the 'Free Derry no-go area' despite the events of 'Bloody Sunday', 30 January 1972, when soldiers shot dead thirteen civilians and fatally wounded a fourteenth during a banned civil rights march, but the IRA continued to maintain street barricades around the enclaves and use the area as a stronghold to mount gun and bomb attacks. A contemporary Army report, from Robert Ford to the GOC described the bombers as:

> ... mostly teenagers carrying small 5–10 lb. devices who operate in the thickness of the shopping crowds and cannot be detected by the considerable number of three-man infantry patrols. Because of the considerable number of ruined buildings and back alleys which lead into the general area from the Bogside . . . it is impossible to contain public movement or control it. In addition the vast majority of the people in the shopping area not only give no help to our patrols but, if they saw a youth with a very small bag which might contain a bomb, they would be likely to shield the youth's movements from the view of our patrols. We now have 52 men patrolling in this very small area constantly.

Thirty years later, two of those involved provided the Bloody Sunday Tribunal with an account of how the IRA carried out its operations from behind the barricades. Martin McGuinness joined the Provisional IRA towards the end of 1970 as a 'Volunteer', becoming first 'Adjutant' and then 'OC' (Officer Commanding) in little over a year.

> I think you have to remember that at that time all of us were very young (our average age would have been around twenty to twenty-three); we were not like a conventional army; we were not well organised; we were making it up as we went along and, of course, we accorded ourselves these grand titles, which bore very little relationship to the reality of life. As far as the strength of the IRA is concerned, it is hard to be accurate. I think there were forty or fifty volunteers in January 1972, and probably closer to forty than fifty. However, a lot of people in Derry were prepared to help us, short of using arms, so when I am asked what the strength of the IRA was, you could say thousands of people would be ready to help in different ways.

McGuinness admitted using 'rather grand phraseology' to paint a picture of a military organisation consisting of battalions and companies. 'In reality they were not battalions at all. We are talking about very small numbers of people who would not have constituted, in my view, anything close to a battalion.' Neither were they as heavily armed as their skilful propaganda stunts encouraged people to believe. 'At the time the IRA had about ten rifles of various kinds, some of them very old, about half a dozen short arms, and perhaps two or three sub-machine-guns.'

In his evidence, Michael Clarke, aged twenty-five at the time of Bloody Sunday, recalled that in the six months after the introduction of internment the Provisionals in Londonderry went from practically nothing to a well-organised group. Indeed the growth was so rapid, he said, there were more members than weapons or explosives for them to use. Clarke became 'Explosives Officer' of the 'patriot army' after his neighbour was interned and two local men were shot dead by the Army in disputed circumstances. At the time he was working at a record-player factory in the city. As a trained electrician, he was immediately assigned to explosives work.

'I was self-trained. I studied books on explosives,' Clarke revealed in his testimony. The first devices he manufactured were nail bombs intended for soldiers during street riots. The weapon consisted of half a stick of gelignite wrapped in corrugated paper to hold the nails in place and was set off by a cluster of matchsticks attached to a length of fuse. Clarke, who went on to become one of the IRA's most prolific bombers and to serve a ten year prison sentence for the massive destruction he caused to his native city, described how he operated. 'Explosives were never kept in the house or in the same area as detonators. I would store them in places where only I would know about them,' he said. He would make up the detonators for bombs at home but never complete nail bombs.

> I would probably get word that we were going into a riot situation . . .
> you would make nail bombs as close as possible to that locality. I took
> the rest of the materials in my Maxi car. Some of the seats were
> removed and the car was used as a mobile workshop. When all the
> materials were to hand, it took no more than five to ten minutes to make
> a nail bomb.

In order to defend the concrete barricades around 'Free Derry', 15 lb. gelignite 'blast bombs' would be put into position overnight, to be set off if there was an Army incursion, and lifted in the morning. 'It never actually happened, but that was the theory,' said Clarke. Early in 1972, he told the tribunal, the bombing campaign was intensified with fertiliser-based explosives being processed in bomb factories. Asked by counsel if he 'knew nor cared' about the lethal potential of the various weapons, he replied: 'I did not, no, I was not going to stand and start measuring out.' 'Did you really care about the risk to civilians?' asked the barrister. 'Of course I did,' Clarke answered. 'We were not in the business of using people for cover; this is our community we are talking about. We were a fledgling organisation at the time. We relied on the people's support. If we had put people, our own people from the area at risk, we would not have lasted very long.' He added that people were given 'the Republican nod' as an indication that they should get out of the way.

A report prepared in 8 Brigade Headquarters calculated the cost of bomb damage in the city between internment in 1971 and June 1972 at £6 million. The existence of the Derry 'no-go area' was a major embarrassment for the authorities. Senior figures talked of the need for action to counter 'the growing hopelessness of the situation'. Towards the end of July 1972, after the failed ceasefire and 'Bloody Friday', it was decided the political circumstances were at last right to mount a military operation to retake the Londonderry streets and impose control in similar IRA heartlands throughout Northern Ireland. Major Army reinforcements were drafted in for the task, with 4,500 troops and equipment bringing the garrison to an all-time peak strength of 21,200. Despite fears of disorder and more loss of life, the operation met little resistance and the Army rapidly achieved all its objectives. As Clarke would later tell the Bloody Sunday Tribunal: 'We would not engage the British Army, they would have wiped us out.'

Within weeks, heavily-guarded 'forts' had been built in many areas to serve as bases for surveillance of suspect premises and individuals. More systematic patrolling was introduced to dominate the streets and inhibit IRA activity. That month there were still 126 explosions throughout Northern Ireland but the IRA's capacity to strike at the commercial heart of Londonderry was swiftly reduced when three large caches of explosives and an array of chemicals and other bomb-making equipment were uncovered. The haul weighed over two tons and included fully assembled devices in oil drums. In Armagh, 1000 lb. of explosive was uncovered together with detonators, fuse cord and other paraphernalia in a similar bomb factory and back in Londonderry, a few days later, an ATO cleared yet another explosives cache during a twelve-hour operation.

Meanwhile Loyalist paramilitaries imposed a parallel reign of terror with the random assassination of Catholics. Many of the killings were direct reprisals for IRA attacks and were marked by an extraordinary brutality. Victims were tortured or slashed and mutilated with knives and other implements before being shot or stabbed to death. There was some arson and bombing activity against Catholic property, especially pubs, but the devices used were crude pipe bombs or beer-keg or gas-cylinder bombs which failed more often than not. On one infamous occasion, a gang lugged a heavy gas cylinder into the porch of a Catholic-frequented pub only to find that none of them had thought to bring matches or a lighter. Such events were disparagingly referred to by the police and Army as 'Prot jobs'.

The effort to impose firmer control of events was only partially successful. At 22.35 p.m. on 2 August, a caller to the RUC at Strabane reported seeing two men moving an oil drum from a white 1100 car at Meetinghouse Road, Clady, about five miles from the town. An Army patrol confirmed there appeared to be a bomb at the location and just after 5 a.m. a Royal Welch Fusiliers patrol, followed by a pair of Saracen armoured personnel carriers, closed in on the suspect drum which was sitting some feet off a narrow country road with wires trailing into the hedge.

That morning, WO2 William Clark, the Number One on call at Ebrington Barracks in Londonderry, was starting the ninth day of his tour of duty. When he reached the scene at 7.30, his Bleep carried out a series of checks and found no evidence of any radio-controlled initiation device. Having satisfied himself there were no tripwires or pressure plates in his path, Clark, in full uniform and flak jacket, went forward to take a closer look at the ten-gallon drum. Using a hook and line, he pulled it onto the surfaced road and then removed the lid from the drum with an eight-inch Cordtex charge. After a pause, he approached the device again and cautiously removed two plastic bags reeking of marzipan, the distinctive smell associated with explosives. He pulled a detonator and yellow wire from one of the bags, each the size of 2 lb. of sugar according to one of his colleagues. At this point Clark told his Number Two he was going to look at 'something wooden' remaining in the drum, but as he turned to do so a secondary bomb detonated, blowing a crater five feet in diameter and three feet deep in the road. The brave ATO died instantly.

A week later, thirty-four-year-old Clark, described by his instructors as 'a very steady EOD operator with a sound theoretical knowledge', was laid to rest at Acklam, Middlesborough. His distraught wife had to be supported by a soldier and relatives as she walked to his graveside after the service. His four sons, aged from five to twelve, did not attend. Again a great cloud of grief descended over the closely knit community of 321 EOD and their associated formations back in Britain.

By now the officer with the task of choosing officers for postings to Northern Ireland had become known as the 'Grim Reaper', but nobody turned him down when he called. ATOs downplayed any notions of courage and heroism, insisting they were merely professionals doing their duty and their job. Foolhardy crowds gathered daily on the streets to watch these exceptional men battle with bombs abandoned ever more recklessly and ruthlessly in every conceivable place by every available means. On one occasion, a woman accompanied by three children dumped a 20 lb. bomb in a pram which caused massive damage to a Londonderry garage. Another pram was used in a bid to bomb Telephone House in Belfast but soldiers on guard at the main door pushed it away before it caused any damage. Even a hearse was used to evade security checks, and a coffin packed with 150 lb. of explosives caused widespread damage when it exploded at Church Lane, Belfast.

The IRA's bombing campaign, intended to inflict such economic damage that the British government would give up and withdraw from Northern Ireland, continued without abatement throughout 1972. In one of the most extensive attacks, eight bombs exploded at the Courtaulds manmade-fibre plant at Carrickfergus, killing one man. An unsuccessful attempt was made to cripple 'Goliath', one of the two 4,500-ton shipyard cranes which dominate the Belfast skyline, by exploding a 250 lb. device in an underground switchgear chamber at its base. Pubs, restaurants, hotels, shops, factories, old people's homes, churches, hospitals and schools all faced evacuation when bombers struck nearby. One night, thousands of viewers watched as the Ulster Television news reader had to flee the studio when the emergency alarm sounded. The news resumed thirty-five minutes later after a search of the station.

The EOD report for August noted a new record monthly poundage of explosives: 15,978 lb., of which 5,855 lb. had detonated in 126 explosions. Regular targets now included pylons, transformers and sub-stations in rural and urban areas, causing frequent interruptions of the electricity supply. Culverts and manholes continued to be used to conceal groups of beer kegs, gas cylinders, milk churns and oil drums packed with HME. Wicker baskets, duffle bags and large sweet jars were commonly used for smaller devices.

George Styles believed one or two bomb 'designers' were at the head of a pyramid supporting this effort. Below that, he said, were three or four carpenters and eight or ten electricians who put in the circuits, 'and then you have the blokes that place them'. Increasingly the 'blokes' were being joined by women, especially to place small incendiary devices which, the Army believed, they concealed beneath their skirts. Army intelligence learned of at least one training session in the Irish Republic at this time, where twelve female operatives from Belfast were instructed in the use and handling of various explosive devices.

Recalling how his own interest in explosives had developed as a schoolboy, Styles said handling them was 'an elementary science' but that the dangers for the bomb-makers were 'hair-raising'. In 1970, according to Army records, five people died in premature explosions while making or delivering bombs and ten lost their lives in 1971. The toll included a boy aged seventeen and an eighteen-year-old girl who were killed in September that year in a house in the Lower Falls area when a 5 lb. bomb exploded. Another young man was killed on 2 October when he triggered a Castlerobin-type device he was planting at Lisburn council offices. At the end of the year, the organisation lost one of its most expert bomb-makers in a premature explosion in the Dublin suburb of Swords. The fifty-five-year-old veteran of earlier IRA campaigns normally mixed explosives on a large sheet of plywood but on this occasion, as he was able to explain before he died from his injuries, he was using the concrete floor of a garage and a spark from his shovel ignited the mixture.

There were thirty-eight further 'own goals' in 1972, a telling commentary on the instability of the devices 321 EOD Unit had to face. The first casualties of the year were two young men, one injured, one killed, while laying a 15 lb. bomb outside the RUC station at Castlewellan, County Down. In February, two men suffered extensive burns during an attack on the council office at Keady, County Armagh. Both were smuggled over the border but later died in a Dublin hospital. The same month two more bombers perished planting a device on sand-barges at Lough Neagh and four died on the south Belfast ring road while transporting a bomb in a car. A few weeks later another four were killed when working with explosives at a house in Clonard Street and after a similar interval three more lost their lives in a premature explosion at a garage being used as a bomb factory in north Belfast. In one of the worst incidents of this type, eight died at Anderson Street, Belfast, when a bomb detonated while being moved between a house and a car, blowing a crater in the street, demolishing two houses and damaging fifty more. In

August 1972 one man died at a Newry filling station, nine people were killed when a bomber dropped a device he was planting at the customs clearing station in the town, and two terrorists lost their lives while placing a bomb at Downpatrick racecourse. Another bomb factory exploded at Balkan Street in Belfast in October 1972, killing three bomb-makers. A journalist at the scene was told by a resident that 'a television set had gone on fire', an unlikely explanation for the blaze which engulfed virtually an entire terrace. Two more terrorists died while working with incendiary substances in the kitchen of a house in Londonderry in November.

Delivering a lecture in Edinburgh in late 1972, Styles said: 'By early 1971 several bomb layers had blown themselves up and this simple fact satisfactorily proved that the men laying the devices were not the same men who had constructed or designed them.' Thanks to the work of the Data Reference Centre a considerable body of knowledge about terrorist methodology had been established. Some bombs were coming north from Dublin in kit form and there was considerable hard evidence that IRA stocks of commercial explosives were being stolen from quarries in the south, the thefts often not even being reported to the Irish police. The 800 lb. proceeds of two recent thefts had been allocated to bombers in Belfast and County Monaghan, but the latter team lost half their haul in a security force seizure at Crossmaglen. In one month of 1972, it was calculated that of nearly 2,000 lb. of commercial explosive deployed by bombers, half was detonated, with over 900 lb. captured by the security forces or defused by ATOs. A marked increase in defusings and bombs failing to go off was put down to the arrest of a key IRA 'Explosives Officer'. There was also a growing confidence among ATOs. The first successful disruption of a car bomb on 27 November was a significant morale booster. By December the monthly poundage used had dropped to 4,920, the lowest since the previous May, but there were still 345 EOD incidents that month, including fifty-seven bombings.

An appalling year for Northern Ireland, with 467 deaths attributable to civil disorder and terrorism, ended with two more tragedies for 321 EOD. The first took place in Londonderry on the afternoon of 28 November when two youths told staff at Long's supermarket on Strand Road that they had twenty minutes to get clear. By the time an EOD team arrived in a Saracen there had been no explosion, so the Number One, WO2 H Kay, instructed the driver to go slowly past the front door of the supermarket and then reverse. After the first pass he asked the driver to stop so that he could take a closer look at a shopping bag by the front door. Royal

Artillery Gunner Paul Jackson, aged twenty-one and married with two children, had one of the vehicle's observation hatches open and was taking photographs. Seconds later the 50 lb. device, just twenty-five feet away, went off, killing him instantly. The explosion brought down a large part of the building and buried the armoured vehicle in tons of smoking debris. The driver, low in the front of the vehicle, suffered pepper-cuts to his face. When Kay was pulled from inside the vehicle he was covered in blood. His skull was fractured and he lost his right eye, but survived his injuries. Scarcely a week later, another of the thirty-strong bomb disposal cadre in Northern Ireland did not.

On 5 December 1972 at 6.15 p.m. Sergeant Roy Hills and his team were in their quarters at Kitchen Hill, Lurgan, County Armagh, when sentries reported two small explosions close by. A patrol from 1 Staffordshire Regiment was quickly mustered and found a home-made three-barrel mortar launcher in the grounds of the Sacred Heart Convent. There was also a small crater in the ground near an undertaker's premises at Church Place and a trail of blood leading to the front of an adjacent solicitor's office, where it came to an abrupt end. Two of the mortar shells had fired. The third was still stuck in the tube and in a 'dangerous unexploded condition', as they radioed back to the control room.

The twenty-eight-year-old sergeant, who was five weeks into his tour, arrived with his team at 8 p.m. The weapon was in a dark corner of the garden, so two of the Staffordshire soldiers held a light so that he could inspect the mortar. He established a pulling point behind the cover of a wall and, running a line from there round the corner and around a tree, went forward to attach it to the mortar. As one of the volunteer torch-holders later recalled:

> He was half standing over the bomb when there was a bright orange flash and I saw him being hurled backwards through the air. I think I was briefly knocked unconscious. I picked myself up and went towards where Sergeant Hills was lying. As I thought the main charge of the bomb was about to explode, I grabbed his shoulders in an attempt to drag him clear and, as I did so, there was enough residual light for me to see from the extent of his head injuries that he was already dead.

Sergeant Hills was the sixth bomb-disposal officer to die that year and the eighth since the campaign started. The death toll could easily have been far higher; two operators had narrowly escaped death or injury in separate incidents that summer. The RAOC calculated that the odds on a bomb-disposal officer being killed were one in every twenty-three four-month tours, compared with one in every 1,142 tours for other operational duties. This casualty rate was, of course, unsustainable, but great strides were being made in reducing the risk to individual ATOs and enabling them to carry out their hazardous missions more safely, rapidly and effectively.

Chapter Five
Pigstick and Wheelbarrow

By early 1972 it was clear that the British Army was unprepared and ill-equipped for the internal security conflict that had developed in Northern Ireland. Its conventional military skills and tactics needed to be refined to cope with the combination of civil disorder and all-out terrorism being encountered in town and countryside, particularly along the border. In a paper on the early stages of the campaign, Brigadier Sir Ian Jardine says the Army was 'barely prepared to do more than fight in the classic internal security pattern of India in the pre- and immediate post-war years'.

> Events moved . . . so fast that the staffs in Northern Ireland became almost totally immersed in the operations of the day. Equipment needs, therefore, were not so much foreseen as stated in arrears to meet the current situation. Unit Commanding Officers fed suggestions to Brigade Commanders and so on upwards. The Ministry of Defence machinery remained essentially the standard peacetime machinery, geared to long-term development and procurement, and totally unsuited to meet a war situation in one small province of the United Kingdom.

In *Bombs Have No Pity*, George Styles put the problem more strongly:

> We had to overcome what the officers' mess had christened 'NIHS' – the 'not-invented-here syndrome'. This was the cloying attitude of mind to be found in any large organisation that effectively prevents efficiency and flexibility. It is the resistance of men to ideas they hadn't thought of, they hadn't invented. The only way to beat 'NIHS' is by making the men at the top think they have dreamed up the idea themselves.

Since early 1970 more effective and innovative ways had been found to cope with disorderly crowds and get new equipment operational but there was no more urgent requirement for a rigorous approach than in the EOD field. By September 1971, despite internment, terrorists were detonating what Styles described as a 'staggering' thousand tons of explosive a month, a figure that increased fivefold by mid-1972. Although bomb-disposal teams had trebled the number of devices neutralised in the same period, from 141 to well over 500 a year, the IRA bomb-makers had made standard methods redundant.

At the outset of the Northern Ireland campaign the EOD operator's main assets were iron nerves, a steady hand and a long, green wooden tool chest containing a stencil kit (for drawing diagrams of bombs), brushes, hammers, crowbars and a selection of drills, screwdrivers, knives, scalpels, fishing hooks and lines, rubber gloves and other basic tools. Also at his disposal was an electronic stethoscope for detecting ticking, a Plasma Arc cutting torch, liquid nitrogen and a 300 kv Andrex X-ray machine with a trailer-mounted generator, the 'contraption' the Northern Ireland government had quibbled about paying for in the years before the Troubles. WO2 Mike Coldrick, who served his first tour in early 1972, says it was a heavy, cumbersome piece of equipment, originally designed for medical purposes and difficult to deploy.

> You had to develop the images with wet chemicals in the back of an armoured vehicle or in a Land Rover. You had the chemicals premixed in two old flare containers. It was also dependent on power and the length of the umbilicals which was only about 25 yards or so. That meant you had to be right on top of a device so by the time I got there, with the big devices that were being used, I never used the X-ray.

Coldrick thinks little of the basic equipment was suitable for the task. Its origins lay in the impromptu development of disposal techniques during the Second World War and the various colonial campaigns, but IRA tactics now far outstripped the capability of the equipment, training and indeed the existing capacity of the operators, whose lives were at growing risk. The first need was for additional manpower to reduce the workload on each team. Tired men, on call night and day, were more likely to make fatal mistakes, so, as the number of bombings mounted, back-up staff were progressively posted in. By the beginning of 1972, despite some jostling by the Royal Engineers for a role, the order of battle in Northern Ireland clearly delegated responsibility for neutralising IEDs to the RAOC.

The Army's entire EOD burden fell on a pool of just 550 highly trained men (there were no women in the ammunition trade in those days) – 200 Ammunition Technical Officers and 350 Ammunition Technicians. After the short 'pretheatre' training course at Bramley, it was from their ranks that personnel were assigned to 321 EOD in Northern Ireland. When not on duty there, many were on standby in Britain to tackle any attacks there or to deploy back to Northern Ireland in an emergency. Some joined 421 EOD, the replacement shadow unit that had been formed to support Army operations worldwide.

By 1972, the front-line EOD formation was a four-strong team: an ATO or Number One supported by a Number Two with a Bleep and a driver/escort. The teams operated within sections. At the beginning of 1972 there was a Belfast section attached to 39 Brigade, another at Lurgan with 5 Airportable Brigade and a third deployed to 8 Brigade, but one team was detached to Omagh and another to Londonderry. An EOD Control Centre was formed at each brigade headquarters and each section commander acted as EOD adviser to his brigadier when necessary. They also provided technical advice and back-up on the ground during a difficult clearance. Later in 1972, as the task continued to grow, a headquarters detachment was established at Thiepval Barracks, Lisburn under the command of a Chief Ammunition Technical Officer (CATO) who advised the GOC and controlled and co-ordinated the entire effort. The new CATO was supported by an ATO and two ATs, accommodated in one of the portable huts that had sprung up around the main building. Elsewhere in the complex the 321 EOD Unit set up its headquarters. From then on, individual 'trickle' posting replaced the previous 'roulement' system whereby entire teams moved in and out. In recognition of the unique strains and dangers of EOD postings to Northern Ireland it was decided that operators and team members would generally serve only four-month tours. The SATO commanding 321 would be replaced every eight months and CATO would serve for one year rather than two as in an equivalent staff job. Team members would be allowed a four-day rest and recuperation break in mid-tour. For all concerned it was a round-the-clock job, with one operator on duty, one on standby and one resting. In the early days, however, this ideal rarely applied and teams could go from job to job for as long as twenty-four hours at a stretch.

As the workload steadily increased the 321 establishment was reviewed. In late 1972 a stores department was added and a quartermaster appointed to cope with the increasing specialisation and quantity of technical equipment. Administrative support was also enhanced as the amount of clerical work burgeoned. The number of incident reports, for instance, soared to 4,800 a year with as many as twenty copies needing to be circulated on the bomb intelligence network within Northern Ireland, the rest of the United Kingdom and further afield.

At this time the Senior Ammunition Technical Officer worked from the HQ Northern Ireland operations room, passing on call-out requests to EOD controllers in the three brigade headquarters. Tasks were then telephoned from the Brigade Operations Room to local sections. On arrival at the scene, military or RUC contacts would show the operator a suspected device. If the situation was unusual or sensitive he could call for a second opinion from a fellow ATO or seek direction from further up the chain. In those days it was not uncommon for the CATO himself to come to the location. There were also contingency plans to form additional teams from CATO's staff, those at the various headquarters and at the Ammunition Sub-Depot at Ballykinler, County Down, where some of the staff responsible for the safety of stored ordnance were also trained for EOD work. By the end of 1972, the Director of Ordnance Services could say:

> Each section is capable of providing an EOD team for continuous
> operation for indefinite periods. It can handle about 10 incidents a day
> in urban areas or in rural areas, where travelling is involved, about 5
> incidents. It can cope with increased activity by producing a second
> team and *in extremis* all personnel can be fielded, but for limited
> periods. This ability to contain sudden increased activity allows time to
> reinforce the section if the situation demands it.

It was during this early period that the EOD teams acquired their 'Felix' call-sign. The frequency of call-outs for EOD assistance required a designation separate from the RAOC's Rickshaw. One version has it that Styles instructed that the new call-sign should be Phoenix, as in 'rising from the ashes', but was misheard. However, Lieutenant-Colonel Malcolm Mackenzie-Orr recalls that it was the Chief Signals Officer who allocated the call-sign Felix. In any case, the teams adopted the famous image of the cartoon cat not least because of its nine lives and ability to survive endless mayhem. A version of the cat first appeared alongside the Red Hand of Ulster and the Europa Hotel logo on a tie commissioned by the hotel manager, Harper Brown, which was presented to all involved in the epic clearances.

Soon further 321 terminology emerged. Radio operators decided that calling for Styles as 'Sunray Felix' was too much of a mouthful, so they unofficially abbreviated his call-sign to 'Topcat'. Thereafter a series of cat signs emerged: the Chief Ammunition Technical Officer remained Topcat, the Senior Ammunition Technical Officer became Bosscat and the Senior Ammunition Technician answered to Wildcat. At first only two of the Belfast teams adopted similar designations, Bearcat and Tomcat, but in due course others came into line with Polecat and other feline sobriquets, these also being stencilled on EOD vehicles.

In another innovation, the Army and the police formed a small, lightly armed covert surveillance team, travelling in plain clothes in unmarked cars, whose priority was to intercept bombers on their way to targets. One of this squad was an RAOC explosives expert with a detailed knowledge of terrorist methods who had been drafted in from Germany. The first undercover squad was deployed by 39 Brigade and similar teams were then formed in the 8 and 19 Brigade areas, though the move stimulated old rivalry when two Royal Engineers were assigned as explosives experts. At a higher level, the development was welcomed. During a conference chaired by the GOC, Sir Harry Tuzo, at his headquarters on 9 September and attended by the Chief of the General Staff, the Commander Land Forces, Major-General Robert Ford, said that the teams acted as a deterrent if not a preventative force. The great need was to block the IRA's sources of explosives and the Irish government needed to do more about this. In the meantime, individuals were being picked up continuously and no organisation could stand such steady attrition. Ford's particular hope was that more explosives experts would be caught.

The undercover initiative reflected some frustration. A 1970 report reveals that wanted men or explosives were found in only ten of over 200,000 cars searched. In 1971 the Army checked well over a thousand vehicles a day and from time to time imposed crackdowns or triggered operations with mysterious codenames such as 'Spondon', which involved 101 cross-border roadblocks, 'Knocker', which sealed Belfast off with thirty-three checkpoints, and 'Fury', which imposed control on all east–west movement within Northern Ireland with 229 roadblocks along the rivers Bann and Blackwater. The Army, strangers in an unfamiliar land, undoubtedly gained useful low-level intelligence from such extensive operations but the return for the investment, in terms of explosives, arms and ammunition captured, remained disappointing. In the belief that terrorist intimidation was deterring people from giving information, confidential telephone lines were set up in eleven major towns. The system worked with some success and was later upgraded to a single number for the whole of Northern Ireland. It was also adopted by the bombers to give warnings.

By the end of 1972 an entirely new EOD philosophy enshrined three priorities: the safety of personnel including the operator, although it might sometimes be necessary to work at speed without regard for personal safety; the protection of property; and the collection of evidence for forensic purposes. With this third guideline in mind, Styles had gathered a body of material from scenes of explosions and dismantled devices and handed the lot over to the embryonic Northern Ireland Data Reference Centre, created to hold and cross-reference information about bombers and their methods, materials and explosives and sources. An ATO was seconded to the Northern Ireland Forensic Science Laboratory to assist in examining material recovered from explosions, dismantled devices and captures from bomb stores and factories, looking for evidence to make arrests and for signs of new bomb-making techniques.

This enterprise had taken off from an unfavourable start. The rudimentary Forensic Science facilities at Cromac Street, Belfast, had no room to accommodate additional work, so an old warehouse at the RUC depot in Sprucefield near Lisburn was converted and Captain Alan Clouter was delegated to get the technical details right. The expertise developed there came to be seen as the most advanced in the world and former operators and scientists went on to share their knowledge, saving lives, preserving property and helping to apprehend terrorists in many other theatres of conflict.

Around this time Styles inaugurated pattern analysis of bombings with a map showing their locations and the sources of explosives. At this early stage the police and the Army knew very little about the bomb-makers except for the distinctive 'signature' each imprinted on his work: the way circuits were connected or the neatness of the soldering and wiring. 'If you gave five people the components for a bomb, no two of them would assemble it in exactly the same way,' said Styles, who used his data to compile a list of the main bomb-makers. Some of them would earn a scintilla of professional admiration for their skill but the bomb-disposal teams held them in contempt nonetheless. Detailed guidance was also prepared about the evacuation of buildings and the factors to be taken into account by an ATO when placing safety cordons. The manual contained details about structural weak points in buildings and the effects of blast on different types of material, based on existing technical knowledge and first-hand observation. This was another area where the textbook had to be hastily rewritten.

At the same time a truly comprehensive EOD support structure was being put in place. Every infantry unit was required to form and train search teams to locate and detect hidden arms, ammunition and explosives and to recognise booby-traps and IEDs when out on patrol. Although excluded from directly neutralising devices, the Royal Engineers entered into an enduring and vital partnership with the RAOC and 321, forming specially trained Explosive Ordnance Reconnaissance (EOR) teams to support the EOD operators by identifying devices and booby-traps. Over the years, as the standard of devices improved and ambushes became more intricate, their skill in route and area clearance would become as critical as the ability to dismantle bombs.

Much of the early EOD response was as improvised as the devices they were dealing with, relying on the skill and luck of the operators. Arranging controlled explosions with detonators, fuse wire and small charges was standard, but sometimes they resorted to Torpex aluminised explosive candles to burn off explosives, an action which usually ensured the safety of surrounding property. In the early days, operators wore ear defenders and standard flak jackets or the basic EOD suit. The first real piece of modern technical assistance was introduced on 1 July 1971 when what was colourfully described as the 'Mechanical Bloodhound' went on trial in the Newry area. Styles had first seen the apparatus demonstrated on the BBC television programme *Tomorrow's World*. In his memoir he recalls:

> One night they showed a device that could detect certain chemical vapours. We went to the manufacturers to discover if it could detect the vapour given off by explosives, particularly gelignite. We bought one machine and took it back to Northern Ireland to demonstrate to Major-General Tony Farrar-Hockley (CLF) and Government research chemists. There was some scepticism about what had been christened 'The Sniffer' but I thought it was better than nothing. I handed a stick of gelignite to the assembled top brass and asked them to pass it round amongst themselves. I told them to remember which hand they'd used to hold the explosive and then I used 'The Sniffer' on them. I was able to tell that some of them had held the gelignite in their right hand, their left hand, both hands, or not at all.

'The Sniffer' was in fact a gas leak detector used in refrigeration plants. In trials at RARDE it was found to respond to the nitro-glycerine vapour given off by explosives. Announcing its introduction, the Army warned bombers that explosive traces on their hands could be detected for twenty-four hours, no matter how thoroughly they had washed, and that it could also pick up explosive vapours in cars and houses. 'It proved a very good deterrent and not a bad detector in spot searches. Quite a number of people had some explaining to do after "The Sniffer" showed they'd recently handled explosives,' recalls Styles. Search capacity was enhanced by a mobile X-ray unit, designated 'Flicker'. Vehicles were winched in and out of a bay mounted on a four-ton trailer to be scanned on all four sides. The images were displayed on screens in an armoured Land Rover parked close by. There were high hopes for the apparatus, according to the minutes of the EOD equipment working party: 'The ability to control movement of explosives was the one field of operations in which the security forces had had almost total failure in spite of the fact that the move towards larger bombs meant that ever increasing quantities of explosives must be moving throughout the province.' In the end Flicker's real value was as a deterrent. Although it was stressed the use of X-rays posed no threat to the public, there was an underlying worry that the continuous wave X-ray required to penetrate a vehicle was far in excess of safe exposure levels. Accordingly strict limits were placed on the use of the equipment until safer systems were brought in.

As the incidence of vehicle-borne bombs increased, 'unattended parking' restrictions were widely introduced early in 1972. The rationale was that terrorists would not leave a person in a bomb-laden vehicle, so empty cars would stand out in the event of a bomb scare. This approach was generally successful, though terrorists used a tailor's dummy during one bombing in Enniskillen. However, as attacks escalated and warning times were shortened, 'control zones' from which all vehicles were prohibited were introduced across Northern Ireland in a bid to protect shopping and commercial centres. In Belfast city centre pedestrians coming in and out were frisked. At first the searches were carried out by the security forces but later civilian searchers were recruited and the original barbed-wire barricades around the control zones were replaced by high fences with controlled entry and exit points. Delivery vehicles were permitted only after extensive searches.

Contemporaneously, a massive security industry developed as every office block, hotel, pub and shop put measures in place. After the distribution of 100,000 leaflets and a newspaper advertising campaign, windows were taped and evacuation procedures and fire points were set up. Every office block and shop designated a 'rendezvous point' so that they could account for everyone in the event of an evacuation. The terrorists' evil ingenuity in defeating the security measures, however, knew no bounds. In the first months alone, the Northern Counties Hotel in Portrush sustained serious damage after four men posing as painters concealed one-gallon tins containing explosive in a toilet. In Belfast an incendiary device was concealed in a settee delivered to a furniture store.

To deal with car bombs, the EOD teams initially turned to a powerful standard army weapon, the Carl Gustav 88 mm. anti-tank rocket. However, firing such a battlefield weapon on the streets of a city raised political and safety issues. Trials at RARDE, which included experiments with a 76 mm. gun mounted on the turret of a Saladin armoured car, found that the anti-tank weapon firing practice rounds was the most successful disruptive method and in April 1972 ministerial approval was given for its use on the grounds that it would disrupt anti-handling devices such as those that had killed Cracknell, Butcher and Calladene. It was used for the first time at Corporation Street in Belfast, where it partially disrupted a bomb, but failed abysmally in a later incident at Bradbury Place. On 1 June a minute distributed from DS10, the Ministry of Defence department which handled Northern Ireland matters, laid down safety conditions governing its use, including that it should only be fired by a trained infantryman or EOD operator. Because of the restrictions imposed on its use in built-up areas its value was limited and it quickly fell out of favour as alternative disruptive weapons became available. In the end, it was new, purpose-built weapons which would not only transform the fight against the bombers in Northern Ireland but would become the prime tools for the task throughout the world for years to come.

With several brave operators dead and others being exposed to an ever more unpredictable threat, it was generally agreed that the priority must be to reduce human risk. While a detonator and small charge could successfully disrupt smaller devices and those in boxes, something altogether more powerful and precise than the Carl Gustav was required to disrupt devices consisting of large quantities of HME, generally set off with a small booster of commercial explosive. The theory of disrupting a terrorist device is straightforward. What is required is something to break the cycle of the blast initiation as the electrical pulse surges from the power source to the detonator to the explosive.

In the mid-1960s the Admiralty Research Establishment in the United States were experimenting with an 'underwater gun' intended to disrupt limpet mines attached to ships. The gun fired a bolt which injected toxic and very corrosive carbon tetrafluoride into the mine like a hypodermic syringe. The Royal Navy was interested in the idea but after a series of trials in 1966 concluded it did not quite meet their needs. What they wanted was a weapon that would disrupt the entire mine, not just knock out the fuse. British scientists therefore returned to the theory that a jet of cool, pressurised water injected into a device at speed might be more effective than a volatile chemical which could react with the explosive. Experiments started in October 1966, directing pressurised water jets through syringes into mines and other projectiles. By trial and error it was demonstrated that with a suitable electric 'squib' as a propellant, water could be accelerated to 5,250 feet per second in a special steel-barrelled gun, at which velocity it was possible to penetrate metal up to five-eighths of an inch thick. As a result of this work, the Royal Navy commissioned the production of Limpet Mine Disposal Equipment (LMDE).

In September 1971, as the EOD fraternity cast around for new ideas to beat the bombers, an urgent study was put in hand to see if this water jet research was relevant to the daunting task of defeating IEDs. The bulky prototype guns were test-fired around the clock against replica devices but the accumulating data had to be recalculated almost daily in response to EOD reports of the escalating complexity and size of IRA bombs. The challenge was to find the point at which the pressurised jet would disrupt the circuitry of a bomb but not detonate the explosive. After three weeks of intensive experiments and modifications the scientists at Fort Halstead produced a workable prototype for active trials. The equipment was demonstrated to Army commanders at a quarry near Belfast and later the same day it was used in action against a device in an electrical warehouse, under the direction of one of the scientists responsible for its design. The reaction was so encouraging that RARDE was asked to produce twelve further weapons as rapidly as possible. The scientists involved described them as 'Circuit Breakers' but the EOD teams initially called them 'Jack Horner'. Phil Yeaman, who started out as an infantryman with the Black Watch before becoming an operator, remembers the cloak of secrecy imposed when the weapon was introduced. 'There was to be no public reference to it and although it was big and bulky and heavy, in three parts, we had to camouflage it with sandbags and give the impression we were simply firing a shotgun at the devices.'

One of the first to use it on the streets was the intrepid WO1 Peter Gurney, who was awarded the George Medal after a tour in Belfast in 1972 during which he dealt with 123 incidents and safely neutralised twenty-five live devices. On 22 August 1972 he was sent to deal with a 50 lb. bomb left by armed men in a pub in Belfast. Despite warnings of an anti-handling device, a customer had picked the bomb up and thrown it outside, where it was lying when Gurney arrived. As his citation says, he placed his classified neutralisation equipment by hand and completely and safely disrupted the device. A month later he dealt with a bomb in an empty social club in Belfast in the same fashion.

With experience gained from operations like these and assistance from a university professor in Belfast, the performance of the disrupter was fine-tuned, but the outcome of trial firings on the ranges at Magilligan Point in September was disappointing. Having fired it four times against bags of sand fitted with mocked-up clock timers, the testers concluded: 'If this method of attack were used on a live device it would be successful only if the position of the clock could be judged to within 2–3 inches. Outside this limit only the charge would be scattered and there would be no guarantee that the initiation system had been broken.' As a result of this trial and other research data, in early 1973 EOD teams were given a smaller and lighter weapon with a breech, barrel and modified muzzle. At 10 lb. it was just a sixth of its predecessor's weight and far easier to deploy and aim. Since many clearance operations were watched by television and newspaper cameras, and terrorists, sometimes concealed in the morbid crowds that gathered at bomb scenes, were analysing the operators' every move, it became standard practice to use vehicles and screens to conceal procedures and equipment. Explaining the process to the media, the Army began using the unspecific term 'controlled explosion' which was later widened to include any attack method of neutralising an IED.

The codename for the lighter version of the disrupter weapon was 'Pigstick', but whether this was culled from the MOD's list of names for weapons and operations or an impromptu designation during development remains unclear. What is clear is that it transformed the fight against the bombers, enabling more and more devices to be swiftly and safely disrupted with a greatly reduced risk to operators. Despite technological advances since, it remains the operator's most significant asset to this day. The efforts of Mike Barker, one of those most closely involved in its development, were recognised with the MBE in 1971. In due course, the basic Pigstick was again modified in the light of experience and reappraisal of ballistic properties. The final version is now regarded as standard, even lighter at just 6.5 lb. and more compact with just two stainless-steel components.

Operators were still required to swathe the new Pigsticks in sandbag covers when in use, though as time wore on the Army became less sensitive about it being seen in action. Understandably they went to great lengths to ensure it never fell into the wrong hands. On more than one occasion, search teams had to pick through tons of rubble to recover Pigsticks. An operator recalls losing one when it shot into the air on firing. 'Such were the rules that I spent literally hours searching for the weapon and was nearly court-martialled when I failed to find it,' he says.

Inevitably the terrorists tried to counter Pigstick. One of their most successful techniques was to wrap a device in several layers of polythene, but this was overcome by fixing an annular wax disc to the muzzle of Pigstick. On firing, this cut a hole through the plastic. An 'elephantine Pigstick', codenamed 'Python', was developed in 1974 in the hope of more effectively disrupting car bombs, but theory and practice did not match and after a handful of unsuccessful operational firings the project was abandoned. A more successful variation later developed by EOD operators was a miniature Pigstick, later known as 'Needle', to render safe small incendiary devices. When terrorists introduced bombs in hard casings, such as beer kegs, gas cylinders and oil drums, another relative of Pigstick was conceived: 'Hotrod' was powerful enough to penetrate such containers.

As Pigstick was being developed, so too was initially rudimentary remote-control technology. The deaths of Captain Stewardson and others had underlined the need for operators to be close to unpredictable devices no longer than necessary. Clearance tasks were complicated by the need to open a car boot or door in order to examine bombs which might be operated by time-delay or command-controlled switches and incorporate anti-handling or anti-opening devices. What was needed was a way of operating from a safe distance, as Styles and Alan Clouter agreed after a hair-raising effort to save Lisburn police station from a holdall bomb abandoned on the front step in November 1971. As they pulled the bag clear from across the street, the line broke and Clouter had to run up and attach another one. Styles said he thought it was ridiculous, with men having recently landed on the moon, that bomb-disposal officers still had to risk their lives walking up to a device and attaching a string to it. Back at his office he made a drawing of a mechanical 'tortoise' that could be remotely manipulated. The following day he consulted Bernard Crossland, the professor of mechanical engineering at Queen's University, Belfast, and within days his team had produced a design for a battery-powered invalid chair steered by ropes, with a black-and-white television camera mounted on the seat. Over the next fourteen days engineering staff at the University built the contraption on a wheelchair chassis designed to deploy either the camera or the unwieldy 'Jack Horner' disruptor. This prototype was called 'Little Willie' from the name daubed on the backrest of the wheelchair 'borrowed' from a local hospital. The new toy was brought out to Lisburn where Styles steered it around the officers' mess to demonstrate its capability to local officers and top brass visiting from London. The following month it initiated the age of remote-control explosive ordnance disposal when it was used to tackle a device at the central post office in the city. Soon afterwards, approval was given to buy five vans to convey 'Willies' to incidents.

Motivated by this development, back at Didcot Lieutenant-Colonel Mackenzie-Orr drafted the first specification for a self-powered device which could be remotely controlled over a range of 100 yards, fitted with a means of viewing an IED and placing diagnostic or disruptive equipment. The concept was simple: 'We wanted a device to place the hands and eyes of the bomb technician 100 yards safely in front of his brain.' By now the collective ingenuity of the military research and scientific establishment was being applied to the task. The need for a delivery mechanism became more urgent once the Torpex candle was developed early in 1972. This device consisted of 108 grammes of aluminised explosive in a plastic tube, initiated by an electronic detonator. It was designed to be placed underneath or inside a car, alongside the firing pack of a bomb, and to burn off the explosive when detonated. Work at the Atomic Weapons Research Establishment at Aldermaston and the Atomic Energy Research Establishment at Harwell resulted in 'Dalek', a development of 'Little Willie', in the autumn of 1972. This four-wheeled contraption, four feet high, had an arm which could reach inside a vehicle to place a Torpex candle or even fish out a suspect package, but, according to Major R McDermott, it was 'sent to Belfast where it died a heroic but predictable death soon after'. Next came 'Rollerskate', a flat wheeled trolley designed to trundle a candle underneath a suspect vehicle so that it could be burned out and cleared. It rolled out from Fort Halstead, the home of Pigstick, but had qualified success, for it would only work to best effect on smooth ground or in a building and its electronics proved too fragile to be transported in a Saracen.

In the meantime, Styles and his men had been thinking about remote methods of hitching a line to a suspect vehicle so they could tow it away to render it safe or minimise damage if it went off. The first device tried was a Royal Marine Commando cliff assault grapnel propelled by a two-inch mortar. They also experimented with a .303 rifle adapted by the

Royal Navy for throwing a line between ships and a Schermully rocket-propelled grapnel. None proved sufficiently effective or accurate, and research turned to the possibility of developing a robot which could be sent up close to a vehicle. On 8 March 1972 Styles, who was now attached to the headquarters of the Director of Ordnance Services at Didcot, travelled to the Military Vehicles and Engineering Establishment (MVEE) at Chertsey in Surrey for informal discussions. There Brigadier HT Pierson, the Deputy Director for Trials and Evaluation, introduced him to Peter Miller, a retired lieutenant-colonel in the Royal Tank Regiment now working on weapons trials. His most recent projects had included improvements to the portable shield and remote handling tools first developed for EOD operators in Hong Kong, and he was also testing a shelter under which an operator could hunker down and work at a device. Firing tests showed that it was strong enough to protect an operator wearing ear-defenders from the effects of a 200 lb. explosion at fifteen metres and that it could withstand a ton of rubble falling from ten feet above it. (In the end twelve were built for use in Northern Ireland but quickly rendered obsolete by the development of other equipment.)

The deaths of Cracknell and Butcher on 15 March emphasised the vulnerability of the operators. What they needed, Styles told an urgently convened meeting next day, was a means of remotely attaching a towing system to cars and vans so that an ATO could drag them from a distance and remain safe even if an explosion took place. The minimum number of men should be required to operate it and, given that the system would be damaged or destroyed in the event of an explosion, the components should be relatively cheap. Although the government and Army had ruled out the deployment of tracked armoured vehicles in Northern Ireland, because of the 'invasion' image they would create and the damage they would cause to road surfaces, the use of a 432 armoured fighting vehicle for towing was not ruled out. It would protect a crew in the event of an explosion and was powerful enough to pull a vehicle laden with a heavy bomb.

After discussion, it was decided to put two ideas to practical evaluation. For the longer term, military engineers were to develop a small remote-controlled vehicle which could position an airbag 'sledge' under a car or van to lift it clear of the ground so it could be towed away. Hopes of more immediate help for the hard-pressed bomb-disposal teams were raised by Miller, who told the meeting how he had tethered a lawnmower to a post so it could be set to cut his grass in ever decreasing circles. By modifying a similar mower, he was sure he could build an appliance that could be remotely guided underneath a suspect vehicle to release a hook or grapnel. Miller recalls, 'The undertaking of this project on an ad hoc basis by a member of the Weapons Trials Branch was contrary to the normal and well-established rules for design and development procedure but was accepted, albeit reluctantly by some, as being a quick and effective means of meeting an urgent operational requirement.'

The next day, Friday 17 March, Miller travelled up the road to Andrews' garden centre at Sunningdale, where the sales manager, CG Chance, suggested that a Unispec Packhorse, at a cost of £102, might meet his requirements better than a lawnmower. Built at Cowbridge, Glamorgan, this was a three-wheeled battery-powered chassis steered with a single handle, to which could be fitted a flat platform with optional hinged sides or a steel barrow-bucket. It could run for about four miles when fully charged. Miller left with it in the boot of his car. Over the weekend he produced a series of working drawings. The technicians at Chertsey, although more used to working from full technical drawings, responded to the urgency of the task and by the Friday afternoon a prototype was ready for testing. Over that weekend and succeeding days the modified Packhorse was put through its paces. Initially it failed to attach tow ropes to an old Ford, but succeeded after additional modifications and further tests on 29 March. That evening the death of Major Bernard Calladene on a Belfast street emphasised again the urgency of the project.

The equipment was demonstrated to Major AT Robertson, Captain RKH Williams and WO2 M Ritchie at Chertsey late the next day. Despite limitations with steering, the power of the motor and the reliability of the on/off switch, they deemed it workable enough for more rigorous trials and so the prototype, officially designated 'Wheelbarrow', was flown to Northern Ireland the same night. According to Miller:

> This was a classic example of a device being accepted on the grounds
> that it was 'good enough'. It was very crude and could well have been
> rejected but the acceptance of it created a precedent and pattern for
> continuing development which had significant and far-reaching effects
> in boosting morale, saving casualties and minimising damage. Without
> the imprimatur of Major Robertson and Captain Williams it is certain
> that Wheelbarrow would never have come to fruition.

The bomb-disposal teams in Northern Ireland were so impressed by the 'motorised grapnel' that Lieutenant-Colonel Paul Crosby, the CATO, immediately requested five more. On 11 April Miller went back to Andrews of Sunningdale with an order for six Packhorses – the extra one for the Army School of Ammunition at Kineton. With an improved on/off switch, a fire-hose drum adapted to house the tow rope and a counter-weight to improve stability, the additional Wheelbarrows were shipped within weeks. Following a request from Crosby, they included another important modification: the facility to replace the hook at the end of the boom with a quick-release device for remotely placing a demolition charge. Wheelbarrow was on its way to becoming much more than a remotely driven tow bar. At first ATOs preferred to call the new equipment 'Goliath' or 'Joshua' in honour of the Biblical figures renowned for defeating vast enemies, but before long they fell into line with the designated name.

Meanwhile, work had been continuing on the airbag-sledge, now known as 'Wheelbarrow 2'. The practicalities were not as simple as the theory and the trials had not gone smoothly, but one element that was working well was an electrical steering system devised by Winter 'Lofty' Pattinson of the Fighting Equipment and Electrical Branch at Chertsey, a larger-than-life character who had served as an engineer with the Royal Navy in the Far East during the Second World War. His team had bolted two Packhorses side by side and Pattinson had come up with a fully electronically controlled steering system. Miller attended a trial on 6 May and realised the system would rectify one of the main weaknesses of the first Wheelbarrow. The vehicle sent to Kineton was recalled and refitted with Pattinson's system, enabling its operator to drive it forward and in reverse, steer left and right, collapse the car hook boom and deposit a charge. The commands were conveyed from a control panel along 100 metres of ten-core cable. Pattinson then joined the first Wheelbarrow team with Miller to effect further improvements enabling the boom to be adjusted for vehicles with different ground clearances. A spotlight was fitted and, again borrowing a development from Wheelbarrow 2, a release mechanism enabled the delivery vehicle to be withdrawn once the hook and line was attached, thus protecting it from the effects of a premature explosion. The first Wheelbarrow was now designated Mark 1 and this latest version of it Mark 2.

Over in Northern Ireland, however, events had overtaken these breakthroughs, as Crosby reported to Miller on 12 June 1972. Advising him that 'because the terrorist bombing techniques have changed' the shelter Miller had developed was not in full use, he went on to say:

You should also know that your 'motorised grapnel' has not been used in anger for similar reasons because of changes in bombing techniques. Car bombs are being set to explode at shorter and shorter timings. Where they do not explode, it is frequently because of design failure. We can deal with these after suitable waiting periods. Were we to use the Grapnel, there is a danger of exploding them by the action of pulling. Should a car bomb be placed on a vital bridge, however, we would certainly use the Grapnel to remove it. We have modified your design to give us greater control over the Grapnel and to prevent the motor burning out should it not be switched off automatically.

Despite this cool reaction, the Chief Inspector Land Service Ammunition organised a demonstration of Wheelbarrow 1 Mark 2 and Wheelbarrow 2 at Kineton on 18 June. The audience was markedly sceptical. Those with experience in Northern Ireland felt that the trolley was too heavy and cumbersome for transportation and was further limited by its inability to go over rough ground. No one could foresee a situation in which it could be used in town or country and anyway, they said, countermeasures would soon be taken once their opponents saw it in action. There was a similar lack of enthusiasm for Wheelbarrow 2. In the right circumstances, it was grudgingly conceded, it could be used to move a vehicle to a prepared area but ideal circumstances were not common in Northern Ireland, where rutted, obstacle-strewn roads and steep hills were the norm. In any case, with time often a decisive factor, there were doubts about the practicality of transporting such a large vehicle and cumbersome piece of equipment as a matter of course. Miller recalled later: 'It seemed to me that a reactionary policy existed whereby the bomb-disposal officer preferred to pit his personal expertise and technique against the wit and deviousness of the bomber with the laudable aim of obtaining forensic evidence in mint condition and avoiding material damage.' In a letter to Styles the next day he sought to address one of the main criticisms, suggesting they could give Wheelbarrow cross-country capability by mounting it on tracks. Whilst at Kineton, he added, an ATO had suggested the capability to pick up an object by remote control would be useful.

In his reply on 29 June, Styles said cross-country performance could be developed but should not be pursued for the moment. However, he added, 'A remote claw or grab which could be carried on Wheelbarrow would be a useful item. It must be capable of being stored separately from the prime mover and rapidly fitted if needed. In this way one prime mover can have a range of "bits".' Until this point bomb-disposal operators had viewed remote-control vehicles only as a means of towing cars away, but Styles's idea was to have lasting significance. It set Miller, Pattinson and others on course to develop a more comprehensive robot, using Wheelbarrow as a platform for a range of 'bits'.

Three days earlier one of the Wheelbarrow 1 Mark 1s had 'died heroically', as Crosby put it, during its first operational deployment in Belfast. At 3 p.m. on 26 June, an EOD team was sent to investigate a Ford Cortina which had been left in the Star Garage at Landscape Terrace. After a lengthy soak period the ATO started to deal with the car, but as he removed a blanket from the back seat it became apparent that the car was booby-trapped with its rear door-handles wired to a device behind the front seats. The ATO decided to remove the car from the garage using Wheelbarrow. After some failed attempts, a tow rope was attached to the car, looped round a lamp-post almost opposite the garage and, on the other side of the road, hooked to a Humber Pig. There was no difficulty pulling the Cortina out into the centre of the road, but at this point the Wheelbarrow turned almost on to its side. Because it could not be disconnected remotely, it had to be left in place while several Carl Gustav rounds were fired at the car, detonating the explosive on board and destroying both the car and the Wheelbarrow. The official report of the incident stated:

> This episode clearly showed that the Guided Grapnel [Wheelbarrow] could carry out its function to enable a car bomb to be moved. By moving the car bomb in this instance we were able to deal with it remotely in the road and to prevent complete destruction of the Star Garage. Had the car bomb not burnt to detonation, damage to the front of the garage and to some houses in Landscape Terrace would have been completely prevented. Had the tow bar been able to disengage from either the grapnel trolley or from the car, this very useful EOD tool would not have been destroyed.

Preventing what could have been a large fire and the destruction of forty cars at the expense of a piece of equipment worth £150 rekindled enthusiasm for the Wheelbarrow. On 10 July Crosby wrote again to Miller, mentioning the incident and remarking that the improvements made to the Wheelbarrow 1 Mark 2 'do appear to be very impressive. One Motorised Grapnel will be sent back for you to modify.' Miller made his first visit to Northern Ireland soon afterwards and Crosby asked him if a jib could be fitted to Wheelbarrow 1 Mark 2 to enable incendiary devices to be deposited through a car window. Miller said that this would be looked at along with continuing stability problems when the Wheelbarrow 1 Mark 2 being evaluated at Kineton was returned to Chertsey.

By now Miller was in fact considering an entirely different model with four wheels which would be inherently more stable than its three-wheel predecessors and more efficient in its use of the two electric motors fitted to the Wheelbarrow 1 Mark 2, one each for driving and steering. On 28 July he returned to Andrews at Sunningdale to commission a four-wheeled version of the Packhorse chassis. The same day, he wrote to Crosby that the Wheelbarrow 1 Mark 1 sent from Northern Ireland was already being updated and he hoped it would be returned in about ten days with the improved features. In fact Andrews exceeded all expectations and produced the four-wheel chassis in four days. It was kitted out at Chertsey with a hook, jib and the remote controls already developed, tested on 8 August and dispatched, with the modified three-wheeler, to Northern Ireland five days later.

The new Wheelbarrow 1 Mark 3 was an instant success, the fourth wheel giving it the stability to climb kerbs and operate on rough terrain. Andrews were asked to provide four more chassis as soon as possible. They produced the first within a week and after additional work at Chertsey and a proving test it was in service before another week had passed. At the end of September a further nine units were requested. At the same time, after protracted trials the airbag-sledge was abandoned, thus simplifying the series of numbers and marks assigned to the Wheelbarrow family. Henceforth the vehicle was simply named Wheelbarrow and given a Mark number.

Between 3 September and mid-October, Wheelbarrow was used on twenty-one operations. Crosby, his team of ATOs and the EOD training staff at Kineton produced a flow of suggestions and requests, such as a window-breaker 'gun' which could be raised and lowered remotely and an addition called 'scissors' to grab and lift objects by remote control. Winding and unwinding Wheelbarrow's 100-metre cable was an early problem, first addressed by Miller who developed a 'flaking tray' in which the cable was wound tidily around forty pegs. However, Pattinson came up with a cable drum which took up less space and performed the same function. In another important modification, a two-speed drive motor control was developed which gave greater manoeuvrability for accurate positioning of disruption weapons.

By the end of October 1972, versions of Wheelbarrow had been used successfully in more than thirty-five clearances. Hard experience, technological advance and ingenuity had forged an entirely new approach to the disposal of improvised explosive devices. Thanks to the 'one-man risk' policy, new procedures and the growing range of options available with Wheelbarrow, the odds in favour of the operator's safety were significantly improved. By now the Mark 3 Wheelbarrow was recognised throughout the EOD constituency as an unprecedented breakthrough. With favourable reports and ideas flowing in, Miller and Pattinson applied at the end of October to produce two more models of the Mark 3 for development work, but the request was turned down. Instead, from the inexplicable protocols of bureaucracy, came authorisation to produce two for 'maintenance' purposes.

A very public mishap involving a Wheelbarrow in Belfast followed on 2 November. At 12.15 p.m. a three-man team, WO1 Peter Gurney, Sergeant W Barnes and Private P Sweeney, the driver/signaller, with their customary four armed escorts, were called to a side street off Clifton Street, between a paint warehouse, a petrol station and a block of council flats, where a Riley Elf car had been abandoned by three armed men who shouted a five-minute bomb warning. It was a traditional flashpoint area and the bomb-disposal task was complicated by the fear that the car might have been positioned to draw them into the line of sniper fire. The five-minute warning had long expired so Gurney, the Number One, decided to draw the vehicle from the narrow street, where it was surrounded by parked cars, to the middle of the main road where he could more easily examine it and where there would be less damage if it went off.

Working from a control point by their Saracen, they put the Wheelbarrow through the customary operational checks and sent it on its way, playing out the control cable and rope. When the car had been towed to precisely where Gurney wanted it, the robot was trundled back to the control point. The tow rope, horizontal boom and hook were removed and his assistants prepared the robot for a second approach to the Riley, this time to place a Torpex candle inside. Again the standard safety drills and checks were carried out before Gurney took the controls, but seconds later the release mechanism for the explosive candle functioned too early. In his memoir, *Braver Men Walk Away*, he recalls:

> The candle dropped from the barrow's arm and lay still less than a yard
> away. I was still staring at the candle when the blue flash came. The
> candle had fallen to the ground in such a way that the main force of the

blast went away from me but there was still enough force to pepper my
stomach with road gravel and to leave me bleeding from nose and ears.

Two other members of the team were injured in the blast and were rushed
to hospital, but Gurney was able to resume the operation with the help of
a back-up team, though his hearing was permanently affected. The entire
incident was shown at length on that night's television news bulletins.

An immediate investigation was launched to establish why the
Wheelbarrow had malfunctioned. Pattinson was summoned urgently to
Belfast and quickly confirmed that abrasion from its drive chains had
exposed wires and caused an electrical short circuit. There was much
relief that the fault had been caused by accidental damage rather than a
fatal design flaw and, in his report, Pattinson laid down a new set of
failsafe rules to ensure the same thing never happened again. In future the
firing cable would not be connected until the Wheelbarrow had deposited
the charge and the operator had taken cover.

On 14 November yet another variation of Wheelbarrow was sent to
Northern Ireland, this time with an adjustable clamp on the front of the
jib to enable it to carry a Pigstick. This innovation was another significant
aid for the operators and, in the latest of a series of triumphant dispatches
about the Mark 3 Wheelbarrow, Crosby wrote to Miller on 25 November:
'The scissor attachment was successfully used for the first time yesterday
by Captain A Millorit of the Lurgan detachment. He skilfully extracted a
milk-churn containing a bomb which had been left in a narrow alley
between two houses.'

Peter Gurney raised the need for the vehicle to have some sort of
climbing capacity after two incidents on his Belfast patch in which he had
to make manual approaches to devices up stairs. Wheelbarrow could
climb single kerbs but going up more than one step was beyond its
impressive capabilities. Pattinson was thinking along similar lines.
During one of his many visits to Belfast he had accompanied an EOD
team on a mission to deal with a stolen car abandoned on waste ground.
The Wheelbarrow, loaded with the window breaker and Torpex candle,
was rolled out towards the car but failed to climb a kerb and toppled over,
drawing jeers of derision from hostile onlookers. Mortified, Pattinson
went forward to plant the candle himself, narrowly escaping injury when
the main charge exploded. These events put Miller's original idea of a
tracked vehicle back on the agenda and soon afterwards Denis Fry, one of
the craftsmen in the Rig Bay where the Wheelbarrow work was done,
drew Pattinson's attention to the toothed fan belts on the engine of a

Chieftain tank in an adjacent workshop. Miller learned they were manufactured by Uniroyal at Dumfries in Scotland and obtained two 60" belts to experiment with. Support staff ingeniously manufactured running wheels and other fittings to produce the first tracked Wheelbarrow. The initial running showed that a longer track was needed so two 84" belts were ordered.

Three main problems persisted in subsequent trials. To give the vehicle sufficient power to climb stairs and other obstacles, Cyril Luger and the electronics team upgraded it from twelve to twenty-four volts and added a third battery, as well as more ribs to the track for better grip, but the stability of the vehicle was affected when it was tilted to climb. After more trial and error, they added a 30 lb. counterweight and a new mounting for the jib at the front. Fingers were tightly crossed when the new design was taken to the Barrow Hills Officers' Mess for testing, but Wheelbarrow Mark 4, as it was promptly designated, comfortably negotiated a long flight of carpeted stairs which included two sharp right-angled turns.

Miller and Pattinson reported on their latest breakthrough when they went to Northern Ireland on 3 January. During visits to the 321 units at Belfast and Lurgan they handed over a belated Christmas present – closed-circuit television kits for three Wheelbarrows, purchased from Dixon's in London's Soho Square in November. The small camera, an Ikegami medium-definition model, was modified to work off Wheel-barrow's batteries and send live pictures back to the operator at his control point where they could be viewed on a 625-line, nine-inch black-and-white monitor. (Colour television was still in its infancy.) With remote-controlled spotlights soon to be standard on Wheelbarrow, this was another major advance.

There were now ten Wheelbarrows of various types in use, with the original three-wheeler now withdrawn. Two of the Mark 3s were converted into tracked Mark 4s and six more Mark 3s were on order. Wheelbarrows had been deployed on eighty-eight occasions, saving the taxpayer an estimated £800,000 in personal injury costs and property damage. More importantly, after the injuries on 2 November nobody further had been killed or hurt in any incident involving Wheelbarrow. Indeed, such was the level of confidence and satisfaction in it that the slower, less manoeuvrable 'Rollerskate' and 'Dalek' were phased out.

By the first anniversary of Miller's trip to Sunningdale on 17 March, a new Mark 5 version was being trundled out of the Chertsey workshops. Despite the triumphant ascent of the mess stairs at Barrow Hills, it was apparent that the drive from the Mark 4's four wheels to its tracks was not always adequate and the counterweight needed frequent adjustments. In the Mark 5, which set the standard for all subsequent Wheelbarrows, the track was lengthened from 84″ to 98″ and the driving wheels were repositioned. This overcame the grip problem and improved stability, making the counterweight unnecessary.

At the same time, Miller was trying to find ways of making bomb-disposal kit more compact and easy to handle. During his new year visit he had noticed how the team at Lurgan struggled to load the car-hook attachment on to their Land Rover, so he devised an easy-release attachment which Wheelbarrow could deliver instead. Taking up a suggestion from Styles, further attachments were designed to fit Wheelbarrow with an Anti-Riot 5 shot Repeater L32A1 gun which could be fired remotely. This became the standard way of shooting open suspect packages and breaking car windows. Following representations from the teams, a small general-purpose grapnel was produced – operators called it the 'carpet-grabber'. Its value was soon proven when an operator used it to extract bundles of laundry from a van to expose a booby-trapped device.

On 2 April an incident in Londonderry demonstrated some short-comings. Just before 3 p.m. Sergeant T Smith and his section were sent to deal with a suspect device left on the counter of Madden's, a tobacconist in Waterloo Place. By the standards of Northern Ireland at the time it seemed a straightforward clearance, so the sergeant decided to attack the device using a Wheelbarrow equipped with CCTV and Pigstick. The vehicle easily gained entrance but once it had cleared the shop door a heavy return spring operated, trapping it inside. Worse still, as the operator could see from the CCTV picture, Pigstick had been knocked out of alignment. With the help of the shop owner he located the device and fired but the disrupter attack was unsuccessful, as were his attempts to extricate Wheelbarrow, whose umbilical cord was now trapped under the door. Having no alternative, Sergeant Smith approached and manually attached a Cordtex charge to the device. When it was detonated the entire bomb went off, extensively damaging the shop and leaving the Wheelbarrow buried in debris though largely intact.

The incident gave impetus to some important developments. Miller heard that ML Aviation Ltd had developed a gun which was fitted to the underside of Nimrod aircraft to fire blobs of paint along the ground to mark out runways. The firm was asked to produce a modified gun to be fitted on either side of Wheelbarrow to fire nails by remote command. In a situation like that in the Londonderry shop, the operator could fire a nail into the ground to hold the door open. In the end two types of nails were supplied, one for concrete floors, the other for wood. At the same time a clamp was added to the Pigstick mounting to keep it precisely aligned even if a Wheelbarrow was jostled.

After just over a year of informal, breakneck development dictated by the threat level in Northern Ireland, the Army decided the time had come to put the Wheelbarrow project on a more formal footing. The Mark 5, incorporating all the lessons learned, had already proved that it could save lives and prevent the destruction of property by going where an operator could only go at great risk. Wheelbarrow had also been deployed several times on the streets of London as the IRA threat moved beyond the shores of Ireland, beginning with a series of bombings in London in March 1973.

The speed of Wheelbarrow's development was a considerable achievement for all involved. Military procurement procedures for even innocuous items are traditionally protracted, yet a small team, working by skill, instinct and word of mouth and using models built on Miller's or Pattinson's kitchen table, had adapted and improvised a series of pioneering inventions that transformed the way one of the most dangerous jobs in the world was done. Of course there remained a considerable risk for the operator, and Wheelbarrow could not assist in every operation, but for the first time the ATO had a significant countermeasure and a range of bespoke tools to assess and neutralise a device from a distance. By mid-June 1973, from a concept intended only to tow cars away, the Wheelbarrow had evolved to carry an impressively versatile list of attachments: the two-piece car hook, a candle-charge dropper, window-breaking gun, incendiary release, Pigstick clamp and sensor, Scissors, nail-gun, shotgun mounting, 'carpet-grabber', towing pylon, CCTV and a Beguine emplacement device. The Beguine was an explosive metal plate used to open up vehicles with a charge fired by a cable played out from Wheelbarrow's jib.

A great sense of urgency had acted as a catalyst to bend or ignore the rules. Miller recalled: 'There was no inhibition about hours of work and, in spite of the inevitable strain and confusion over rough sketches and broad specifications, there was no lack of good humour.' One Wheelbarrow sent out to Northern Ireland on 4 May 1973 had been blown up three days later. The parts were gathered up and returned the next day to Chertsey. One track had been blown off, the lamp was broken and bodywork had been torn off and twisted. Nevertheless, it was repaired and returned to 321 EOD three days later. A key factor in this quick turnaround was the transport support network. Wheelbarrows were shuttled to and from RAF Aldergrove aboard the regular Hercules services to Brize Norton. Smaller packages with spares were carried on the VIP aircraft plying ministers and senior officials back and forward between Belfast and RAF Northolt. On occasion British European Airways (later British Airways) captains flying commercial flights from Heathrow to Belfast were recruited as trusted couriers.

On 11 May 1973, Lieutenant-Colonel Mackenzie-Orr, who had taken over as CATO at Lisburn, wrote to Miller:

> We are very grateful to your tremendous support in producing and providing bits for our increasingly battle-scarred Wheelbarrow fleet. Your men are doing a magnificent job for us and I would be grateful if you would pass on the thanks of all ATOs in Northern Ireland for their help. Wheelbarrow is almost as popular with the press and local populace as it is with the ATOs. Its appearance is always greeted with a popping of flash bulbs, whirl of cameras and applause from bomb-scene spectators.

By mid-1973 all twenty-two virtually hand-built models had been updated to Mark 5 and Wheelbarrow completed its six hundredth operational deployment. With the concept proven in action and attracting worldwide attention, it was time to put it on a more conventional and commercial footing. Meanwhile a Mark 6 emerged, the main addition being a new lighting system to improve the quality of CCTV pictures. Subsequently the camera mounting was modified to pan ninety degrees left and right. These modifications were standard on the first commercially manufactured Wheelbarrow, the Mark 7, in 1975. It also had a gearbox and drive system to replace the chain-drive of earlier models. A Mark 7A version was lighter and had an extending boom and, most significantly of all, a remote-control drive facility which did away with the cumbersome umbilical cord. This aspect alone was a considerable technical achievement given that real breakthroughs in microcircuitry and cordless communication were still to come. The process began early in 1973, when the Royal Artillery asked to borrow a Wheelbarrow to use as a model tank on their range at Larkhill in Wiltshire. As Miller manoeuvred it by command wire among the scaled-down houses and obstacles he realised how much more versatile it would be for its real job if it was radio-controlled. The proposition was put to the REME element attached to the Royal Artillery and they were lent a Wheelbarrow for development. The incident in the tobacconist's shop in Londonderry underlined the need. In August 1973 experiments with a Skyleader radio-control installation and a Mark 5 Wheelbarrow began. The electronics firm EMI became involved in developing an integrated radio-control/ video link, completed in October 1974 when the vehicle was taken to the Royal School of Signals at Blandford in Dorset for proving. As terrorists were more frequently using radio-controlled devices to detonate bombs, and the operators themselves relied on radio communications and other electronic devices for their safety, Wheelbarrow would have to be able to operate in an independent radio environment.

Another important addition to the basic platform was an infrared ranging device. Operators had had difficulty estimating distance from CCTV alone and sometimes had to send a Number Two or escort to make a visual check. They requested a sensor which would indicate when they were within 1 metre or 2.5 metres of the target. EMI went one better and produced infrared ranging accurate to +/-75 mm. over a range of twenty metres, achieved by projecting and receiving two pencil thin infrared beams from either side of the television camera. The first version of the kit was too bulky to be carried on the Wheelbarrow but more work was done to split it into two main components, with the measuring equipment being adapted to transmit the readings back to the operator at his control point.

All of this made the Mark 7, manufactured by Morfax of Mitcham, Surrey, so durable and popular with operators that it remained in service until the early 1980s. The overall weight and dimensions remained the same: 430 lb. and four feet by twenty-seven inches with a two-hour endurance from its various battery packs. Further ingenious modifications included variations of the grabs and clamps and a non-slip aiming bracket for Pigstick, modelled on the mounting used for an 80 mm. mortar in the FV432 armoured vehicle, which prevented it being knocked out of alignment and enabled the operator to set it confidently at any bearing throughout the 360 degree circle.

In the eyes of most in the EOD world, the primary credit for inventing Wheelbarrow belongs to Miller and his labour-saving lawn-mowing arrangements. In 1972, 321 EOD presented him with unit tie number 169, an accolade usually reserved for those who have actually faced live bombs. Peter Gurney says:

> The inventor was as distinctive as his invention: you could ring Peter
> from Belfast and say the barrow didn't cope too well today, and
> somehow he'd wangle a flight out the next morning and solve the

problem. It was the kind of behaviour which probably didn't suit the orthodox minds that ran MVEE because when Peter retired there was virtually no recognition of his work, nor has there been any since. His invention has saved many a life. He deserves far more acknowledge-ment than he has received.

The history of the long campaign to recognise and reward Miller as the inventor of Wheelbarrow was recounted by Nick Hawkins, his Member of Parliament, in the House of Commons on 21 October 1998. Hawkins quoted from a tribute, supplied by a former ATO:

> Wheelbarrow had profound effects on both terrorist tactics and the safety of bomb disposal operators. It is impossible to give hard and fast statistics regarding just how many lives Colonel Miller's machines have saved but, in the period 1972–8, and taking into account machines which had been exported, over 400 Wheelbarrows were destroyed while dealing with terrorist devices. In many of these cases, it can be assumed that the loss of a machine represented the saving of an EOD man's life . . . Having heard that, Mr Deputy Speaker, you will understand why I feel very strongly that my constituent deserves the recognition that he has been denied.

Replying for the government, the Parliamentary Under-Secretary of State for Defence, John Spellar, said that the work of Miller and others had 'without question saved many lives and the destruction of much property'. But, he continued, Miller was barred by reason of his position from receiving any financial award, 'as he was carrying out work that he was paid to do, and the invention, although useful, and vital . . . was not considered to be of exceptional utility and exceptional brilliance.'

'Lofty' Pattinson, Miller's principal collaborator who provided much of the electronic ingenuity and played a similar hands-on development role, was made an 'honorary ATO' and awarded the MBE in 1972. Dave Williams, who served the first of three tours in Northern Ireland in 1973, remembers that 'Pattinson spent a long time camping with us in Albert Street Mill and was out on the dangerous streets at all hours of the night and day with the operators troubleshooting problems as they arose and watching Wheelbarrow at work to see how it could be made even more effective.' After a bomb exploded nearby, drowning out his voice on the radio, he was even given his own call-sign: 'Lofty 24 Boom Boom'. His daughter Margaret remembers her mother back home in Surrey anxiously watching television news bulletins during his absences. 'There were few opportunities for him to phone home so that was how she knew he was all right.' In 1983, Pattinson was awarded the Roger Goad Trophy by the International Association of Bomb Technicians, a recognition from his peers that he valued even more than his MBE. The award was all the more poignant for him because Goad was a close friend. When he retired from the Ministry of Defence in December 1991, he was presented with a brass cannon and an engraved silver salver on behalf of all the ATOs and ATs he had worked with. 'I have seen so many young men go to Northern Ireland and other operations as boys and return as men in a very short time and, alas, several never to return,' said Pattinson, who died in 2002. His funeral became a reunion for 'the old and the bold' of the bomb-disposal world.

While Pigstick and Wheelbarrow fundamentally transformed the way IEDs were tackled, they were not the solution for every situation. Bombs were regularly placed in highly inaccessible places such as culverts under roads where only an operator could go. In the final analysis, as Pattinson said, 'It is only the "Mark One Eyeball" of the operator that will allow him to declare a vehicle, building or area clear to enter.' So, in parallel with the development of remote handling capability, many other EOD projects were pushed ahead to provide operators with better personal protection, improved diagnostic capability, alternative methods of disruption and dismantling and better communications. Like Pigstick and Wheelbarrow, these were pushed through far more speedily than the usual snail's pace of defence procurement because of the urgent operational requirement. The Vice-Chief of the General Staff, Lieutenant-General Sir Cecil Blacker, underlined the gravity of the race in a letter to the GOC on 13 July 1972, a month in which nineteen soldiers died and seventy-eight were wounded in shooting and bomb attacks, bringing the military death toll since 1971 to 122:

> I am particularly distressed at the casualties you are now suffering . . .
> because a lot of combat development and scientific thought and
> discussion has gone on here for months . . . with the main object of
> foreseeing, forestalling or remedying just such a situation as this. This
> is why I am keen on as much scientific analysis in Northern Ireland as
> can be done without getting in your way.

The general added that Dr Bondi, the Army's Chief Scientist, and his senior colleagues wished to help the effort 'all they can'. The Internal

Security Equipment for Northern Ireland Committee, established by Blacker in February 1971, was empowered to muster the technical, scientific and purchasing resources of the defence establishment to answer the needs of the troops. It was also the forum where new EOD equipment was considered, but such was the volume of work that these specialist judgements were soon hived off to a sub-committee. Brigadier Jardine comments that hitherto 'research and development into EOD equipment, although active, was mainly devoted to the heavier equipment appropriate to war. The advent of the IRA bomber in mid-1971 and the rapidly increasing scale and sophistication of his activities gave a spur, which ought, perhaps, not to have been so necessary, to the special requirements of EOD in an internal security situation.' Thereafter, he says, 'crash programme after crash programme was put in hand', first to meet the existing situation but later, from 1972 when an officer was specifically appointed to the task, to wrest the initiative by predicting the bombers' future techniques and developing equipment to foil them. The research programme was both comprehensive and open-minded. Military attachés worldwide were instructed to pass on details of any technology, equipment or ideas that looked promising. As a result, by the end of 1973, the EOD sections were provided with modern, effective equipment. An improved EOD suit was the main contribution, but it was hot and cumbersome, especially during protracted clearance operations, and many operators still preferred to take their chances with only a standard helmet and flak jacket.

By this point, many new bits of kit were either in service, on trial or being developed in response to ideas and demands generated by ATOs. Teams now had no-shadow illumination and floodlights and a powerful Swiftscope and binoculars to see at night or in low light. The range of diagnostic equipment had been considerably improved. A new IED stethoscope and the Scanray Radiographic diagnosis system, with Polaroid plates for instant processing, allowed operators rapidly to inspect suspect devices, as did two new explosives detectors. The 'Sniffer' had been overtaken by a hand-held device, the Explosive Detector Mark 2, which was said to be one thousand times more sensitive to gelignite and nitro-benzene. It was complemented by a 50 lb. Mark 3, said to be a thousand times more sensitive again and able to sniff traces of nitroglycerine and TNT in large spaces.

From mid-June 1973, a Beaver aircraft fitted with both black-and-white and infrared photographic equipment was deployed over areas where the presence of landmines was suspected. The photography could indicate where ground had been disturbed to bury mines or command wire. Each team had a range of cameras and lenses to record every feature of the devices they encountered. Their vital electronic countermeasures capability was under constant review and there were constant modifications to keep the top-secret 'Lilliput' equipment as effective as possible against the ever-expanding range of bomb initiation techniques.

As well as a growing range of attachments for Wheelbarrow, thirty-six tools had been developed to deal with incendiary devices remotely. While Pigstick had transformed the disrupting of a bomb, its capabilities were limited where it could not be aimed directly. This problem was alleviated by the introduction of the Beguine, but this was ineffective against the industrial gas cylinders used by the IRA to accommodate larger quantities of HME. A Remington 12-bore automatic shotgun had better success in disrupting certain types of device and there was some experimentation using a captured Armalite high-velocity rifle, dubbed 'the widow-maker' by the IRA, to disrupt soft or non-metallic containers such as shopping bags. Up at the Magilligan Point ranges in County Londonderry, there were tests to see if 'Co-Op Mix' could be burned off by either high or low-velocity bullets. The low-velocity and tracer rounds were ineffective but high-velocity 7.62 mm. ball rounds fired from a standard SLR rifle proved capable of detonating the explosive.

There was also rapid progress in communications. More powerful long-range radio sets enabled teams to liaise with aerial support. More importantly, pocket phones, primitive forerunners of the mobile telephone, allowed teams to communicate privately with each other and headquarters. Recording equipment was procured so that commentaries could be analysed afterwards.

Another innovation was a tool consisting of a rimmed wheel, a key clamp, a handle and two lengths of cord, designed to open a pillar box with the minimum of risk. The operator had to approach the pillar box and insert the key in the lock. He could then use the various grabs and clamps attached to Wheelbarrow to unlock the box and clear it from a safe distance.

The twelve search and seven tracker dogs already deployed by EOD had already scored what commanders described as 'results out of all proportion to their numbers'. During one cross-county search operation, Jerry, a tracker dog, unearthed a command wire and followed it for 300 yards to a firing point. Prince, another search dog, cast in the opposite direction and discovered a 100 lb. milk-churn bomb. Dogs could also play a vital role in tracking culprits. One Saturday afternoon, a handler and his dog were dispatched to Letterbreen, County Fermanagh, after a Saracen was blown up by a roadside bomb. The dog quickly tracked the path of the command wire to the firing point. 'There was still a good concentration of scent there and the dog picked up the escape route straight away,' said the handler. The pair crossed open fields, a rough wooded area, marshy ground, more woods and a main road for some two miles until the trail ended at the front door of a farm house. Within minutes, reinforcements arrived and arrested the suspected bomber. Impressed by this record, Headquarters Northern Ireland asked for a major increase from nineteen to ninety-one dogs, each with a dedicated handler. As well as tracker and search dogs, there were also pointer dogs trained to sniff a human up to 300 yards away. However, dogs could be distracted or have off days. They were only at their best for about forty minutes at a time before their concentration wandered.

It is a measure of the thoroughness of EOD research at this time that the idea of using rats in EOD work was raised. The suggestion came from the GOC's Scientific Adviser, JD Culshaw, who wrote: 'Although it sounds far-fetched I believe it is well within the limits of practicality to train rats to detect explosives and to attack wiring associated with the explosives.' British diplomats in the US were asked to find information on the suitability of rodents in general, but nothing more was heard of this particular idea.

The EOD teams' transport was another source of concern. Their Land Rover Safaris had insufficient space for team members and their escorts together with the newly increased array of equipment and they offered no protection from mobs with stones and bottles, much less from the large roadside bombs being laid with increasing cunning. In Belfast, the EOD teams operating from Albert Street Mill, the unit with the toughest workload, deployed in a Saracen and three Pigs. The Londonderry teams travelled in a Saracen with two Pigs. In each case, one of the Pigs was the Bleep's vehicle, fitted with Lilliput. Elsewhere, the teams used a mix of Pigs and lightly armoured Land Rovers but Derek Pickford, who was based at Ballykinler, County Down, recalls going out in a Land Rover towing a horsebox with a Wheelbarrow aboard.

From time to time EOD teams were required to deploy by helicopter and came to ridicule the ultra-cautious approach of the RAF pilots who, they said, wouldn't fly unless they needed sunglasses. The Army Air Corps pilots, by contrast, frequently operated in unfavourable weather. Perhaps the most spectacular of the many EOD contingency plans was that to tackle a bomb scare on any of the cross-channel ferries, which frequently carried military as well as civilian passengers and vehicles. The idea was to drop the CATO, another operator from 321 and some basic equipment onto the vessel. The plan was rehearsed early in 1974, to the entertainment of passengers, when a hovering Wessex winched Lieutenant-Colonel John Gaff and a colleague onto a Larne–Stranraer ferry in the middle of the North Channel.

By the end of 1973, these combined efforts meant that bomb-disposal officers could do their hazardous job more safely and effectively than ever before, but as Lieutenant-Colonel Maurice Tugwell said, the security forces had been conspicuously unsuccessful in capturing bombs in transit. Attention therefore turned to control of explosives.

Chapter Six
Control of Explosives

The escalation of the IRA onslaught gave a new urgency to finding ways of blocking the conduits through which explosive materials were pouring into terrorist hands. Efforts to check the flow had begun with the Explosives Act (NI) in 1970, when the Northern Ireland government reintroduced the controls on the supply, movement and discharge of commercial explosives which had worked relatively well during the 1956–62 IRA campaign. Police officers were appointed to check inventories, escort explosives in transit and supervise blasting operations.

The legitimate explosives trade relied on two main distributors, one importing explosives by sea from Scotland to Carrickfergus while the other brought them by rail and road from the Irish Republic. Altogether there were five main storage magazines, 103 licensed stores and 1,900 suppliers in Northern Ireland, the latter usually farm and builders' merchants stocking a maximum of 60 lb. at a time. However, as much as sixty per cent of the explosive used in the province was legally acquired from suppliers in the Republic, where the price was lower. There were calls for all explosive being used in Northern Ireland to be code-marked but the Ministry of Home Affairs discounted the idea because of the administrative burden. Instead, in August 1970, substantial rewards were offered for information about thefts of explosives and the identity of bombers. As the intensity and frequency of the attacks increased, with little or no information forthcoming, so too did the amount on offer until it reached £50,000.

It is safe to assume that the reward money produced little result, for the Ministry continued to think about more effective controls. An official study concluded that only about 0.1% of locally consumed explosive was used illegally, that users were not leaking supplies and that with no hard evidence of misappropriation from Northern Ireland sources, the terrorist stocks must be coming in on cross-Channel ferries from Britain or over the border from the Irish Republic. (This report appears to have ignored the outcome of a formal inspection of magazines in Northern Ireland the previous January by the Home Office Inspector of Explosives. He found them frequently in poor repair, with defective locks, inadequate alarms, faulty doors or loose hinge bolts, while many held considerably more stock – up to half as much again – than they were licensed for. One building had so deteriorated that the Inspector doubted whether it would withstand a break-in long enough for the police to arrive after the alarm system had functioned. As a result of these shortcomings, two magazines and forty explosives stores were shut down.)

On 16 May the crackdown widened with a thorough search of every known quarry in Northern Ireland, but this yielded only 87 lb. of illegal explosive, although the capture of 510 contraband detonators was a success. From the results of similar quarry searches, which rarely resulted in finds, and the lack of any really large seizures of commercial explosive in Northern Ireland, experts concluded that the IRA must be obtaining their supplies from south of the border. 'If this is so, an effective means of cutting off their supplies would bring the bombing to an abrupt halt,' one Army report stated. Residues gathered at the scenes of bomb blasts confirmed that a considerable proportion of the gelignite was indeed coming from sources in the Republic of Ireland.

On 11 November 1970, for instance, a vehicle using an unapproved cross-border road (without a customs post) was stopped near Keady, County Armagh. After the driver ran off, 60 lb. of open-cast gelignite, manufactured in the Republic, was found. In a similar operation on 9 April 1971 the RUC seized 50 lb. from a van just north of Aughnacloy, subsequently traced to an industrial plant at Kingscourt, County Cavan. The same month, detonators found in the Andersonstown area of Belfast were sourced to a civil engineering contractor in County Wicklow. In June two suitcases, each containing 45 lb. of Republic of Ireland gelignite, were found dumped in a ditch outside Newry, County Down, hastily abandoned when smugglers encountered an Army checkpoint.

Diplomatic action was already under way. After a meeting of the Joint Security Committee in Belfast in February 1971, Ronnie Burroughs, the UK government representative in Belfast, wrote to John Peck, the British ambassador in Dublin, on 2 March asking him to investigate whether the government there would be prepared to co-operate. He ended his letter:

> It is common knowledge that there is an IRA training camp at Scotstown in Co. Monaghan. Graduates of this and other camps are now putting the future of Ireland, both North and South, at risk. We recognise that the IRA is a sensitive domestic issue, but it is more than

that. It threatens all the patient policies of Westminster, Dublin and Stormont and threatens to plunge this province into civil war. Is it really too much to ask of the Dublin authorities in their own interest as much as ours to clamp down on these illegal and highly dangerous training camps under their own jurisdiction? A raid on Scotstown alone would help. Moral cowardice is a national industry on both sides of the border but there are times when it is too dangerous to be cowardly.

As at previous times of crisis, the question of border security was high on the political and diplomatic agenda. Faced with a Republican threat, the traditional catch-cry of the Northern Ireland authorities was to call up the vision of a mustering IRA and demand the sealing of the border – as happened in August 1969, with the Stormont government and the police utterly convinced that a full-scale 1916-style IRA uprising was on the way. Almost as soon as the Army had deployed in Londonderry and Belfast, sceptical military commanders were required to mount armoured patrols on the border, when a more sober assessment of the situation would have confirmed they were unnecessary. Sir Albert Kennedy, a former inspector-general of the RUC, told the Hunt Commission, which was charged with reforming the police, that some border police stations were kept open mainly because 'the locals like to see the bricks and mortar'. He shared the widely held view that such stations were a liability, maintained only for political reasons because 'the government sees them as showing the flag'. Brigadier Tony Dyball, then the Army's Chief of Staff at Lisburn, agreed: 'There are much easier ways of importing arms into Northern Ireland than the use of unapproved roads and attacks have been carried out on police stations in border areas which stand out like something of a sore thumb. It is a matter for consideration', he said, 'whether there is a real police need for such stations as Crossmaglen and Forkhill.'

After the traumatic summer of 1969 another attempt was made to crack down along the border, but 'sealing it', to use the politicians' vernacular, was impossible. The frontier meandered for some 280 miles along the boundaries of five northern counties, zigzagging through fields and criss-crossing rivers, streams and paths. Many homes, farm buildings and business premises actually straddled the frontier, some of the latter deliberately sited by smugglers to aid and abet the movement of contraband. There was one rail and 252 road crossing points; the British Army had cratered and spiked many minor roads, inconveniencing the local community on both sides. It was a pointless gesture, for there were still many ways in which weapons and explosives could be infiltrated. A military appreciation prepared in late 1971 estimated that to restrict cross-border movement to authorised points and impose continuous effective surveillance along the rest of the frontier would require a force of twenty-nine battalions, or nineteen 'by cutting some corners'. That would number between 11,500 and 17,500 soldiers, the latter figure equating to one for every twenty-eight yards of the border. Because of other commitments, the study noted, this was the absolute maximum force the British Army could assemble, and then only by withdrawing the entire Hong Kong garrison and reassigning troops from the British Army of the Rhine. Furthermore, such a force could only be sustained in place for very few months because of the lack of replacements.

The existence of the border was, of course, a major factor in the rapid destabilising of Northern Ireland, but the 'players', as the British Army had come to term their terrorist opponents, were all home-grown northerners, the vast majority having no connection with the few diehard Republican families that traditionally provided the IRA with its active membership in Northern Ireland. This was in stark contrast to the failed 1956–62 crusade, when IRA activists from all over the Irish Republic had travelled north. Moreover, this time many young women were involved as bomb-makers and layers. Some even took part in gun battles and at least one was seriously wounded and spirited away to a hospital across the border. She was taken under the wing of the extensive support organisation that had sprung up there, openly and with apparent immunity organising training camps, safe houses for rest and recuperation and hiding places for arms, explosives and propaganda.

Many of the active northerners had 'gone on the run' from the RUC or Army, basing themselves in border towns like Monaghan and Dundalk where the locals were overwhelmingly unsympathetic but too frightened to oppose them. After the introduction of internment, cross-border attacks on the security forces in the north became more and more frequent. From 9 August until 5 November 1971, for instance, there were sixty-six incidents in which two soldiers were killed, nineteen customs posts bombed and two elaborate cross-border booby-traps set up. Brian Faulkner, Northern Ireland's prime minister, told the parliament in Belfast that there were between three and seven cross-border incidents every week.

There were historical and political reasons why Dublin governments had long turned a blind eye to the IRA's activities. The Irish political world was still deeply scarred by the events around Partition, and from

Dublin's perspective there was no simple equation that the IRA were in the wrong. This ambivalence went to the very heart of successive governments, the political establishment and the population. In the way that Britain had its 'smoked-salmon socialists', Ireland had its sympathetic 'prawn-cocktail Provos' who provided practical, moral and often financial support. During the 1956–62 period, a Foreign Office mandarin in London had recorded that a senior Irish figure was 'more voluble than convincing' in his protestations that there was no safe conduct for the IRA in the Irish Republic, and while some activists were indeed brought to justice, the impression persisted that it was a grudging and reluctant process. Indeed, the murder of a member of the security forces in the north was deemed by the southern authorities to be a 'political' offence and thus immune from extradition.

The Irish police and army were run on the tightest of political reins, very much obedient to their political masters, and lacked equipment and even basic training. There had been fanciful talk in August 1969 of the Irish army 'internationalising' the situation by 'invading' the Catholic Bogside and Creggan in Londonderry or 'taking' the border town of Newry. In reality they only had half a dozen vintage armoured vehicles and, it was said, could only deploy numbers of soldiers on the border by taking the buses off the streets of Dublin, so it was not surprising that the Irish security forces appeared complacent about border incidents. The state of affairs was summed up in a dispatch from Ambassador Peck to the UK representative in Belfast on 27 May 1971:

> The harassment of IRA activists has been going on but at a low level. The Irish clearly do not wish to draw accusations of complicity with the British and of instituting an active campaign against the IRA . . . Nevertheless, a number of men have been picked up for the illegal possession of arms and the death of a Provisional during training in County Wicklow in April this year was treated strictly according to the book. I do not think we can hope for the Irish to be much more militant unless the IRA commit serious offences in the Republic and a case can be proved, or unless they become a threat to the security of the Republic. Moreover, I do not believe that anything short of a major security crisis would induce the Irish to co-operate openly with the security authorities in the North. The Gardai may be willing to co-operate, if mutual advantage is likely, with the RUC, but only if secrecy is maintained over the link.

After some research at the Dublin Embassy, Peck reported to the Foreign Office in June 1971 that the only Irish legislation relating to explosives was the 1875 Explosives Act, which was more concerned with safety than misuse. He also revealed that of the 4,500,000 tons of explosive imported into Ireland each year, all but 130 tons came from the UK. Much of the material was manufactured in France and supplied to a sister company, Irish Industrial Explosives Ltd, who reprocessed it at the only gelignite-manufacturing facility in the country, a plant in Enfield, County Meath, set up in 1967. Peck said the Irish government intended to bring in new legislation, but concluded: 'Whether the measures they take would be effective is a different matter – the Irish coastline is ideal for smuggling.'

The Irish dimension of the IRA bombing campaign became publicly evident in an ITV news bulletin on 11 September 1971, when a soldier held up a case of Irish Industrial Explosives gelignite for the camera. It had been used in an unsuccessful attempt to kill soldiers on the border. But the Irish attitude, as Peck reported to London on 20 July, was that IRA supplies were being siphoned off from exported gelignite being used in Northern Ireland. Any notion of lack of control in the Republic would be firmly discounted for years to come, despite explicit evidence to the contrary.

Official attention in the north had come to focus on devising a foolproof method of marking explosives and detonators at the point of manufacture, so that leakages could be traced. In May 1971 George Styles, who quickly emerged as the public champion of the initiative, took part in a fact-finding mission to the ICI plant at Ardeer near Stevenston on the Ayrshire coast, the origin of much of the explosive legitimately imported into Northern Ireland. The team watched explosives being mixed and packed for distribution and talked to production staff about the practicalities of marking and the latest methods of detecting the presence of explosives. ICI suggested supplying a specially coloured Primacord exclusively for Northern Ireland and offered to consider packaging gelignite by sticks rather than by bulk weight, for stricter stock control. Some consignments had been found to have as many as six or seven extra sticks to make up the weight. Clearly these could be skimmed off without trace from legal stocks. ICI also agreed to consider some form of tracing procedure for electrical detonators but said that numbering and marking gelignite was impracticable. Styles accepted that coding explosives was both a costly and complicated business, but, he went on to argue, without a detonator there could be no explosion. At first he canvassed the idea of putting a simple alphanumeric code on the case of each detonator but abandoned it when he discovered the code could easily be removed. Guns reaching the terrorists from the USA and other sources had their identifying serial numbers obliterated with powerful metal grinders.

Styles next suggested incorporating a hidden identifier during manufacture. These would be two small metal discs stamped with a code and dropped into the detonator case before filling. One disc would carry two letters, the other a letter and a digit. If they were packed in lots of 1,000, this system would allow 351,520 lots – a total of 350 million detonators – before the first code sequence ran out. Then the letters could be changed from upper to lower case for another 350 million. With some individual bombs in Northern Ireland now causing as much as £500,000 damage, the idea found favour with the authorities in Belfast and Styles was allowed to campaign publicly for its implementation. There was some consternation in London after he appeared on a BBC Television news programme on 27 July to promote the cause and again in mid-September when he prepared a hard-hitting letter to be printed in the influential Edinburgh-based paper *The Scotsman*, accusing ICI of being unwilling to mark detonators 'at some small inconvenience' because of 'profit motivation'. The Ministry of Defence forbade publication in order to protect its relationship with ICI. Officials anyway preferred for the idea not to be publicly ventilated in case the IRA were alerted and took steps to build up stocks of detonators.

Government scientists were in fact looking at an acidic paint which would etch the metal detonator case and be readable even if the paint had been removed, or small discs marked with coded dots and visible only by ultra-violet light. The government needed a foolproof technical solution before approaching ICI, the sole annual producer of 30 million detonators for United Kingdom use. The company was far from enthusiastic about individually marking this vast output. In a note in September 1971, DF Bayley-Pike, scientific adviser to the GOC Northern Ireland, said: 'The manufacturer would be put to additional expenditure and his natural resistance is such that we should probably need legislation to compel him to do it as well as financial compensation.' The Chief Inspector of Explosives took a similar line: 'To go to them prematurely would risk them finding many reasons why what was proposed was impracticable.'

For its part, ICI was concerned about the perception that it was dragging its feet on the matter. Writing from the factory at Stevenston on 1 October, AG Short expressed the company's frustrations in a letter to

Major-General Phelps, the Director of Ordnance Services (Styles's ultimate boss):

> I am concerned about statements which continue to appear in the Press and on TV attributed to Major Styles (Northern Ireland) which suggest that ICI is failing to co-operate with the military and police authorities in respect of detonator identification. Such a suggestion is far from the truth and in no way indicates ICI's attitude to this problem . . . Our attitude to the press has been that such matters are strictly security issues and therefore we are not prepared to comment on statements made by any official. We should welcome such an attitude by all authorities concerned.

The tensions found their way into the newspapers and there were stories that a senior military officer, obviously Styles, had been disciplined. The matter thus took on a political dimension, but ministerial briefings show that Styles 'had not been reprimanded or disciplined in any way' and that official frustration actually centred on ICI. A military minute prepared for senior officers noted:

> I find it astonishing that a Major should be at the van in this pressure on ICI. The battle has raged some one and a half years and ICI, the major distributor, has not been brought to heel . . . If Northern Ireland stopped all imports of explosives and dets, Bayly-Pike reckons that almost overnight they would introduce the schemes.

By now Whitehall had decided to impose its own technical solution on ICI with the incentive of financial assistance. At the same time legislation would make the traceability schemes compulsory. The first priority was to establish overt marking schemes; covert marking could come later if the first scheme proved unenforceable. Hints of all this had changed ICI's 'unhelpful attitude to one of grudging co-operation', according to comments in the files of the time. Meanwhile the MOD research establishments at Woolwich, Fort Halstead, Waltham Abbey and elsewhere were working to find the elusive technical solution, formally defined as a foolproof accounting mechanism to trace material from the factory through the supply chain to the user. Numbering of explosives wrappers was quickly excluded because terrorists could erase the marks or remove the wrapping altogether. The Atomic Energy Research Establishment at Harwell came up with a scheme of mixing batches of gelignite with quantities of 'rare earths' in coded proportions which could be traced even from residue recovered from an explosion. However, because of problems with creating a foolproof audit trail, the focus returned to the option of inserting coded UV-visible microdots into detonators. Styles, Bayly-Pike and EG Whitbread, the Chief Inspector of Explosives, were due to visit ICI again on 12 November and it was decided to use the occasion to pressure the company with an incentive of £20–30,000. So that ICI were not let off hook by refusing to develop the technology, the Royal Ordnance Factory at Chorley was also given a similar research brief. The delegation visited the factory as planned but little progress was made. ICI remained unenthusiastic about the whole business despite the offer of the research grant. The company would not contemplate introducing radioactive materials into explosives and the most it offered was to code detonators destined for Northern Ireland with 'spectrographically identifiable' paints.

On 3 September, while these events were still unfolding, Des O'Malley, the Irish justice minister, had announced tighter controls on the use of explosives including more supervision by the Garda Siochana. Although the police did not yet maintain an explosives register and little actual supervision took place, the minister did not accept that explosives had been smuggled across the border in any quantity. He conceded that in view of the recent explosions in Belfast and elsewhere, every precaution should be taken to guard against illegal traffic, however small. The statement was timed to pre-empt British representations on the subject, for Edward Heath was holding a groundbreaking summit with his Irish counterparts, Jack Lynch and Brian Faulkner, on 6 and 7 September at Chequers. The Irish well knew that Faulkner would make a big issue of border security and the control of explosives and expected that Heath would support him.

During the summer and autumn of 1971 Heath was almost totally pre-occupied by the political and security fallout from events in Northern Ireland and was well briefed on the subject of explosives. He had only reluctantly sanctioned internment and was determined to crank up a major political initiative to bring the divided factions together as rapidly as possible, an objective given more urgent impetus with every new death and atrocity. The first sign that the Irish were really sympathetic to British and Northern Irish concerns came at the end of September when the Dublin government contacted Whitbread in London asking for help in improving security at explosive stores. The Foreign and Commonwealth Office in London gave the go-ahead to this and to a parallel request for

EOD assistance. On 11 November the Assistant Chief of Staff of the Irish army, Colonel Harry Byrne, wrote to Brigadier Frank McMullen, the military attaché at the British Embassy in Dublin:

> I have had a request passed to me from our Ordnance Corps via QMG [quartermaster-general] concerning bomb disposal. Director of Ordnance states 'It would be of immense value if information were made available on developments in the EOD field. For example it would be a help to know how and why the British Ordnance Officer was killed recently in Belfast and also details of the mechanisms met with in the two devices recently dealt with in the Europa Hotel.'

McMullen forwarded the letter to the Foreign Office and commented:

> If it is possible to give the Irish some information (perhaps even by suggesting that their expert makes a trip to the North or the appropriate MOD establishment in England) we would very much like to do so. The Irish are certainly worried about a possible spread of IRA activity to the South, as their recent enquiries for riot gear show. Their anxiety over bomb disposal is more urgent; there have been a number of explosions this year in the Republic and they have every reason to wish to be up to date in their techniques. Our experience would be especially valuable to them since, as with us, the threat they face comes from the IRA. The main factor in deciding whether or not to help is, I imagine, an assessment of Irish willingness and ability to keep anything we give them to themselves. We think it most unlikely that any material we pass them, if necessary with a suitable caution, will get into the wrong hands.

It took until mid-January 1972 for Charles Henn at the UK Ministry of Defence to reply to Kelvin White who ran the recently formed Republic of Ireland desk at the Foreign Office in London.

> We are not prepared to give the Irish anything that could help the IRA. Even though the individuals to whom we released such information might be perfectly trustworthy, they would have to tell others in the Irish Army if the information was to be of real use. The Defence Intelligence Staff are convinced that, sooner or later, something would leak. As I'm sure you appreciate, this is a very sensitive field and information on those features of design that have been particularly

difficult (or easy) to counter could prejudice the lives of our own people.

All the Ministry of Defence was prepared to offer was two places on a forthcoming EOD course run for Foreign and Commonwealth officers at the Army School of Ammunition. 'I ought to make clear that the Irish should not expect that these courses will reveal sensitive Northern Ireland material,' Henn concluded.

Exchanges also continued between the two countries about the use of southern-originating explosives in the north. Heath, who had taken a close personal interest in the issue since the summit, said in answer to one of the many rebuttal telegrams from Dublin on 12 October, 'Why do we not stop all this and control supplies ourselves from ICI?' What he had in mind was amplified by one of his staff in a minute to the Home Office on 25 October:

> The Government of the Irish Republic argue that although significant quantities of explosives pass from the Republic into Northern Ireland these are for legitimate purposes. The Prime Minister has been wondering whether we might consider prohibiting the private buying of explosives from the Irish Republic either in Northern Ireland, or, if this proved necessary, in the United Kingdom as a whole. The State would then buy the explosives from the Republic and resell them only to authorised persons for legitimate purposes.

The prime minister's personal intervention provoked a flurry of drafting in Whitehall but the results were far from compelling, as Kelvin White wrote to Sir Stewart Crawford, his Permanent Secretary in the Foreign Office, on 23 November: 'The flaw in [the] draft is that it is adequate to persuade reasonable people who know where the "probability" of guilt lies but it lacks conclusive and quantified proof which will have to be rammed down Irish throats if they are ever to concede that they ought to be doing something.' But a potentially more productive line of communication was opened when the RUC wrote to the Garda, referring to the political talks and suggesting a meeting of experts. The Garda were wary but a meeting took place in Dublin on 29 November. These exchanges persuaded the Irish authorities to remedy weaknesses in their explosives-control regime and they quickly introduced a Dangerous Substances Bill providing for a licencing system operated by the police. Six tons of stored explosives were recalled from smaller users and lodged in the Irish Industrial Explosives magazine at Enfield under heavy military guard.

Styles made another startling proposition during a two day visit by the Home Secretary, Reginald Maudling, on 13 December. For as long as necessary, Styles declared, no southern-produced explosives would be imported into Northern Ireland. All Northern Ireland customers would be required to use ICI explosives and components supplied through Carrickfergus. 'Should southern explosives still be found in the north then pressure on control south of the border could be properly exerted,' Styles wrote in an associated memorandum for the GOC and the Home Office. 'The need is to recognise the present design and distribution system as a national danger.' Maudling was impressed and told officials to examine Styles's ideas urgently, but they drew an unflattering response elsewhere in the Home Office. 'Major Styles has something of a reputation for seeking publicity and because of it causes the Ministry of Defence a certain amount of trouble,' wrote JTA Howard-Drake. 'I do not think it will be helpful to encourage Major Styles to pursue his own line outside the [informal interdepartmental working] group of which he is a member.'

Styles had a strong point about banning all cross-border imports, for quantities of a particular brand of explosive called Gelamex (later rebranded as Frangex) were still turning up in Northern Ireland, but, as we have seen, while early bombs consisted almost entirely of gelignite, the IRA was now augmenting it with alternative explosive substances. As the bombing campaign gathered force after internment and throughout early 1972, HME became as urgent a priority as gelignite. With agriculture such an important industry in North and South, fertiliser and weedkiller were easily available, as was fuel oil of various types, another component of the improvised explosive mixes. A top-secret survey by the Army warned of economic consequences of restrictive measures, but imports were halted before the spring surge of use and farmers were encouraged to use up the 2,000 tons then in stock.

A report to the Joint Security Committee at Stormont on 9 March 1972 said that as supplies of gelignite had become more difficult for the IRA to obtain, they were resorting to ammonium nitrate, the main ingredient of fertiliser. In one recent week, according to the report, half the 1,000 lb. of explosive detonated was estimated to be fertiliser-based. Manufacturers had already agreed to replace the normal mixture over time with alternative ingredients which had a lower ammonium nitrate content. At the same time regulations were being drawn up to prescribe the maximum proportion of the chemical to be used in fertiliser mix to reduce its explosive potential. Soon after this meeting, direct rule from Westminster was introduced, and it fell to William Whitelaw, the secretary of state, to bring forward the planned legislation in May 1972 enforcing rigid controls on the sale and acquisition of ammonium nitrate, sodium chlorate and associated products such as weedkiller. Later in the year the terms of the Northern Ireland Explosives Order were extended to licence use of nitro-benzene, a highly toxic ingredient of HME.

Meanwhile, the British government acquired a first-hand account of the true state of affairs at the Irish Industrial Explosives plant at Enfield when the Chief Inspector of Explosives 'contrived' a visit, as he put it in a subsequent report: 'The "cover" was that as a private individual and a friend of a Mr D Rumble, a director of IIE, I would be shown by him round the factory and would, in return, comment on their safety standards.' What Whitbread found was far from reassuring and very much at odds with the picture painted by the Irish government. 'Security in the factory itself is very poor indeed,' he reported:

> As we approached I was 'warned' that a military unit guarded the factory and we would be stopped. When we arrived I found an impressive drop-arm military barrier with a large notice warning that the army were guarding the factory. The general effect was spoiled because the fence on either side of the gate and round the factory generally varies from rudimentary to nonexistent and at the time the gate was up (i.e. open) and a considerable amount of horn-blowing failed to produce the sentry.

He was told that the guard consisted of a corporal and six men, two of whom should be on guard at any time on a two-hours-on, four-hours-off basis, but during the whole of the visit he did not see one soldier. Whitbread was unimpressed by Commandant Gerald McDevitt, the Irish Inspector of Explosives, whom he described as 'dispirited'. McDevitt confessed that he was 'waiting to take my pension and get the hell out of it' to retirement in Spain.

Whitbread was told that over the previous weekend four shots had been fired at a figure in an adjacent field. 'Since this field belongs to a neighbouring farm such an action seems somewhat hasty but the story fits in well with the generally somewhat unreal atmosphere,' he reported. Describing the state of the premises, he noted the magazines were built with concrete blocks and fitted with steel doors and locks of a lower standard than in the UK. At the very edge of the site he spotted a large barn in which ammonium nitrate was stored. 'I took the opportunity to acquire a small sample of this thinking that it might be useful as a reference material by both the Home Office lab and by Forensic labs Ulster.' IIE claimed their 'accountancy' (i.e. loss) rate in the factory to be one per cent of the 32-ton annual throughput. Whitbread disagreed. 'I would say that the standard of accuracy I saw corresponds with possible errors of nearer five per cent. Certainly anyone working there, who was not greedy, could get a case [50 lb.] a day out without the loss showing up.' After Christmas 1971, Whitbread was told, security had been tightened and all explosives and detonators moved to portable steel stores in barracks. 'Material for a blast is transferred under escort which, I was told, is constant until it actually goes into the shot holes,' he said, but some slip-ups were admitted.

> I was told of 1,200 pounds which should have been returned late one night to Kilkenny barracks but was left in the Quarry Magazine overnight from whence it was stolen. Two reasons were given. A lazy Sergeant disobeyed orders and was disciplined but, more seriously, the locksmith who fitted the locks to the magazine had thoughtfully provided the 'opposition' with a duplicate key.

Despite such failures and political sensitivities, these efforts and the parallel pressure from the RUC on their police counterparts appeared to bring results. At the beginning of May, a minute prepared for White in the Foreign Office and Sir John Peck, now ambassador in Dublin, noted that in previous two weeks no gelignite had been found by the British Army and that the amount of ammonium nitrate and nitro-benzene seized had risen to nearly 1,000 lb. 'The IRA are also detonating bombs made of fertilisers by using bundles of detonators instead of gelignite,' it reported. 'They would not do this if they could get gelignite; this proves that the tighter laws which were enforced in the Republic during January this year are beginning to show results. It is time to start cutting off the supply of detonators in the same way.' The minute further recorded that ICI was finally ready to go ahead with the government's system for overtly and covertly marking detonators. 'The system will involve numbering batches of a minimum of 1,000 detonators externally. Inside the detonators will be plastic micro-discs, also with numbered codes, both sets of which will be mated to a much tighter accounting system.' A detailed telegram was sent to Peck in Dublin outlining the scheme and instructing him to seek the co-operation of the Irish authorities.

The Republic did take a major step to curb the IRA in August when they brought in an Explosives (Ammonium Nitrate and Sodium Chlorate) Order copied from that earlier introduced in Northern Ireland. At an RUC–Garda meeting at the Phoenix Park headquarters in Dublin on 15 August, RUC delegates advised their colleagues how they had called in existing stocks of controlled substances for reprocessing and encouraged farmers to spread their stocks on their fields where possible. To illustrate the scale of the problem, the Irish police said that one manufacturer in Cork alone was holding 1,300 tons. 'This was a very useful and frank discussion and there appears no doubt that the Eire authorities are anxious to have control of explosives similar to that which exists in Northern Ireland,' one of the RUC officers recorded in a formal report the next day.

However, when the group reconvened a month later little progress had been made. The firm in Cork was still holding its entire stock and there was fresh concern about five tons of nitro-benzene which had been imported by a bogus firm linked to a man known to the Garda Siochana. Progress in seizing prohibited fertiliser had been delayed by the government's unwillingness to pay compensation. Instead they had proposed that farmers keep stocks in liquid form by adding water, until it was pointed out by the RUC that the water could be dried out or boiled off. The RUC also raised concerns about Irish-marked detonators which were already turning up in the north. The Irish side conceded further security measures would have to be considered.

In his report the next day, the RUC inspector repeated that there had been 'useful and frank discussion and there appears no doubt that the Gardai are anxious to have strict control of explosives and explosive substances . . . It is felt, however, that full power had not been given to them at government level.' He suggested that 'pressure in this direction could be brought to bear on the Eire government'. But even the potential threat to the south, graphically illustrated by a series of bomb attacks on targets in the Irish Republic that autumn by the Ulster Defence Association, failed to make a serious impact. In a minute to Sir Stewart Crawford, the permanent secretary at the Foreign Office, on 3 November Kelvin White noted that the Irish had said 'nothing to us formally' about the UDA raids. 'Probably too embarrassed,' he commented.

The Foreign Office recognised that their representations to the Irish would be vulnerable to challenge unless everything possible was being done to seal Northern Ireland's border in both directions and to secure the air and sea routes from Britain. The issue was addressed in a letter to the Home Office and others on 13 November:

> Now that Protestant extremist elements in Northern Ireland are beginning to mount a campaign of violence not only in the North but also across the border into the Republic, we need to take another look at this problem. Firearms, ammunition and explosives for the Protestant extremists may quite possibly come from or through Britain and, in particular Scotland, where they have strong connections e.g. with the Scottish Orange movement. The Irish Republican authorities publicly pointed out that the explosives used in the raid at Carrigans, County Donegal in October originated in Scotland, and although there is no indication that they were smuggled into Northern Ireland, as opposed to being stolen from licensed explosive stores in Northern Ireland, we would like to be able to say if pressed by the Irish Republican authorities that we have intensified our efforts to prevent the smuggling of explosives etc. from Scotland into Northern Ireland.

Despite all these apparently positive exchanges, the underlying reality was still one of great difficulty for the Fianna Fail government, instinctively sympathetic to the Irish Republican cause. The state of play was summed up by White after a visit to Belfast early in November. The Gardai, he told the embassy in Dublin, engage in 'obvious and deliberate obstruction of justice' and do not reply to RUC requests for extradition, even for 'straight' criminals. They would not provide the RUC with pictures of IRA men who had recently escaped from the Curragh internment centre in County Kildare. On border incidents, White reported, co-operation 'varies according to individuals but it would be silly to pretend that it amounts, in any informed observer's view, to a wholehearted effort responding to a firm injunction from Dublin'. On explosives, he concluded, 'Irish co-operation is good. Stopping things going wrong in the Republic seems to be uncontroversial; hence our progress on explosives; helping the British deal with the IRA is something very different.'

Meanwhile renewed UDA threats to bomb targets south of the border and responsibility for the earlier attacks were mired in a series of claims and counter-claims and an exasperated telex from the Dublin Embassy to London and Belfast on 27 November ended: 'Between the IRA, the UDA and the Irish authorities, the true facts are becoming more and more obscure.' What was not in doubt was the cost of a year of remorseless violence. Despite the profound technical and tactical innovations that had taken place in battling the bombers, the new year of 1973 was greeted with a strong sense of foreboding.

Chapter Seven

'Think Like a Terrorist'

Just before Christmas 1972, Major-General Robert Ford, the Commander Land Forces, set out the Army's priorities for the coming year. In a widely circulated 'Directive for Future Operations', he wrote: 'Vigorous and successful action by the security forces has seriously reduced the IRA's morale and made most encouraging inroads into their command structure.' Analysing the twin threat from the IRA and Protestant extremists, he concluded the Army's task 'is to ensure that we do everything in our power to reduce sectarian tension'. 'If the extremists have too great a grip on the community,' he warned, the province could face 'a period of unprecedented violence'.

Although Operation Motorman the previous July had reversed the upward trend of death and destruction, the security forces continued to face attacks directed from new IRA bases. The leaders of the Londonderry IRA, having been dislodged from their commandeered headquarters at the gasworks in the Bogside, relocated to a cottage at Buncrana in Donegal, a few miles across the border. From there they continued to control gunmen and bombers in the city. Elsewhere, from places like Dundalk and Monaghan, regrouped IRA units sallied back and forth across the border. In Belfast, harried in their heartlands by intensive military surveillance, the IRA set up a network of safe houses in less troubled areas of the city. The increase in the average size of bombs illustrated the persistent threat: 10 lb. in 1971; 40 lb. in 1972; 50 lb. in 1973.

Despite the valiant efforts of 321 EOD Unit, the bombing campaign was having increasingly debilitating social and economic consequences. In a bid to curb the vehicle bombers, the entire city-centre business area in Belfast had been fenced off by the Army in an operation codenamed 'Segment'. All traffic was banned and essential delivery vehicles could only get in or out through checkpoints where they were searched by male and female soldiers. (In time a Civilian Search Unit took over this task.) Every pedestrian was searched and all shops and office buildings were obliged to employ security staff. Outside Belfast, traffic was routed away from town centres. Steel barriers and concrete 'dragon's teeth' designated the 'control zones' where parking unattended vehicles was prohibited.

Despite the constant destruction, removing many historic landmarks in Belfast and other towns, the terrorist threat failed to paralyse commerce by day. Shoppers and workers became used to the disruption caused by checks, bomb scares and attacks. In the midst of the turmoil, a new retailing phenomenon was unveiled: the bomb-damage clearance sale. In the early evening, however, when the shops and offices closed, Belfast city centre was deserted save for security patrols. Cafés, bars and restaurants began to shut early and the city's once teeming nightlife evaporated. Off-licences prospered as people took to doing their entertaining and drinking at home.

Against this background Paul Crosby, soon to be honoured with a DBE, completed his term as CATO in January 1973. His departure was eventful. As he headed for the Larne ferry his car was intercepted by police and escorted back to Belfast where the IRA had abandoned a 5,000-gallon petrol tanker with a device in the cab outside the offices of the *Belfast Telegraph*. Apart from the potential blast and fire damage to the building there was the possibility of petrol draining into the various systems underneath the street and setting off explosions over a much wider area. A larger than usual safety zone had been cleared around the vehicle and volunteer council workers were spreading lorryloads of sand around the tanker. Crosby watched from the incident control point as Captain Nelson Gunson severed the wire linking the cab and the tank with a well-aimed shot. Then Gunson and Major Mike Newcombe, the 321 commander, defied the 'one man risk' rule and approached the vehicle together. While Gunson clambered up the ladder on to the tank and neutralised a plastic container of explosive, Newcombe entered the cab and recovered the timer that the shot had halted with just three minutes to run. Given a thumbs-up to show he need not intervene, Crosby resumed his journey home.

The incoming CATO, Lieutenant-Colonel Malcolm Mackenzie-Orr, articulated the priorities for the EOD teams under his command as being to neutralise car bombs, detect and neutralise radio-controlled devices and improve methods of explosive detection to deter bombers and capture explosives and devices in transit. Mackenzie-Orr set out distinctively different approaches for rural and urban areas. In the countryside, the priority was to 'take away the initiative from the terrorist' by choosing when and how to respond to a bomb warning or an apparent lure. He advised organising the maximum amount of cover with ground troops and using the Irish Army and Gardai to cover possible fire positions in the

Republic when working at or close to the border. Before going in, teams should obtain the maximum intelligence from aerial photography, police sources, questioning of local inhabitants and detailed surveys of the area. Operators were advised to make full use of specialist search dogs and search teams to trace command wires and clear the approach to a bomb before attempting dismantling operations. All of this should be done under the protective umbrella created by their electronic equipment. 'Think like a terrorist,' declared Mackenzie-Orr. 'Do not use obvious positions or drills and never repeat the operation mounted against a particular bomb on a previous occasion.'

In the urban environment, where risk to life was greatest, Mackenzie-Orr said EOD action must be immediate. 'The number of people in a city centre at risk from a car bomb can run into many thousands unless evacuation drills and clearance operations are swiftly and carefully mounted.' However, the protection of property would never receive higher priority than the protection of life, including that of the EOD operator. At bomb scenes, operators were instructed to evacuate the area to at least 100 metres from a device and to ensure that onlookers stayed away from windows and out of lines of sight. Where it was safe, operators were encouraged to dismantle bombs and preserve evidence. They were also encouraged to establish co-operative relations with the media so that television news bulletins did not 'become training films for the IRA who watch EOD operations aimed at dismantling their bombs with avid interest'.

By early 1973, forty ATOs and 100 ATs had served in the EOD role in Northern Ireland, supported by ever-expanding security operations. Army visibility in Northern Ireland had become all-pervading with the average soldier working between sixteen and twenty hours a day. The main objectives were to reassure law-abiding people by their presence and to deter illegal movement with a minimum of inconvenience and delay to normal traffic. This entailed a mixture of patrolling on foot and in vehicles, aerial surveillance, establishing covert observation points and carrying out checks in depth on traffic using the main roads. Over 1,000 vehicles a day were screened on main routes to and from the border. A regular unpleasant task for the ATOs was to check for booby-traps around the bodies of victims of the murder gangs. ATOs were also required to clear all arms and explosives after a police officer who lifted a booby-trapped shotgun lost an arm, a leg and an eye. Some dumps were protected by sound or light-sensitive devices, evidence of the IRA's accelerating technical development. Based on such incidents, EOD

Branch at Headquarters Northern Ireland produced bulletins 'to illustrate the features of good counter-terrorist operations and the penalties for being incautious', as Mackenzie-Orr wrote in a preface to the first pamphlet.

As ever, the bombers tried to thwart the constantly escalating security measures. Bombs were laid with short or no warnings. Devices were regularly passed over the Belfast city-centre security fences at unmanned points. Meanwhile larger and larger HME bombs were being directed against targets outside the control zones. The lessons learned from all these incidents, successes and mishaps, were analysed in detail by the EOD Branch, the various intelligence-gathering organisations and at the Data Reference Centre (later the Weapons and Explosives Research Unit), a joint police–military unit. An experienced ATO, Captain Andy Collis, was seconded to the Centre to work with the scientists examining recovered devices and remnants from explosions to identify bomb-makers and find hard evidence to prosecute them. Some bomb operations were minutely reconstructed, from sourcing the materials, through construction, planning, laying and outcome, to identify weak points in the process. Another priority was to spot new types of device or technical innovations. All this information was fed into the wider intelligence-gathering machinery along with covert surveillance of suspects, community screening and interrogation of suspects, all designed to identify and capture the most active terrorists, whether Republican or Loyalist.

After the original Forensic Laboratory was bombed in 1971, the service eventually moved to a larger, purpose-built complex at Newtownbreda in south Belfast. The annual caseload had soared from 200 to almost 11,000 and every device encountered was the subject of a 'quick look' report circulated through the police and military networks. The aim was to ensure that every EOD team was aware of every type of device being used, whether it turned up in Londonderry or London. This shared expertise became increasingly important after the IRA campaign was extended to the British mainland in March 1973, creating the need for a nationwide expansion of EOD capability and the rapid exchange of bomb intelligence. The RAOC assumed the brunt of the task, deploying personnel who had served in Northern Ireland to support regional police forces in Britain. The London Metropolitan Police had its own bomb-disposal capability with four ex-RAOC officers, led by Geoffrey Biddle, who each spent a week with 321 EOD. They were soon joined by Peter Gurney, fresh from Northern Ireland.

The violence in Northern Ireland and growing international terrorism prompted a strategic MOD review of the armed forces' worldwide counter-terrorist capability. A five-strong study team, which included George Styles, set out the fundamental principles for minimising the threat. Urging that specialist police and military vigilance be maintained at all times, they warned: 'The initiative always rests with the terrorist, who will achieve the greatest effect against an ill-equipped or unsuspecting society.' They also cautioned that bomb-disposal operations alone, even by a properly trained and equipped EOD organisation, could never defeat the terrorist bomber. There must also be an effective denial of resources, such as explosives and chemicals, enforced by legislation.

In June 1973 the total number of EOD incidents recorded since the outbreak of the IRA and Loyalist terror campaigns passed the 10,000 mark. Despite the increasing complexity of the devices they were encountering, the EOD teams were having steady success, but sometimes the scope of the terrorist operations overwhelmed their resources. Of fifteen car bombs planted in different areas on a single day only three were defused before they went off. Another day, teams had to treat every one of sixty-five simultaneous alerts as a live threat until proven otherwise, even though this played into the terrorists' hands by prolonging the disruption.

The terrorists had become more and more indiscriminate in their choice of targets. Complex ambushes were laid in urban housing areas regardless of the risk to residents or passers-by. Much larger bombs were placed in rural areas, primarily aimed at the security forces but with a reckless disregard for anyone else who might be caught in their path. Innocent civilians found their homes, businesses and vehicles being taken over to facilitate bomb attacks. On one occasion in south Armagh, armed and masked men ordered a woman from her home, which was later demolished in an explosion aimed at security forces. Attacks were well thought out, carefully prepared and patiently sprung. Analysis demonstrated that some ambushes had taken between six and twelve hours' hard physical work digging in command wires, often over distances of several hundred yards, and positioning heavy loads of HME in inaccessible culverts or hedgerows. Sometimes wires were dug in and left for long periods before being connected to a bomb. One such wire spotted by search teams lay dormant for two months before terrorists moved to use it. The discovery of food and drink at ambush and firing points showed that bombers lay in wait for long periods for a suitable target.

At this stage, the IRA believed that if it could exact a high enough price in terms of destroying Northern Ireland's infrastructure, Britain would baulk at the bill and withdraw. This belief was founded on the long outdated notion that Britain remained in Ireland purely for its economic and strategic value. The IRA also calculated that a constant procession of coffins carrying dead soldiers would further tilt British political and public opinion in favour of withdrawal. It was these convictions which influenced the choice of targets, some of which were hit repeatedly to impose a heavy social and economic levy while others were singled out for their headline-making potential. The public utilities and transport networks fitted both categories and in the early 1970s the authorities became increasingly concerned about their vulnerability.

The cross-border electricity interconnector in south Armagh had first been severed in 1970, isolating the Northern Ireland grid from that in the Republic, so the electricity supply depended on internal generating and distribution capacity. We have already seen that only swift repairs after the attack on a power station in summer 1971 prevented electricity cuts the following winter. After a pattern of such attacks by an IRA bomber with specialist knowledge, orders were issued for patrolling troops to pay special attention to pylons carrying power supplies and a specialist military group was established with the task of 'eliminating the IRA expert'. There had also been serious attacks on the water supply system. In October 1971, for instance, a million gallons had flooded Belfast's Whiterock Road after the pump house at a reservoir was blown up by the IRA.

Isolated from the rest of the United Kingdom by water, Northern Ireland is far more reliant on air services than other parts of the country. Its main civil airport at Aldergrove, eighteen miles north-west of Belfast, shares runways with the RAF. With its extensive troop movements and economic significance as the sixth busiest civil airport in the UK, Aldergrove inevitably became a focus for the IRA. In July 1970, the airport pub and restaurant was destroyed by a bomb. Security checks were introduced because of the fear of hijacking and intensified in June 1971 with searches of passengers, luggage and freight, but soon afterwards British European Airways decided that it was no longer safe to position aircraft and crews overnight. Instead they flew out to Glasgow. In December 1972, a senior BEA pilot was suspended after refusing to fly to Aldergrove because of 'the lack of security there', a fear apparently justified two months later when two bombs exploded on outlying runways inside the supposedly secure perimeter fence. On 17 May 1973 the IRA declared the airport a 'legitimate target', prompting some crews to refuse to fly there at all. Late on the evening of 3 June, before another security check was even completed, an RPG7 rocket aimed at a fuel tank exploded harmlessly when it hit perimeter fencing. Next day, the authorities announced that the airport was to be screened by radar twenty-four hours a day, but the cover was clearly ineffective for just twenty-six days later a huge vehicle bomb was driven into the bay of the cargo terminal where it exploded without warning, causing extensive damage. Eight people were injured and passenger aircraft movements were disrupted for several hours. The next major incident came on Friday 14 September when a warning was given by telephone that two parked cars at the airport contained bombs. The terminal was cleared and passengers were confined inside inbound aircraft while an EOD team checked the suspect vehicles. One was clear but a 200 lb. device in the other exploded while the team was working at it. By then the airport had been closed for the evening, causing disruption to thousands of passengers.

The Northern Ireland authorities and the Army were exasperated. A note prepared for the Chief of the General Staff in June 1973 commented that the plans to defend the airport were satisfactory and that it was the BEA pilots and cabin crew 'who were making the most trouble', forcing the profitable Northern Ireland run into a £100,000 annual loss. By this time, the prospect of the airport being closed by a major explosion or a boycott by civil aircrew was under close study at the Northern Ireland Office and the Ministry of Defence, who feared that apart from such an event being 'a severe setback to commerce and industry', it would be 'a great triumph for the IRA'. As a result a plan was drawn up for the RAF to maintain skeleton services to London Heathrow, Birmingham, Manchester and Glasgow using Britannia trooping aircraft, the passengers being selected on a first come, first fly basis with seats reserved for government officials, MPs and other essential travellers. (The plan was never needed.) At the same time more security measures were taken at the airport. A search area was constructed in a warren of portable buildings well away from the main terminal. Vehicle movements and parking were restricted and the perimeter was ringed by a rocket-proof, floodlit fence with roads all around the area sealed off and access confined to one heavily guarded checkpoint.

However, it was a breach of security at Heathrow which led to potentially the most serious aviation incident of the entire Troubles. On 23 July 1974, several Members of Parliament and the chief constable of the RUC, Sir Jamie Flanagan, and his wife were among the eighty-three passengers and crew on board a Belfast–London flight leaving Aldergrove at 12.38 p.m. As it crossed the Irish coast, a girl telephoned the *Irish News* in Belfast warning that four bombs on board would go off in fifteen minutes. The plane was quickly diverted to Manchester, where it put down at 1.18 p.m. Passengers were rushed off and police found a 2 lb. high-explosive device concealed under a seat with a timer made from an analogue wristwatch. The device had functioned as planned but failed to detonate because the bomb-maker had neglected to scrape a thin layer of paint off a drawing pin in the watch face. The paint had acted as an insulator and frustrated the electrical contact with the watch hand, thus saving eighty-three lives.

Given their aspirations for a united Ireland, the IRA's repeated attacks on another vital transport artery were a perversion of logic, for the Belfast–Dublin service run jointly by the northern and southern railway undertakings was one of the few all-Ireland institutions in existence. The 100-mile line was used by just four passenger trains a day and a similar number of freight services carrying newspapers, kegs of Guinness, bulk fertiliser and cement. The first serious explosion derailed a freight train near Lurgan in July 1972 but the most vulnerable stretch was south of Newry where the line meandered through the south Armagh countryside to the border and then on to Dundalk – what became known as 'bandit country'. Another attempt to sever the line was made in September when a bomb went off at Kilnasaggart Bridge on the border, after which some drivers demanded danger money.

Events took a more serious turn during the night of 15 August when armed men took over a signal box at the Meigh crossing point close to the border, signalled the northbound goods train to stop and placed two large milk churn bombs inside the engine, connected by 'Geoflex' to an initiating mechanism tied between the front bumpers. A carefully considered EOD operation was mounted soon after daybreak, once troops had imposed a 300-yard exclusion zone. As the Irish army and Gardai staked out high ground overlooking the train from their side of the border, troops using low stone walls for cover adopted similar positions on the Northern Ireland side. Sergeant Graham Lightfoot, leader of the EOD clearance team, who eventually became a Senior Explosives Officer at Scotland Yard, deduced from aerial surveillance that the wire across the bumpers was an aerial for a radio-controlled detonation. He set out together with Mackenzie-Orr, Major John Jackson, commander of 321 EOD, and Lance-Corporal Wills, a sniper from the 1st Battalion, Light Infantry, to a position in a ditch some ninety yards from the train. There the lance-corporal, who had not been able to zero his rifle, was ordered to start shooting by Mackenzie-Orr acting as fire master through a sniperscope. The first shot did not even hit the train, but by the ninth shot the wire moved and the tenth severed the wire and ignited the explosive. Mackenzie-Orr and his three colleagues thought they were going to be decapitated when they saw the radiator from the £120,000 locomotive flying towards them but it went over their heads and landed some distance away. 'We learnt many valuable lessons about securing the area and planning EOD operations in open rural areas from that operation,' he recalls.

Another locomotive was hijacked in exactly the same position on 23 October. On this occasion the terrorists set fire to the signal box and the rear coach. In line with Mackenzie-Orr's dictum never to repeat the pattern of an operation, aerial reconnaissance was carried out to plan a different approach and the EOD operation was held over until late in the following afternoon. Meanwhile troops were discreetly moved into stake-out positions in different fields. Some hours after the hijacking four gas-cylinder bombs detonated without warning in a dry-stone wall near the helicopter landing site used during the earlier operation. At 12.23 p.m. a further ring of four charges totalling 200 lb. detonated under another wall and an hour later the train itself suddenly blew up. If the pattern of the first operation had been followed, EOD and Army personnal would have been caught in all three blasts. Periodic attacks continued throughout 1973 and by the end of the year the overnight mail and newspaper service was ended.

Even off duty, as the Army was reminded at great cost on 18 May, it could not afford to drop its guard. That evening, five soldiers based at Lisanelly Barracks, Omagh, travelled by car to a dance at the Knock Na Moe Castle Hotel on the edge of the town. When they returned to their vehicle at 1.15 a.m. and drove off, this tugged a cord taped to the underside of the car and pulled a wedge from the jaws of a clothes peg. The peg snapped shut, bringing together two drawing pins which completed an electrical circuit and set off a massive explosion in a device concealed behind the wheel. Four of the soldiers, attached to 652 Squadron of the Army Air Corps, died instantly; the fifth, a recruiting officer, died later in hospital. From that point on, soldiers were advised not to leave vehicles unattended, or if they had to, to carry out checks when they returned. They were advised to use threads to monitor if a door, bonnet or boot had been opened, or to position objects inside the car which would have to be moved by anyone placing a bomb. The need for the utmost caution on the part of security forces and civilians was again reinforced by the death of six people when a car bomb exploded outside a wine shop in Coleraine on 12 June 1973.

At this point the EOD teams were dealing with an average of twelve or thirteen tasks a day. For the team of twelve attached to the 39 Brigade area, which was commanded from Lisburn and roughly corresponded to a twenty-mile radius from the city centre, the main forward Belfast base was Girdwood Barracks on the northern fringe of the city centre. Other teams were based inside the Belfast segment. Outside the city, nineteen teams were assigned to the 3 Brigade area, which covered the south and west parts of Northern Ireland. The most demanding posting was to the team located at Bessbrook Mill, just west of Newry, dealing with the constant run of incidents and alerts in the adjacent south Armagh area. The headquarters of 8 Brigade was in the Ebrington Barracks complex in Londonderry, and eleven teams were deployed from there and outposts including Omagh. There was a constant rotation of personnel on four or six-month tours, with about one in four replaced each month.

Supervisory officers and team leaders had become very conscious of the need to monitor morale. 'A lot of nervous energy could be spent dealing with an incident and it was not until the final moments that it became clear it was a hoax or a false alarm,' recalls Ian Jones, who served several tours in Northern Ireland at different ranks before becoming an explosives officer at Scotland Yard. It became the practice to accompany operators on their first jobs and those coming to the end of stressful tours, as insurance against a rash decision or a lapse of concentration. Senior officers kept a close eye on whether operators observed the render-safe and technical procedures, on occasion 'reeling in those that were getting too confident and cocky and hence dangerous,' as Ian Jones says. Inevitably the public spotlight fell on the senior officers and the operators, but without the support of the rest of the team working from the anonymity of the EOD vehicles they would not have been able to succeed. The Number Two ensured everything that was needed for the job was to hand and often acted as a tactical consultant. The Bleep's expertise in identifying danger from the electronic environment was of life-and-death importance, but other members of the team – drivers, escorts and the technical staff who supported them on the streets and back at base – played a similarly essential part. Although Wheelbarrow and other technical aids had considerably reduced the operators' exposure to direct danger, it was still frequently necessary to make a manual approach to a device.

One such occasion arose in Londonderry about 6.30 p.m. on 10 March, when Captain Jeff Gordon was called to deal with a bomb in a paper bag left against the counter of a jewellery shop. Having just used Wheelbarrow to clear a car in another part of the city, Gordon and his team confidently trundled it towards the shop but it could not push the heavy door open. The ATO decided to go in and place the disrupter himself, but as he turned to come out of the shop there was an explosion. His Number Two immediately ran forward and found him unconscious, trembling with shock and covered in blood. Next day Mackenzie-Orr visited Gordon in the Altnagelvin hospital and found him sitting up in bed surrounded by flowers and chocolates brought in for him by the nurses and medical staff and he eventually made a full recovery.

As Sergeant Thompson found a couple of months later, also in Londonderry, ATO's were not only at risk from bombs. He suffered concussion and a head wound requiring ten stitches when he was struck by a stone while approaching a suspect car. Later the same year, again in Londonderry, Captain Richard Hourahane lost two teeth and needed twenty-two stitches when a mob stoned his team as they were examining a suspect car in the Bogside. On another occasion some years later, Captain Ian Magee earned a round of applause from onlookers when he headed away a brick.

The people of Northern Ireland were also trying to frustrate the bombers. Staff and customers in a Belfast pub took advantage of a ten-minute warning to lift a bomb to the street outside where it caused far less damage than intended. In another case a man kicked a bomb into the street after terrorists hurled it into a pub doorway. A seven-year-old boy had a narrow escape when he carried a bomb from the village hall to his nearby home; the initiation mechanism had functioned, but the main charge failed to detonate. After a spate of thwarted attacks the IRA in Londonderry issued a public warning that all future bombs would incorporate an anti-handling device. In another incident at Portadown a man was killed when he opened the booby-trapped door of a cottage. Soon afterwards, on 19 June, an Army major drove a hijacked mail van away from the sorting office in Londonderry and jumped clear after steering it into the nearby river Foyle, where the bomb on board exploded harmlessly.

The next day 321 suffered its ninth casualty when Captain Barry Gritten, aged twenty-nine with six years' service as an ATO, was killed while examining an IRA bomb factory. About 10.45 p.m. an Army patrol passing along an alleyway heard voices from some Nissen huts and challenged two youths inside, who attempted to get away but were quickly apprehended, one on the spot, the other by a back-up patrol. A fifty-strong crowd quickly gathered, threw stones, bottles and a blast bomb at the outnumbered soldiers and freed the youths. Meanwhile other members of the patrol, alerted by the marzipan-like smell from eight foot-long, sausage-shaped white bags in the hut, had called for an ATO. Captain Gritten and his team arrived just before midnight and after questioning the patrol and reconnoitring the area, he decided to go in and inspect the scene for himself by torchlight. The original patrol leader, close by outside the hut, heard him say, 'What a wonderful find.'

The ATO then emerged and asked for assistance. With the patrol leader holding the torch he went back into the hut and began collecting empty bags. 'These will be very good for fingerprints,' he remarked. Working with the caution drilled into him during his long hours of training, the captain moved methodically through the hut, examining and recovering bomb-making components such as an alarm clock with wires attached. After thirty minutes he turned his attention to a large bag bound with rubber straps. According to the patrol commander, when Gritten hunched down and gently moved the bag there was a large explosion. The ATO was killed instantly. The patrol commander lost an eye and suffered ear and other injuries including the permanent loss of his senses of taste and smell. Nearby the hostile crowd cheered and began singing Republican songs while corrugated iron and other debris swirled around in a cloud of choking dust and smoke.

Captain Gritten, from Darlington, County Durham, was survived by his wife and three small children. Before his death he had successfully dismantled an extensively booby-trapped bomb at the local football club ground, one of fifty-four incidents he attended. Eighteen months later one of the two young men who had been inside the Nissen hut, twenty-two-year-old mechanic Liam Coyle, appeared at the Belfast City Commission where Mr Justice Gibson sentenced him to twenty years' in prison for a series of terrorist offences, including possession of the explosives which killed Captain Gritten. After his arrest, he boasted to police that as the 'Engineering Officer of the Derry Brigade' he was responsible for between 150 and 200 bombings. Asked if he had maintained a record of them, Coyle replied: 'No but I take a pride in my work.'

Earlier in the year a disturbing development had illustrated how widely the IRA was casting its net. Just after 9 p.m. on 27 March, an RAF Nimrod signalled the Irish patrol ship *Deirdre* that a vessel under surveillance, the MV *Claudia*, was entering Irish territorial waters off the

County Waterford coast. With two other Irish patrol ships, the *Grainne* and *Fola*, in close support the *Deirdre* intercepted the *Claudia* and a boarding party found that it was carrying over five tons of munitions bound for the IRA from the Libyan leader Colonel Muammar Gaddafi. Also on board were a number of senior IRA figures making for a rendezvous near Dungarvan to deliver the arsenal: 750 rifles, handguns and sub-machine guns, 100 antitank mines, 100 cases of anti-personnel mines, 500 hand grenades and 5,000 lb. of military explosive and Cordtex. The 300-ton, Cyprus-registered *Claudia* was escorted into the Irish naval base at Cork, where the Irish passengers were arrested and the cargo unloaded. Afterwards the ship was sent back to sea with what Patrick Donegan, the Irish defence minister, described as 'a kick up the transom'.

Back in London the scale of the haul was both disappointing and embarrassing. The original tip-off to the Irish, passed on to newly elected prime minister William Cosgrave by the ambassador in Dublin, Sir Arthur Galsworthy, had talked of a 100-ton cargo and there were fears that some of the hardware might already have been run ashore or dumped at sea. The British, however, were most interested in the content of the £100,000 shipment for they feared British-made weapons legally exported to Libya could have been on their way to Ireland to be used to kill British soldiers. The fears proved to be unfounded, and in later years it emerged that the original intelligence anticipating a 100-ton shipment was accurate. The mercurial Gaddafi had changed his mind at the very last minute, as the *Claudia* was being loaded in Tripoli. The episode is doubly significant because it denied the IRA an important boost and coincided with a thaw in political relations between London and Dublin. The Fine Gael–Labour coalition government, although strongly hostile to the IRA, was distinctly timorous about saying so publicly. In a bid to stimulate them to tougher anti-IRA action, Edward Heath telexed fulsome but secret praise for the skill with which Irish forces had carried out the operation.

The next move in the security co-operation between Britain and the Republic was to channel secretly marked detonators to suspect suppliers in the south, as was already being done in Britain. The issue was discussed in London on 22 January 1973 after the RUC captured a single cache of 500 detonators, an indication that terrorists were having little difficulty in obtaining this vital component. A senior RUC officer said the Irish police control was good in theory but weak in effect and he thought they would be willing to implement the scheme without involving their political masters. The meeting was also told that a machine to cut open retrieved detonators and check for markings had been supplied to the Data Reference Centre in Northern Ireland, where all recovered detonators would be taken for examination. Another machine would be provided for forensic scientists in Britain, who would inform the RUC if any marked items turned up. It was agreed that prosecution would not necessarily follow the discovery of marked detonators, to prevent details of the scheme becoming known and to enable the IRA's supply network to be more thoroughly unravelled. It was especially important to find out how IRA bombers in Britain were obtaining gelignite manufactured by Irish Industrial Explosives.

It was not long before the first of the marked detonators worked their way through the system. On 7 May, seven detonators examined at the Data Reference Centre were sourced to two firms working on a tunnelling contract in County Dublin. The lead was passed to the security service who were asked to go about 'cultivating somebody in one of these two firms' with a view to discovering more. However, after examining 600 captured detonators over the next three months the evidence suggested they were old stock rather than the more recently marked items.

Before he became CATO, Mackenzie-Orr had addressed participants on an explosives course at Bramley, including the Irish Commandants Denis Boyle, the head of their EOD unit, and Gerard Bates, Inspector of Explosives. Mackenzie-Orr knew Boyle from his attendance at an earlier course at Bramley and the three got talking about common interests. Contact continued once Mackenzie-Orr took up his new posting in Lisburn, and Boyle and his colleague unofficially invited him to visit them in Dublin. Mackenzie-Orr knew they were playing with political and diplomatic fire, especially as he had ignored the advice of his own superiors to inform Brigadier Frank McMullen, the military attaché in Dublin. So at the end of April 1973 he set off covertly for Dublin in a hired car. He passed himself off as a reporter at both a British Army checkpoint in the north and a Garda one in the south, where (to the subsequent alarm of diplomats in Dublin) his registration number and driving-licence details were recorded. Nobody paid any attention to the top-secret equipment he had in the boot – a device for etching codemarks on detonator cases. Mackenzie-Orr recalls:

When I got to his home in Dublin, Denis was very keen to get my hire car with Northern Ireland number plates off the street and we put it in his garage. I showed him how the equipment worked in his garage and we went to the New Jury's hotel for a wee dram. The following day he took me into Army HQ where I met his boss, the Director of Ordnance Services and the Irish Army Chief of Staff. All promised maximum assistance but wished it to remain entirely covert.

In due course Mackenzie-Orr submitted a written report to the CLF, saying that he had laid the foundations for a working relationship with his two Irish contacts which would enable EOD operators on both sides to exchange information. However, the fact that the proposed relationship was to be personal and unofficial set alarm bells ringing loudly at the Ministry of Defence and the Foreign Office in London, where there was particular concern about a plan to exchange intelligence using the public mail. Kelvin White, head of the Republic of Ireland desk at the Foreign Office, had doubts about whether Mackenzie-Orr 'was the best person to be playing J. Bond', as he colourfully put it. He summed up the concerns in a letter to the MOD on 2 May about the 'rather odd way' in which Mackenzie-Orr had carried out his visit.

> To summarise the exercise, it now transpires that the Irish officers had not cleared their invitation with their own superiors (not Mackenzie-Orr's fault); nor apparently had the Embassy been properly consulted (I am not sure whose fault this is – Mackenzie-Orr's, MOD's, the Embassy's, or ours, so let us forget it on this occasion); nor had Mackenzie-Orr, despite MOD's request, contacted the MA [military attaché] on his visit (Mackenzie-Orr's fault); and finally that Mackenzie-Orr made up for himself a story of being a freelance news reporter and blarneyed his way past police checkpoints in the South (very much Mackenzie-Orr's fault).
>
> You will realise the considerable embarrassment that would have occurred had his bluff been called by the Gardai . . . It therefore seems to me essential that any officer travelling to the Republic, officially or privately, should follow a set drill, informing you of his intention, and not moving until you, we and the Embassy all know and agree. I would be most grateful if you could ensure that this is done, though personally I rather hope you can do it in such a way that Mackenzie-Orr does not feel that the substantive gains that he apparently achieved have been ignored.

White concluded that he 'would be careful not to press for a neat and orderly Anglo-Irish committee structure just to satisfy our bureaucratic souls'. A few weeks later, in a letter to Allan Rowley, the Director and Co-Ordinator of Intelligence at the Northern Ireland Office, he said that while Mackenzie-Orr's visit was perhaps a little disorganised, they should try to build upon the initiative. 'But as so often in seeking co-operation with the Irish it is a case of one step at a time.'

After all the diplomatic fuss, Mackenzie-Orr decided he would make no more visits to Dublin:

> I deemed it too risky for Denis to continue the direct liaison and saw him only once more in my tour in Northern Ireland. I was in the cabin of one of two articulated lorries which had been hijacked and used to block the main Belfast-to-Dublin road right at the border. As I was placing Pigstick to disrupt a wooden box, a voice said, 'Is that yourself Mac?' Denis Boyle, resplendent in service dress, Sam Browne belt and riding mac, was standing by the door of the cab about two feet from the bomb. I told him that it was a real bomb and that I was about to disrupt it and that he should retire to the Garda post about 200 metres down the road and that I would call him to have a look when it was rendered safe. He pulled himself up onto the access step, peered through the window and said, 'I have never seen a real bomb,' got down and retired to the Garda post. The disruption was successful and he did come to look at the pieces . . . Since that encounter, we have never met although we continue to exchange greetings through mutual friends in the world of EOD.

The issue was so sensitive that Whitelaw had ordered knowledge of the talks on cross-border co-operation to be kept within 'a restricted circle'. Diplomatic reports from Dublin to London repeatedly emphasised that Irish ministers' willingness to help must not be disclosed. Writing to Galsworthy, the British ambassador, on 2 May, White noted: 'The Irish seem to have the right attitude but I agree with you that we will have to take this step by step avoiding any impression of hustling them.' A week or so later, following a meeting with Paddy Donegan, the Irish defence minister, Galsworthy sent a telegram to London outlining what had been agreed. Donegan had emphasised again the absolute need for secrecy. Any leak would cause them maximum political embarrassment and greatly inhibit what they could do to co-operate. They must 'mute down the method but at the same time provide the service', through contact between Galsworthy, Donegan and the Taoiseach. The normal channel for the exchange of information and intelligence would be through the

Director of Intelligence of the Irish Army or the military attaché in Dublin. The Irish rejected the British offer of scrambling equipment for cross-border contact between the two police forces, again for fear of politically compromising leaks. The poor standard of communication was a particular concern for although there were a few privacy sets in Garda stations, some lines could only be connected through manual exchanges, which was not only a security risk but also far too slow for effective action. A Foreign Office progress note to Downing Street recorded: 'More remains to be done but so far so good.'

In fact what developed from all these exchanges was a series of personal and unofficial encounters. One-to-one police relationships flourished as did informal contacts between EOD specialists. For years the CATO regularly visited his counterparts in Dublin and welcomed them at Lisburn in return, both parties often travelling incognito by train. During the frequent political and diplomatic squalls that would punctuate the British–Irish relationship in the years ahead, the individuals concerned learned to keep their heads down until the air had cleared and, in the long run, more was achieved informally than might have been the case by official channels.

The importance of border security was underlined by Mackenzie-Orr's monthly report for July 1973, describing how the 'use of ingenious ambush and booby-trap bombs continues in border areas'. In a later report, he said: 'Whilst no completely new techniques have been used by terrorist bombers greater use has been made of combination bombs together with hoaxes as lures to attract the security forces into areas where they will be killed by ambush bombs detonated by command systems.' Not long afterwards, on 20 July, Major Richard Jarman of the Royal Engineers was killed by an explosion during a search operation near Keady. Within two days, Corporal Bryan Criddle, an Army dog handler, died in a similar blast in the border area near Clogher. His dog was searching a road frequently used by security forces when it 'marked' and became very excited, refusing to leave the hedgerow. As the handler went forward, the bomb was detonated remotely, killing him instantly. The dog survived virtually unscathed and some hours later was recovered and 'adopted' by one of Criddle's colleagues.

In his report for the year, Mackenzie-Orr noted that despite increased activity by the southern forces, as well as British Army helicopter surveillance, ground patrolling and intensive covert surveillance by small teams concealing themselves in the countryside for several days at a time, terrorist teams up to ten strong were still able to spend many hours planning, preparing and digging in ambushes. One of these elaborately planned cross-border operations, on 30 August 1973, cost the life of Staff Sergeant Ron Beckett, the tenth 321 EOD soldier to die. It began at 11.15 a.m. when an armed man confronted a garage owner in the Fermanagh border village of Pettigo. A shot was fired but the garageman ducked and it missed, slightly wounding a thirteen-year-old boy nearby. Another raider then put down a cardboard box and said: 'You have one minute to get out.' Meanwhile at the nearby post office a second party of raiders abandoned a plastic shopping bag after holding up staff and customers and stealing money and stamps, and two customs officers were held up in their caravan – in use because their permanent post had been destroyed by terrorist attack – while another bomb was laid. By now the garage owner, who was also a part-time soldier in the Ulster Defence Regiment, had defied further gunfire and run the 150 yards from the garage forecourt to his dwelling, where he kept a Sterling sub-machine gun legally issued for his protection. He emerged in time to fire a burst of shots at a Ford Cortina and Fiat fleeing across the border carrying the eight raiders, who returned fire. Later their cars were recovered, the Fiat with a conspicuous bullet hole in the roof.

It was just after noon when the first assistance arrived. The RUC officer and Royal Tank Regiment patrol arriving by helicopter could see smoke rising from the garage and the customs caravan, where the bombs had exploded. On landing they learned there was a third unexploded device in the post office and called for Staff Sergeant Beckett and his team. After questioning the postmistress, Beckett ruled out using Wheelbarrow because of the post office's high entrance step and at 1.30 p.m. he went into the building himself, set up a Pigstick and fired it once he was safely outside. Fifteen minutes later, with the device still unexploded, he decided to go in again to attach a hook and line. During this soak period he had remarked to his Number Two that a clock attached to the bomb had been ticking.

Almost as soon as Beckett had gone into the building for the second time, there was a large explosion and the roof and rear wall of the building collapsed, burying him under rubble. Members of the security forces dug frantically to rescue him but when they reached the seat of the explosion they found his lifeless body. Thirty-seven-year-old Beckett left a wife and two young daughters. A soldier since 1954, he had served in the British Army of the Rhine, Jamaica and the Middle East.

As ever, triumph counterpointed tragedy in the 321 story. Staff Sergeant Alan Glasby was awarded the George Medal after a year's tour during which he neutralised eight out of nineteen live bombs among the fifty-seven incidents he attended. When he was posted to 321 EOD headquarters in October 1972 his primary task was to record intelligence and prepare bomb statistics but he was also on standby as an ATO. It was in this capacity that he was called out on 17 May 1973 after a telephone warning of a bomb in the ladies' toilet at Lisburn Railway Station. Glasby saw he would not be able to use Wheelbarrow to approach the bomb remotely because of restricted access, so he went in and found a 50 lb. bomb, set to be initiated by a cooker switch, wedged behind the toilet bowl. He neutralised the device and recovered the detonator and circuit board, which yielded fingerprints. His work not only saved the station and prevented what would have been a lengthy closure of the Belfast–Dublin railway line but led directly to the arrest of the man who made the bomb and the woman who planted it.

On 2 July Glasby carried out another successful clearance. When the master of a barge used for collecting sand from Lough Neagh boarded his vessel at 8.15 a.m. he found it smelling strongly of marzipan and reported a suspect bomb. Glasby traced the device to a greasy catwalk in the poorly lit engine room ten feet below deck, only approachable through a cramped hatchway and down a steep ladder. Carrying his equipment, he made a second hazardous visit to the device and then used his disrupter to separate the firing pack from the explosive. Re-entering the barge, he cut out the detonator and recovered the explosive, discovering that only poor electrical contact had prevented the 50lb bomb exploding, which would have sunk the barge and killed him. Glasby's citation noted the intelligence and skill with which he performed his primary duties and his cheerful willingness to volunteer for arduous additional work. It recorded that his exceptional practical ability and calmness in difficult and dangerous situations earned him the admiration of his fellow ATOs and all security forces with whom he worked.

In the latter months of 1973, as the prospect of a major political breakthrough gathered momentum, the IRA again intensified its campaign. In the spring, its core objective of a united Ireland had been predictably rejected in a referendum. Moderate Catholic political leaders called on their supporters not to vote, for given the Protestant majority in the North the result was a foregone conclusion. When the poll took place on 8 March, only 6,463 voters (0.6 per cent of the total electorate) said they wanted to join the Irish Republic, while 591,820 (57.5 per cent) voted to remain part of the United Kingdom. Forty-one per cent of the electorate abstained.

The Army considerably raised its profile to ensure the IRA did not upset arrangements for the referendum and the publication, soon afterwards, of a government white paper outlining new governance proposals for Northern Ireland. In all 26,000 soldiers and police officers were on duty and 321 EOD played a key role in the operation. With an additional two sections and equipment drafted in temporarily from Britain, a dozen disposal teams with vehicles, equipment and escorts were fielded throughout Northern Ireland. A reserve team was formed from 321 EOD headquarters and another was called up from the Ammunition Depot at Ballykinler, County Down. There were no major incidents in Northern Ireland over the period, although one ATO was hit by a brick thrown from a crowd. However, IRA teams from Belfast exported the campaign to Britain for the first time by planting four car bombs in London on polling day. Two were neutralised, the third exploded during EOD action and the fourth went off before it could be disrupted by Scotland Yard's SO13 explosives officers. Because of the prevailing threat level, five RAOC EOD teams were assigned to duty in London and deployed within minutes. Within a few hours 421 EOD, which had replaced 321 as the shadow formation for emergency deployment, was activated and 20 EOD sections were on immediate call throughout mainland Britain.

Thereafter, events in Northern Ireland were dominated by politics as secretary of state William Whitelaw presided over groundbreaking negotiations designed to enable Unionists and Nationalists to share government at Stormont for the first time. That autumn, Mackenzie-Orr noted a marked increase in the size of bombs and repeated use of mass disruption tactics in co-ordinated operations mixing a handful of live bombs into a series of bomb scares, often right across Northern Ireland. On 30 August, for instance, the railway system around Belfast was paralysed for hours by five bombs, one of which demolished a key signal box. Early in October, the entire city ground to a lengthy standstill as EOD teams worked flat out to clear sixty alerts. On a single evening later in the month over 100 vehicles were hijacked and roads disrupted throughout the six counties with explosions in Belfast, Derry, Rostrevor, Cookstown and Dungannon. Over the following twenty-four hours there were another seventy-eight incidents including seventeen explosions and fourteen devices successfully defused, but no casualties.

Later in the autumn IRA units recruited from the Irish community in Britain, reinforced by activists sent over from Ireland, carried out a series of attacks in London, southern England and the Midlands. In September, a Birmingham-based team planted a device at an office block in the city's Edgbaston area which went off as the ATO, Captain Ronald Wilkinson, inspected it. He died from his injuries six days later and was buried with full military honours after a service at Deepcut Barracks, the RAOC's headquarters in Surrey.

Back in Ireland, the political moves were aggravating Protestant suspicions that the British government intended to make concessions to the IRA and from spring 1974 onwards this provoked an upsurge in the activities of extreme Loyalist groups. Their early bombs had been crude efforts, but a new generation of more reliable devices now appeared, although they never fully rivalled those of the IRA. They mainly consisted of a mixture of gelignite (usually pilfered from quarries and road workings in Scotland) and home-made chemical explosive packed into beer kegs and gas cylinders, which would be manhandled from a car and lit by the bombers before they made their escape. Their chosen targets were relatively soft: isolated Catholic homes in Protestant areas, churches and associated premises, schools and Catholic-owned pubs and businesses. In September CATO noted the 'high level of Protestant activity against church property' in his monthly report.

On 12 November 1973, afterwards known as 'Mindless Monday', twenty-four explosions in twenty-four hours formed a rare concentrated outburst of Loyalist violence which led to the proscription of the Ulster Freedom Fighters and the Red Hand Commandos. Their targets were Catholic-owned public houses in Belfast and Armagh, a bookmaker's premises and the recently vacated headquarters of the Catholic Social Democratic and Labour Party, which was completely demolished. Any lingering doubts about the culpability of militant Loyalists for much of the violence were dispelled on 18 November when a UVF bomber killed himself in a premature explosion at a farmhouse near Desertmartin, County Londonderry. That month, for the first time, Loyalist factions planted more bombs than the IRA: twenty-seven to twenty-six.

There was another multiple IRA disruption operation on 6 December, with sixteen car bombs among more than seventy vehicles hijacked and abandoned all over Northern Ireland. That day Brigadier Dutton, the Chief Inspector Land Service Ammunition, was visiting Mackenzie-Orr, who planned to take him to Albert Street Mill and later to a birthday party for the wife of a forensic scientist. Reports of the hijackings were coming in before they left the Lisburn headquarters and as they travelled along the M1 motorway towards Belfast, they heard that all five Belfast teams were called out, including that led by Staff Sergeant Len Grey, who had just finished a twenty-four-hour spell of duty. He had been tasked to deal with a van under an M1 bridge so Mackenzie-Orr diverted to offer him support. 'On arrival I found that his Wheelbarrow was unserviceable, that he did not have a bomb suit and he looked tired out.' Mackenzie-Orr decided to take over the clearance himself. Clad in his civilian clothes and a helmet and flak jacket, he approached the van with a charge to open the rear doors and two hooks and lines to pull them ajar. Inside was a box large enough to hold up to 50 lb. of explosive which the driver said was not part of his consignment. Mackenzie-Orr recalls:

> Len had no Pigstick so I decided to use the two hooks and lines to attach to the box and jerk it out of the van, hoping to disrupt the firing circuit or at least reduce the potential damage to the bridge if the bomb went off. As I approached the van I noticed that one of the hooks had been blown off the door and was in the gutter near a drain. I knelt with my back to the van to pick up the hook and the bomb went off hurling me into the side of the tunnel and ruining my jacket and flannels. Having checked that all my bits were still attached and functioning, I called out that everyone was to stay where they were and that I was all right. The bomb and the van were totally disrupted so I returned to the control point, handed over the mess to Len Grey to do the report, apologised to Brigadier Dutton for setting a bad example by being blown up in front of him and continued on to Albert Street Mill.

Mackenzie-Orr was lucky, only suffering superficial lacerations. The bomb had only partially detonated and the helmet and jacket had protected his head, neck and torso. He was also partly shielded by the corner of the van. 'I suspect that my door-opening charge had restarted a stopped clock, which completed the circuit just as I knelt down, presenting a minimum target to the blast and fragments. Lesson learned; after any disruptive EOD action recommence the soak time.'

The wave of disruption was designed to overshadow the final round of political talks at Sunningdale, Berkshire, which culminated in a formal agreement a few days later. The euphoria that greeted the political breakthrough was not shared by the IRA. EOD reports from the time show that plentiful supplies of Republic of Ireland gelignite were still available as booster charges for large HME devices. The reports also note the proliferation of detonators originating from the United States, an early indication of a supply conduit that would become more serious in the years ahead. The year was also marked by nineteen 'own goals' by both Republican and Loyalist bomb-makers and deliverers, one a Republican from County Cork who perished when a bomb detonated while he was helping prepare an elaborate ambush at Rosslea, County Fermanagh.

A cruel act of intimidation and a devastating explosion at Omagh police station on 12 December 1973 demonstrated that the new accord had not nourished any peaceful intentions among the terrorists. The incident began when four armed men arrived at a house of a local van driver. Two of them held his wife and daughter hostage while the others escorted him to a farm near the town. There they loaded a 1,000 lb. bomb into his van, set the timer and ordered to him deliver the bomb to the police station and then 'leg it'. Failure to do so, he was warned, would mean his wife and daughter being hurt. The driver did as he was told and shouted a warning to the sentry. By the time the device went off, the station had been cleared and there was only damage to property.

Attacks continued right up to Christmas Eve. That night, and into the early hours of Christmas morning, firefighters and two ATOs struggled to save a large building from destruction in Londonderry. While the firefighters fought to control a blaze caused by an explosion in a dry-cleaning shop on the ground floor, a further bomb in a black rubbish sack was discovered outside a photographer's studio on the second floor. Sergeant Keith Negal, who was the most experienced operator in the city at the time and was coaching a recent arrival, took this 10 lb. device apart with Pigstick. Having had two bombs in the same building Negal decided on a precautionary search of the other rooms on his way back downstairs. His suspicions were justified when he found another black bag under the sink in a hairdressing salon on the first floor. After letting it soak for two hours, he returned early on Christmas morning; but as he was setting up Pigstick to disrupt it, the timer ran out and the device detonated. Negal, a married man from Doncaster, was hit by the full force of the blast, suffering multiple burns and lacerations, compound fractures of his legs and hands, and the loss of the little finger on his left hand. Thanks to his helmet and visor, his face only received flash burns and although he was blinded for six months he later recovered his sight.

Elsewhere in the city, Captain 'Tug' Wilson, another ATO, heard the radio messages asking for 'Starlight', the code for a medical evacuation helicopter, to lift injured Felix and rushed to the scene, as did Mackenzie-Orr, who learned about the incident as he was travelling to Londonderry to begin his Christmas visits to the five EOD sections. 'I got there just after the firemen had dragged him clear although they knew that there were other bombs in the building,' he remembers. Wilson made safe the device outside the studio and at 4 a.m. successfully dealt with a fourth incendiary bomb, this one in three plastic bags with the timer still running. In the subsequent incident report, Wilson stated the devices had been dispersed throughout the building and set to go off at intervals, not only to burn it down but to kill or maim the ATO and firefighters responding.

At the year's end, although the number of explosions was significantly down from 1,339 in 1972 to 978, the EOD teams had answered 4,416 calls compared to 4,323 the previous year. They had also neutralised 32.15 tons of explosive, a substantially greater quantity than the previous year. This was in fact their busiest year of the entire campaign, but the Chief Inspector Land Service Ammunition felt they were getting insufficient credit. In his annual report he complained:

> The public rarely hears of our successes; the picture most often seen on TV screens is the spectacular sight of a shop front disappearing in a hail of glass and brick splinters. In fact 35% of IRA devices are neutralised by RAOC EOD teams and more than 50% of enemy effort in the explosives field is negated by the action of the Security Forces if the amount of explosives and their accessories captured is taken into account.

Chapter Eight
The Toss of a Coin

The IRA's strategy of constantly varying targets and tactics took an utterly unpredictable twist on 24 January 1974 when an RUC station was attacked from the air with a hijacked helicopter. The aircraft was hired from its base in Dublin by an apparently respectable Englishwoman who said she wanted to photograph seals on the Atlantic coast, but when it landed near Letterkenny in County Donegal, ostensibly to collect a photographer, it was taken over by an armed gang. The pilot, an ex-RAF wing commander, objected to the weight of four milk churns filled with explosives being loaded, so two were left behind. He was ordered to cross the nearby border and hover over the police station at Strabane, but as one of the gang attempted to manhandle the first churn out, it got jammed in the door and the pilot was instructed to head for the adjacent Foyle River, where the churn was dumped without exploding. The second bombing run was no more successful. This time the churn struck the wall of the police station and fell in the garden of a neighbouring house, also without exploding.

By coincidence, Mackenzie-Orr was airborne in a Sioux helicopter bound for Londonderry when the attack took place. On hearing of it he ordered the pilot, Sergeant Sid Pryke, a former ammunition technician, to divert and put down close to the police station. As the aircraft came in to land, Pryke said: 'Shit, somebody is shooting at us.' While Mackenzie-Orr was examining the milk churns, the sergeant had heated words about aerial target identification with the commander of the infantry detachment guarding the station. Meanwhile the hijackers had escaped.

Early in February, Mackenzie-Orr departed after an action-packed tenure. Among the most demanding of the many tasks he had been involved in was an eight-hour operation the previous September in which Telephone House in Belfast was saved from destruction. The incident began with the hijacking of a van which routinely delivered roller towels to the building. When it turned up to make its delivery three hours later than usual, it had been fitted out with over 500 lb. of ANFO, a booster charge of Gelamex and two timed initiating circuits, one of which incorporated an antidisturbance device. In addition nine mortar bombs, each connected to a chain of Cordtex detonating fuse several hundred feet long, had been packed into the area behind the driver's seat and the rear wheel arch. The van was parked against a wall in the central quadrangle of the complex where the explosion would cause maximum structural damage.

Staff Sergeant Graham Wells was in charge of the team called to the scene and he set a small charge on the rear door of the van to blow it open. However, the blast upset the van's cargo of roller towels which cascaded out all over the ground. Wells could now see the horrible complexity of the bomb and realised that as Wheelbarrow could not traverse the carpet of towels, he was faced with making a series of manual approaches. Sensibly he asked for advice and before long Mackenzie-Orr and another senior colleague arrived.

Mackenzie-Orr knew, and chose not to tell Wells, that the IRA had phoned newspaper offices in Belfast claiming that the bomb was so sophisticated it could not be defused. Over several hours, with Mackenzie-Orr consciously deferring to Wells as incident commander, the two patiently unravelled its complicated circuitry strand by strand. Mackenzie-Orr completed the final stages of the render-safe procedure and Wells took the rest of the device apart, bagging samples of the explosives and key elements of the components for the forensic science laboratory. For his skill, concentration and coolness, Wells was subsequently awarded the British Empire Medal. Mackenzie-Orr's epic endeavours during his tour of duty earned him the George Medal and OBE for his distinguished service. He went off to a new job conducting guided weapons trials at Woomera in Australia, where he developed an international reputation as a counter-terrorist and security consultant.

The bomb-disposal career of the new CATO, Lieutenant-Colonel John Gaff, had begun in Singapore in 1944 when he was called from the mess in full dress uniform to defuse a Japanese mortar bomb which a gardener had found in a coconut tree. After an eventful career in several parts of the world, he was facing a formidable explosives threat in Northern Ireland while the means to combat it were still far from totally effective. 'My tour from February 1974 to April 1975 covered one of the most active periods of the whole campaign in spite of there being two truce periods. The tactics and methods used by both the IRA and the Protestant factions varied almost daily,' he recalls. The surge of incidents frequently caused the deployment of the entire EOD capability including the backups from the Ammunition Inspectorate at Lisburn and the Ammunition Depot at Ballykinler. The two emergency teams formed by CATO and the commander of 321 EOD Unit were frequently called on and both officers carried basic equipment in their cars. 'The established practice was for trains, important tanker and multiple device incidents to be reported to me and then I would decide on the operator,' says Gaff, who thought it was unfortunate but inevitable that his teams almost always had to react to new tactics and could very rarely take the initiative. 'There also came a stage when the speed of reaction by the EOD team assumed much greater importance than ever before and required frequent reviews of procedures and changes of location.'

There was a tragic outcome to an elaborate incident only a couple of days after Gaff took up his post. On Sunday 17 February, six explosions were heard in the Moybane area, close to the border in County Armagh. The explosions could have been radio-initiated unintentionally by terrorists or even model-aircraft enthusiasts, but calculating that they were probably designed to lure him into an ambush, Staff Sergeant Allan Brammah waited until morning before going in to investigate. Instead he overflew the scene in a helicopter and concluded the explosions were all linked. Early next morning, after the area had been secured by the Welsh Guards, Brammah along with Captain Iain Moore and an EOD team began the clearance plan they had devised overnight. A specialist Royal Engineers search team was involved and Gaff, still new to the job, decided to travel down from Lisburn to help. He recalls how he and Brammah traced the path of a buried command wire through a small marsh, along a stream and up to a stone wall where the wire divided in two directions.

> We paused at this spot and tossed a coin to decide which of us would go right or left. I went to the right and the ATO went left to follow the path of the yellow wire. I saw him approach an area of disturbed earth. I called to him but he could not have heard me. He then bent down and I saw him lift a piece of turf. At that instant an explosion occurred.

The escort from the Welsh Guards, Allan Millar, later recounted how Brammah had lifted a corner of the piece of turf, which was raised and of a different colour to that around it, to reveal a white wrapping. 'This could be another device or a Claymore,' he remarked. The second time he lifted the turf, the blast was triggered and he was killed instantly. Brammah, aged thirty-one, a married man from Hatfield, near Doncaster, was a keen sportsman and had been selected for promotion on his return from Northern Ireland. Millar, who had been standing only a yard or so behind him, was lifted off his feet but only slightly injured. Gaff was badly shaken by the fact that but for the toss of the coin he could have perished. The blast, caused by some 200 lbs. of explosive, scattered debris over seventy-five yards and blew an eight-foot crater at the side of the road. According to Gaff, subsequent examination of the scene suggested a radio-controlled device. 'It was concluded that the incident was a rather devious "come-on" by the South Armagh IRA.' During the follow-up operation some five or six gunmen fired an estimated 600 shots at the troops involved. Fire was returned but there were no injuries.

Soon after this incident, the secretary of state, Merlyn Rees, painted a depressing picture at a cabinet meeting in London on 10 April:

> The pattern of violence had changed and consisted largely of attacks with fire bombs prepared and placed by women, and the placing of car bombs by civilians who were not themselves terrorists but who were acting under extreme duress. The prevention of violence in these forms was a virtually impossible task for the Army; and it was a misuse of the armed forces to employ large numbers of them on the task of searching people.

The new tactic of the 'proxy bomb' had been used with increasing frequency since January 1974 when two armed men stopped a twenty-year-old technician near his home in Andersonstown, Belfast and forced him to drive his employer's van to nearby Suffolk. A large bomb was put aboard and he was told to park outside the local police station. He did so, alerted the sentry and was still being questioned inside the station when the device exploded. In following weeks similar attacks took place on other police stations and proxy vehicle bombs were also taken into the Belfast segment. In a twist on the tactic, the terrorists began commandeering vans and lorries with two people on board, holding one hostage while the other was ordered to drive a bomb to a target. At Randalstown, County Antrim, a man was held up and ordered to take his car and a 100 lb. bomb into the village while his wife was held hostage. In Belfast a man was taken into a church by armed men and forced to sit through a Mass while his workmate positioned a bomb. As soon as his captors heard the anticipated explosion they left the church.

More 'proxy' incidents followed and after a soldier drove away a car bomb from outside his base before it functioned, the terrorists started ordering hijacked drivers to throw away the vehicle keys once they had stopped and to drive well inside security force bases before parking. Gaff came up with the idea of 'panic pits' dug out of the ground and lined or built from walls of sandbags adjacent to the entrances of bases. Sentries could direct a proxy device into the pit where a blast would be contained. He also provided bases with Carl Gustav anti-tank practice rounds and a launcher which could be fired from fifteen or twenty yards if an ATO was unable to reach a base in time.

By the end of 1974, total compensation for criminal injuries and damage as a result of terrorism had exceeded £100 million, £40 million that year alone. As a result of the growing incidence of multifaceted terrorist operations, every aspect of the Army's operational and tactical effort in Northern Ireland was subjected to in-depth scrutiny. EOD, with its particular problems and continued high risk to operators, was no exception and there was a constant flow of ideas from other arms of the military infrastructure. Many were superficially plausible, such as a plan to lift vehicle bombs from the street by helicopter and drop them into the sea where they could explode without causing damage. The author of this one had, however, failed to think through the consequences for the helicopter and its crew, as well as those on the ground below, if the device were to go off in transit.

Where once ATOs were instructed to let vehicle bombs soak, new shorter warning times now forced them to consider means of acting faster without putting their lives at greater risk. Gaff says, 'The IRA watched all our operations and they calculated that we had a "bogey" time to attack any suspected car bomb and began to shorten fusing and warning times. This meant that the operator usually had a maximum of ten minutes to set up Wheelbarrow, do his appreciation, place and fire a disrupter.' Improvisation continued to drive the development of much EOD equipment, but some impromptu measures were fairly crude. After one incident in which a captured bomber was roped and sent back along the cleared Belfast street to defuse his device, there was a spate of copycat behaviour by some units until it was ruled out by commanders who feared the outcry that would follow if a bomber was sent to his death in this way.

To make life even more difficult for the EOD teams, terrorists next took to planting bombs in vans, inhibiting the effectiveness of EOD weapons which depended on line of sight. The problem was highlighted by an incident in Belfast city centre involving an abandoned refrigerated truck with heavy insulated doors. After blowing open the driver's cab with a small charge and finding nothing suspicious, the ATO used another small charge in a bid to open the rear compartment. When this failed, three Carl Gustav rounds were fired, blowing the vehicle open and showering the street with frozen chickens.

A number of more practical and effective steps were taken. In March, a new set of Explosive Regulations licensed the use of ammonium nitrate and sodium nitrate, the main chemical constituents of the agricultural fertiliser which was the mainstay of the bombing campaign. At the same time, the Northern Ireland Office circulated thousands of leaflets to the business community reminding them of the 1971 compensation legislation which obliged them to have proper security precautions in place at all times and to take steps to minimise looting and other damage in the aftermath of an incident. A propaganda film was also designed to raise their awareness of the incendiary threat. However, the film-maker found himself under conflicting pressures about what to include in it. During a visit to Northern Ireland he called on Major Clive Pickard, the OC of 321 EOD Unit, who demonstrated various devices and outlined possible security measures. In contrast, the film-maker reported, 'retailers are trying to keep normal life going and profitable commerce. All security measures cost money directly or indirectly by man-hours used in drills or reduction of customer throughput.' Others involved in the concept wanted a 'shock, hard sell' film but some retailers objected in case it frightened the shop girls 'who keep functioning because of a certain ignorance'. In the end a script was agreed and the film was produced. The commentary concluded:

> Compensation means time consuming enquiries and government forms and applications. The compensation rarely equals your estimate and doesn't restore goodwill or lost custom. Lack of security precautions can mean you are entitled to less compensation. Surely prevention is better than compensation.

The sixty-three explosions in January 1974, ninety in February and 111 in March reflected the rising tension. In January, IRA gunmen wounded a Londonderry businessman who had carried a bomb out of a shop in the city centre. 'The same punishment will be inflicted on persons who are guilty of similar actions,' an IRA statement said. Both Republican and Loyalist bombers were highly active, the latter suffering a setback in February when security forces recovered half a ton of explosive chemicals stolen from a warehouse by a gang of armed and masked men. Every aspect of daily life continued to be battered by the bombs: supermarkets, factories, pubs, hotels, car showrooms, cafes, garages, shops of every description, newspaper offices and cinemas. Everywhere buildings were surrounded by fences of concrete-filled oil drums and scaffolding to prevent car bombs being driven close to them. Hotels, pubs and clubs employed 'bomb-watchers'; factories and warehouses created double 'airlock' gates to control access. Searchers frequently moved bombs or suspect vehicles, sometimes with tragic consequences. One man, however, came to be regarded with a mixture of annoyance and admiration by EOD teams. He was Werner Heubeck, a German who had been a prisoner of war and had settled in Northern Ireland in 1966 when he was appointed to run the publicly owned bus services. Since the outbreak of the Troubles, buses and depots had been a prime target for rioters and terrorists. Buses were still allowed to traverse the Belfast 'control zone' after being searched, so they were inevitably exploited by terrorists aiming to breach the security crackdown. By 1988 1,100 buses had been destroyed and eleven transport staff killed.

However, ATO teams arriving to 'ventilate' Heubeck's vehicles began to find that he had removed the devices by the time they got there. The staff of Ulsterbus and Citybus calculated that by the time he retired in 1988, Heubeck, who was awarded an OBE and then a CBE, had personally handled close to 100 incidents. One morning in Londonderry he removed a beer keg from each of three buses abandoned outside the police headquarters, and he frequently ignored Army and police cordons to get rid of suspect packages. On one occasion an EOD team got the shock of their lives when, as they were using Wheelbarrow's camera to line up a Pigstick disrupter, Heubeck suddenly came into shot, walking along inside the target bus. As they watched astonished from the control point, he calmly removed the device to the street and asked the ATO to neutralise it there. The majority of the devices he moved were hoaxes, but he was not to know that when he lifted them and it is something of a miracle that he survived unscathed. He would never talk about his daring-do. 'My job is just to run the buses,' he would say.

The authorities, of course, actively discouraged such heroics and advised citizens to call the experts to deal with any suspicious devices but some people continued to take action themselves, perhaps out of frustration and anger as much as bravery. Everyday life continued to be interrupted by security checks and alerts which sometimes gridlocked traffic for six or eight hours. People became expert at distinguishing various types of weapon. That's an SLR or an Armalite, they would say with great authority as the sound of gunfire rattled over the Belfast skyline. Even the youngest became connoisseurs of urban guerrilla warfare. One day in Belfast city centre, a five-year-old was heard reassuring his mother after yet another loud bang. 'Don't worry. That was a controlled explosion,' he insisted and he was right.

There were constant reminders of the destructive power of the bombs. In Belfast, vehicle bombs continued to devastate landmark buildings. One such was the former Grand Central Hotel, which had been taken over by the army after the commercial effects of the Troubles had caused it to close. Luxury accommodation by military standards, it was an ideal patrol base for the city-centre guard and an EOD team. As such it was an even more inviting target for the terrorists, who struck on 7 March causing severe damage to the hotel and surrounding shops and offices with a 500 lb. bomb in a hijacked van. The bombers returned on 28 March, this time causing another £750,000 of damage to the area with a 600 lb. bomb conveyed by a lorry driver who was held up and forced to park outside the building. Brian Faulkner, the chief minister of the power-sharing executive, raised his frustrations about security during a meeting with prime minister Harold Wilson at Downing Street on 1 April.

> I receive an impression of bafflement and drift when I talk to those responsible for security. There is a feeling that everything conceivable has been done and still there is no end to the violence. The political progress, far from lightening the sense of anger and frustration, has deepened it because . . . political change was presented to the public as a means to draw off support from the terrorists and now they see them still able to devastate Belfast city centre.

Since the turn of the year there had been a mounting toll of destruction attributable to new incendiary devices. The first sign that the IRA was trying to produce a more effective incendiary came on 19 August 1973, when a fierce fire engulfed a house at Elaine Street in the University area of Belfast. A twenty-nine-year-old man was critically injured and died eleven days afterwards, and a nineteen-year-old woman died a further forty-eight hours later. She was a known incendiary bomber and forensic examination of the house confirmed the IRA had been using it as a bomb factory. More significantly, there was clear evidence that they had been experimenting with a more sophisticated form of incendiary device that had gone badly wrong.

The setback for the IRA was only temporary. In the run-up to Christmas 1973, the new device made its first appearance in Londonderry and Belfast, where two were recovered before they went off. They consisted of a wristwatch timer, a battery and an igniter – a torch bulb with the filament exposed or the top of a domestic gas lighter – embedded in a small quantity of explosive and chemicals. The glow of the igniter, when the timer ran out and activated the battery, was sufficient to set off the mix. The entire device was contained within a plastic tape-cassette box. Use of this device, the 'Mark 2', accelerated through 1974 causing considerable damage: 'as much as the largest car bomb', one ATO reported. An even more powerful version entirely gutted six shops in the seaside town of Bangor in the early hours of 30 March.

Gaff and his teams remained in the forefront of the intellectual and physical battle with the bombers, but thanks to the frantic development work of the early years, vital support equipment was now coming through in sufficient quantities. The most welcome items were the EOD communications system and a much improved protective suit. At the outset of the campaign EOD teams had had no mobile short-range communication facilities and relied on police or the civilian telephone system. In the very early days, Styles recalls his operators ringing in from call boxes or other telephones near incidents.

> What could you say on the telephone to a man who was dealing with a bomb? My rules were very, very simple. If you find something that you think is strange, do not call me and say that you do not know what to do. Neither do anything. Instead ring me up and ask for a second opinion, just like a doctor. This way we solved many dismantling tasks successfully.

There was one occasion, however, when the duty officers in the operations room at army headquarters attempted to stop Styles having a highly classified conversation over a military radio network because an offshore Russian spy trawler was eavesdropping. 'You and the Russians can both fuck off,' said an exasperated Styles after the bomb had been successfully dismantled.

Under the Felix call-sign the EOD organisation was at last fully linked into the RUC and Army's radio networks but still lacked its own secure inter-team communication facility. There were two main technical problems to be overcome in developing such a system. It had to be secure to prevent eavesdropping by terrorists, who could learn of EOD methods and make future devices even more problematic to neutralise, and it had to be safe. The electrical impulses powering a communications system could set off a detonator or a timer-power unit if not properly suppressed.

This question had been wrestled with periodically since the Second World War, and the IRA's ever more commonplace use of radio-controlled and command-detonated devices further aggravated the problem. However, spurred on by the grave risk to operators in Northern Ireland, radio experts came up with a secret system of scrambled receivers and transmitters with a range of only 200 yards – the extent of most bomb scenes – which allowed the operator and Number Two to talk freely. Other members of the team were linked by a specially designed cable. The operator had a hands-free microphone and a single earpiece built into his helmet, which could be used without pressing any switches to speak or listen. At first all exchanges were recorded so that the handling of an incident could be reconstructed in the event of a mishap but this practice was eventually discontinued. Some ATOs found it distracting having to give a running commentary of their actions, but a more compelling reason was the unsettling effect of hearing a colleague injured or killed. Instead, it became standard operating procedure for the Number One to tell the Number Two everything he had found and everything he intended to do.

The new state-of-the-art EOD suit protected virtually the entire body and face, and team members were also given ear defenders. The old EOD suit, cynical operators said, was only good for holding your body together so that you could be buried in one piece but the new version, it was claimed, provided good survival capability within two to three yards of a five to ten-pound detonation. Moreover, the suit was easier to put on and far less restrictive. John Gaff was one of the last to wear the old suit during a clearance operation in Woolworth's in Belfast.

> It was a cumbersome suit and, quite rightly, operators were reluctant to don the motley collection of bits and pieces from which it was made up. The introduction of the Mark 2 suit, with the new helmet and the communication system linking them to the incident control point, helped the operators gain confidence through not having to be truly alone at a device. None the less it was a trying task to ensure that operators wore the new suit when required for they had little or no confidence in its predecessor.

Thanks to Gaff, there had been one critical addition to the suit before it was issued. 'At first it had no back protection, its designers seemingly unaware that an operator can actually spend more time approaching and retiring from a device than he spends working at it. I managed to get a quick response from the powers-that-be and a back apron was introduced before distribution of the new suit to all detachments.' Gaff claims that in 1974 he established an unbroken world record for running 100 yards in the EOD suit, which weighs almost 50 lb.

There were still occasions when the suit could not be worn. Late one evening, standing in for an ATO who was away on mid-tour rest and recuperation break, Gaff was called to an incident in Belfast involving a suspect device in the roof space of a combined house and restaurant.

> I had to enter the roof space up a ladder and through a small trapdoor. In the restricted space it was impossible to get in or work in an EOD suit but as it was mid-winter I was wearing a parka over my flak jacket. I was therefore fairly bulky even before I loaded myself up with any of my gear, a disrupter, with the cable trailing behind me, a sandbag to fix the disrupter when fired, a torch hung around my neck, a pocket full of tools and a trailing hook and line. Despite the bulk, I managed to force myself through the loft opening and up into the roof space. As it turned out, I only needed to place the disrupter and then tried to make a dignified exit down the ladder. Going down the parka caught in the sides of the loft opening and rose up all around me. As I tried to go up again to pull myself free the hook of the hook and line jammed itself in my right hand. At this point I began to sweat, knowing that a possibly live device with an unknown fuse timing was only a few feet away. It was only by dint of some desperate contortion of my hands and arms that I managed to free myself but despite the setback, I successfully neutralised what was indeed a live device.

On another occasion, Gaff was asked to clear a hijacked petrol tanker without the protection of the suit. Indeed, the job was to be done covertly in civilian clothes. The tanker had been left outside a local infant school in a dangerous area for a few days and been assured by the local IRA that it contained no explosives. The local priest was pressing for it to be taken away. Gaff says: 'As a Protestant, I was no less apprehensive when the priest gave me a blessing but when he did insist on standing alongside me as I searched the tanker it was much more reassuring. He was as good as his word and I was quickly able to confirm that the tanker was safe to move.'

The 'Foaming Pig', which Gaff describes as 'the most exotic piece of EOD equipment ever', was introduced on a trial basis in mid-1974. Ever since the start of the campaign, there had been suggestions that

1. and 2. Aftermath of explosions in Belfast, 1972. *(Public Record Office Northern Ireland)*

3. Barn near Coalisland when ATO arrived. *(Mike Coldrick)*

4. Explosion in barn near Coalisland. ATO's line can be seen at right of picture. *(Mike Coldrick)*

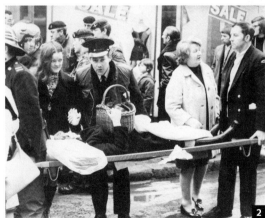

5. *(left to right)* TOP ROW: Captain David Stewardson, WO2 Colin Davies, Staff Sergeant Christopher Cracknell. MIDDLE ROW: Sergeant Anthony Butcher, Major Bernard Calladene, WO2 William Clark. BOTTOM ROW: WO2 Edward Garside, Sergeant Martin Walsh, WO2 John Howard.

6. EOD Suit developed for Hong Kong in the 1960s. *(Defence Press Office Northern Ireland)*

7. Newspaper advertisement, 1972, announcing control of explosive substances.

8. Lieutenant-Colonel Malcolm Mackenzie-Orr GM OBE picks through the rubble at Omagh police station in December 1973.

9. Poster warning soldiers to watch out for booby-traps. *(Defence Press Office Northern Ireland)*

EXPLOSIVES

CONTROL OF NITRO-BENZENE

THE EXPLOSIVES (NO. 2) REGULATIONS (NORTHERN IRELAND) 1972

1—The above Regulations impose control on nitro-benzene.

2—It will be an offence for anyone to manufacture, sell, acquire, transfer, store, transport, handle, use or dispose of this substance from **18th SEPTEMBER, 1972** except under licence.

3—Persons who have special reasons which require them to manufacture, etc., nitro-benzene as outlined above from 18th SEPTEMBER, 1972, should apply WITHOUT DELAY for a licence to the Ministry of Home Affairs, Room 309, Dundonald House, Upper Newtownards Road, Belfast BT4 3SU.

ISSUED BY THE MINISTRY OF HOME AFFAIRS

NO!

DON'T
END UP AS
A BOOBY
PRIZE...

10. The ruins of RUC Tynan after an IRA mortar attack and fire in December 1985.

11. EOD officers inspecting the crater after the ambush of an armoured police car.

12. The hijacked Seddon Atkinson 300 truck, fitted with ten mortars, which was used to attack RUC Carrickmore in November 1983 and kill a policeman.

13. The Mark 15 Mortar in its launcher tube bolted into a stolen builder's van which broke down on its way to RUC Pomeroy in August 1994.

14   15

16

14. The 321 mascot, Felix – the cat with nine lives.

15. The flaming bomb – the trade badge of the British Army's 'ammunition family'.

16. Crest of the Royal Army Ordnance Corps.

17. A Wheelbarrow attacks a suspect vehicle outside RUC Belcoo, 1991.

18. Balter airportable EOD vehicle.

19. A Tactica (*left*) and one of the new 'Wedgies' (*right*), January 2005.

(All pictures: Defence Press Office Northern Ireland)

20. Crest of the Royal Logistics Corps.

21. Captured nail bombs, 1972.

22. HME spills from the mouth of a neutralised Mark Ten Mortar.

23. Explosive-filled milk churns buried at a roadside.

24. Empty milk churns after a successful EOD clearance operation.

(All pictures: Defence Press Office Northern Ireland)

25. An EOD Saracen passes through the Belfast 'control zone' gates, 1978.

26. The long walk – Oldpark Road, Belfast.

(All pictures: Defence Press Office Northern Ireland)

27. Winter 'Lofty' Pattinson.

28. George Styles GC revisits the Belfast Europa, June 2004. *(Hastings Hotels)*

29. Captain Colin Whitworth. *(Kelvin Boyes)*

30. Professor Sir Bernard Crossland. *(Kelvin Boyes)*

31. Tony Blair presents letter of commendation for 321 EOD Squadron to Lieutenant-Colonel Mark Wickham. *(David Cutherbertson – Defence Press Office Northern Ireland)*

32. Tony Blair greets delegation from 321 EOD at Downing Street. *(David Cutherbertson – Defence Press Office Northern Ireland)* explosions could be smothered with a heavy blanket or with foam. Experiments with a blanket were unsuccessful but trials using foam were more encouraging. The idea had come from South America where foam was pumped into streets full of unruly crowds. After reports that it had also smothered an explosion during one riotous gathering the tactic was picked up in Britain and thus the 'Foaming Pig' came into being. It took its name from the aqueous foam generator and dispenser which was developed at RARDE and built into the back of a one-ton Humber which was added to the EOD fleet in Belfast in April 1974. Experiments had been encouraging in controlled laboratory conditions, but there was considerable apprehension among the EOD teams in Belfast when they learned that the Pig had to operate at not more than thirty yards distance whilst applying foam. Gaff set up an experiment to reassure them that no harm could come to the operator or driver.

> I found a suitable quarry, obtained a large amount of HME and detailed an ammunition technician and a driver to come with me. I intended to set off 100 lb., then 200 lb. and finally 400 lb. of the explosive. On the first firing I sat alone in the Pig but this shamed the other two and wearing riot helmets with the visors down and ear plugs, they joined me for the other blasts. The effects inside the Pig were minimal.

Emboldened by the experiment, Gaff formed a Foaming Pig Team and put it through its paces at the Royal Naval Air Yard on the eastern outskirts of Belfast. On 7 May it had its first outing after a van loaded with explosives was parked on top of three large underground petrol storage tanks on a garage forecourt at Chichester Street. The device, containing a massive 1,100lb. of explosive and shrapnel, was successfully blanketed with foam and later defused. Buoyed by this success, the foam team became a frequent sight in Belfast and notched up a number of successes but the concept was far from perfect in practice. Wide streets and wind played havoc with the effort to envelop a vehicle in eight feet of foam. Attempts were made to stiffen the foam and, inspired by the cricket screens on the sports ground at Thiepval Barracks, high hessian screens on wheels were constructed to contain it, though they were used only once. Within months, however, the Foaming Pig was also declared redundant. Weather conditions were rarely ideal and its deployment had become an unwieldy exercise involving a vulnerable, slow-moving convoy of up to a dozen vehicles. Apart from the core EOD vehicles and escorts, there was the Foaming Pig itself, three-ton trucks to carry the screens and other vehicles for more guards and assistants. Traffic tangles developed as the vehicles arrived at incidents and there was confusion about what should be parked where. Foam generators remained in place on the roof of the Grand Central Hotel for a time, intended to lay a foam curtain around the building if another vehicle bomb was parked outside, but were never used.

Loyalists were as rampant as the IRA at this time but their main tactic was the shooting of mainly innocent Catholics, who were either ambushed or abducted. They did carry out a number of arson bomb attacks, the targets usually being Catholic businesses, churches, schools and sporting clubs. Protestant tempers were generally at breaking point as a result of the seemingly unstoppable IRA atrocities and what they saw as unacceptable political arrangements at Stormont. There was particular resentment of the provision for a Council of Ireland which greatly buttressed Loyalist opposition to the Sunningdale pact. While moderate Catholics were represented in the new power-sharing administration, opposition continued in the hardline Republican community which was fighting for a united Ireland or nothing.

The instability was exacerbated by political events in Britain, where a strike by coal miners had caused widespread power shortages and industrial unrest, undermining Edward Heath's Conservative government. When it became clear that there would be a national general election in February 1974, before the new Belfast institutions had had any real chance to demonstrate their worth, the terrorists on both sides intensified their violence. The fledgling power-sharing executive took the brunt of the blame and its slender political credentials were fatally weakened by the outcome of the 28 February election. With polling time marked by twelve IRA explosions throughout Belfast in one hour, electors voted overwhelmingly for unionists opposed to the Sunnningdale Agreement, presenting Merlyn Rees, the new secretary of state, with an intractable inheritance.

The final confrontation came on 14 May 1974 after the Northern Ireland Assembly voted forty-four to twenty-eight to condemn power-sharing and the Council of Ireland. At 6 p.m., when the result was announced, the Ulster Workers' Council declared that a general strike would start the following day and continue until the Sunningdale Agreement was ended. With the support of key technical personnel in the electricity supply industry, the Council, an unholy coalition of leading politicians and loyalist terrorist representatives, imposed widespread power cuts bringing what remained of normal life throughout Northern

Ireland to a standstill. Fourteen days later, as a phalanx of farmers in tractors and trailers blockaded the roads in and out of Stormont, the Executive collapsed, the strike was called off and direct rule from London was resumed.

As the daily round of shootings and bombings continued, the Belfast control segment was extended early in July with even tighter restrictions on vehicles. The Provisionals responded with a mass proxy-bombing on the afternoon of 26 July. Five vehicles were hijacked, loaded with bombs and their drivers ordered to park them at specific locations. The first exploded outside the Europa Hotel, shattering all the windows and setting cars alight while an ATO was preparing to fire Carl Gustav rounds at it. Another went off outside the Ministry of Commerce in Chichester Street while a third damaged more government offices in Bedford Street. Within an hour a fourth car exploded outside government offices and commercial premises at High Street, but an ATO defused the final 1,000 lb. device at Bridge Street after a two-hour operation. On 2 August, River House at High Street, Belfast, mainly occupied by government departments, suffered serious damage in an explosion and the Foaming Pig was deployed to help contain the flames.

The year also brought a series of alerts on the railway system. The first came at 10 p.m. on 21 March when three armed men held up the signalman at Dunloy Halt on the main Belfast–Londonderry line and took over his box. Two of the raiders carried an oil drum into the ground-floor rest room and then placed a galvanised iron dustbin on the railway track. The signalman was told that both contained bombs which would explode if he lifted the phone.

When Gaff arrived at the scene his initial suspicions focused on a parked car which he quickly found to be clear, as was the dustbin on the track which he attacked with a Wheelbarrow and disrupter. Next he examined the exterior of the signal box with binoculars and ordered the telephone and power lines to be cut as a precaution. Meanwhile a search team had cleared a path into the signal box. Gaff checked the signal-operating rods for any signs of suspicious wiring to the phones or levers, then entered the box where he immediately noticed an unusual bulge on the linoleum floor. He concluded it was a pressure plate which would set off a device if stepped on.

> I made up a lasso consisting of a three-foot loop of Cordtex, affixed an electric detonator and placed the loop on the floor around the bulge. I then retired to a safe distance and fired it. After waiting a short time I

returned to find that the Cordtex loop had cut a neat hole in the floor. I decided not to open the door and approach it but instead to cut a hole in the landing overhead to get a better look. So I made up a square cutting charge from four 18-by-1-inch strips of SX2, a plastic sheet explosive, and placed it on the landing floor. Again I retired to a safe distance, fired the charge and after a suitable pause entered the building once again. Through the hole in the floor I could now see a five-gallon oil drum with a cardboard box on its top and wires leading from the box to the door and out underneath. I carefully examined the door and could see nothing suspicious from my vantage point and so decided to open the door with a hook and line. I then initiated a small anti-handling charge and the oil drum, which was filled with ANFO explosive, was neutralised. By this time it was quite dark and with no power there were no interior lights, so I asked the search team to clear the rest of the building but they would not do so using only torches. I therefore cleared the rest of the building myself and handed it back to Northern Ireland Railways.

Gaff's account modestly underestimates the scale and gruelling duration of the task, for over a period of fifteen hours he was constantly exposed to extreme danger. This was recognised soon afterwards by the award of the George Medal. The citation records: 'Throughout the long potentially dangerous time that Lieutenant-Colonel Gaff was neutralising the bomb he displayed outstanding personal courage and technical skill which were an example to the men of his unit and also to the general public as a whole, as his operation attracted the attention of the media.'

Perhaps no other target in Northern Ireland was so consistently attacked as the Belfast–Dublin line, with at least eight direct bomb attacks among many false alarms. On 3 August at 4.45 a.m. a cadre of masked and armed men halted the northbound Dublin/Belfast mail train 300 yards south of the border, ordered the driver and guard off and loaded four heavy milk churns into the locomotive cab. The driver and guard were then released and raised the alarm. In line with standing practice, CATO was informed of the incident and given a map reference. On reaching it he was horrified to find an RUC sergeant standing immediately under the Kilnasaggart railway bridge with the train a few feet above him. 'He seemed blissfully unaware of the fact that it might have exploded and buried him under itself and the bridge.'

Despite the interruption of train services, the team was in no hurry to move in and, covered by stake-out teams, found a vantage point near by.

Through his powerful binoculars Gaff could see a length of Cordtex leading from the driver's door to the front nearside buffer. The fuse and some fog signals were attached to the buffer with brown tape. Later he overflew the train in a helicopter and in late afternoon, having let the train soak for almost twelve hours and with his protectors still in position, decided on a plan. Having conclude there were no obvious booby-traps to prevent the train moving, he called for a locomotive to be brought up from the south. 'What I intended to do was push the hijacked train into a cutting further along the line to the north, where I could deal with the device in my own good time without easily being observed by the IRA spotters, but this proved impossible as the brakes of the hijacked train were applied and could not be overridden.' The next option was to approach the train from the north, so a Northern Ireland Railways engine was summoned. When it arrived, pushing in front of it a 100-yard buffer of flatbed wagons, Gaff put a Wheelbarrow fitted with CCTV on the front wagon and placed the monitor in the engine cab before it was slowly trundled towards the booby-trapped train. However, he was unable to manipulate the Wheelbarrow from the engine cab and reluctantly decided that there was no other option than to make a manual approach.

He could hear the hijacked engine still running as he tramped warily along the trackside. After a check, he disconnected the explosive cord and fog signals before starting to climb up into the cab. 'But as I put my foot on the first step of the ladder there was an almighty explosion. My immediate reaction must be left to the imagination but I was mighty relieved when I realised it was only the air compressor safety valve which had blown.' Inside the engine cab he saw four milk churns, each containing some 200 lb. of HME and a booster charge of Frangex, which he disconnected from the timer-power unit. Northern Ireland Railways staff would not drive the train away until they were convinced it was safe, so, after a hurried briefing on how to drive a train, Gaff managed to get it going. It would not stop when he applied the brakes, so he 'let go of everything' and the emergency brake engaged. It was the first of a very few occasions on which a targeted train was handed back to the railway company completely intact.

There was only seventeen days' respite before the next attack, on 20 August. This time the same early service was halted at 5.05 a.m. in the same locality but a set of radio-controlled bombs were placed at different points along the train and were set off later as, with Gaff on leave, Major Clive Pickard was operating on board. He concluded that the terrorists had watched the procedures used during the earlier operations and that if they had been repeated he would undoubtedly have been killed. On 8 November, the early-morning train was targeted yet again. After ordering the driver and guard off, one of the terrorists set the train in motion before jumping off. The eighty-ton locomotive and carriages careered along the line for thirty miles until they approached the station at Portadown. Travelling into a sharp bend at an estimated speed of 70 mph, the train jumped the rails, turned on its side and slewed to a halt alongside the track. After a telephoned warning every available police officer and soldier was called to the scene to rouse hundreds of people from their beds in houses backing onto the railway line. Although the driver and guard told the ATO that they had seen nothing being put aboard the train, he was still forced to check through the precariously balanced engine and carriages to declare them safe and enable engineers to clear the wreckage. Trains were interrupted again on the afternoon of 22 November after the crew of a Sioux helicopter spotted a milk churn on the line north of Jonesborough. Two days later ground troops secured the area for an ATO and search team, who discovered several devices on the line designed to lure them into the range of another one buried under the track.

Earlier in the year, a party of Royal Marines manning a hilltop observation position at Drummuckaval near Crossmaglen, 300 yards from the border in south Armagh, had been the victims of a similarly well-planned ambush. For some time the post had been manned four days on, four days off, the last patrol having pulled out on 8 August. When the replacement unit arrived a few days later, they conducted their usual checks before moving in and all was quiet until about 3 p.m. on the afternoon of 13 August, when Marine Michael Southern, aged twenty, and Corporal Dennis Leach, twenty-four, were changing guard. A radio command from across the border detonated a 200 lb. device hidden in a beer keg and killed them instantly.

Though soldiers and police officers continued to lose their lives in such ambushes, the blend of caution and experience that had come to inform EOD operations was increasingly frequently preventing death and injury. In a typical instance, on 23 October at Captains Bridge, near Belleek, County Fermanagh, skill and patience outwitted terrorists who had carefully planned an attack. The trap was to be sprung by an observer in a house with good view of the main road who would alert an accomplice by short-range 'walkie-talkie' once a patrol came into sight. However, suspicious movements in the area were reported to the local security forces and a covert reconnaissance found five milk churns concealed in a culvert under the stretch of road clearly visible from the house. The area was staked out by an undercover unit for eight days before an ATO was tasked to clear the the churns, which contained 120 lb. of explosive linked to a command wire buried along the course of a stream leading to a good vantage point.

As he criss-crossed Northern Ireland, travelling to incidents or making morale-boosting visits to EOD teams, Gaff was driven everywhere by Lance-Corporal John Eboral in a nondescript, discreetly armoured saloon car. 'He looked after me as if I was a somewhat mentally deficient and wayward son,' says Gaff, who had such trust in Eboral that he spent much of the travelling time catching up on sleep. One day however, waking from a nap, Gaff had cause to be alarmed. Travelling from Strabane to Londonderry, Eboral had taken a wrong turn and they had somehow crossed into the Irish Republic. At the checkpoint, Gaff recalls, 'It was with considerable embarrassment that I identified myself to the Officer Commanding who turned out to be very understanding. But for weeks afterwards I expected a summons to the GOC's presence which fortunately never came.' The pair got into another scrape one day when Gaff happened to mention that the toilet paper provided in the officers' mess was very hard and that he preferred the more delicate Andrex. At that moment, although they were taking a short cut along the notorious Falls Road, Eboral spotted a suitable shop and pulled up for Gaff to go in and make his comfort purchase. To his horror, the young shop assistant immediately called out: 'Can I help you, soldier?' 'I quickly denied being a "soldier", picked up my purchase and paid for it but as I fled for the door, she smiled at me and said, "Whassamatter, do we scare the shit out of you?"'

Despite the apparent vacuum after the collapse of the Sunningdale Agreement, significant political moves were afoot. Secretary of State Merlyn Rees, a close student of Irish history, did not subscribe to the view that there was a military or security solution to the Northern Ireland problem and even before the Agreement foundered he had ordered top-secret initiatives geared to bringing about a negotiated settlement, this time a fully comprehensive one including the IRA and Loyalist hardmen and their supporters. At the height of the 1974 strike, few had noticed the unsung passage of a piece of legislation at Westminster legalising Sinn Fein (the political front for the IRA) and the Ulster Volunteer Force. (The other main Loyalist grouping, the Ulster Defence Association, had never been proscribed.) The aim was to draw them into ceasefires and encourage them to pursue their aims through political channels. Even before the strike, the Army was involved in this putative peace process, for its reaction on the ground to any scaling-down of violence would be crucial. In May a document classified 'Secret' was prepared at Headquarters Northern Ireland articulating what the Army response would be in the event of the Provisional IRA declaring a unilateral ceasefire. It said the IRA were probably aware 'that, should the campaign be continued for much longer, they may separate themselves still further from the main body of Catholic opinion'. Military concessions would be needed to sustain a ceasefire which could be either a tactical expedient or a change in policy. 'Even if the reasons are the latter, rather than the former, there will remain the very real possibility that the Provisionals will take up arms once again at a moment which they judge to be suitable,' the paper stated. 'It would therefore be folly to make concessions to preserve a ceasefire if these concession prematurely reduced the effectiveness of the security forces or eroded the integrity of the law and of Her Majesty's Government.'

As the military analysis highlighted, Rees's strategy was fraught with great difficulty. Ever since the abortive IRA ceasefire in July 1972, which foundered on its unrealistic demand for immediate British withdrawal, mutual distrust remained. In any case, majority public opinion in Britain and especially Northern Ireland was firmly opposed to withdrawal or indeed any move that would seem like a surrender to IRA violence. Rees created a constitutional convention to fill the political vacuum left after Sunningdale but at the same time insisted that the IRA and Loyalists had to be included in any political settlement for it to have durability. Secret contacts with terrorist sympathisers, virtually amounting to political tuition, were conducted at arm's length, and in July Rees signalled that internment without trial would be phased out.

After the UK general election in October 1974 and a series of IRA attacks on the mainland, culminating in simultaneous no-warning bomb attacks on two Birmingham public houses in November which killed nineteen people and injured almost 200, Rees increased the pressure for an IRA ceasefire. The proposition was promoted at a secret forum between senior IRA figures and Protestant clergymen at a small country hotel in Feakle, County Clare. Within ten days the IRA, scenting major concessions, announced a unilateral ceasefire from midnight on 22 December to midnight on 2 January. Before the truce ended, Rees said that the British government would respond positively to a 'genuine and sustained cessation of violence'. At the same time he permitted his officials to meet Sinn Fein openly to explain British policy. As a result of these exchanges, the ceasefire was renewed and then temporarily halted again for a few days before an open-ended truce was announced on 9 February 1975.

That month, amid renewed optimism that the dark days were at last over, Gaff left Northern Ireland. His service, which he had begun as a young infantryman at Palace Barracks, Holywood, in 1944, had ended back in the province after thirty-one years in many theatres of operations. In the preceding five years of violence there had been 20,387 shooting incidents and 4,133 bomb explosions in which fifty-six police officers, 271 soldiers and 760 civilians had lost their lives. If the security forces had not captured 73.7 tons of explosives and 5,037 weapons, and if the men of 321 EOD had not neutralised a further 1,896 bombs, the toll would undoubtedly have been far greater. During the preceding year alone, the Army revealed, 6,500,000 cars had been checked and searched by soldiers who were now generally working an eighty-hour week.

While the closing months of 1974 were vibrant with optimism that peace was at last on the cards, the year ended on a tragic note for 321 EOD with the loss of two more operators. The first was Staff Sergeant Vernon Rose, aged thirty, a married man with two children. Early on 7 November he first cleared a suspected booby-trap at a derelict house near Cookstown, County Tyrone, then went on to examine an electricity transformer at nearby Stewartstown, where there had been an explosion late the previous evening. Having checked around the damaged transformer, which was in a compound surrounded by two fences, Rose gave the all clear and, accompanied by several other soldiers and police officers, went to inspect breaches in the fence where the bombers had gained entry. Constable Charles McConaghey said afterwards that they had just spotted two plastic fertiliser bags inside one of the fences and a footprint nearby when there was a massive explosion. He was permanently blinded and suffered other injuries. Staff Sergeant Rose was killed, as was thirty-five-year-old Staff Sergeant Charles Simpson of the Royal Hussars, who was married with four children. Seven other soldiers and three civilian workmen waiting to clear up after the first explosion were also injured. One of the victims was eighteen-year-old Private Stuart Davies, attached to 321 EOD, who suffered perforated eardrums and facial lacerations.

About three weeks later, on 27 November, an elderly woman spotted a milk churn in the corner of a field about ten yards from her home at Gortmullan, County Fermanagh. The suspicious object had already been reported to the police but apparently no action had been taken. Three days later, concerned about her safety, her son and a neighbour attached a long rope to the churn and pulled it out into the centre of the field where it remained for two days. The Army then deployed a number of foot patrols and put the churn under covert observation from a distance. The area was also overflown by helicopters and photographed from the air for any sign of command wires or firing points. Meanwhile the EOD task had been assigned to WO2 John Maddocks, just over a month into his tour of duty in Northern Ireland, who set to work with a Royal Engineers search team to plan a clearance operation. Having let the situation soak for several days, they finally moved in and, as they suspected, found severed command wires where the churn had originally been left. After this area had been checked, the search team cleared an approach route to the churn in the middle of the field. Protected from a radio-controlled or command-wire detonation by a cordon of troops in the vicinity, Maddocks approached the device to look for anything suspicious and to take photographs and X-rays. From what he saw, he was convinced the device had been booby-trapped since being moved to its new position and he discussed with his team the possibility of setting it off with the 12-bore automatic shotgun that was a standard part of the EOD kit. In the end, after further scrutiny of the device and X-rays, he told his Number Two that he was going to make another manual approach to remove some Cordtex from the around the churn. It was a fatal mistake, for what looked like Cordtex was in fact a coaxial cable connected to a detonator. As Maddocks severed it, his metal cutters completed an electrical circuit, detonating the bomb and killing the father of three instantly. In the aftermath of the tragedy, the search team discovered yet another command wire. As they were tracing it there was another huge explosion, but this time nobody was harmed. Gaff later concluded that 'on this occasion the terrorist bomb-makers took advantage of a pattern in our behaviour'. Through their careful study of EOD methods the terrorists had observed that operators frequently cut Cordtex when neutralising devices.

Maddocks' was the thirteenth name inscribed in gold on the memorial board now prominently displayed at the 321 quarters in Lisburn, but alongside the roll of honour was another board with a lengthening list of those who had been honoured for exceptional bravery. In the previous year alone, members of EOD teams had been awarded ten George Medals and five British Empire Medals and another eleven were mentioned in dispatches. Their task was still far from over and their expertise and gallantry would be needed for a considerable time still to come.

There is one further landmark to be recorded in the history of 321 EOD for 1974. Staff Sergeant Bryan Shepherd was a self-taught cartoonist who whiled away his free time during a tour in Londonderry that year producing a series of cartoons based on day-to-day events in the team. Many of them featured the character of Felix the Cat as an ATO. They were more widely published in 'Pigstick', a frequently scurrilous internal newsheet for 321, started by Shepherd but later compiled by Major CR Pickard and edited by former CATO John Gaff. Within a short time, the image was adopted by the unit and appended to every conceivable object. Today Shepherd's Felix adorns the 321 EOD vehicles, paperwork, signs and computer screensavers and is also to be found on a range of ties, T-shirts and other clothing, ashtrays, doormats, computer mousemats and more.

Chapter Nine

The Long War

Theobald Wolfe Tone, the radical Protestant barrister who led the unsuccessful rising against British rule in Ireland in 1798, is widely deemed to be the founding father of Irish Republicanism. Every June, there are factional gatherings around his grave at Bodenstown to hear addresses from modern leaders. In 1977, the Provisional IRA's speaker was Jimmy Drumm, a veteran Belfast Republican whose main claim to fame was that he had spent more time interned without trial than any of his contemporaries. After eight years of all-out conflict, what he had to say was, from the IRA's point of view, far from encouraging. 'The British government is not withdrawing from the six counties . . . indeed it is committed to stabilising the six counties and is pouring in vast sums of money to improve the area and secure from Loyalists support for a long haul against the Irish Republican Army.' Drumm went on, 'We find a successful war of liberation cannot be fought exclusively on the backs of the oppressed people in the six counties nor around the physical presence of the British Army. Hatred and resentment of this army cannot sustain the war.' It was everything but an admission of defeat, a recognition that eight years of bloodshed and destruction had brought them no nearer to a united Ireland.

The 1975 ceasefire and subsequent semisecret talks with senior British officials, in which Drumm participated, were not popular within the IRA. With Drumm now openly admitting that 'negotiations' about a British withdrawal were going nowhere, the considerable internal discontent before long triggered both a change of leadership and a fundamental reorganisation of the movement. Out went the veteran Dublin-based Republicans, mocked as 'armchair generals' by the new generation of young northerners who took over. Battle-hardened on the streets, those who had ended up in the Maze prison had used their time there to plan a joint strategy of violence and politics which they believed would be far more effective in ultimately forcing the British government into serious negotiations. Martin McGuinness and Gerry Adams were prominent among this new generation but their names were little known and their authority unestablished, so they had chosen Drumm, although one of the derided old guard, to be their mouthpiece.

In line with what he had to say about the new policy of a long and expanded war, the traditional military structure of the IRA, grandly modelled on the brigades and battalions of the British Army, was quietly abandoned. Instead, in a bid to prevent terrorist operations being betrayed by informers, a new cellular configuration was introduced. The theory was that members of the cells would only know each other and any penetration by an informer would therefore be limited to a single cell. At the same time, a ruthless internal security unit was created to root out informers. The young leaders believed the British had lured them into a ceasefire to weaken and demoralise them. Their intention was to escalate the campaign of violence, this time to a point where the cost, in terms of life, finance and property, would be unacceptable to the British government. Simultaneously they would build a political arm and when the British were ready to surrender they would step into the arena, claim the spoils and fulfil the Republican dream. Thus the indefinite IRA ceasefire declared on 9 February 1975 rapidly proved to be a false dawn.

In its immediate aftermath there had been some respite. Explosions dropped to their lowest since the Troubles had started: forty-six in February, nineteen in March, twenty-six in April and seventeen in May. For the first time some EOD team members completed their tours without encountering a live device. Although a minority of incidents were undoubtedly attributable to IRA elements hostile to the ceasefire strategy, the majority of the recurring violence was sectarian and, for a time, Protestant outrages outnumbered those of the other side. One of the ugliest of these tit-for-tat exchanges came on Grand National Day, 5 April. During the afternoon, a car pulled up outside McLaughlin's Bar in the Catholic New Lodge area and one of the occupants planted a gas cylinder bomb, of a type used by the Loyalist UVF, in the front porch. As the stolen car raced away, onlookers shouted warnings and people watching the racing in the crowded bar had just enough time to crouch down before it exploded. Two of those nearest the device were killed and five more injured. The reprisal was swift. Within hours, at 6 p.m., two IRA terrorists entered the crowded Mountainview Tavern in the strongly Protestant Shankill area of Belfast. One opened fire indiscriminately on the drinkers while the other placed a box inside the main door. Moments later the package exploded, killing four of the customers instantly and grievously injuring a fifth, who died the next day.

The number of explosions increased to twenty-five in June and twenty-six in July, including one tragic episode on 10 July after a Green Howards foot patrol reported a suspected IED south of the Cortreasla Bridge crossroads, near Forkhill, County Armagh. It appeared to be a cone-shaped object in a plastic bag attached to a five-gallon oil drum. This was most certainly not the kind of device or location to which an ATO would rush openly. Over the next four days covert surveys were carried out from the air and on the ground while WO2 Edward 'Gus' Garside, whose thirty-fifth tasking it was since arriving in Northern Ireland nine weeks earlier, planned the clearance operation with his Number Two.

It got under way just after dawn on 17 July, when a Wessex helicopter from the joint police–Army base at Crossmaglen dropped in the sixteen-strong picket who would protect the search and EOD teams. With the cordon in place, at 9 a.m. the EOD party were landed in the field some eighty yards from the suspect device, where Garside planned to establish the incident control point. He knew that, whether false or live, the suspect oil drum could well be a lure designed to bring him within range of a far more deadly device. With this in mind, he had identified a milk-churn collection point, a post box and a pile of rubble for careful checking but he remained equally cautious about every building and hedgerow.

What none of the military party knew was that the helicopter activity had attracted the interest of a twenty-one-year-old man who lived close by and who had been waiting for a fortnight for a target to present itself. A week earlier a number of soldiers had come within range of his concealed bomb but he decided not to act. This morning, however, he set off for the area. He was spotted in the fields by a corporal in one of the cover teams, who was scanning the area with his magnifying rifle sight, but when the soldier tried to contact the control point his set would not transmit.

The ATO and four other members of his party were preparing a hook and line and other equipment and the electronic countermeasures operator was carrying out his customary radio sweeps when at 9.50 a.m. there was a huge explosion and a massive cloud of smoke, soil and debris erupted into the air. One of the cordon team later described how he saw Clive Evans, a Royal Military Police sergeant, stagger from the inferno and then collapse. Despite the clear risk to their safety, some of the soldiers ran to his aid while others summoned medical assistance. Evans later gave his account of the incident for the book *The British Army in Ulster*:

The next thing I remember is lying in the field face down with my hands over my head and feeling all the mud dropping on my back, and I could hear stuff falling out of the sky. Then I realised that there had been an explosion. My ears, God, terrible. It's hard to describe the sound in your ears. And my eyes they just stung like hell. I didn't remember any flash . . . Apart from my ears and my eyes one hand was quite painful. I could open my left eye after a little while and I stood up and I could see a bloody great hole and I could see a body nearly next to me. I heard someone running towards me and I felt pretty giddy at that point, and sick, and I sat down again. Then I felt someone picking me up and I heard a voice saying, 'This one is dead,' and I was just dragged off across the field to the corner of the field. By that time my other eye, the eye I could see out of, was stinging again so I closed both of them. In fact someone, one of the soldiers put a field dressing on the bad eye. I knew it was bleeding. I could feel the blood. But he put the bandage over both eyes so I couldn't see anything. I just lay there and I could hear people on the radio requesting a helicopter and telling them exactly what had happened and I still just lay there hurting like hell.

Fifteen to twenty minutes later, as the helicopter was evacuating casualties, the cordon team halted a car at a snap checkpoint they had established nearby. One of the team immediately recognised its occupant as the man he had seen a short time before the explosion and arrested him. He had wet shoes, apparently from running across the fields, and fresh scratch marks on his arms and forehead. Meanwhile Captain Bicknell, another ATO, was flown to the scene, where he unearthed a command wire and traced the firing point. He found that a metal beer keg containing 75 lb. of explosives had been dug into a gap in the hedge right beside the control point.

The final death toll was four soldiers, two of them members of 321 EOD. The first was the operator, WO2 Garside, aged thirty-five, married with four daughters and a son, from Ashford in Kent. Also dead was his Number Two, Corporal Calvert Brown from Lowestoft, twenty-five years old and married but with no children, who had just completed the fourth week of his tour. Their deaths brought the 321 EOD fatal casualty list to fifteen. The other victims were Major Peter Willis, aged thirty-seven, of the Green Howards and Sergeant Robert McCarter, thirty-three, of the Royal Engineers. At the end of a seventeen-day trial in March 1976, the arrested man was convicted of the murders and given a life sentence.

After his arrest he confessed to the police that after a gang of IRA men had dug in the bomb he had volunteered to lie in wait to detonate it because he 'hated Brits'. Reflecting later, Clive Evans deplored the 'waste of life'.

> I don't think anyone wants to come to Ulster, but Gus Garside was sent and he came in to do a job of saving life and property by neutralising devices. That's all he had to do. So why kill a man like that? He's got no political motives in what he's doing and all the people in the patrol, none of them were sort of out-and-out – they didn't have any political views – they were sent there to do a job. I mean, the week before he had been down to Derrybeg, in Newry. He had done a couple of jobs in Derrybeg, actually. It would have been so easy to not risk his life; to put a charge underneath the suspect car and blow it to pieces and admittedly, a few of the windows of houses in the area would have been damaged. But he didn't do that. He went out and risked his own life to save the property, and neutralised the device in the car.

The incident effectively marked the end of the ceasefire, which was never formally renounced. The number of explosions rose from twenty-five in August to forty-seven in September, when Lieutenant-Colonel Peter Underhill, now CATO, reported a 'large increase in Provisional IRA activity aimed at prestige industrial and commercial targets'. The figure increased again to seventy-two the next month and although it tailed off again towards the end of the year, Underhill's monthly report for October talked of 'more and more sophisticated types of devices' being encountered. The principal problems for the security forces at large were a continuation of internal IRA feuding between the old guard and the new 'Northern Command' and a series of further tit-for-tat sectarian incidents. The primary thrust of the IRA campaign had in fact moved to mainland Britain. While 321 EOD had endured another gruelling year, the 2,643 taskings and 635 explosions showed a reduction from the 3,834 taskings and 1,113 explosions in 1974. Forty-two teams were still being fielded.

Ever since the Army had deployed to relieve the overwhelmed police force in Northern Ireland in August 1969, the General Officer Commanding had been Director of Operations, effectively in charge of the Army and the police for the purposes of the counter-terrorist campaign. However, early in 1976, a report entitled 'The Way Ahead' was produced for the government by a team of security advisers, defining the doctrine of 'police primacy' or 'Ulsterisation': retraining and re-equipping the RUC to take the lead in a new policy of 'criminalisation' designed to capture and convict terrorists through the courts. (Detention without trial had been ended in December 1975 and the remaining detainees released.) The Army would remain in support of the police for as long as necessary, retreating to its barracks again as soon as the police could handle the security situation on their own.

Until this point, the Army had maintained a high public profile. Senior officers regularly featured in the news explaining military objectives and policy while soldiers involved in incidents were allowed to be interviewed and attract public credit for their good work. The EOD teams had benefited from this policy and every CATO from George Styles on had become well known. Under the new relationship, however, the Army was not only to take a back seat to the police but also to adopt a vow of silence, so that although the EOD teams continued their highly visible work on the streets, it was a police officer rather than a soldier who would explain what was going on. Newspaper reports and broadcast news bulletins, of course, still referred to clearances carried out by 'Army bomb-disposal officers' and there were frequent pictures of suited ATOs on the long walk, but none was ever interviewed and the CATO became an anonymous figure.

A joint directive to give effect to the new security policy was signed by the GOC, Lieutenant-General Sir David House, and Sir Kenneth Newman, the Chief Constable, on 1 January 1977. Privately both commanders, in common with IRA strategists, knew the Army was still undoubtedly there for a long haul. In 1976 nearly three hundred people had died in sectarian outrages. At the beginning of the year, in a bid to ease fears on both sides, Harold Wilson had announced the official deployment of the SAS. Despite their fearsome reputation, they were unable to do much to halt the violence. Republican and Loyalist killers struck at victims in their homes, often gunning them down in front of their families. Public houses were targeted by killers on both sides who carried out 'spray jobs', opening fire indiscriminately. Sometimes gunmen would lie in wait to fire at those fleeing from blasts. With the number of explosions increasing to 1,192 in 1976, EOD taskings for the year totalled 3,831. The teams were now scoring a 50 per cent success rate in neutralising devices, speed being the principal factor, but as one ATO recalls, 'The bombers just kept shortening the time. Twenty minutes was once the minimum [before timers expired], then it became the maximum.'

Detonators of US origin were now turning up in considerable

quantities, showing that controls on the home-manufactured items were having some effect, but Irish-sourced explosives were still coming through in regular quantities and also turning up on mainland Britain. There was growing evidence that bomb components, especially timer-power units, were being produced in 'factory' conditions at various locations in the Irish Republic. In January 1976, Irish police raided a light engineering works at Ballyconnell, County Cavan, where they found equipment being used to make bomb casings. Other parts of the manufacturing chain were located at a factory in north Dublin. Advances in micro-electronics were already being incorporated into IRA bombs and timer components and initiation circuitry were traced to a factory at Dundalk, where they were being manufactured on equipment intended for producing video-gaming and amusement machines. In December, a new model of timer-power-unit was captured which could run for five days and fifty-seven minutes. Terrorists were also working to counteract the controls on fertilisers and other chemicals by setting up plants in remote farms and other buildings. The fertiliser was heated with Bunsen burners, and when the materials cooled and separated, the additives were discarded to leave purified ammonium nitrate. Later the IRA discovered that adding sugar considerably enhanced the explosive effect.

By now the violence, although worse than its previous peak in 1972, had reached levels that the majority of the population found tolerable if not acceptable. Belfast people took to comparing themselves with the legendary Londoners who had refused to be bowed by the Blitz. People went to work, children went to school and normal social and entertainment patterns resumed. As ever, criminality flourished amid disorder and the unofficial drinking clubs that had sprung up to replace bombed and burned-out pubs hosted a black market in goods looted from hijacked vehicles and bombed out buildings. This was the background for 321 EOD's only scandal during its marathon deployment. Early in 1976, a twenty-five-year-old former lance-corporal with the Argyll and Sutherland Highlanders told a national Sunday newspaper that while he was serving at Albert Street Mill with one of the EOD teams, they had regularly looted items from premises cleared because of alerts or explosions. The story was picked up by other newspapers, especially in Belfast, and RUC detectives travelled to Scotland where the soldier gave them a full account. After the follow-up investigation, fourteen soldiers appeared before the courts in Belfast. They admitted a series of thefts and the handling of stolen goods and received suspended prison sentences ranging from one to six months and fines totalling £400. The court heard how items were removed from evacuated city-centre shops, pubs and two hotels and then shared out back at the team's quarters. The most serious incident was the theft of a camera and lens valued at £370 by an RAOC Staff Sergeant who had answered 150 bomb alerts during his tour of duty. Ironically, one of the bombs he dismantled was a 450 lb. device outside Musgrave Street police station in Belfast from where the investigation of the looting was being conducted. If it had gone off, details of the thefts might have been lost. The other offenders, two RAOC privates and nine soldiers from the Royal Corps of Transport and the Argylls, pilfered and shared bottles of spirits, cigarettes, clothes, an electric drill and cash. Sentencing the soldiers, John Fox, the resident magistrate, said: 'The community owes a debt of gratitude to the bomb-disposal squads which can never be repaid but looting is reprehensible and the courts have a duty to impose penalties which will act as a deterrent.'

In March 1976, two more members of 321 were killed, this time in a road accident. Sergeant Michael Peacock and Corporal Douglas Whitford were travelling from Poyntzpass towards Newry on a Saturday evening when their vehicle collided with a local bus. The corporal had been nearing the end of his tour with the Bessbrook detachment.

Soon afterwards, in June 1976, Lieutenant-Colonel Derrick Patrick became CATO. Born and brought up in the London Docklands, he had a conventional post-war Army career with the RAOC before moving into the exclusive world of EOD. He had been friendly with three of 321 EOD's operators who had been killed and at the beginning of 1975, when he was first told he would be going to Northern Ireland as CATO, it was some months before he could bring himself to tell his wife and three children. In the end, it was only the necessity to make a will and arrange his affairs, in case the worst happened, that forced his hand.

In his final monthly report the departing CATO, Peter Underhill, noted that the current pattern of terrorism emphasised commercial and sectarian targets in urban areas and ambushing security forces in the countryside. Intelligence assessments indicated that the IRA had eighteen explosives recipes, only two of which required complex chemicals. 1976 saw increased use of large incendiaries, as one of Underhill's reports had noted: 'Devices utilising large quantities of petrol becoming common-place in attacks on business establishments.' Four such devices planted in the County Antrim holiday resort of Portrush on 3 August completely devastated shops and other accommodation, but a similar attack on the market town of Ballymena on 9 October went badly wrong. As four raiders entered the town by car, one of their incendiary devices ignited prematurely. One of the men lost part of a leg. Despite this setback, other raiders pressed on and laid at least fourteen devices at various shops in the town. One of the targets was the Alley Katz boutique in Bridge Street, where Yvonne Dunlop, the owner's daughter, noticed that two girls had left a shopping bag at the back of the shop. Mrs Dunlop examined it and shouted to her nine-year-old son, 'There's a bomb, get out.' Just as she finished speaking, a massive fireball engulfed her. Her son escaped with his hair singed. (Thomas McElwee, a twenty-three-year-old motor mechanic later convicted for the killing, was the ninth of the ten hunger strikers who starved to death at the Maze Prison in 1981.) In December, thirteen shops were destroyed and nine more damaged, at a total cost of over £1 million, by up to sixteen devices in Londonderry. By the end of the year there had been 236 incendiary attacks.

In November 1976, twenty-eight-year-old Sergeant Martin Walsh had arrived in Northern Ireland for a four-month tour of duty with the 321 section based in Omagh. He had joined the Army from school and then became a military policeman but later transferred to the RAOC, became an ammunition technician and qualified as a bomb-disposal officer. After a Christmas break with his wife, Eve, and two children in Hereford, Walsh returned to Omagh and on 9 January he was called to North's filling station and shop at Drumully, a hundred yards from the border near Newtownbutler, County Fermanagh. The previous evening, four armed and masked men had placed a milk churn on the premises which they said contained 100 lb. of explosives and was set to go off in twenty minutes. A police patrol evacuated everyone from the area and sealed it off. It was with great difficulty that they persuaded the owner of the business to stay away from his home, about thirty yards away. Poor weather prevented helicopter patrols and the possibility of a secondary device on the only road to the scene ruled out driving in an ATO, so the decision was made not to examine the device until morning. At 9.15 a.m. a Puma helicopter brought in soldiers to form a cordon around the scene while two Royal Engineers search teams clearing the road with special attention to bridges and culverts. Walsh and his escort, Lance-Corporal Watson, were then flown in with some equipment, landing close to the incident control point by the filling station. By then members of the Garda Siochana had taken up positions on their side of the border.

While his escort readied the equipment, Walsh quizzed the owner of the filling station about the layout of the shop and the forecourt, especially the location of the pumps and petrol storage tanks. He then went forward and inspected the scene through the side window of the shop to establish precisely where the churn, without its lid, had been placed. He ran back after ten or fifteen seconds and reported: 'There is one in there. I can see a clock on top and something that looks like a safety fuse.' Unable to reach the device with a Wheelbarrow, Walsh prepared a hook and line and went into the shop, where he attached the hook to the churn. He and his assistant then started to pull the churn but the shop door swung closed, trapping it inside. After thirty minutes' soak time, Walsh made another approach and found the churn had toppled over. Again with the help of his escort, this time he pulled the churn out of the door and across to the edge of the road, well away from the petrol storage tanks. There he left it to soak for another thirty minutes. Some spilled ANFO and a clock with a battery taped to it could be seen hanging out of the churn.

Back at the device just before 12.40 p.m., Walsh pulled on a pair of rubber gloves, picked up the clock and shouted that it had stopped. He put it down before leaning over the churn, reaching inside and pulling out a bundle of wires. He shouted to his assistant: 'I can't make head or tail of this.' Seconds later, there was a bright red flash followed by a cloud of grey smoke. Walsh died instantly from multiple injuries. Even if he had been wearing the EOD suit, it would not have saved him. Later examination indicated that an anti-handling mechanism, independent of the clock, had triggered the blast.

As soon as the new CATO, Derrick Patrick, learned that Sergeant Walsh had been killed, he took off for the scene. While in the air, he ordered that all EOD operators should phone home and tell their families they were safe before news of Walsh's death was released. (In the past, early reports of the death of a bomb-disposal officer had caused every family with a relative serving in 321 to worry.) The news was broken to Walsh's wife in their married quarters in Hereford. Later, a police car drew up outside his parents' house in Rhyl, north Wales, where Martin, the eldest of four sons and two daughters, had grown up. The door was answered by Sean, then aged eighteen, who thought one of the family was in trouble with the police and called his mother. Outside, another brother, twelve-year-old Mike, who had been training his dog to halt on command before crossing the road, called for his mother to come and see the trick. 'Suddenly I saw that she was crying,' he remembers.

Sergeant Walsh's family never recovered from their grief. Their Irish-born father could not forgive the fellow-Irishmen and Catholics who had so cruelly deprived him of his beloved son. 'It tortured him for the rest of his life and he put himself through hell about it,' says Mike Walsh. His mother remained upset until her dying day in February 2005. 'A few days before his birthday in August and his anniversary in January, she would go quiet. She was still badly affected by losing him as are his children. His son, who was only a baby at the time, really resents losing his father.'

At the time of his death Martin Walsh had been preparing for life after the Army. Among the possessions returned from his quarters in Omagh were the textbooks he was using to study for an Open University BA. Ironically, a few days after his death, a letter arrived saying that he had been awarded the degree.

Five days after the incident he was buried with full military honours in his home town. The 300-strong congregation in St Mary's Catholic Church heard the Army chaplain Lieutenant-Colonel Father Hugh Beattie, who conducted the requiem mass, say that Martin Walsh belonged to 'an elite and heroic band'. Later at the graveside in the town cemetery a bugler sounded the Last Post and a twenty-one-gun volley of shots was fired.

The second eldest of the Walsh family, Alan, was already in the Army at the time of Martin's death and two more of his brothers later joined up, although none of them served in bomb disposal. Every year on the anniversary of Martin's death they travel to Northern Ireland to lay a wreath at the spot where he died. The family who lived there at the time always share a glass with them in memory. So, too, do the police at Newtownbutler station, where the brothers have erected a plaque alongside the memorials to police officers murdered in the locality by the IRA.

In his memoir, *Fetch Felix: the fight against the Ulster bombers 1976–77*, Derrick Patrick recalls that 'the Walsh tragedy had an unpleasant aftermath':

> The sergeant who took over immediately did a fine job in holding the Omagh team together and rebuilding their morale. (He and I did a clearance in a snowstorm shortly afterwards.) Then he was replaced by a staff sergeant from England who spent two days with us at Lisburn. He was given every assurance and told there were no bogeymen in Northern Ireland. Provided that he stuck to the rules, all would be well. He was sent to Omagh to do a clearance operation which had been held back specially for him and after he had completed it successfully he was left to take command of the team. That same night he was on the phone to the OC of 321 EOD Unit. The conversation must have been the most painful to which an officer in charge of a unit can be

subjected. The man on the other end of the phone broke down and confessed that he was frightened – so frightened that he could not do the job. Coming from a senior rank that was a very serious admission. But it was serious also for the troops serving in the area and for the public, too, for that matter. For the second time in a matter of days the FOD team was leaderless and the area was exposed. The OC of 321 EOD Unit had no option but to order another NCO to take over (the sergeant who had done such a good interim job) and to send home the staff sergeant who had cracked. In less sympathetic days, the staff sergeant might have been dealt with severely – the kindest comment from operators in Northern Ireland at the time was that he should have been court-martialled for cowardice in the face of the enemy. Someone suggested he should have been sent to a psychiatrist but we didn't have one in the Province at the time. In any case, when he saw one later he was found to be perfectly normal, and I am pleased to say that later he returned to Northern Ireland and completed a four-month tour satisfactorily. Perhaps the one thing one cannot fault is the man's decision to phone his OC – an act which, in itself, must have taken some courage. But having done so, the OC had no alternative but to relieve him. He could not possibly have left a man who had broken down to lead an EOD team into a deadly area, or any other area for that matter – for their sakes as well as the man's.

This breakdown highlighted the sustained pressure that the bomb-disposal teams had to face and the strain and self-doubt that followed the death of a colleague in a small, closely-knit professional community. Many ATOs confess to private moments of fear or panic, but they say they were steadied by their training or by words of encouragement or warning from a colleague. There were indeed occasions when ATOs were taken off jobs or even sent back from Northern Ireland, sometimes following a misjudgement or because of a personal or family crisis. In contrast, WO2 K Adams, posted to Omagh on 1 February 1977, proved more than equal to unusually difficult circumstances. He had already completed a tour some five years earlier, so he had some sense of the ground. On 19 February he was called out to the Drumcard Road about two miles from Kinawley, County Fermanagh, to check out a rifle clip and 8 rounds of matching ammunition found after a police officer had been shot and wounded in the area. It took Adams two days to uncover a bomb consisting of 5 lb. of Frangex explosive connected to a timer and a micro-switch which would have set it off had the rifle clip been moved.

His meticulous care enabled weapons and intelligence colleagues to decode the markings on the explosive wrapper and pinpoint the quarry in the Irish Republic from where it had been stolen.

Within a few days Adams was called out to another complicated clearance. This time a pipe bomb packed with eight ounces of explosive was jammed between the outside mesh and the frame of a window in the Community Centre in Omagh. A previous telephone call had warned of a booby-trap in the area so great caution was again called for and the operation lasted five hours. During another operation, following an explosion at a border crossing on 23 April, Adams identified two booby-trapped devices over six hours, both found to contain some 50 lb. of HME. Another bomb encountered soon afterwards contained only 11 lb. of explosive, but it took Adams three risk-filled hours to clear because it had been planted under a precarious catwalk on top of a 12,000-gallon fuel tank at a depot in Omagh. If the bomb had functioned at any time the result would have been a catastrophic explosion and the certain death of the ATO.

By the time he had completed his tour in the notorious Fermanagh–Tyrone area Adams had been tasked sixty-five times and neutralised thirteen out of twenty-five devices, four of which were booby-trapped. His citation for the George Medal noted his high levels of technical skill and personal courage. 'Adams was always in complete control of the situation and by his example, confidence, and professional skill earned the respect of all those with whom he served. His actions are all the more outstanding because he was fully aware that his predecessor had been killed whilst carrying out the same tasks.'

Towards the end of Adams's tour 321 suffered another fatal casualty, although this time terrorists were not directly to blame. On 31 May, the ten-ton Saracen vehicle carrying Lance-Corporal Michael Dearnley overturned and tumbled down a steep embankment. Thirty-year-old Dearnley, from Reading, Berkshire, who had two sons and a daughter, was sitting in the command turret with his head and shoulders out above the vehicle. Despite wearing a safety helmet, he sustained multiple skull fractures. The Royal Military Police investigation of his death concluded that it had been caused by 'an unfortunate, unforeseeable accident'. In a letter of sympathy to his 321 counterpart, the commanding officer of another unit wrote: 'We simply cannot afford to lose such brave men in this way.'

At this time, EOD commanders were involved in top-secret planning for the first visit of the Queen and the Duke of Edinburgh to Northern

Ireland for eleven years, as part of a Silver Jubilee tour. On the last occasion, in 1966, a concrete block had been thrown at the Queen's car in central Belfast, so apprehension about the visit now dominated Patrick's last months as CATO. The two-day itinerary in August was kept secret and the plan was to create two security zones around the Queen. Three extra EOD teams were temporarily drafted in to help with the operation. The entire tour could have been threatened in advance by two incidents at the University of Ulster in Coleraine, which she was due to visit. On 29 July a device concealed in a lavatory was uncovered during a search operation and neutralised. Examination revealed that it was a new type of 'sleeping bomb' with a long-delay timer of the sort used in video recorders. Then on 9 August, the day before the Queen arrived, another device of this type exploded in the grounds of the University, but the danger was not considered sufficient to halt the visit or even amend the schedule and early next morning the Queen arrived by helicopter at the first 'sterile zone', around Hillsborough Castle. There was yet another scare on 11 August, a few hours before the Queen was due at Coleraine for a garden party. Search teams, sniffer dogs and ATOs were hastily called in, one of their tasks being to comb at speed through thousands of volumes in the library. Nothing was found. Later that afternoon the arrival of a fleet of ambulances caused some alarm, but they had only come to remove to hospital some young people taking part in a display, who had become ill after eating sandwiches. In the evening, hours after the Queen's departure, another long-delay device buried on the edge of the campus exploded harmlessly. The success of the visit in the teeth of the IRA's threats was a triumph for the security forces. One senior man summed up their glee by saying that the caterers had caused more casualties than the Provos.

Thus ended perhaps the most fraught royal visit of the Queen's long reign. It also marked the end of Patrick's tenure as CATO and within days he departed into retirement after twenty-five years in the Army. An OBE followed, earned in considerable part for dealing with an an epidemic of petrol-tanker bombs, three of which he personally neutralised. The attacks began on 18 September 1976 when a hijacked tanker was planted at the customs post on the main Belfast–Dublin road at Killeen, just south of Newry. It exploded while the EOD team were travelling to deal with it. A great ball of fire engulfed the building and consumed five parked cars, while the cab of the lorry was hurled into a field across the road. Then just before Christmas a car exploded at the H21 border crossing near Crossmaglen. Covert surveillance found no sign that anybody had been killed or injured by the blast, but with two milk churns clearly visible in what remained of the boot the Bessbrook ATO rightly feared a trap and let the scene soak. Meanwhile the road was passable for those who wanted to risk it, until on 22 December a petrol tanker was hijacked nearby, driven to within thirty yards of the car and abandoned across the road.

With the road now completely blocked and a school, a farm and other local residents being inconvenienced, the EOD organisation had little choice but to mount a clearance. The risk was clearly considerable. The tanker posed a considerable threat on its own; there could be any number of subsidiary devices and terrorists could have laid command wires long in advance or could simply be waiting across the border to transmit a radio command. It was an appallingly difficult situation and Patrick decided he would take the lead in tackling it, early on Christmas Eve.

The morning before, Patrick went to one of the main fuel import and distribution firms at Belfast harbour to inspect the innards of a petrol tanker, clambering over the tank and body, examining the cab and learning all the systems for pumping and discharging the fuel load. By the time he arrived at Bessbrook soon after dawn on the 24th, patrols were staked out, the Royal Engineers' search team had cleared a path to the tanker, ATO equipment was ready at the control point and the Bleep was electronically sweeping the area. Irish police were positioned across the frontier as an additional safeguard. Apart from the desire to wrap up in time for Christmas, the window of daylight was short at that point of the year, and Patrick wanted to get it all over with before dark to minimise the exposure of soldiers on the ground.

Using a hook and line, Patrick pulled each of the tank lids open, revealing the vehicle to be full of petrol but with no device aboard. The cab and body were similarly cleared and Patrick and one of the EOD drivers climbed aboard the tanker and drove it away to a safe distance. He was now sure that the tanker had merely been hijacked to draw in an ATO after the ploy with the burned-out wreck had failed. The most obvious danger area was the churns in the car boot, so he used a hook and line to pull one from the wreckage before setting a small charge to both to blow them apart. The second churn did not move as he expected, and he inspected it again and found it packed with explosive and cunningly booby-trapped. After that, the clearance was uneventful and everyone concerned was safely back in Bessbrook by dusk. Before leaving for Christmas, Patrick produced a bottle of Irish whiskey that had been slipped to him by one of the locals at the end of the operation and they all had a celebratory glass.

It is the slaying of what he called 'the Donegall Pass dragon' for which Patrick is most remembered in EOD circles. In *Fetch Felix* he records the sequence of events after a petrol tanker was hijacked on 8 February at a garage in the IRA's west Belfast heartland. After delivering the fuel, the driver took his delivery documents into the office, where he was held up by a masked man with a gun. Other masked men appeared and after about twenty minutes he was instructed to drive his vehicle to the RUC station at Donegall Pass, Belfast. As he moved off, a black London-type taxi pulled in front of him and a battered Cortina moved in behind. The drive through traffic, slowed down by unusually persistent thick fog, took about ten minutes. Outside the station, one of the men got out and indicated where the tanker should be positioned, before jumping back into the taxi and driving away. The Cortina had disappeared. The driver jumped from his cab and ran into the station to raise the alarm.

By chance Patrick was only a short distance from the scene and reached it while the surrounding area was still being cleared. From his vantage point a hundred yards away he could just see the outline of the tanker shrouded in the persistent fog. The Belfast EOD team's arrival was delayed by gridlocked traffic, so Patrick began questioning the driver about his load and what, if anything, he had seen of the device. The driver told him the tanker had seven 500-gallon sections. The front three were empty, the others full of fuel. He was adamant nothing had been left in the cab. The only other thing he had noticed was that the man who had got out at the police station had seemed to pull a string leading to the top of the tanker.

While this conversation was going on there was a loud crack, like a shot, which triggered a flurry of radio exchanges about whether anyone had fired a shot or been fired on. 'Negative, negative,' one position after another reported, leaving the sound a mystery for the moment.

The hijacking of the tanker had triggered the now well-established major incident procedure. Fire chiefs, the owners of the tanker and officials from the city council and public utilities were converging on the scene. At Patrick's request, several lorryloads of sand were brought in. With everything in position and armed with all the information he could glean, Patrick conferred with the EOD team, telling them he thought the explosive was in one of the vehicle's empty but vapour-filled tanks and linked to an arming mechanism and timer-power unit, probably on top of it. All agreed they needed a closer look at the vehicle. Wheelbarrow was thus trundled into action but thwarted by the lingering fog and the restricted height of its camera. Patrick now called for 'Eager Beaver', an armoured, remote-controlled forklift truck conveniently based at the Grand Central Hotel, but when it arrived there were technical problems and it proved equally useless. He then decided there was no option but to go into the police station, from where he would have a clear view of the tanker. 'This was against the rules,' he writes in his memoir, 'but as CATO wrote the rules there was no one better to break them.'

Patrick and the EOD sergeant were guided through the deserted station and up by two RUC officers. From the roof they could clearly see the seven tanker caps all in position and a box on top of one of them which Patrick recognised as a typical IRA timer-power unit. Back at the control point, he was helped into the sergeant's bomb suit with its distinctive whiff of sweat and explosive. 'If anyone wonders why I bothered to cocoon myself against the inferno which would result if thousands of gallons of petrol went up, I can only say that at the time, any protection seemed better than none. Besides the device might go up when I was some distance away.'

Well over two hours since the incident had begun, a radio alert went out that CATO was going forward. The firemen made their pumps ready and the infantrymen providing cover against snipers curled their fingers around their triggers and clamped their eyes to their sights. A large crowd had gathered at the edge of the cordon, for watching bomb scares was still something of a spectator sport in Belfast. Such was their appreciation of the finer points of the trade that all knew this was an exceptionally hazardous clearance. As they sensed the expectation among the security forces and emergency services, many people crossed their fingers or said a silent prayer for the tiny figure in the distance shuffling forward in the heavy bomb suit, carrying his pouches full of tools.

The fog had almost dispersed now and Patrick walked carefully round the tanker, looking into the cab before climbing the ladder to the top of the tanks. He went up stiffly, rung by rung, encumbered by the bomb suit, until the watchers could see his silhouetted figure on top of the vehicle. Treading carefully along the slippery catwalk, Patrick was now certain that the rectangular plywood box was a piece of IRA equipment. He attached a hook and line and retreated carefully down the ladder. When he was 100 yards to the rear of the tanker he pulled, but nothing happened. After a time he ascended again and found that he had completely dislodged the box from the side of the tank cap. A blackened detonator with two wires hanging from it explained the earlier 'shot' noise. The terrorists had intended 'to send up the whole show at the time we heard the crack', but the device had failed to detonate. Now faced with clearing each tank compartment, Patrick opened the first cap, looked inside and saw 'a pipe which, according to my knowledge of tankers, should not have been there'. After consulting the driver, he climbed onto the vehicle again and, kneeling over the hole, untied a length of fishing line wrapped around the hinge and extracted two feet of grey plastic pipe full of explosive. Patrick checked the other tanks and finally declared the operation over after a nerve-racking five hours. Next evening, in its editorial, the *Belfast Telegraph* commented: 'Without the skill and courage of Colonel Derrick Patrick and his men, who regularly are dismantling Provisional IRA bombs, the people of Northern Ireland would stand naked against the threat of a holocaust. It is all too easy to let the sound of one explosion deaden the many successes of these men.'

All too rapidly, however, the tanker bombers struck again at the same target. On 24 March a diesel tanker exploded before the ATO could get there, devastating the station and surrounding property. Patrick himself endured two more torments by petrol tanker before the end of his tour. On 28 March one was hijacked and abandoned outside a church hall on a busy village street at Kingsway, south of Belfast. Patrick was there within ten minutes. The driver told him there were 1,000 gallons of petrol on board in two of seven tanks and that the bomb was in a paint tin rolling loose in tank number five. He had been made to lower it in on a string which was dropped in after it, and had then been ordered to drive the vehicle to the centre of Belfast but had become so frightened that he simply stopped and raised the alarm. Patrick got suited up, took the long walk to the tanker and climbed the ladder to the top gangway. With a hook and line he deftly retrieved the tin and lowered it to the ground, set up the disrupter and fired, splitting the paint tin and separating the 5 lb. of HME from the timer-power unit and US-made detonator.

Patrick's final battle against a tanker came on 18 April 1977 when a vehicle was abandoned outside a former mill at Flax Street in the Ardoyne area of north Belfast, then occupied by the Army. As he confessed in his memoir, he was consumed with apprehension as he was driven to the scene and what he heard from the trembling driver did nothing to allay his anxieties. The man, just back to work after suffering a heart attack, had been hijacked and detained for three hours before the terrorists told him to drive his vehicle slowly to the base and not to go over any bumps. His state was not improved by the attitude of the sentry who told him at rifle point and in strong terms to move the vehicle well away from the base before halting.

From Patrick's perspective, the most relevant aspect was what had been done to the tanker during that three-hour interval. In all the previous incidents the set-up had been quite swift. This longer one, he feared, could spell trouble. In *Fetch Felix* he says: 'I walked away from the Saracen with the realisation dawning that I was very frightened indeed.' He had learned from the driver that there were two devices, one in the cab, the other in one of the tanks. This would be the most dangerous, he felt, for the bomber surely intended to do more than just blow up the cab.

At 5.30 p.m., three hours after the first alert, he was finally suited up and ready to go forward. Despite his apprehension he had calmed himself and was once more the cold professional. The rear bomb was in a putty bucket dangling at the end of a string from a piece of wood jammed across the mouth of the tank. Patrick secured the hook, played his line back to the control point and began pulling with the help of one of the officers, but the line went taut and the bucket would not come clear. 'There's nothing else for it, I'll have to do it by hand,' he told the crew.

Once more he laboriously climbed the tanker steps and positioned himself over the open tank. He was now sure that there was an anti-handling switch inside the bucket which would go off if even slightly tilted, so he freed the piece of wood and began lifting the bucket with supreme care. When it was clear he set it down on the gangway, fixed a hook and line and, again with the utmost caution, descended from the vehicle. Not wanting to go all the way back to the control point he played his line around the street corner, where the building would cover him, and pulled the bucket off the top of the tanker. There was an immediate explosion, as he had expected. The blast knocked over the second box in the cab, which appeared to be a hoax device filled with rubbish. However, Patrick took no chances, set up his disrupter and blew it apart 'according to the book'. After a final check he gave the all clear nearly four hours after the operation had started.

Patrick's success had a profound effect on him. Army intelligence learned that the Belfast IRA had imported a booby-trap specialist from Strabane in a direct bid to kill him. 'This was no amateurish affair with home-made blast mixture but 2 lb. of powerful industrial explosive,' he wrote later. 'I never felt the same after the Crumlin Road tanker incident. I began to realise just how much I wanted to stay alive and see out the rest of my tour.' Some of his closest friends spotted how deeply the incident had scarred him and next morning the GOC himself told him: 'You've done all we could ask of you and there would be no stigma attached if you decided to go home now.' Patrick immediately declined. 'Well,' said the general, 'the next time you are called out to anything like that, you are to let me know. I insist on going with you.' But there were no further incidents before the end of Patrick's tour.

The next CATO, Lieutenant-Colonel Peter Istead, who had first enlisted as a boy soldier in the Scots Guards in 1952, was no stranger to danger. According to *The History of the RAOC*, on the evening of 25 June 1965, while Istead was a young captain, a Belgian ammunition train caught fire in a cutting near Minden in what was then West Germany. The train was halted and four of the wagons uncoupled but the fire still raged and two of the wagons exploded, scattering ammunition. Major CW Smith, a Senior Ammunition Technical Officer, and Istead, his second-in-command, were called to the scene and found a third wagon on fire and the surrounding area covered with burning propellant and dangerously hot 90 mm. artillery shells which might have detonated at any moment. They quickly arranged for water to be played on the burning wagon and managed to move its explosive contents away from the blaze. They then uncoupled the third and fourth wagons, each containing about ten tons of 90 mm. ammunition, and trundled them down the track. Having prevented a further major explosion, they set about dealing with the other ammunition in and around the first two wagons, which were still burning. The long and hazardous operation was not completed until the morning. Afterwards both officers were awarded the George Medal.

Istead's first month as CATO presented only two ambush bombs and a booby-trap device. 'No car bombs, mortars or rocket attacks,' his report noted, but the lull was deceptive for incendiary attacks had been increasing in frequency over the preceding months. Over the same January weekend when Sergeant Martin Walsh was killed, firebombs damaged two shops in Keady and another in Londonderry and experts from 321 neutralised incendiaries in four other towns. Days before the arrival of the Queen in August £1 million worth of damage was caused by co-ordinated attacks on six shops, two garages and an office block in Belfast and Lisburn. For the rest of the year, incendiary attacks became so frequent that, just as 1972 had been the year of the car bomb, 1977 can clearly be described as the year of the firebomb. In the autumn, when firefighters struck for improved pay and conditions, vintage 'Green Goddess' appliances were issued to the troops assigned to provide fire cover, a task which exacerbated the dangers they already faced in hard areas.

Not surprisingly, the bombers set out to exploit the strike, targeting the troops manning fire pumps. After a spate of incidents in which devices were placed in litter bins close to fires and fire hydrants were booby-trapped, EOD teams had to clear areas around fires before the firefighting troops could move in. Some of the ambushes were particularly callous. On 17 November an ATO neutralised a nasty device in Londonderry: a 5 lb. charge concealed in a traffic cone packed with ball bearings which would have functioned when lifted. After another fire ignited by incendiaries, an ATO found a 100 lb. device concealed under a fire-hydrant cover which exploded during action to neutralise it.

In November the IRA unveiled what became known as the 'blast incendiary': a length of metal pipe filled with commercial explosive and aluminium filings, taped to a one or five-gallon container of petrol with a timer-power unit. They were also known as 'meat-hook bombs' because they were frequently packed into bags and attached to metal security grilles with a butcher's hook or wire clothes-hanger. Once the explosive detonated, the petrol formed a rolling fireball which incinerated everything in its path. Bomb intelligence experts believe the device was developed to eke out supplies of explosive but that once the IRA realised its destructive power and that of the cassette incendiary, both were used with increasing frequency.

Two further pieces of EOD equipment made their debut about this time. One was a variant of the hook and line, designed to enable fire hydrants to be prised open from a safe distance. The other was a Saracen armoured personnel carrier with a turret adapted to fire a water slug to disrupt 'meat-hook' incendiaries. The vehicle only operated in Belfast and with limited success. The theory was good: the water slug was powerful enough to dislodge or even disrupt a device and the operator was protected. However, the cumbersome vehicle could not always be manoeuvred into a good firing position and most ATOs preferred to use a shotgun.

Between August and October, incendiaries were causing damage calculated at £4 million a week. The annual compensation bill for damage to property jumped from £28 million in fiscal year 1973–4 to £40 million the next year, then £45 million before peaking at £50 million in 1976–7. The destruction continued into January 1978 with twelve explosions and seventy-eight blast incendiaries of which twenty-two were neutralised. A few weeks later the blast incendiary exacted a price in human life in one of the worst massacres of the entire Troubles. On the evening of Friday 17 February, as the members of the Irish Collie Club gathered for their annual dinner-dance at the La Mon House Hotel on the south-eastern outskirts of Belfast, blast incendiary devices were hung on the iron grille protecting one of the windows. At 9.03, as the guests were beginning their meal inside, the bombs exploded. Moments earlier there had been a muddled warning to Newtownards police station but when an officer called the hotel to pass it on, he was told the bombs had already exploded. A direct anonymous warning to the hotel was also too late.

As the ATO who attended the scene wrote in his report: 'Complete carnage resulted in the room concerned. Evaluation of blast effect was not possible due to fire damage.' Twelve people, all Protestants, were burnt to death and twenty-three badly injured. All the bodies were so badly burned that two could only be named by elimination after medical and dental records had identified the others. Survivors, other patrons and staff gave harrowing accounts of the aftermath as rescuers were beaten back by the intense fireball which rapidly gutted the building.

There was an unprecedented wave of revulsion throughout the entire community, but just forty-eight hours later thirty-one buses were torched at the Londonderry bus depot and similar attacks continued, usually with warnings. In many cases hoaxes were set up alongside live devices to delay firefighting work so that buildings blazed as firefighters watched helplessly.

The exceptional work of 321 EOD was recognised in July 1978 by the award of the prestigious Wilkinson Sword of Peace. The company, sword-makers to the British armed forces for over 200 years, instituted the award in 1966 to recognise outstanding efforts by military units in fostering good relations in areas where they are stationed or operating. Recommendations for the award are made each year by the Admiralty, Army and Royal Air Force boards to the Ministry of Defence, which decides the winner. The specially engraved sword and a citation was presented to the unit at a ceremonial lunch in the Cutlers' Hall in the City of London on 21 July 1978, a few weeks before Istead departed. The citation read:

> It is self-evident that the operations of the Unit have saved human life, and there is no doubt that they have both prevented damage to a vast amount of property and helped to prevent terrorists achieving their aim of totally disrupting the economy and society of Northern Ireland.
>
> Since 1969 (to date) the Unit has dealt with some 24,500 calls of which some 9,500 were actual terrorist bombs – adding up to 296,000 lb. of explosives. 3,509 calls were to deliberate hoaxes and 3,419 to finds totalling 125,260 lb. of explosives. Of the actual bombs, 3,800 containing 110,250lbs of explosives were successfully neutralised.

A statistician has estimated that every pound of explosive detonated by terrorists in Northern Ireland causes £1,000 worth of damage. Using this figure it can be estimated that the Unit has prevented about £100 million worth of damage to property in Northern Ireland since 1969. There is no doubt that this saving of property has prevented untold human misery in the form of lost homes and loss of places of work and, in the words of a former Chief Constable of the RUC, has done much to promote goodwill and friendly relations between the community at large and the Security Forces.

Obviously something as intangible as goodwill is very difficult to quantify, but it is an indisputable fact that the actions of the EOD operators, which can be seen by everyone to be totally peaceful in intent and to have no sectarian bias whatsoever, have created a bond between them and the community. To the EOD operator a terrorist bomb, regardless of which terrorist faction has laid it or what the target might be, is something to be rendered harmless with the least possible detrimental effect to people or property.

The number of EOD operators in the Unit at any one time is approximately fifteen. During their four-month tour they are on constant call. In mid-tour they get four days' leave. On average an EOD operator answers calls to approximately 120 incidents during his four-month tour, of which about twenty are live devices. Because of the individual nature of their task there is no doubt that the EOD operators are subject to personal stresses during their tours far greater then those experienced by an average member of the Security Forces.

To date 397 ATOs and ATs have carried out EOD tours in Northern Ireland, including 45 second tours. Their successes have not been achieved without terrible cost nor have they gone totally unrecognised. To date sixteen EOD operators have been killed carrying out their duties and ten injured, three seriously. Their gallantry has been recognised by the award of one GC, three OBEs, six MBEs, twenty-four GMs, twenty-two QGMs, fifteen BEMs, thirty-one MIDs and two GOC's Commendations.

These awards have almost invariably been made to the team leaders, who make the actual approaches to explosive devices. The Unit consists, however, of these and some other men who support them in various ways on operations. It is clear, therefore, that the achievements of the Unit are based on team efforts and not isolated individual actions.

This point was stressed by Brigadier DFA Cowdry, the Director of Land Service Ammunition, who congratulated 321 on the distinction they had earned and said that as far as he was concerned, credit was due in part to every ATO, AT, driver, storeman, clerk, signaller and escort who had ever served with the unit in Northern Ireland. Felix the cartoon cat added his own wry tailpiece in the *RAOC Gazette*. Sword in hand he said: 'Oh my Gawd. This is going to be difficult to swallow.'

Peter Istead was succeeded by Lieutenant-Colonel BR Fox, at a time when the emphasis of the bombing campaign was switching from destruction by incendiary to attacks on the security forces using radio-controlled IEDs. Near Dungannon on 19 July, just before Fox's arrival, eighteen-year-old Private Mark Carnie, serving with the Black Watch, died when a 5 lb. radio-controlled device planted behind a stone wall was detonated as his patrol walked past. A local priest described the murder as 'foul and inexcusable'. A month later, on 17 August, Corporal Robert Miller of the Royal Marines was killed and a colleague injured when a similar device exploded in the boot of a car outside their base at Forkhill.

The 'cat and mouse' threat, with terrorists waiting to pounce on the slightest lack of operational rigour, was all too evident. On 3 November, a grey Renault was stopped by two men who placed a parcel in the car and told the driver to park his vehicle outside the Savoy Cinema at the junction of Merchants Quay and Monaghan Street, Newry. Instead he drove it towards the RUC station and reported the incident to the police. A full clearance was mounted but the parcel was found to contain only candles wrapped in brown paper attached to a battery. Two days later, security forces investigating an explosion near Merchants Quay found a car had blown up about sixty yards from where the terrorists had intended Friday's hoax car to be left. The debris revealed a radio-controlled device had been planted at what would have been the incident control point.

Reacting to what he described as 'the greatest current threat to our soldiers', Fox ordered an in-depth study of the ninety-two incidents involving radio-controlled devices since 1972. The study found that the devices had evolved in three stages. The first utilised the components of a model-aircraft radio-control system, the command passed by the transmitter to the receiver which was wired to activate a switch and complete the firing circuit. The system worked, but stray signals could prematurely detonate the devices, so pulse coding was introduced to provide greater safety for the bomber. With an encoder on the transmitter and a decoder on the receiver, the bomber could set the device to operate only on a given code. This system was still not foolproof and was superseded by codes of tones rather than pulses.

The IRA had also become more proficient at selecting ambush positions. The most vulnerable targets were foot patrols in small villages such as those along the border or in close proximity to their bases where their movements were comparatively easy to predict. The devices were also easy to conceal, especially in cars familiar to the security forces. Sometimes the bomb was put in a hijacked car of the same make, repainted and renumbered to match that of, for example, the local doctor. In August 1976 Private James Borucki, a nineteen-year-old member of the Parachute Regiment, perished in such circumstances. As his patrol were returning to their base in the middle of Crossmaglen, none of them paid more than passing attention to an old-fashioned black bicycle leaning against a wall because they thought they recognised it as belonging to a local man. However, that day the rear carrier of the cycle held a parcel containing 5 lb. of explosive which was detonated by radio control as the patrol passed by. By the end of 1978, there had been eleven radio-controlled bomb attacks in south Armagh, four in Belfast, three in rural border areas of Fermanagh, one in Dungannon and one in Limavady. Another Marine Commando, nineteen-year-old Gareth Wheedon, was killed and two of his colleagues seriously injured in one of these attacks at Crossmaglen on 12 November.

A major upsurge in IRA activity began two days later when six blasts within a thirty-minute period injured thirty-seven people and caused serious damage in Armagh, Belfast, Castlederg, Cookstown, Derry and Enniskillen. The car bomb reappeared as part of the offensive and over the course of the next week another fifty attacks took place. On one day alone ATOs were called to twenty elaborate hoaxes in Belfast and Lurgan. A week later, on 30 November, there was another co-ordinated incendiary and bomb attack in fourteen towns and villages followed by a further eleven attacks on 1 December. An IRA statement admitting the attacks warned that it was prepared for a 'long war'. The year-end statistics showed they had the capacity to sustain it. In the 3 Brigade area, which included a long stretch of the Irish border, the amount of explosive expended was six times higher than in the previous year. The number of EOD taskings for the year dropped from 2,611 to 1,913, the lowest since 1971, but the number of explosions was up from 377 to 465, reflecting the greater frequency of no-warning attacks.

Early in 1979, as bombings continued daily, the security forces scored a notable success. In the early hours of 7 March, they raided a house at

Kilmood Street in east Belfast where they found forty-two 10 lb. explosive charges and timing devices packed into gas cylinders. It was the largest ever haul of operation-ready bombs, but this new record was quickly surpassed by one far less welcome: the largest bomb detonated to date. Trooper Gordon Scott, aged nineteen, was on sentry duty outside the police station at Kinawley on the evening of Sunday 18 March when a car pulling a horsebox halted outside the building. He immediately threw himself to the floor, sounded the siren and shouted through his intercom telling everyone to clear away from the front of the station. He had hardly finished speaking when the 1,000 lb. device went off, bringing down the blast protection wall around the building and blowing a crater six feet deep and more than twice as wide in the road. On 22 March another unwelcome record was set when the IRA mounted the biggest co-ordinated bomb attack of its entire campaign, targeting banks and public buildings in twenty-one towns across Northern Ireland with forty-nine devices which all went off within ninety minutes. The Army estimated that it must have required 100 people to mount the operation.

Operations like these kept the EOD teams at full stretch. Apart from trying to defuse bombs before they went off, finds of arms and explosives had to be cleared by an ATO and the bodies of murder victims could not be removed until they had been checked for booby-traps. On 2 August 1979 the Lurgan-based EOD team were returning from Benburb, where they had been checking a car thought to have been used in the murder of an RUC constable. As their three-vehicle convoy passed over a small bridge at Lisbane, four miles from Armagh, one of two men watching from seventy yards away used a buried command wire to detonate a 500 lb. bomb under the bridge. The two members of the EOD team in the first vehicle heard a loud explosion. One hundred yards behind them, they saw the second vehicle, an armoured Transit, nose down in a massive crater rapidly filling with water. The third, a Land Rover which had been travelling two hundred yards behind, was stopped on the brink of the crater. Immediately after the blast terrorist gunmen fired about four or five shots at the scene and the escort soldiers returned fire while the two surviving members of the EOD team plunged into the fifteen-foot crater, forced open the battered doors of the rapidly sinking Transit and pulled out their two badly injured comrades. A doctor arrived by helicopter within twenty minutes but despite first aid efforts he could only pronounce them dead from multiple injuries. In a follow-up search, a Suzuki 250 motorcycle, two helmets, a .38 revolver and batteries were recovered at the firing point and a farmer later came forward to say he had seen two men running away across a cornfield after failing to get the motorcycle started.

The soldiers' deaths brought the number killed in Northern Ireland since 1971 to 301, and the EOD roll of honour to eighteen. Gunner Richard Furminger, aged nineteen, one of the team's escorts from the Royal Artillery, had been travelling in the passenger seat of the Transit. From Colchester in Essex, he had only been in Northern Ireland for a week, and had told his family during a telephone call that he was 'as happy as a sandboy'. He was the son of a soldier, and had grown up in Singapore, Hong Kong and Gibraltar before joining the Army at sixteen. Signaller Paul Reece, also aged nineteen, was the team's Bleep and had been driving the Transit. He had only been in Northern Ireland for nine days. Hours before the fatal tasking he had posted a letter to his Irish-born mother in Crewe, saying what good mates he had in the unit and how much he was already enjoying the work. The letter, the envelope emblazoned with SWALK, was delivered to his home the day after he died. Six days later he was buried after a Requiem Mass in St Mary's Church, Crewe. His family turned down the offer of a military funeral and the only ceremonial was the sounding of the Last Post by two buglers from the Sea Cadets, in which Reece had served before joining the Army.

Two weeks after the incident, the RUC arrested twenty-year-old Eamon Burns, who initially denied the murders. Midway through his trial in January 1981, he pleaded guilty to manslaughter and was sentenced to ten years' imprisonment.

Chapter Ten

'Every Night is Gelignite'

'Every night is gelignite,' scrawled a Republican graffiti writer in Londonderry at the height of the 1979 bombings. The boast was more propaganda than fact for by then the terrorist bombing campaign in Northern Ireland had peaked and would progressively decline thereafter. The steady fall in EOD taskings over the period, from 1,590 in 1979 to 768 in 1985, reflected the much improved security situation but, comforting as the figures appeared, events on the ground continued to demonstrate an all too familiar ruthlessness. Indeed some of the incidents during these years count among the most notorious of the campaign.

On 27 August 1979, Lord Mountbatten, former supreme commander of Allied forces in south-east Asia during the Second World War, then the last British Viceroy of India, was murdered by the IRA. The Queen's cousin, aged seventy-nine, was out in a small fishing boat at Mullaghmore, County Sligo when a radio-controlled bomb previously smuggled on board exploded, killing him and three others: eighty-two-year-old Lady Brabourne, Nicholas Knatchbull, Mountbatten's fourteen-year-old grandson, and fifteen-year-old crew member Paul Maxwell. Three other close family members were seriously injured. Worse was to come that day. About 4.30 p.m. two lorries and a Land Rover carrying members of the Parachute Regiment were travelling along the northern edge of Carlingford Lough at Narrow Water. As the last lorry passed a trailer of hay in a lay-by, a 500 lb. bomb concealed in the load was detonated by radio control from a firing point across the waterway, which marked the border. Six members of the regiment were killed.

Surviving and arriving troops established an incident control point by the Gate Lodge of nearby Narrow Water Castle while others halted traffic on the busy dual carriageway and maintained cover positions. Almost exactly at 5 p.m. as a Wessex helicopter was taking off with casualties, a second huge explosion took place. Despite the blast the aircraft got airborne but on the ground below another twelve soldiers lay dead amidst swirling smoke and debris. The terrorists waiting across the border had placed a secondary device in the Gate Lodge, correctly calculating that the follow-up operation would be co-ordinated from there. Ten members of the Parachute Regiment and two of the Queen's Own Highlanders, one of them the Commanding Officer, Lieutenant-Colonel David Blair, perished in this 100 lb. blast. The incident remains the British Army's greatest loss of life in a single attack during the Northern Ireland campaign.

It confirmed that the IRA still posed a deadly threat through continued innovation of their IEDs and tactics as well as sheer ruthlessness. There remained a powerful threat from militant Loyalists also but their crude, unstable bombs were as much a danger to the people making and laying them as to their intended victims. Their prime activity continued to be gun attacks on Catholic individuals, premises and organisations. Thanks to advances in technology and equipment, the EOD battle was far from one-sided but the initiative was always in the hands of the terrorist.

Christmas Eve 1979 was a rare occasion when the Number One was not the pivotal figure in a clearance operation. The hero this time was Corporal Derek Chidlow of the Royal Corps of Transport, who earned a GOC's commendation for his skill and concentration in remotely manoeuvring the Eager Beaver forklift in a narrow mews off Donegall Street, Belfast, so that an ATO could deal with what turned out to be a 300 lb. device in a stolen van. On New Year's Eve, recently promoted Sergeant John Anderson demonstrated outstanding qualities of skill and endurance when dealing with seven milk churns near Carrickmore, County Tyrone. In freezing weather conditions, he was forced to haul himself in and out of a cramped culvert to dismantle them. After a clearance lasting two days, the team had just returned to base at Omagh when they were immediately called out again to deal with a blast incendiary attack. The clearance, requiring extreme physical exertion and constant personal risk, earned the ATO the George Medal.

Within a few days, the overall Troubles death toll reached 2,001 when three UDR soldiers, travelling in the first of two Land Rovers, died in a landmine explosion near Castlewellan, County Down. Four others in the second vehicle were injured. Later in January, WO2 Arthur Burns completed a four-month tour at Bessbrook during which he responded to fifty-one taskings and dealt with fourteen live devices. He was mentioned in dispatches for clearing a hijacked petrol tanker at speed so that firefighters could move in to tackle a fire caused by blast incendiaries in Newry. That month, too, WO2 Kevin Callaghan, who had already won the George Medal as a sergeant in 1973, was awarded the Queen's

Gallantry Medal for dismantling a radio-controlled device on a lorry. The vehicle was stolen in the Irish Republic and parked at Cloghogue, near Newry, where the police spotted it and contacted the owner. He noticed a new aerial had been fitted and on closer examination a wire was found running from the cab to the truck body. The main Belfast–Dublin road and railway, which run side by side at that point, were immediately closed and an EOD team was summoned from Bessbrook. During a ten-hour clearance, Callaghan found that 600 lb. of fertiliser-based explosive had been packed into six milk churns and lined up in the lorry on the side nearest the road. The terrorist intention was to detonate them as a suitable target passed just yards away. It was only the second time a radio-controlled device had been recovered intact and it was an important prize for the forensic scientists. Lieutenant-Colonel Peter Forshaw, the CATO, said the device would have 'completely destroyed any passing vehicles and their occupants'. The next day, the *Belfast Telegraph* paid tribute to the bomb-disposal teams.

> The brave man who has to make the long, lonely walk up to a suspect vehicle cannot afford to take any chances. If he fumbles, or makes the wrong decision, there is no second chance, just the certainty of sudden death. It takes a special kind of courage and coolheaded professionalism to be a bomb-disposal officer in Northern Ireland, where the deeds of devilish minds must be undone. The routine announcement that a suspect vehicle has been cleared by Army experts is something that we all take for granted. The sinister details of a device, where one slip would have led to a horrendous fireball or explosion, reminds us of the appalling risks which a group of brave men must take to protect the community from ruthless men. It is right that such heroism should be saluted.

Such sentiments merely spurred the bombers to new excesses. Twenty-five-year-old Captain Mark Wickham and his team spent two days over Easter 1980 clearing a 650 lb. landmine in a cluster of milk churns in a culvert running underneath the main road south from Armagh to Middletown and over the border to Monaghan. If security forces had not been tipped off about the device and the firing point 150 yards away, the detonation would have entailed certain death for any drivers passing over it as well as substantially damaging houses near by.

The body of a man murdered by the IRA became the macabre centrepiece of another fraught clearance operation. About 10.30 p.m. on

11 May, fifty-seven-year-old Anthony Shields, a caretaker in a paper factory, was abducted by four armed men near his home in Crossmaglen. At 9.30 a.m. the following Tuesday morning, his hooded body was discovered at the side of the road at Mounthill, County Armagh, a few yards north of the border. The IRA said they had killed him because he had provided information to the Army about a landmine. Recovering his body was a perilous operation and it was agreed there would be no hasty action. There had been a large explosion in the same area not long before, on 1 May.

The usual surveillance and planning took place and there was evidence that terrorists were watching closely when three shots were fired at a covert patrol on 14 May. Despite this, the operation went ahead as planned at 7.30 the next morning but was quickly frozen when the Bleep detected a radio-controlled device somewhere between the incident control point and the body 100 yards away. It was decided to try and recover the body using a radio-controlled Wheelbarrow but the radio and CCTV signals were interrupted by a crest of high ground. Another attempt was made with a second Wheelbarrow but the result was the same and both vehicles were now stranded. A cable-controlled Wheelbarrow also encountered problems and the operation was ended for the day. During the night an Eager Beaver remote-controlled forklift truck was brought in, but its drive failed. Finally WO2 Malcolm Boscott, the ATO, managed to attach a triple hook and line to the body and establish that it was not booby-trapped, and it was removed from the scene at 9.30 p.m.

Early the next morning Irish police uncovered a firing point and a command wire leading north. After a series of checks, the ATO went forward to the border where he cut the command wire and found that its circuitry was still complete. Everyone within range was ordered to take cover before the senior ATO present passed current into the wire, which triggered an explosion some distance away.

When the operation resumed next morning, the stranded Wheelbarrows were finally recovered by Captain Wickham. Only one of two gas cylinders had gone off, so he cleared the other 200 lb. device before focusing on unearthing the radio-controlled device that had originally threatened the recovery of Anthony Shields's body. Thanks to the skilled work of the Bleep and the Royal Engineers' search team, it had now been pinpointed to a spot a few yards away from where the body had been dumped, where those involved in recovering it would have been within range. By 6 p.m. the ATO had neutralised it, recovering 100 lb. of ANFO with an ANNIE booster from two milk churns linked to a Tupperware box containing a timer-power unit, tone decoder and radio-control receiver. The search team were now able to look for the aerial, which turned out to be a length of black wire concealed in the hedge. The operation was completed by 9 p.m. Lieutenant-Colonel Forshaw, the CATO, remarked: 'This now makes an interesting case history proving that caution pays off.'

As Captain Wickham would soon confirm, caution needed to be tempered with a high proportion of good luck. In the early hours of 8 June 1980, terrorists descended on the Cohannon Inn complex at the end of the M1 motorway near Dungannon, County Tyrone, and laid three blast incendiaries which went off soon afterwards. They also left at least one further device in the mini-supermarket next to a nearby petrol station. Wickham and his team arrived at the scene at 2.30 a.m. to find the pub completely gutted, so they established a control point to deal with whatever had been left in the supermarket. The Bleep found no indication of any radio-controlled device, and Wickham decided to send Wheelbarrow into the shop, but it could not negotiate the steep concrete step. Wickham then put on his EOD suit without its helmet and went forward, but his view in through the shop window was blocked by boxes stacked inside. Going straight in through the front door was the obvious thing to do, but with the caution drummed into him during his hours of training he returned to the window and broke the glass with the padded elbow of his suit to remove some of the boxes.

At this point, for reasons he could not later explain, Private 'Burge' Burgess, the team driver, went to the rear of one of the Transits and brought out a carbon-dioxide fire extinguisher. By then Wickham had removed seven cardboard boxes and was reaching for an eighth when a sheet of flame erupted, followed by a loud explosion. 'I saw the fireball engulf him and the blast lifted him and threw him backwards a couple of yards onto the forecourt,' one of his team remembered later. As Wickham lay there with his EOD suit burning, Burgess rushed forward and doused him with the contents of the fire extinguisher. The Bleep also ran to his aid and pulled away smouldering sections of the suit. As waiting firemen moved in, soldiers gave first aid to the ATO who had extensive burns to his face, hands, chest and abdomen as well as bruising, lacerations and perforated eardrums. A helicopter arrived twenty minutes later and he was flown to the Military Wing of the Musgrave Hospital in Belfast where he hovered on the brink of death for several hours. His condition stabilised within forty-eight hours and he was soon well enough to be evacuated to the specialist burns unit at the Queen Elizabeth Military

Hospital at Woolwich in London, but it was months before he completely recovered. Apart from the driver's intuitive decision to fetch the fire extinguisher, which earned Burgess a formal commendation from the GOC, he believes his survival depended on a further piece of good fortune. 'I am sure that I was exhaling rather than inhaling at the moment the device functioned, which prevented me breathing in flame and therefore minimised my internal injuries.' During his three-month tour of duty Captain Wickham had dealt with thirty-three incidents and was later awarded the Queen's Gallantry Medal for consistent 'courage of a high order'.

Patience as much as caution and concentration were necessary qualities for ATOs. In September 1980 WO2 Malcolm Boscott, serving at Bessbrook, was confronted with a lorry containing fifty-five milk churns. Through repeated approaches he identified the one carrying the device and a booby-trap and set it off with a controlled explosion. Having rendered safe twenty out of the twenty-seven devices he encountered during his tour, he was awarded the Queen's Gallantry Medal. The same month, Staff Sergeant Martin Nicholson was called from Omagh to the Lisnaskea–Newtownbutler road where a bomb had been uncovered in a water-filled culvert. During a twelve-hour clearance he neutralised seven milk churns, each containing 100 lb. of explosive, linked by a command wire running to a firing point with a clear view of the road. About the same time, at Silverbridge, County Armagh, just north of the border, another ATO was dealing with an equally complicated device. After four explosions at telephone junction boxes, which were interpreted as terrorist come-ons, a search and clearance operation quickly focused on two derelict farm buildings. Inside the ATO discovered a 300 lb. bomb buried in the earth floor in gas cylinders, designed to function when any soldiers entered the building.

Although there were many similarly successful operations during the year, there were other setbacks and explosions in which both civilians and members of the security forces died. The IRA's bombs were now consistently reliable and they had made up for the scarcity of commercial explosive by greater reliance on fertiliser-based mix with a booster charge of commercial explosive when they could get it. The recovery of traces of Russian military explosive indicated how far they were now casting their net for supplies, although some explosive was still leaking from the Irish Republic. The controls on detonators had been partly compensated for by a supply from the United States and a switch to other methods of setting off bombs, such as light-bulb elements which could ignite inflammable material. 'Own goals', while rarer than they had been, still occurred. During the year a bomber travelling by train from Lisburn to Belfast killed himself and two passengers when the device on his lap exploded. An accomplice, who survived with disfiguring burns, was nicknamed 'Crisp and Dry' when he eventually was sent to prison.

Over this period, the Army's strength and responsibilities were changing as the expanded and reorganised RUC continued to reclaim the prime role in maintaining law and order. The military force level of 13,000 early in 1979 was steadily reduced to 11,300 over the year and dropped to 9,000 in 1985. The reduction was accompanied by the withdrawal of 3 Brigade headquarters and the reallocation of operational boundaries between 39 Brigade in Lisburn and 8 Brigade, which was run from Ebrington Barracks, Londonderry.

For the EOD teams, from 1980 onwards the Northern Ireland commitment entailed long periods of inactivity punctuated by short periods of intense work. Bombings and shootings declined as the IRA concentrated on street protests to improve prison conditions, while intensified undercover work by police and Army units also contributed to the lull. 'We came out of hibernation and were tasked five times in one week,' the Belfast team reported at one point to the *RAOC Gazette*. The Londonderry section also reported little activity. 'We picked up four jobs in a month, one of them real.' After a bomb attack on the Fort George base, the EOD section there relocated to Ebrington Barracks. By now, all the armoured Pigs and Saracens had been replaced by specially adapted Transit vans. In 1980, as the Army handed the Grand Central Hotel back to its civilian owners for redevelopment, the Belfast teams were relocated to Sydenham and Girdwood, described as 'the last outpost of the British Empire' in one dispatch to the *Gazette*. At the end of a ten-year deployment in Northern Ireland it was calculated that 546 ATOs had served with 321 and during the year its designation was changed from 321 EOD Unit to 321 EOD Company.

The lulls enabled teams to catch up on administration and maintenance and commanders made training more enjoyable with Wheelbarrow races around obstacles such as traffic cones and parked vehicles. Teams also competed to see who could suit up an operator fastest. Watching television and catching up on sleep remained the most popular recreational pastimes but one captain put his leisure to more purposeful use building a one-eighth scale Wheelbarrow out of matchsticks. But the teams still yearned for action, or 'street heat'. 'Skip is getting near to the end of his tour and is sweating on getting a real one,' read another frustrated missive to the *Gazette*. Inevitably the downtime was frequently interrupted and the 321 teams would be back in the thick of the action and danger.

The established campaign pattern continued into 1981. In February a 600 lb. culvert bomb was neutralised near Bessbrook, but five soldiers died in an almost identical ambush near Newry in May. That month another ATO lost his life while following up the murder of a policeman. On 27 May 1981, Constable Mervyn Robinson had been ambushed and shot dead while leaving a public house at Whitecross, County Armagh. The killers were reported to have escaped in a pale blue Ford Cortina and three days later a similar car was found parked at at Drumalane Road, Newry. WO2 Michael O'Neill, serving with the Bessbrook team, arrived to take a look at the vehicle but decided to let it soak for a couple of days. The area was cordoned and a clearance operation began at 4.20 the next morning. First on the ground were the Royal Engineers' search team and the Bleep. Within an hour they declared the area around the car and its underside clear for the ATO to approach. O'Neill first sent forward a Wheelbarrow to open the tailgate of the estate car but the lock was jammed. He then used Wheelbarrow's boom to break the rear window and rock the car from side to side but still could not get it open. After a fault interrupted the CCTV feed from Wheelbarrow, he decided to look around the car himself, with active cover from the Bleep. On his return to the control point he reported nothing visible on the seats or in the luggage compartment.

He then began to ensure the car was completely clear, blowing open the doors with small Cordtex charges and checking for any sign of a device after each one. He then used a hook and line to pull out the carpets and the rear seat cushion, again leaving a precautionary pause after each step. It was the textbook operating procedure, methodical and cautious. Next he opened the bonnet in the same fashion and checked the engine area. Back at the control point, he said he was 'ninety per cent sure' the vehicle was clean and told the team to start packing up and get a tow line ready to remove it for forensic examination. Making his eighth approach to the car for a final check at 7.45 a.m., he removed his EOD helmet because it was misting up. One member of the team recalls O'Neill looking along the side of the car and then leaning in the front passenger door. What happened next cannot be established beyond doubt. The most likely explanation is that the ATO pulled open the glove compartment which was wired to set off a bomb concealed there or in the footwell. Such was the force of the blast that he would not have survived even if he had been wearing his protective helmet. The bomb blew a crater in the ground and shattered the car, throwing large sections of the bodywork, wheels and engine block a considerable distance.

By now, the police had established that the suspect car had been hijacked on the border, resprayed and fitted with false number plates to twin it with a local car. The terrorists also adapted the electronics – probably the glove-compartment light – to trigger the concealed 15 lb. explosive device before the car was used in the murder of the policeman. The booby-trap was intended for anyone investigating that murder. O'Neill, aged thirty-five, was the nineteenth member of 321 EOD to lose his life. He was from Sunderland, married with a son and daughter, and had joined the Army in 1964, becoming an AT before going on active service in Aden. He was two weeks into his second tour in Northern Ireland and had been selected for promotion to WO1.

WO2 Paul Mitchell had the unenviable task of replacing him. Soon after his transfer from Londonderry to Bessbrook, a local radio station broadcast a terrorist taunt challenging the Army to find and defuse a bomb. Despite this added pressure, Mitchell uncovered and dismantled the carefully concealed 700 lb. device which was linked by a 500-yard command wire to a cross-border firing point. Soon afterwards in the same vicinity he neutralised a pressure plate designed to set off another bomb consisting of 20 lb. of commercial explosive and metal shrapnel. The efficiency with which he carried out both jobs earned him a mention in dispatches.

On 17 June a soldier patrolling in Crossmaglen had a fortunate escape after he pulled at the corner of an anti-Thatcher poster attached to the door of a derelict building. A commercial mercury tilt switch was glued to a corner of the poster and linked through a detonator to 5 lb. of Frangex in a pouch on the back of the door. Fortunately for the soldier only the detonator exploded.

The year was marked by a number of significant captures of explosives but in tandem with their continued attacks in Northern Ireland, IRA teams continued to cause regular explosions in mainland Britain, mostly in the London area. They believed that such outrages were more likely to inflame public opinion now that people had become so tired of hearing about the endless conflict in Northern Ireland that the deaths of soldiers were often not even reported in the national newspapers. One such attack was mounted at a Wimpy fast-food bar in London's busy Oxford Street on 26 October 1981 and Kenneth Howorth, one of Scotland Yard's explosives team, was sent to deal with a 5 lb. bomb left in a men's toilet. The bomb's anti-handling device functioned, killing fifty-year-old Howorth instantly. Like the other members of the Yard team, he was a veteran of 321 EOD in Northern Ireland. (Howorth was the third of three bomb-disposal experts killed by the IRA outside Northern Ireland. The first had been Captain Ronald Wilkinson in 1973 and the second was another ex-RAOC officer attached to Scotland Yard, Captain Roger Goad, who died on 29 August 1975 while attempting to defuse a bomb in Kensington High Street in west London. Goad, already decorated for bomb-disposal gallantry in Cyprus and Northern Ireland, was post-humously awarded the George Cross.

Just in time for Christmas 1981, cars were allowed back into Belfast's closely guarded city centre at night for the first time in seven years. The offensive against the terrorists was succeeding and the majority of people of Northern Ireland, with the help of 321, had refused to be beaten by the bombers. The slow march back to 'normality' had begun. The first major incident of 1982, however, focused attention back on the Belfast–Dublin railway. On 17 January a hijacked tanker was placed under the railway bridge at Meigh and burned out after a large explosion during EOD action. On 8 February the IRA mounted its first no-warning car bomb attacks for some time, in a return to the strategy of attacking civilian targets and threatening the economy. Staff Sergeant Lee Hayter thwarted their intentions in Lurgan on 8 February when he dismantled a 100 lb. device in the boot of a car against a thirty-minute timer. His mention in dispatches said he achieved the 'rapid render-safe through ingenious improvisation and professional expertise, making the bomb safe with five minutes on the clock and avoiding massive destruction of life and property'. About this time another team defused a 200 lb. car bomb in Lisburn. The four of them were later presented with shields bearing the borough coat of arms as a mark of appreciation.

There was a more concerted effort at destruction on 15 March with simultaneous evening strikes in Belfast, Newry, Newtownards, Armagh and Banbridge. An eleven-year-old boy waiting for a lift home from school was killed and thirty-four people injured as the last device went off in a crowded shopping street. The frequency of terrorist outrages had dropped significantly by now but they were more thoroughly planned and ruthlessly executed than ever before, with gunmen and bombers, often in combination, exploiting every vulnerability they could find in the security forces' operations. Every effort was made to avoid routine movements, create a pattern or respond to 'come-ons', but, as a triple killing on 25 March 1982 illustrated, terrorists were all too adroit in spotting any opportunity to strike.

For years Springfield Road police station in west Belfast, jointly occupied by police and soldiers, had been a virtual fortress. A blast wall had been built around it, surmounted by high wire screens to prevent missiles being thrown over and to thwart snipers operating from high buildings in the densely populated residential area, but those coming in and out of the station were at high risk. Their vehicles had to slow down on a busy road to come in and out and frequently had to wait for traffic. Late on 24 March a nearby house was taken over by gunmen who held the occupants hostage overnight. Next morning, when two Land Rovers pulled out of the base, they opened fire with rifles and an M60 heavy machine gun. Three soldiers from the Royal Green Jackets, due to return to their base in Germany only forty-eight hours later, died in the hail of gunfire and five other people were injured. A corporal who had been driving the first vehicle managed to reach the house, but the gunmen escaped through the rear. The corporal was later awarded the Military Medal. In line with standard practice, before the firing point could be combed for any forensic evidence an EOD team was called in. They found a booby-trapped explosive device containing six-inch nails concealed at the rear of the house to maim or kill any police officer or soldier pursuing the gunmen. WO2 Roger Davies was mentioned in dispatches for 'displaying courage above and beyond the normal requirements of his duties' during the three hours it took to neutralise the bomb.

On 9 April there was a renewed incendiary blitz when seventeen cassettes with new electronic ignition and seven-hour timers made their debut in Belfast. Only five caused fires and the rest were neutralised. Eleven days later there was another concerted bombing operation with eight attacks right across Northern Ireland. The first came at 4.45 p.m. when armed men placed three blast incendiaries at Auto Supplies in Lower Irish Street, Armagh. The building was destroyed by fire before the ATO arrived. At 5.32 the Ulster Bank in Strabane was evacuated after a warning and suffered extensive damage when the 200 lb. car bomb exploded. At the same time a similar device went off at the Linen Hall in Ballymena, but the area had been cleared after a twenty-five-minute warning and there were no injuries. At 5.55 p.m. a Wheelbarrow was damaged at Tuffel Street, Londonderry, when another 200 lb. device exploded while the ATO was working at it. A couple of minutes later yet another 200 lb. car bomb exploded at a garage at Millvale Road,

Bessbrook. Thirty minutes after that came the first of two attacks in Belfast. A 100 lb. device exploded at James Street South in the city centre. An ATO then neutralised two beer-keg bombs, each containing 100 lb. of HME, in a car abandoned in Donegall Street. The final attack came at a minute before midnight when a car bomb went off in Market Street, Magherafelt. Two men were killed while moving their vehicles from a nearby car park.

On 25 June, twenty-six people were injured by another car-bomb attack in Belfast and the next day a record 1,600 lb. IRA car bomb went off on the Springfield Road. Attacks on security forces continued and on 27 October three members of the RUC were killed at Kinnego Embankment, Lurgan, when 800 lb. of HME was set off by command wire, destroying their armoured patrol car. Another officer and his female civilian companion died on 9 November when a booby-trap bomb attached to the underside of his car exploded outside the Lakeland Forum Leisure Centre in Enniskillen, County Fermanagh. Earlier in July, the police had warned of just such a device, inserted into black plastic piping and attached with powerful industrial magnets.

The breakaway Republican group, the Irish National Liberation Army, was responsible for the worst outrage of the year. For some months they had become steadily more active and indiscriminate. In September they laid a booby-trap ambush for an Army patrol in Belfast's Divis Flats complex. When the device concealed in a drainpipe was set off, a fourteen-year-old schoolboy was killed, an eleven-year-old was injured and died the next day and twenty-year-old Lance-Bombardier Kevin Waller died from his injuries three days later, on 20 September. Another soldier was very seriously hurt but survived. On 19 October the headquarters of the Ulster Unionist Party in Glengall Street, Belfast, was badly damaged by a bomb attributed to the INLA.

At this point, INLA terrorists from Londonderry were paying weekly visits to the Droppin' Well pub and disco at Limavady, frequented by off-duty soldiers from Ballykelly barracks nearby, to assess if the risk of civilian casualties was balanced by the presence of enough soldiers to mount an attack. At 11.15 p.m. on 6 December, while about 150 people were drinking and dancing in the disco, 5 lb. of commercial explosive concealed next to a stanchion supporting the roof exploded without warning. The thick concrete roof slab collapsed on the crowd, killing or injuring many who had been out of the range of the blast. Altogether eleven members of the Cheshire Regiment were killed and six civilians, four of them women. Margaret Thatcher, the prime minister, described it as 'one of the most horrifying crimes in Ulster's tragic history'.

The annual toll of death and destruction would have been much worse but for the continued hard work of the security forces. Among their successes was the capture of 1.5 tons of gelignite in a lorry at Banbridge, County Down, on 28 August. Two ATOs were awarded the Queen's Gallantry Medal. Staff Sergeant Michael Berridge was called to the Cobweb Inn at Crumlin where he found a petrol can and a sports bag from which ticking could clearly be heard. Despite the time that had elapsed since the bomber's shouted warning, he decided the can was a decoy and so he approached the bag, set up the Pigstick disrupter and neutralised it. WO1 David Walker was decorated for recovering a new type of radio-controlled device intact. It had been built into a dry-stone wall along with 400 lb. of explosives and he had to make seven approaches during the eleven-hour operation. His citation stated: 'The Warrant Officer was well aware of the added risks to his life which the recovery of the device undamaged imposed but disregarded them in the justified hope that analysis of the device would enable safety measures to be discovered.'

After 321 EOD's annual inspection in 1983, Major AJ Taylor, the commanding officer, congratulated the company on the 'very high standard obtained'. The second-in-command of the Army in Northern Ireland, Major General Peter Chiswell, the Commander Land Forces, said that the EOD teams were 'greatly admired and respected by every member of the security forces in the province. They also enjoy a world-wide reputation for their professional excellence and skill. I am also pleased to note that they are supported by a competent administrative team without which their effectiveness would be severely limited.' In step with the reduction in violence and the steady run-down of the garrison in Northern Ireland, 321 EOD was now fielding only ten teams.

Among the setbacks in 1983 was the murder of a policeman on the street in Armagh by a command-wire device. A soldier was killed by a radio-controlled device in a lamp-post on a Belfast street; four UDR soldiers were killed in a command-wire landmine blast near Dungannon and three RUC officers died when a long-delay timer triggered a bomb in the ceiling of a lecture theatre at the Ulster Polytechnic in Jordanstown (now the University of Ulster). There was concern about the growing threat from advances in electronic technology. For instance, a package intercepted in the post had been found to contain 5 lb. of Frangex with an electronic timer that could be set for twelve days, three hours and sixteen minutes, according to a bench test at the Weapons and Explosives Research Unit (formerly the Data Reference Centre). In other incidents, one soldier was killed in Belfast and another in Londonderry by remotely-detonated bombs in derelict buildings on their patrol routes. Another soldier died in Omagh when his car was booby-trapped while he was off duty drinking in a bar with a colleague, who lost a leg and suffered other serious injuries. In a similar attack, Charles Armstrong, a fifty-four-year-old part-time major in the UDR and Ulster Unionist chairman of Armagh District Council, died when his booby-trapped car exploded after a council meeting.

There were ninety-eight finds of explosives, 106 devices dismantled and over five tons of explosive captured during 1983. One of the main police establishments in Belfast, Castlereagh, was saved from serious damage in August when a 500 lb. device on a milk lorry was intercepted and neutralised. WO1 Richard Warner was mentioned in dispatches for preventing the destruction of a timber yard in Newry after terrorists planted blast incendiary devices; five ignited, but in an eleven-hour overnight operation eight were neutralised by the ATO, who had to work on foot along narrow gangways between the timber stacks. WO1 Alexander Calvert handled one of the year's most gruesome EOD tasks on 13 July when he was called to clear a car abandoned close to the border near Crossmaglen. There were two bodies in the boot, those of local Catholics who had been shot dead in the Irish Republic. The ATO had every reason to fear a booby-trap but he earned a mention in dispatches for clearing the area and car by manual rather than explosive means to avoid disfiguring the bodies, a process that took him several hours. Lieutenant Gary O'Sullivan, on a tour in Belfast, earned himself a similar honour after a Ford Transit van was abandoned near a routine RUC checkpoint on the Falls Road in Belfast on 26 April. Inside he found 500 lb. of explosive. Over six hours he succeeded in neutralising the unseen device, linked to a method of initiation never seen before, and recovering it intact for analysis. It consisted of two copper plates insulated by greaseproof paper and was intended to be initiated by a sniper firing a shot through the plates.

Although the company did not lose any members in action during the year, one serving member died after a motorcycle accident. Sergeant Leslie McKenzie, aged thirty and married with a daughter, was attached to 321 from the Royal Signals. He was injured on a scrambling track near Hillsborough on 23 May and died next day in the intensive care unit of the Royal Victoria Hospital without regaining consciousness.

1984, according to one ATO, was 'a quietish year' but only by the brutal standards of the early Troubles. Eight soldiers and policemen died in five landmine attacks, four soldiers died in under-car booby-trap incidents, two civilians were killed by other booby-traps and in Londonderry a 200 lb. roadside bomb killed a Royal Military Police officer driving a minibus to collect a party of military wives for a day out. Two terrorists lost their lives in 'own goals', one of them, in Londonderry, being hit by debris thrown up by the landmine he had just detonated which injured patrolling soldiers but inflicted no other fatalities. An undercover soldier was killed, as were two terrorists, in a shoot-out which foiled the laying of an ambush for the police on a country road near the border in County Fermanagh. The Loyalist UVF were responsible for two deaths when a holdall bomb planted outside the home of a Catholic woman in south Belfast detonated while she and a police officer were examining it.

From the EOD teams' perspective, the most significant operation of the year was a six-day clearance operation on the border, the longest of the campaign to date. After Royal Marine Commandos spotted a petrol tanker abandoned a few miles from Crossmaglen, WO1 Frank Smith and his team from Bessbrook were assigned to clear it on 15 October. Mindful that the IRA had had plenty of time to work on the tanker, which had been missing for several days, and of the history of complex, multi-device ambushes laid in the area in the past, the ATO was in no hurry to approach. The first step was to obtain high-quality aerial photographs of the area. Armed with this data and other surveillance reports, he and his team got to work with a specialist Royal Engineers search team and the CATO, Lieutenant Colonel MD Hall GM, as consultant. Their first target was the tanker itself which, after a painstaking examination, Smith found to be empty. It was clear that the vehicle was a lure to draw him into a trap. In the words of his citation for the Queen's Gallantry Medal, 'despite the dangers and difficulties of terrain, weather and sheer mental and physical exhaustion, Warrant Officer Smith went about his render-safe procedures in a cool, efficient and unhurried manner which reassured all those about him and undoubtedly saved the lives of a number of the security forces.' In all there were three elaborately booby-trapped devices surrounding the tanker, each containing 700 lb. of explosive, which he safely neutralised and destroyed in a series of controlled explosions. One of the devices incorporated a pressure plate, while another was intended to be set off by radio command. The Army spokesman later commented, 'The terrorists had gone to an awful lot of trouble to catch us out with particularly fiendish devices.'

Chapter Eleven

'A Squalid Act of Multiple Murder'

On the evening of 28 February 1985 eleven police officers were relaxing in the canteen at the rear of the bomb-battered police station at Corry Square in the town centre of Newry. Some two hundred yards away to the south, across a complex of buildings and a row of shops, was crowded Monaghan Street and opposite that again was the dark, deserted yard of the former Armaghdown creamery. There a group of furtive terrorists were aligning a red Ford flatbed lorry, its payload covered by a black tarpaulin, with the winking red navigation lights on the station's communications mast.

Preparations had begun five hours earlier when the lorry was hijacked near Crossmaglen by a man wearing a Ronald Reagan mask. The driver was still being held hostage to prevent him reporting the theft. During the afternoon, a steel frame holding nine launcher tubes had been bolted to the rear of the lorry. Each tube was angled forward over the cab and there was a layer of pallets to the front and rear of the frame, all concealed under a tarpaulin. Wires ran from the bottom of each tube into the cab, through a thin section of black pipe, to a detonation unit in a wooden box on the passenger seat. It consisted of two one-hour Memopark timers, two microswitches, an electrical motor, relay switches and batteries. Finally the heavy mortar bombs themselves, with stabilising fins welded on the rear, were loaded into the tubes. Made from four-foot lengths of heavy duty seven-inch metal piping, each contained an explosive charge of 45 lb. of ANNIE and up to a yard of Cordtex fuse to accelerate detonation. At the base of each mortar bomb, connected to the US-made igniter and firing pack, was a separate propellant charge of sodium chlorate mixture which would get the weighty mortar bomb into the air. Threaded to the top end of each mortar was a separate fuse to set off the main explosive charge on impact. In late afternoon, with the work complete, the lorry was driven the short distance to Newry and the timers were set running. At 6.36 p.m., when the timers expired, the pack of a dozen batteries powered up the firing switch in the cab, set off the igniters and sent the mortars arching high over the roof tops towards their target at one-and-a-half-second intervals.

Inside the canteen, one of the police officers recognised the sudden series of thuds as the sounds of a mortar launch and shouted for people to move. As he did so he heard the thump of the larger blasts as the mortars landed and exploded. He ran from the canteen with debris falling around him as another mortar plunged into the flimsy portable building and exploded. Eight of the other nine officers in the canteen at the time were killed; the ninth, a woman officer, was pulled from the debris by frantic colleagues, but her legs and one arm had been blown off and she died before reaching hospital. Another thirty-seven people were injured in the incident, the majority by flying glass and debris. It was and remains the largest RUC death toll in a single terrorist incident.

The improvised mortars were known as Mark 10s by the bomb-disposal teams and had been used eighteen times since 1979. The weapon was notoriously inaccurate and therefore indiscriminate. In this attack only one device hit the station, accounting for all the fatal casualties. The other eight mortars landed in adjoining streets where six exploded. If any had fallen short they could have devastated any of the shops or a restaurant under the flight path. The attack was described by the Northern Ireland Secretary, Douglas Hurd, as 'a squalid act of multiple murder'.

The origins of the mortar threat lay back in the earliest days of the conflict, when troops could go back to their bases and relax in comparative safety after even the most bruising confrontations on the streets. Although many were originally billeted in far from ideal conditions, determined efforts were made to provide more comfortable accommodation. Soldiers were no longer sleeping in commandeered factories, parked buses, school halls or the corridors of police stations. Instead they were living in converted mills, factories and other quarters, which had been fitted out with dormitories, bunks, showers, kitchens, television rooms and other facilities to make life comparatively congenial. Subsidised telephones enabled them to keep in touch with their families, mainly in Britain and Germany. As we have seen, by conventional military standards the Grand Central Hotel in Belfast provided sheer luxury for the units in residence, including a 321 EOD section. Where some still had to live in cramped conditions for operational reasons, such as along the Belfast 'peace line', they were regularly rotated so that the discomfort was shared around. At the main barracks, which pre-dated the Troubles, prefabricated buildings had been hastily erected to provide not only living but administrative space for a garrison that had almost quintupled in size.

In the very early days, there were almost two hundred police stations in Northern Ireland. Although they were fortified with steel window shutters with firing ports, sandbags and barbed-wire entanglements during the IRA's 1956–62 campaign, these had long since been taken away and for years most stations were protected by nothing more than sturdy front doors. Once the Troubles started, round-the-clock sentries and the usual sandbagged posts were put in place, but to begin with the most serious threat they faced was from stones or bottles. In due course blast bombs and grenades were also lobbed at the bases and suitcase bombs were even planted in the front offices of police and Army posts. Whatever the weapon used, the attackers had to come close and were therefore highly vulnerable to capture or fire. However, as the level of fortification increased they tried to find ways of attacking from beyond the perimeter fences and stand-off areas created around vulnerable locations. The first device they improvised, the 'spigot grenade' as the Army christened it, was projected from a standard shotgun. Consisting of up to a pound of gelignite packed into a six-inch pipe taped to a wooden dowel, it was primitive and highly hazardous to the person firing it and soon fell out of favour.

During the evening of 21 June 1972, however, the equation for protecting sleeping and resting soldiers changed dramatically when two makeshift devices were fired into the yard at Albert Street Mill, where they fell without exploding. An ATO from the resident EOD team recovered the containers for detailed examination. Four nights later a car which failed to stop at a checkpoint was chased by soldiers who found six similar mortars together with a launcher barrel. This capture enabled EOD and forensic science staff to test the weapon, which was designed to be held with one hand, aimed and then fired with the other hand from a rotating barrel. On impact, a chisel-pointed striker was driven against a .22 cartridge setting off a charge of about ten ounces of blasting explosive in the main body of the mortar, constructed from twelve inches of two-inch-diameter copper pipe. Three metal fins fitted to the base contained the propellant charge, a .303 ball round. The entire device was fired from a launch tube and ignited by a shotgun cartridge. The design was far from reliable. The mortar could wobble or spin in flight and would fail to detonate on landing if the angle of impact damaged the nose fuse, which the experts said was of 'ingenious design'. The lack of a safety mechanism or a delay circuit meant that it could kill its user if it was dropped. Probably because of these drawbacks it was used only once more, twelve months later. By then another model, the Mark 2, had taken its place.

Meanwhile a conventional and far more threatening military weapon came into the hands of the IRA: the RPG7 shoulder-launched rocket which, according to a contemporary military report, was 'the most significant escalation during the period', providing the IRA with 'long-range attack capability'. On 28 November 1972 it was used for the first time when terrorists opened fire on the RUC station in the border village of Belleek, County Fermanagh. Fifty-five-year-old Constable Robert Keys was coming down the stairs to go off duty at 9.25 a.m. when the rocket penetrated a steel shutter, hit him and killed him instantly. The weapon was used in eight other attacks that day against two Army bases in Belfast, police stations at Strabane, Crossmaglen, Pomeroy and Lisnaskea, a Saracen armoured personnel carrier in Belfast, which was not hit, and a four-ton lorry in Lurgan. Six soldiers were injured in that attack and another at Crossmaglen. The next day it was again used against an Army base and a Saracen in Belfast, and at another base in Newry where two shots missed.

Despite the misses, the weapon posed a serious threat to security forces both in their bases and out on patrol and immediate steps were taken. High wire-netting screens and canopies were erected around and over police stations and Army bases so that warheads would explode harmlessly in the air. The vulnerability of even armoured vehicles was concealed from personnel on the ground for a time until a programme of up-armouring was completed, but even that offered only limited protection. Over the next twenty years the RPG7 would kill or injure another five security-force personnel. RUC Constable Alexander Beck was killed and Constable Michael Paterson injured in Belfast on 28 September 1981 when an RPG7 round smashed into the side of their Land Rover. The last recorded use of the weapon was in May 1991 when another policeman, Sergeant Stephen Gillespie, was killed while his Land Rover was fired on during a patrol in the Falls Road area of Belfast. Over the years it was used in some 200 attacks but about three in four rounds missed. In one such case in February 1984, when a stray shot narrowly missed a classroom full of children, there was a considerable community backlash against the terrorists.

On 5 December 1972, just after the initial assaults with the RPG7, the IRA made first use of the Mark 2 mortar at the Bligh's Lane Army post in Londonderry. The warhead, with a 2 lb. explosive charge, was not hand-launched but fired from an L-shaped base plate. There was a built-in firing pin with a five-second delay and the nose-cone fuse was simplified to help ensure detonation on impact. Twenty-five of them were used in the next four months but their reliability was no greater than the first design, for the basic aiming problem was compounded by the violent movement of the base plate on launch. Their inherent instability was demonstrated in December 1972 by the incident at Lurgan in which Sergeant Roy Hills was killed, but they continued to be used for another eight months while another variation was produced.

The Mark 3 made its debut on 20 June 1973 when sixteen were fired in Londonderry and Omagh. The accuracy of the aiming had been improved by strengthening the base plate and introducing an aiming quadrant which set the line of fire by rotating the barrel and locking it into position. This proved quite effective and in one attack the mortars all fell in within thirty yards from a distance of 300 yards. This was partly achieved by halving the filling of the main charge to 1 lb. of ANAL – ammonium nitrate and ground aluminium – with a length of detonating cord as a booster. The device was not entirely foolproof: on 16 August 1973 a flash-through set off the main charge in the launching tube and killed two terrorists who were carrying out a multiple mortar attack on the RUC station at Pomeroy. The same fault made the bombs liable to tumble or even explode in flight. Army intelligence learned that such was the loss of confidence among IRA activists that threats had been made to kneecap any 'Volunteers' who refused to carry out attacks. Nevertheless 105 mortars were fired in fourteen attacks in the six months after its introduction.

By now CATO John Gaff, as the main explosives adviser to the GOC, was becoming concerned. With the IRA conducting its own trial-and-error process to develop a more viable weapon, he needed to know more about the probable range, accuracy and effects of mortars. Recovered examples were evaluated at Fort Halstead in Kent where the experts concluded: 'The probability of striking a specific target such as a house or command post is low even when the mortar is rigidly clamped at a fixed angle of elevation but the probability of striking an "area" target [within 200 yards' maximum range] is much higher.' The Royal Engineers were commissioned urgently 'to investigate methods and to recommend suitable measures to protect service hutting against improvised mortar bombs'. A conference of all available experts came up with a number of possible solutions including waterproofed mattresses, slabs of concrete, sandbags, concrete foam and glass-fibre reinforced concrete (GRC). Further research into these and other materials was conducted at Fort Halstead, the Building Research Station at Watford and the 22 Engineer Regiment base at Tidworth. More captured IRA mortars were shipped over, refilled with Gelamex and tested against GRC on 29 June at Fort Halstead. The trials showed that the mortar shell could fragment into as many as 400 pieces and that the smaller the fragment, the greater was its penetrating effect. None of the test panels of GRC provided complete protection but the best results were obtained from combining panels in a 'sandwich'. A further series of firings using eight other building materials on 19 July demonstrated that the best results were obtained with needleloom, chipboard and hardboard 'sandwiches', a combination that was lighter, cheaper and more easily installed than GRC. A third series of proving tests was arranged, this time using two huts specially erected for the purpose on Salisbury Plain. After five Gelamex-loaded mortars were detonated against a hut roof, it was unexpectedly found that two layers of standard one-inch chipboard provided as much protection as the more expensive 'sandwich'. Recognising that complete protection could not be guaranteed, the Engineers concluded that a stand-off screen and the chipboard layers provided the best solution. A further set of firings to compare results between two and three layers of chipboard showed that the third added little extra protection.

Based on this research, the go-ahead was given in early September 1973 for the Royal Engineers to begin putting protective measures in place on the Nissen and Twynham huts that had been thrown up to accommodate the influx of troops since 1969. The EOD headquarters at Lisburn, for instance, occupied a couple of unprotected portable buildings positioned just behind the main three-storey office complex at Headquarters Northern Ireland. An NCO and eight Sappers were given two days to shield each hut using pre-cut chipboard, at an average cost of £500 per building. The project overlapped with the introduction of the Mark 3 mortar in June 1973, which continued to be used until November 1977 although a Mark 4 replaced it as the weapon of choice in February 1974. Thirty were fired at the beleaguered RUC Strabane border station but fourteen failed to function and were rendered safe by the ATO and removed for testing. These contained the same weight of ANAL filling as their predecessor but some included ball bearings and other shrapnel to maximise injuries. Again changes had been made to the design. The safety mechanism had been removed and this model was simply dropped in the launcher tube and sent on its way like a conventional military mortar. This overcame the possibility of a flash-through, but the bomb still could go off in the launch tube if the propellant charge failed to ignite. The last recorded use took place only six months after it was introduced.

Good intelligence work imposed a significant setback on the IRA on 14 May 1974, when security forces raided a small engineering workshop at Cushendall, County Antrim, and found details of IRA mortar experiments and a prototype of the newest model, going back to first principles with a simplified firing mechanism. The design was designated the Mark 5 but because of the capture it was never fired in anger. The IRA's weapons development activities were predictably not confined to one facility and another discovery at a welder's workshop in Belfast on 30 July forestalled the introduction of yet another improvised weapon, the 40 mm. mortar. The warhead, with an 8 oz payload and no tail fins, was designed to be fired from a handheld launcher with a piece of carpet wrapped round it to protect the operator's hand. A launcher and twenty shells were seized in the workshop but a small number of the weapons had already been distributed within the IRA and eight were fired in Belfast over the next four months.

The Mark 6 mortar made its first appearance in spectacular style when thirty were fired from across the border and all exploded on impact inside the Army observation post at Drumackavall in County Armagh on 28 September 1974. Preliminary examination of the fragments by the ATO suggested that it had a greater range and was both safer and more reliable than any previous version. Other attacks on the same target followed in quick succession but on 22 October twenty-eight Mark 6 mortars and three launcher barrels were found at a bakery in Belfast. They were sent immediately for firing trials at RARDE. When the data came back, Lieutenant-Colonel John Gaff commented in his monthly report:

> The equipment and ammunition are the most advanced of their type which have been used up to the present time. Much thought and care has been taken to produce it. Manufacture would require the facility of a light engineering factory or a considerable home workshop including a metal lathe and heavy welding equipment. Excellent workmanship is evident, the best examples being in the production of the bomb outer body and the initiating system. The [handwritten] user instructions give the impression of past military experience of a specialised nature, probably of weapons, although the writer does not register as having had the benefit of a high standard of education.

One of the most novel features of this new seven-inch mortar, which could hold an 8 oz explosive charge, was a wind-driven nose propeller which rotated in flight and armed the device to explode on impact, reducing the danger of it igniting before launch or by if dropped. In-flight stability was improved with redesigned fins. A military report conceded that in just twenty-seven months the IRA had developed a relatively sophisticated device from an extremely primitive start. The Mark 6 remained a basic IRA weapon for the next few years. Early modifications involved a new arrangement of eight rather than three tail fins cut from aluminium heat-exchanger pipe, and the introduction of remote firing. Indications that this version was being produced in substantial quantities in professional conditions were confirmed during 1975 when police in the Irish Republic discovered a factory in north Dublin making firing tubes from industrial piping. In January 1976, again south of the border, Irish police uncovered a light-engineering works at Ballyconnell, County Cavan, where lathes and other specialised equipment were being used to make mortar shell casings. The growing threat accelerated the protection programme for security-force buildings and fuel tanks and soon they were festooned with large stretches of wire-netting 'mortar catchers'.

After a brief period free from mortar attacks, a salvo of bombs fired at an army base from the garden of a nearby house in west Belfast signalled a new phase of violence in February 1976. Eight similar assaults took place elsewhere but another operation was foiled when primed mortars were discovered ready to be fired at Cloona House, Dunmurry, the residence of the GOC, Lieutenant-General Sir David House. Soon afterwards he moved inside Thiepval Barracks, a couple of miles away. CATO's monthly report recorded that 'mortars are rarely successful due to inaccuracy, failures and poor fragmentation'. However, an attack in March on Aldergrove airport was the first time a non-security target had been chosen for mortar attack and it marked a significant new means of delivery. In a method that would quickly become standard, the mortar tubes were embedded in sand on the back of a hijacked ten-ton lorry and the propellant charge was initiated electronically by a purpose-built timer-power unit rather than a shotgun cartridge. Another innovation was revealed when nine bombs were seized in Dungannon in February 1977. The casings were made from cast iron, a change that increased fragmentation on detonation and exposed anyone in the vicinity to deadly shards of flying metal.

More significant developments had been revealed on 31 August 1976 when ten mortars were fired at the security-force base in Crossmaglen. They were launched electronically in pairs at 2.5-second intervals from tubes in a wooden frame on the back of a lorry, another first that would become standard. This variant, designated the Mark 8, incorporated features from earlier warheads: Mark 3 tail fins, the Mark 6 wind-driven propeller and a casing elongated from seven to thirty inches to accommodate a sixfold increase in the explosive charge, to 3 lb. Weapons intelligence concluded the terrorists had taken a significant step forward by increasing the payload but that this version was:

> . . . the result of bastardising a mortar bomb from existing material by persons other than the designer. The terrorist is displaying a require-ment to deliver an increased warhead for greater material damage with scant regard to accuracy, flight, ballistics or range. All the technical advances which culminated in the Mark 6 have been rejected in favour of inaccurate delivery of large charges the propaganda effect of which outweighs that achieved by many Mark 6s on the target.

These words proved all too prophetic. On 23 October 1976, five double salvoes of mortars were fired at the joint RUC-Army base at Crossmaglen. Five soldiers were injured, there was extensive damage to buildings and one mortar actually pierced the roof of the main building and destroyed living quarters. 'This is the most successful mortar attack by the PIRA so far in terms of accuracy, reliability and damage to per-sonnel and equipment,' reported Derrick Patrick, the CATO. However, when the warheads had been more thoroughly evaluated and designated Mark 9, the conclusion was that the terrorists had been prepared to use the most hazardous system yet in order to inflict maximum casualties. The warhead body was an adapted industrial gas cylinder packed with 10 lb. of explosive. Because of the danger of premature explosion the array of mortars had been fired from a distance by command wire.

With the advent of the Marks 8 and 9, all the indications were that the IRA was now prepared to forgo accuracy and range in an effort to achieve headline-making results.

In January 1977 this high-risk strategy became all too clear when five warheads were fired at a security base in west Belfast. Although they landed a hundred yards short in the grounds of a school where a youth club meeting was taking place, there were no serious injuries. Attacks continued intermittently, including a number of similar near-misses in terms of casualties, but it was over two years before the next upgrade was used, this time with a disastrous result.

During the afternoon of 19 March 1979, a volley of mortars was fired from a lorry close to the joint RUC–Army base at Newtownhamilton,

County Armagh. Seven landed inside the base, one killing twenty-one-year-old Private Leslie Woolmore of the Queen's Regiment, the first death caused by a mortar. Four more soldiers and police officers were injured as well as civilians in nearby shops and houses. Seven mortars detonated in all, each four feet six inches long and containing 40 lb. of explosive. This was another new model, designated the Mark 10, the most lethal, and indiscriminate to date. Its weaknesses were vividly demonstrated on the afternoon of Saturday 19 April 1980 when ten were fired on the police station at busy Corry Square in Newry. Twenty-six people were injured and there was extensive damage to adjoining property. A blast incendiary in the lorry cab was set to go off five minutes after the main volley. Though this failed to detonate, the tactic became standard, intended to destroy any debris of evidential value.

The growing threat to the lives of police officers and soldiers prompted the development of a prefabricated blast-resistant building, the 'Mark 10 cube', made from layered panels of steel and concrete. A list of the most vulnerable stations was drawn up and over the next few years about a dozen of the new buildings were erected. Such was the continued concern about the threat of mortar attack that in August 1981 the police took the highly unusual step of warning the public of the risk. They said that in the previous eight years there had been eighty attacks using 466 mortars, of which three out of four had fallen off-target on houses, school grounds, sports fields and a car park adjoining security-force locations.

The prospect of civilian casualties arising from overshoots appeared not to concern the IRA. Just before lunchtime on Saturday 12 November 1983, six armed men halted a heavy Seddon Atkinson 300 truck near Pomeroy, County Tyrone and took it and the driver to a shed near Carrickmore. There over the next five hours a group of men drilled six holes in the tipper body of the truck and set up a steel frame supporting ten mortar tubes. The mortars, Mark 10s each holding 45 lb. of ANNIE with a 10 lb. booster, were then loaded into the tubes and wired up to the launching mechanism. During the afternoon a seven-months-pregnant woman cooked food for the terrorists while they worked.

Just before six, the lorry was abandoned close to the perimeter wall of the newly-built Pomeroy police station. Almost immediately, at one-second intervals, the mortars were lobbed up into the sky across the helicopter landing pad towards the buildings inside the base. Only nine of the ten launched and only two fell inside the target area but one of these penetrated a prefabricated building where it killed Constable Paul Clarke, a twenty-nine-year-old father of three, and injured several of his colleagues. The other seven bombs overshot the base, one exploding in mid-air, the others landing and going off in a wooded area well beyond the perimeter wall.

On 4 September 1985 eighteen devices were launched against the RUC Training Centre at Enniskillen, a record for the number of warheads launched in a single strike, but there were no serious injuries. This attack came on the eve of the first significant political development since the collapse of the Sunningdale Agreement in 1974. In the late 1970s successive efforts to break the political deadlock by both Labour and Conservative governments in London had foundered. When Pope John Paul II made the first ever papal visit to Ireland in September 1979 he made an impassioned plea for progress: 'On my knees I beg of you to turn away from the paths of violence and to return to the ways of peace.' That too was ignored. The British government thus pressed on with the twin policies of Ulsterisation – building up the RUC – and criminalisation, a drive to convict terrorists through the courts and imprison them as 'ordinary criminals'. Republicans in particular took exception to this policy and insisted that they should enjoy political or prisoner-of-war status. In pursuit of this demand, newly sentenced prisoners refused to wear prison clothing and mounted what became known as the 'dirty protest' by smearing their cells with their own excrement. When this failed to achieve any results, a small number commenced a hunger strike in late 1980 but with one of them at the point of death just before Christmas the protest collapsed in disarray, with the British government insisting it had made some concessions.

Early in 1981 the prisoners decided they had been deceived, and led by Bobby Sands, serving fourteen years after being captured with a firearm during a bombing raid in Belfast, a second hunger strike began. As Sands's condition deteriorated, his plight attracted international attention after he was elected to the British parliament in a by-election caused by the sudden death of the sitting MP. The Pope sent an envoy, but that and other initiatives failed and Sands died on 5 May after a sixty-six-day fast. Over the summer another nine prisoners starved themselves to death before the authorities caved in and granted virtually all their demands. The episode proved a major turning point for the IRA, which cashed in on its gains with a carefully co-ordinated strategy of both political and terrorist action succinctly articulated by Sinn Fein's Danny Morrison at a conference in Dublin: 'Who here firmly believes we can win the war through the ballot box? But will anyone here object if, with a ballot paper in one hand and the Armalite in the other, we take power in Ireland?'

Despite the ongoing violence there was a surge of support for the IRA and its political mouthpiece, Sinn Fein. This deeply alarmed both the British and Irish governments, who began a protracted political dialogue. By the summer of 1985, the heads of a new accord were clear and the final touches were being shaded in. The results of the recent local council elections in Northern Ireland, when Sinn Fein came from nowhere to win fifty-nine council seats with an 11.8 per cent share of the first preference vote, encouraged the two governments to finalise a deal which was formally signed at Hillsborough Castle on 15 November 1985. The Anglo-Irish Agreement, as it was known, for the first time since Partition enabled the Irish government to establish a diplomatic presence in Belfast and enjoy formal rights of consultation and input into the future governance of Northern Ireland, especially concerning the treatment of the minority Catholic community.

The IRA was unimpressed by the ground-breaking all-Ireland initiative and showed its contempt by detonating a 300 lb. device near Crossmaglen at about 10.20 a.m., as Margaret Thatcher and her Irish counterpart Dr Garrett Fitzgerald were arriving at Hillsborough for the signing ceremony. Twenty-five-year-old Constable David Hanson, a member of an eight-strong joint Army and police patrol, was killed and another police officer injured. It was the start of a major offensive against the police and security force bases, many of the attacks using the Mark 10 mortar. An 800 lb. van bomb damaged RUC Toomebridge on 5 December 1985. Two days later two RUC officers were held up and shot as they opened the gates of the RUC station in Ballygawley, County Tyrone. The killers placed a 100 lb. beer-keg bomb on the station forecourt but three officers inside escaped through a rear door ten minutes before it went off. The station at Castledawson was attacked a day later, then on 11 December RUC Tynan was set on fire by one of four mortars fired from a hijacked van. Four injured police officers inside the station escaped but firefighters could not move in until the ATO had accounted for the other mortars. By that time the building had been reduced to a shell.

Mortars were fired at RUC Cullybackey on 19 December and at the joint police–Army post at Castlederg later in the day, where the completely indiscriminate nature of the weapon was evident. One of three mortars launched from a stolen van in a nearby car park fell short of the base but the other two burst in the air, sending glass and debris flying. Meanwhile a fourth mortar exploded in the launch tube, damaging nearby houses. A police officer was injured and a mother and her two daughters, aged five and seven, were also hurt in the blast. There was a similar assault at RUC Carrickmore on 21 December and two days before Christmas seven mortars were launched from a hijacked van at the Camel's Hump checkpoint at the Strabane–Lifford border crossing. Police admitted that of fifteen stations damaged in the previous twenty months only one had been repaired because of a campaign of murder and intimidation against civilian construction contractors. The first victim was Seamus McAvoy, a forty-six-year-old Catholic shot dead in Dublin, whose northern-based firm supplied prefabricated buildings and other materials. Soon afterwards it was revealed that 300 workers had been laid off by employers unwilling to complete security contracts. Over the next decade nearly forty civilian workers would be murdered by the IRA.

Meanwhile there was strenuous opposition to the Anglo-Irish Agreement among the majority Unionist community. Eight days after the signing at Hillsborough a crowd estimated to exceed one hundred thousand gathered at Belfast City Hall to register dissent and some demonstrators clashed with police. At the same time, extremist Unionists mounted attacks on the homes of police families. Amidst this fury, the disclosure that the bill for Troubles destruction had reached £600 million – the equivalent of £2 million a month – went unremarked. Total damage to property, principally from explosions, amounted to some £489 million while compensation for personal injuries totalled £98,500,000. Claims going back two years remained unsettled and those from one recent car bomb in Chichester Street, Belfast were estimated at well in excess of £1 million.

There was still no real sign of an end to the destruction. In fact the violence was continuing with a replenished arsenal of both imported and ever more effective home-made weapons. On 15 March 1986 two mortar bombs exploded at the Ulster Defence Regiment base at Kilkeel, County Down. WO2 Ernest Bienkowski, who was one month into his tour, found that six of the 40 lb. mortar bombs remained unfired in the launch tubes and that the ignition system was unfamiliar. As with many previous mortar attacks, there was no alternative but to render the unexploded shells safe manually. At great risk to themselves, Bienkowski and his team worked for eighteen hours through the night to neutralise the devices. Their courage and skill enabled weapons intelligence experts to study the new firing system and devise a render-safe procedure. For his courage in dealing with this and other incidents, Bienkowski, who had been mentioned in dispatches during an earlier tour, was awarded the Queen's Gallantry Medal.

Chapter Twelve
Street Heat

Just before 6 p.m. on 28 October 1986 the terrorist campaign in Northern
Ireland took another sinister turn. Not long after dark, terrorists launched
six mortars in quick succession across the border at an Army observation
post in an old pigsty at Drummuckavall, south Armagh. The sandbagged
forward post was occupied by four infantrymen from the Prince of Wales'
Own Regiment who were there to help protect 'Golf 20', the hilltop
observation tower half a mile behind them. This sixty-foot construction,
with its array of antennae, state-of-the-art image intensifiers and infra-red
vision aids, was one of four similar hilltop installations on the south
Armagh border which played a vital role in maintaining frontier security
and providing cover for police and soldiers on the ground by day and
night. As the mortars landed and exploded, despite the protection of the
sandbags, the force of the blasts knocked the four soldiers inside off their
feet. Three gunmen then fired an estimated 100 shots at the post with
high-velocity and automatic weapons. The soldiers returned fire in the
direction of the muzzle flashes they could see in the darkness. In the
comparative safety of daylight the follow-up operation began as an ATO
checked the area around the post for 'blinds', unexploded mortars. After
seven hours' work, WO1 RD Clay took away samples of the mortars that
had exploded and recovered the unexploded bomb intact for examination
by weapons intelligence and forensic experts.

To all appearances it was just another cross-border skirmish which
would be added to the statistics and, with nobody hurt or killed, otherwise
be rapidly forgotten. However, when the weapons and explosives
specialists got to work they made a troubling discovery. Each of the the
mortar bombs had contained about 1 lb. of Semtex, a Czechoslovakian-
manufactured military explosive never before seen in Northern Ireland.
The implications for the security forces were considerable. Semtex was
twice as powerful as Frangex, the high explosive most commonly used by
the IRA until then. ANFO, the most frequently encountered HME, was
only up to 70 per cent as powerful while ANNIE and other mixes had only

forty per cent of the explosive potential. That was why the soldiers had been blown off their feet. The new threat was frankly summed up in a briefing note prepared by an Army explosives expert: 'Its lethality is such that even a small quantity can cause immense damage. The ease with which the terrorist can lay and conceal it confers enormous advantage over the familiar HME and exposes the operators to much greater risk than hitherto.'

With the arrival of Semtex the long-drawn-out Northern Ireland campaign had reached one of its most significant turning points. The IRA now had not only an arsenal of modern weaponry and powerful explosive but the state-of-the-art technology and expertise to maximise its effect. For years the United States and European countries had been trying to tighten controls on the international trade in arms and explosives to frustrate the activities of terrorist groups like the IRA, who had formed alliances to exchange know-how, material and contacts. Official efforts were patchy at best and despite constant vows to increase international co-ordination, successive terrorist atrocities demonstrated how successfully tactics and techniques continued to be exchanged.

One of the most productive of these conduits was between Ireland and the US, where anti-British sentiment and misguided affection for 'the boys' trying to free 'the old country' flourished among many citizens whose parents and grandparents had emigrated over the previous century or so. Many were prepared to donate a dollar or use their connections to help the cause. In the early 1980s the IRA increased its contacts with this reservoir of goodwill. Some of the deals they pursued ended in failure. On more than one occasion, middle-men offering to sell them anti-aircraft guns and surface-to-air missiles proved to be US undercover agents and the IRA sympathisers and gunrunners from Ireland ended up in prison, but, as the weapons and explosives experts in Northern Ireland could tell from finds and the aftermath of incidents, much lethal material was getting through.

Some of the most dangerous material was coming from a US citizen called Richard Clark Johnson, whose technical knowledge and the electronic equipment he sourced would transform the IRA's capability with radio-controlled ambush bombs, especially in south Armagh, and provide the 321 EOD teams with some of their most complex challenges. Johnson had no known connections with Ireland, but some time in the late 1970s he had become involved with IRA activists, visited Ireland and been an active participant in IRA research and development. For them he was a prize catch. After graduating with a degree in electronic engineering he had worked for NASA on the Voyager and space-shuttle programmes as well as in other sensitive areas of the US defence industry. For the IRA he was able to rig up sophisticated bomb-initiation devices from components readily available in electronics stores. He developed a remote-detonation device by adapting a radar alarm originally designed to warn drivers of police speed traps and identified a US weather-alert radio channel as a suitably obscure frequency on which the IRA could set off radio-controlled bombs, outwitting the EOD Bleeps. His activities were finally halted in 1990 after his support network was unravelled by the FBI and he was sentenced to ten years' imprisonment. The FBI had originally been put on his trail by forensic experts in Northern Ireland who identified serial numbers on switches and other components used in dismantled bombs which US investigators traced back to source.

Before the attack at Golf 20, the authorities on both sides of the border were unaware that for some time the IRA had been landing arms, ammunition and explosives shipments at Coggle Strand in County Wicklow. The first consignment came in in August 1985 aboard the *Casamara*, a converted fishing boat, and was shuttled ashore in rubber dinghies. The episode was brought to the attention of the local police who found that the *Casamara* was registered to Adrian Hopkins, a recently bankrupted travel agent, but as he had no known links to terrorists they assumed he was trafficking drugs, reported the matter to customs and no further action was taken. Hopkins meanwhile changed the name of his vessel to the *Kula* and landed another cargo the following October. Like the earlier load, it was taken away by waiting IRA activists to be stored in camouflaged underground bunkers at several locations in the Irish Republic. In July 1986 a third shipment came in, again undetected at the time. That October the Irish authorities boarded and searched the *Kula* but their sniffer dog, trained to look for drugs, found nothing, and the presence of two crewmen with strong Northern Ireland accents, charts of north Africa and documentation showing the vessel had been in and out of Malta raised no suspicions.

The IRA's benefactor was none other than their mercurial old friend Colonel Gaddafi, who had excluded them from favour after the *Claudia* episode in 1973. Whatever his reasons for rehabilitating them, their status with him was radically enhanced by the events of 14 April 1986, when US bombers flying from British airfields attacked targets in Tripoli and Benghazi, including one of Gaddafi's desert encampments where the casualties included at least one member of his family. Recognising that he could use the IRA to take his revenge on Britain for facilitating the operation, he authorised another cargo of arms and explosives. This time it weighed so much, a reported 100 tons, that Hopkins had to buy a new ship, the *Sjarmar*, to transport it. Again evading detection, the massive arsenal was landed in September 1986 and distributed to the storage bunkers. Almost immediately Hopkins and his henchmen were ordered back to the Mediterranean to collect yet another cargo. This one weighed 150 tons, so an even larger vessel, the *Eksund*, was acquired.

In the early hours of Saturday 31 October, a few days out of Malta, the *Eksund* was boarded by French customs and ordered into Brest, from where Hopkins and his four crewmen were taken to Paris for questioning. When the cargo inventory was transmitted to London and Dublin it came as a severe shock to both. The French estimated the value of the cargo at up to £20 million. It included twenty SAM7 surface-to-air missiles, 1,000 AK47 Kalashnikov rifles, 600 Soviet F1 grenades, ten Soviet 12.77 mm. heavy machine guns with anti-aircraft gun mounts, a quantity of anti-tank recoilless rifles, Beretta M12 9 mm. Belgian machine guns, two tons of Semtex explosive with detonators and fuses, RPG7 tubes and rockets, mortars and fifty tons of assorted ammunition. Both governments were even more perturbed when they heard that during interrogation the five crewmen, travelling with false names on stolen Irish passports, revealed that four more loads of weaponry, easily exceeding the total of what had been captured, were already safely in the hands of the IRA. The failure to spot what had been going on was all the more perplexing because of a clue among the proceeds of a major arms seizure from bunkers in Sligo and Roscommon the previous January. There, among substantial caches of armaments of East German, Romanian and Russian origin, were twenty ammunition boxes, all but one unmarked. That one bore the stencilled inscription: 'Libyan Armed Forces'.

Reporting on the capture of the *Eksund* and its cargo to the Irish parliament on 10 November, Gerard Collins, the minister for justice, said: 'The impact which such a cargo would have had upon the campaign being carried out by the Provisional IRA can only be imagined. All the signs are that this cargo was intended to raise the campaign of violence on to a new plane, a plane not hitherto reached in the history of this state since the early 1920s.' The Irish police and army began a nationwide hunt, but despite searching some 70,000 premises, what they uncovered over the succeeding months was only a fraction of the arsenal some official estimates put as high as 250 tons – enough to keep the IRA in the terrorist business for another thirty years.

The potential capabilities of such weapons amounted to a complete redefinition of the conflict. Until this point, despite the IRA's ambitions to bring one down, helicopters had been a comparatively safe way of ferrying troops in and out of areas where movement by vehicle or on foot was too dangerous. The risk of ground-to-air missile attack or proper anti-aircraft fire would dictate a complete review of flying techniques and landing and take-off procedures. Security-force bases, already dangerously vulnerable to improvised mortar attacks, were now exposed to a substantially increased threat from heavy automatic weapons which could easily penetrate all existing defences. Patrols on the ground were in similarly increased danger. The wealth of Semtex apparently at the IRA's disposal presented a fresh challenge for the EOD teams, some of whom were still moaning to the *RAOC Gazette* about the lack of action: 'Another month passes and as yet there is no sign of the fabled big one. Number Two Section feels there is a possibility of missing it altogether so elusive is it. Jobs are at a premium and the daily training routine is beginning to take its toll.' Sadly, the wait was soon over.

A week after the capture of the *Eksund*, the IRA, emboldened by the arsenal already in their possession, committed another multiple murder. The target was the well-attended annual Remembrance Sunday ceremony at the war memorial in Enniskillen. Each year spectators clustered by the St Michael's Reading Rooms community centre, owned by the Catholic Church, to watch the wreath-laying ritual. On 8 November 1987, shortly before 11 a.m., as the military parties took up their positions and the band played sombre music, a 30 lb. charge of HME, planted in a storeroom on the other side of the community centre's gable wall, detonated without warning. Regardless of the risk to themselves from a secondary explosion or the fall of further debris, soldiers and police officers in their best uniforms plunged into the cloud of debris, dust and smoke to rescue those crying for help. Musicians dropped their instruments to assist and homes and shops threw open their doors to offer help to the injured and dying. In all eleven people lost their lives, ten civilians and a police officer, while over sixty bystanders were injured, many needing years of surgery. Tom King, the Northern Ireland Secretary, led the avalanche of criticism from every bearing of the political compass. 'It stands out in its awfulness,' he said. The IRA admitted planting the bomb but denied detonating it. Their plan, they claimed, had been to set it off after the ceremony to hit security forces still in the area. They accused the Army of triggering the device with its own radio equipment, an explanation which was widely ridiculed as an effort to divert attention away from the

IRA's characteristic recklessness with the safety of civilians. At that time the Army's radio-controlled devices worked only with a unique electronic code and they would not have been randomly sweeping the airwaves to detonate any bombs in a built-up area at a time when large numbers of civilians and military personnel were near by.

The ATO who cleared the building after the explosion reported that he had found a Kosangas cylinder in one of the rooms which the caretaker could not account for, but it proved to be full of gas and unopened. A witness said he had heard a large 'crump' as opposed to a sharp crack and that there was 'a lot of dirty black smoke', from which description the ATO concluded that the explosive charge most likely consisted of ANFO. He also judged from the way the debris fell that the seat of the explosion was inside the outer wall of the building. Although glass was shattered over a wide area, none of the adjacent buildings were structurally damaged. Lieutenant-Colonel Hugh Heap, the CATO, later took the highly unusual step of publicly producing fragments of a timing device related to known circuits 'peculiar to the IRA', painstakingly recovered from the debris, to disprove their claim that the Army was to blame for the explosion. At a news conference he said: 'The person who planted the bomb either intended it to explode at 10.45 a.m., when it did, or he made a mistake. The excellent forensic work quite conclusively indicates that this was not a radio-controlled device.'

The Remembrance Day bombing, one of the most horrific attacks attributable to the IRA, is also of enduring significance. From then on, for the first time since the late 1960s, IRA violence would be closely synchronised with what became known as the peace process. At this point the IRA leadership was not being transparent about its strategy. A 'peace process' was already being planned by Gerry Adams, Martin McGuinness and a small like-minded cadre and nourished through secret contacts with leading politicians and churchmen as well as at least one senior figure from MI6, the British secret intelligence service. This new vision was still far too radical for the rank and file, who were simply told that the Libyan weaponry had been acquired to mount a new all-out offensive. The leadership cadre knew that the *realpolitik* of the situation would not be so simple. The 'doves' intended to use the declared 'Armalite and ballot box' strategy more subtly to persuade the movement to swallow its historic objections to seeking political representation in the elected bodies in London, Dublin and Belfast, and to build a powerful political base, through the Sinn Fein front, from which to advance their demands.

Thus after the Enniskillen tragedy the Sinn Fein leader, Gerry Adams, adopted a notably apologetic mode: 'I do not try to justify yesterday's bombing. I regret very much that it happened. On behalf of the Republican people, I extend sympathy and condolences to the families of those killed and injured.' But Adams was as determined as those around him to ensure that any overtures indicating a willingness to talk would not be interpreted as revealing a weakness on the part of the IRA or a desire to surrender. They intended to show that they were talking from a position of strength and that they had the capacity to maintain and enhance their terror campaign if the political signals went unanswered.

The seven years from 1987 would see some of the most deadly and innovative attacks of the entire campaign. While IRA violence continued on the home front in Northern Ireland, its thrust moved abroad to mainland Britain and northern Europe. In Britain there were constant attacks on security forces and premises as well as bombings designed to disrupt economic and commercial life, especially by threatening the international financial institutions in the City of London. At the same time, British forces and bases located in northern Europe, West Germany, Belgium and Holland were singled out for repeated attack and there were both military and civilian casualties, although an attempt to set off a radio-controlled bomb during a military ceremony in Gibraltar in 1988 was foiled by undercover British troops and three IRA terrorists were killed. In northern Ireland, the number of explosions rose from 254 in 1986 to 384 in 1987 and the amount of explosive captured more than doubled, from 2.4 tons to 5.8. The number of EOD tasks jumped from 865 to 1,397. On 25 April Lord Justice Gibson, the second most senior judge, and his wife were assassinated by a 500 lb. roadside bomb at the border in south Armagh. But the IRA suffered a serious setback on 8 May when an SAS undercover unit shot dead eight leading terrorists as they attacked the RUC station in Loughgall, County Armagh.

Staff Sergeant Peter Hurry notched up another notable success for the security forces after midnight on 16 July when he was sent to check a car at Main Street, Portglenone, County Antrim, which had been the subject of a bomb warning. Because of the position of the vehicle he could not make full use of Wheelbarrow and had to approach on foot. As he leaned in through the broken car window he saw a barrel attached by wires to a timer-power unit with two minutes left to run. Despite this time pressure, he carefully placed his disrupter against the device and returned quickly to the incident control point from where the device was safely neutralised. His cool courage earned him the George Medal.

The next day brought the first evidence that IRA 'engineers' had come up with another new weapon, an improvised anti-armour grenade designed to explode on impact with a vehicle. The discovery was made by Acting Captain Christopher Hodder, who was called to a device that had been thrown at a police Land Rover on the Falls Road. Rather than render it safe remotely, he dismantled it by hand so that it could be examined. His action, 'regardless of his own safety', as the subsequent citation stated, was recognised with the award of the Queen's Gallantry Medal.

Staff Sergeant Stuart Hooper was also awarded the QGM after a two-day clearance at Omagh on 17–18 October when he neutralised a bomb containing 3,500 lb. of HME, the largest device yet encountered. The operation began after a trailer-mounted slurry tank was abandoned at Newtownsville, near Omagh. Having let it soak, the ATO and a search team ensured the area round the tanker was clear, but remote action was not possible and the ATO had to climb onto the tank to look in. There he saw a primed initiation device and a pile of fertiliser bags, each apparently containing a quantity of HME. Having made the initiation device safe, over the rest of that day and the next he climbed in and out of the tank to remove the fifty-eight fertiliser bags one by one. Working in cramped, deeply unpleasant conditions, he had to be sure each bag was not booby-trapped before moving it.

The backlash from Enniskillen did not deter the IRA in the slightest and they continued to set up similar ambush attacks, primarily aimed at the security forces but in locations where the risk to civilians could not be eliminated. A few days before Christmas 1987, a Catholic man living in a mainly Protestant-populated area of Londonderry died in the second of two 5 lb. bomb blasts close to his home. A third device which failed to explode yielded firm forensic evidence that the IRA were responsible. On 22 December a prominent Loyalist paramilitary leader, John McMichael, was killed by an under-car booby-trap outside his home at Lisburn.

A week into the new year of 1988, a large vehicle bomb devastated the Law Courts building in Belfast. On 25 January, the IRA killed a police-man in the city with one of their new grenades – home-made from a soup or baked-bean tin, a metal cone and a small charge of Semtex – lobbed at his vehicle from the upstairs room of a derelict house. This confirmed fears that the IRA had developed a viable weapon following the principle that a hollow cone charge could be used to penetrate vehicle armour. An ATO later told the Belfast Coroner that anyone with access to a carpentry shop could make the weapon. A month later, on 24 February, two Ulster Defence Regiment soldiers were killed by a booby-trapped device attached to the security gates in Belfast city centre.

Another victim of a booby-trap device was Corporal Derek Hayes, a dog handler, who died along with his search dog, Ben, after triggering a 100 lb. device during a follow-up to the successful neutralising of a 1,400 lb. roadside bomb at Glassdrumman in south Armagh on 21 May. An under-vehicle booby-trap caused multiple casualties after a fun-run in Lisburn on 15 June which attracted four thousand competitors to raise money for local charities. The participants included 270 soldiers stationed at Headquarters Northern Ireland and elsewhere, six of whom travelled from the 8 Brigade headquarters at Londonderry in an unmarked blue Transit minibus. They had parked in the town's main car park, next to the starting point for the race, at 5.30 p.m. Some time between then and 8.55, when the driver, twenty-two-year-old Lance-Corporal Graham Lambie from the Royal Signals, and his five colleagues returned to the vehicle, 5 lb. of commercial explosive and a timer-power unit with a mercury tilt switch, probably contained in a plastic lunch box, was clamped to a recess on the underside of the van with three diver's magnets. The timer had been set for one hour and was armed to explode after that time when the mercury tilt switch functioned, which it did four minutes later as the driver braked at traffic lights. All six soldiers died as the explosion ripped through the vehicle and the fuel tank ignited. Later in the month, on 23 June, an Army helicopter was forced to land after coming under anti-aircraft fire near Crossmaglen, in another manifestation of the increased IRA threat to the security forces.

Soon afterwards the IRA once again put civilians at risk in an ambush for the security forces. The location this time was the swimming baths on Belfast's Falls Road which were held up by an armed gang, including one woman, at about 5.15 p.m. on 7 July. The staff were first held at gunpoint in an office and the receptionist was ordered to open the safe by one of the gang, who scattered the day's takings on the floor. They were then locked in a changing room and told they would be released after an explosion, but under no circumstances should they return to the building. The promised blast took place some two hours after the raid began, blowing a large hole in the wall of the building and killing two passers-by, a sixty-year-old woman out to buy a carton of milk and a twenty-four-year-old man returning from dropping off his baby daughter at his girlfriend's house. Others were injured and an Army medical team was prevented from reaching the scene by a taunting crowd who said the bomb had been meant for them.

WO2 John Howard, aged twenty-nine, who was two weeks into his second tour of duty in Northern Ireland, was assigned to clear the swimming baths and established his incident control point at North Howard Street, close to the Army base. His first step was to glean what he could from the manager and staff about what the terrorists had done during the two hours they had been in control of the premises. Learning very little except that there appeared to be a command wire inside, he first checked around the scene of the explosion on the street. As his view into the building was obstructed by structural damage he decided to send in a camera. However, as Wheelbarrow could not get through the main doors, the ATO had to suit up and open them himself. He then sent Wheelbarrow into the building to sever the command wire so that he could trace its path. It was a laborious process, for he had to make several manual approaches to open internal doors. Having finally cleared a path, Howard escorted a scenes of crime officer and a forensic expert to the seat of the explosion in the basement, but they withdrew rapidly after spotting a blue nylon sports bag partially hidden under a gym mat. Howard decided to use the route he had already cleared to attack the bag with a disrupter. Once again he put on his suit and made several trips inside to position equipment for the task. During one of these trips, six and a half hours after the operation started, there was an explosion and Howard was fatally injured. He was the twentieth member of 321 EOD to lose his life and his murder brought the total Army death toll in Northern Ireland since 1969 to 400.

During the follow-up investigation, it was concluded that a pressure plate, concealed by three inches of floodwater and rubble from the earlier blast, had functioned when Howard stepped on it and set off the explosives in the sports bag. The Commander of 321 EOD had arrived at the scene just as the blast occurred. In a letter of sympathy to Howard's widow, Beverley, he wrote:

> The exact details of the incident, I am afraid, we will never know. It may be some comfort to know that there is no question of him doing anything wrong or ill-considered during the clearance and he would have known nothing about the explosion as he was killed instantly. In addition, as I was out on the ground at the scene at the time, I can assure you that he was happy and confident in what he was doing and we will remember him that way. Everyone is still stunned by the incident which once again demonstrates the deviousness and callousness of the enemy we face.

Writing from the Directorate of Land Service Ammunition at Didcot, Brigadier JFF Sharland said: 'As head of the "ammunition" family, my concern and sorrow at the loss of your husband on duty in Northern Ireland is as hard to describe as this letter is to write. Your husband was and is respected and admired by all his contemporaries as a man of great courage and resolution.' Chief Superintendent Ian Williamson, the local police commander, said 'John Howard was the bravest man I have ever known.' His bravery was recognised by the posthumous award of the Queen's Gallantry Medal.

For their part, the IRA stated that the first bomb, which killed the civilians, had been accidentally triggered by one of their own men. The same night, another of their men did not escape the consequences of a mistake when a mortar he was aiming at the RUC station in Pomeroy exploded in the launch tube and killed him. However professional, calm and cool ATOs seemed about doing their job, such stark reminders of the consequences of an unconscious slip, the cunning of a callous terrorist or the misfire of a volatile weapon increased the pressure on them and their teams. The rise in the number of incidents imposed additional stress, but for the teams and operators, such as Staff Sergeant Seamus O'Brien, it was literally all in a day's work. In July 1988, he worked against a running timer to force his way into a locked van and neutralise eight dustbins each containing over 200 lb. of explosive. If the device had gone off it would have devastated the police headquarters in Londonderry and shops, homes and offices nearby. A couple of months later, over two days O'Brien prevented terrorists from severing the main A6 road between Belfast and Londonderry when he disrupted a 1,360 lb. device in a cramped culvert under the carriageway. With access only possible down a rough, steep embankment, none of his remote equipment could be used and he was forced to make repeated forays on foot to complete the task. Both jobs earned him a Queen's Gallantry Medal.

The next victims of the violence were further IRA 'mistakes', a man, his wife and their seven-year-old son killed by a huge roadside explosion on the border just south of Newry on 23 July. Their vehicle had been wrongly identified as that of a judge and his family. Their deaths brought the number of IRA 'mistakes' since the bombing at Enniskillen to seventeen.

Not long afterwards, in a similar roadside bombing, the Army suffered another major blow. Several times a week an unmarked hired bus travelled from Omagh to the two Belfast airports carrying soldiers from the 1st Battalion, the Light Infantry and members of their families who were travelling in or out on leave or other business. On the late Friday evening of 20 August, after picking up passengers at the two Belfast airports, the bus started its return journey to Omagh several hours behind schedule, just before 11 p.m. It has never been established precisely how the bus was targeted that night, but spotters with mobile phones may have been in touch with another team of terrorists lying in wait on high ground at Barony Bridge, nine miles short of the safety of Omagh barracks. At 12.30 a.m., the headlights of the bus came into view round a corner and one of the watchers operated a bell-push attached to a cluster of six batteries, sending a surge of power along a 350-yard twin-flex command wire strung across a farm track, along a stream, under a bridge and over to a firing pack and more than 200 lb. of high explosive planted beside the road. As the bus passed within yards of it, the bomb detonated and the vehicle slewed along the road, shedding bodywork and throwing passengers on to the tarmac. By the time it stopped eight soldiers were dead and twenty-seven injured.

Another IRA 'mistake' followed in Londonderry. At the end of August, residents of a block of flats became anxious about a neighbour who had not been seen for six days. Deciding to check up on him, they broke a window and one climbed inside. Moments later there was a massive explosion which killed the man in the flat and a woman neighbour by the front door. Another man standing beside her was critically injured and died seven months later. The occupant of the flat had been abducted by IRA terrorists who had set up a booby-trap in the expectation that police would come to enquire into his disappearance. August also saw the IRA attempt to murder Sir Ken Bloomfield, the head of the Northern Ireland Civil Service, by planting a 'necklace' of eight bombs around his house at Helens Bay, County Down. All but one exploded at 6 a.m. while Sir Ken, his wife and son were asleep. They had to flee from the shattered house by stepping over the remaining unexploded bomb on the front doorstep. The worst damage was caused at the back of the house where one of the bedrooms collapsed. Their daughter, who would have been sleeping there, had returned to university in Britain the previous day.

There were two more civilian deaths in the months after, these from under-car booby-traps. Again the victims had been mistakenly targeted by the IRA. On 31 October an elderly woman died from a heart attack after a mortar attack on the police station at Rosslea and on 23 November a sixty-seven-year-old man and his thirteen-year-old granddaughter were killed when a large van bomb detonated as they were driving past the police station at Benburb, County Tyrone.

Despite the death of John Howard, the ten EOD teams continued with their round of usually unsung heroics. Among the most difficult operations of the year was one in Belfast in September, carried out by Sergeant Jonathan Clarke. He was called to a building site in the west of the city after an explosion was reported in the cab of a crane 160 feet above the ground. With no information available from witnesses and no way of having a look at the scene either from a distance or with his own equipment, there was nothing for him to do but to climb the crane and see for himself. The crane overlooked the perennially troublesome Divis Flats area and there was the clear possibility that the explosion had been set up to lure an ATO onto the crane for a sniper attack. Without the protection of an EOD suit, Clarke climbed the narrow steel ladder, inspected the damaged cab area and ensured there were no further explosives. His courage was recognised with the Queen's Gallantry Medal.

The number of bombings in the year was 458, the highest for seven years. The weight of explosives used was the greatest for eleven years, principally because the acquisition of Semtex gave the IRA a reliable booster charge to set off larger bombs than ever before. More significantly, in 1988 the new range of conventional and improvised weapons and explosives available to the IRA had significantly changed the pattern of violence and resulted in the most fundamental tactical changes for years on the part of the security forces. The advent of the anti-armour grenade, or 'drogue bomb', caused great concern when one blew an armoured vehicle twenty feet. This prompted an urgent programme to reinforce 500 police Land Rovers by adding another sheet of armoured protection over a layer of foam. Patrol methods were also changed. RUC Land Rovers were now sent out in pairs followed by a third military vehicle with two top-cover sentries ready to fire at anyone attempting to throw a grenade. To further reduce the risk to personnel, foot patrolling was intensified in urban areas, with smaller, four to six-strong patrols working in multiples of three or four to look out for each other. To counter the threat of attack from heavy ground fire or heat-seeking missiles, helicopter pilots took to flying at tree-top height to make their craft less easy to target. Previously pilots and crew had carried only personal protection weapons; now automatic weapons were fitted for added firepower in the event of an attack. Increasingly helicopters moved in pairs or even threes, with one flying high to cover the other. Take-offs and landings became faster and steeper, again to reduce their vulnerability to attack. The security forces were very much on the defensive and the promised 'long war' had effectively reached stalemate.

Chapter Thirteen

'A New Threshold of Evil'

By the late 1980s, the IRA's 'Armalite and ballot-box' strategy was paying dividends. Spurred on by Bobby Sands's 1981 by-election victory, efforts to build electoral support steadily increased and by the end of the decade Sinn Fein had secured a ten per cent share of the vote which it intended to use as a bridgehead for further political progress. Just as the IRA was fighting a long war, Sinn Fein recognised that making political progress called for similar patience.

The IRA campaign over the late 1980s and into the 1990s was waged on parallel lines. By far the most effective operations, in terms of propaganda and political impact, were the ongoing attacks in Britain and Europe, which are not a primary part of this story. Meanwhile the overall level of violence in Northern Ireland itself fell short of the peaks of the early 1970s, but it matched them in destructive power as the organisation deployed a range of conventional and improvised weapons employing state-of-the-art technology and effective tactics. The greatest impact came from the successive poundings inflicted on Belfast and other main towns by a series of vehicle-borne bombs, devastating even by the standards of Northern Ireland. These attacks were modelled on the commercial bombings of the early 1970s with the intention of undermining the growing economic confidence that was attracting new investment. Other consistent targets were police and Army bases and court buildings, regardless of the risk to civilian life and property. The late 1980s was the busiest period for the EOD teams for ten years and one operator carried out 111 tasks during a six-month tour.

After Enniskillen, the IRA was clearly more sensitive to the fate of civilians and following an incident in Belfast in August 1988, when a 300 lb. bomb caused damage costing £3 million, announced a warning measure. IRA 'engineers', a statement proclaimed, had developed a system to set off a smoke grenade after a car bomb had been planted to identify it to the public. The statement also contained a claim that future devices would include a micro-switch intended to set off the bomb if the

Army interfered with it. The IRA pronouncement was officially dismissed as 'twaddle' and 'hypocritical nonsense' and nothing more than an attempt to shift responsibility for endangering civilians. 'The ultimate responsibility for injuries or loss of life rest with those who manufacture and plant such lethal devices,' ran an official police statement. In the event, none of the warning grenades was ever seen and the IRA's cavalier attitude to the safety of civilians was demonstrated again in an attack on 12 April 1989 in Warrenpoint, County Down. The main target was the police station but a twenty-year-old woman was killed in the shop next door when the bomb went off without warning. In all 308 properties were damaged and the compensation bill for that single incident reached £1,250,000.

The Law Courts in Belfast were targeted again on 31 July when the driver of a hijacked laundry van was ordered to deliver a bomb to the building. Despite supposedly stringent security, he was waved straight through the checkpoint and the alarm was raised only after he had parked against the main building. Captain Andrew Stevens, the ATO on duty, arrived seven minutes later. The EOD teams had developed rapid-response drills to attack devices more quickly, for the IRA was using shorter and shorter delays to try and prevent them being defused. On this occasion the ATO lost a valuable five minutes as he had to force the locked main gates in order to clear a path to the vehicle bomb just twenty yards away. He finally swung them open and a Wheelbarrow was trundled forward, but as it reached the point between the gates where the ATO had been standing moments earlier, the 600 lb. van bomb detonated, blowing the Wheelbarrow to pieces. The ATO's valiant effort to save the complex, which so nearly cost him his own life, was marked by the award of the Queen's Gallantry Medal.

The Belfast–Dublin railway continued to be an target and in the late 1980s, after a renewed spate of attacks, an all-Ireland 'Peace Train' committee was formed to draw attention to the idiocy of the IRA's constant disruption of one of the few symbols of real north–south contact. The IRA, as always, was unmoved and took a malicious pleasure in disrupting the service for prolonged periods, infuriating passengers and campaigners. The ingenious and complex devices were invariably carefully designed to maximise disruption and endanger EOD teams. They regularly incorporated new and novel features to catch out an ATO adopting anything but the most careful and patient methods.

The vulnerability of the ATOs and the justification for their protracted methods was demonstrated by an incident which began on 3 February

1989 when rail services were halted after an explosion at an embankment close to Kilnasaggart Bridge, four hundred yards inside Northern Ireland. The area was kept under close surveillance and a secondary device located but, fearing a more complex ambush, the EOD team led by Staff Sergeant Mike Knox waited two weeks before going in. Knox decided to use the minimum of manpower and equipment to minimise the danger and avoid helicopters having to run the risk of ambush. This meant that without Wheelbarrow he had to make repeated approaches on foot, silhouetted on the skyline, to neutralise the device. Unknown to him, the terrorists had dug in another device nearby, which they remotely detonated later in the day when he was just fourteen feet away. The force of the 150 lb. explosion blew him thirty feet through the air and blasted a crater eight feet deep and nine feet wide at the side of the line. Despite not wearing an EOD suit, Knox suffered only shock and an injured knee but he was somewhat surprised again when, on getting to his feet, he was rugby-tackled to the ground by his Number Two, who had rushed forward to help without regard for his own safety.

Despite his close shave Knox insisted on returning to the scene next day where he played a key part in the follow-up operation. The first objective was to complete the clearance of the device he had been working on when he was attacked. To their amazement the ATOs could find no evidence that the device which had nearly killed Knox had been set off by either radio control or command wire. As their minute examination widened, they discovered the terrorists had used the railway line itself to carry the current to initiate the bomb. Another identical device was found, so the rail was severed by controlled explosion. When neutralised this bomb was found to consist of 220 lb. of explosive. By any standards this was a spectacularly successful clearance, frustrating a four-bomb ambush designed to kill at least the ATO. For what his superiors described in his citation as 'superb bravery in the face of great danger', Knox was awarded the George Medal. 'The clearance op lasted four days for me but the men of the Royal Regiment of Fusiliers were there much longer,' he says modestly. Following the incident, 'Lofty' Pattinson was called back from retirement to help adapt a Wheelbarrow for use on the railway. Under his guidance, within three weeks the team at Chertsey came up with the 'Railbarrow', a powered platform on train wheels to which a conventional Wheelbarrow could be bolted and then dropped directly onto the line by helicopter.

Staff Sergeant John Franks earned a Queen's Gallantry Medal later in the year for two acts of bravery at Belfast City Airport. The first came on

3 July 1989 when three explosions rocked the complex and two more unexploded devices were found, one against a fuel pipe, the other under a 6,000-gallon storage tank containing highly inflammable aviation spirit. The clearances took over eight hours, principally because remote-controlled vehicles could not get close to the devices. The one under the tank was especially inaccessible and the ATO had to climb a wall and crawl underneath the tank to work at it. The airport was targeted again during the night of 28 November when two explosions were heard soon after a telephoned warning that five bombs with anti-handling switches had been planted. The ATO began work at daybreak and found two unexploded devices, one on the axle of a 1,000-gallon tanker-trailer, the other on the chassis of a 3,000-gallon tanker. Despite the constant risk of the fuel in the tankers igniting, Franks worked for nine hours to render them safe.

WO2 John Grimsley was honoured with a Queen's Gallantry Medal for an action in Londonderry. In the late afternoon of 3 October, only a few days after his arrival for a four-month tour, a vehicle bomb was positioned against the perimeter wall of the RUC station at Strand Road, Londonderry. After a ten-minute telephone warning, part of the station and residential properties opposite were rapidly evacuated as the ATO and his team raced to the scene. Within thirty minutes of the first alert they had fired a disrupter at the vehicle. Nothing happened, but nine minutes later there was a small explosion as part of the device detonated, setting off a fierce blaze. The ATO quickly dragged a fire hose to within about ten feet and calmly directed the jet onto the blazing vehicle. When the fire was extinguished, he made the remainder of the device safe. It was unusually complex, incorporating five separate timing mechanisms and two anti-movement switches. The explosive charge weighed 2,000 lb. The assistant chief constable in the city personally congratulated Grimsley for saving the station from serious damage. His citation recorded that 'the operation was completed in the finest traditions of EOD' and that Grimsley's 'determined and courageous actions undoubtedly saved many casualties among the security forces and civilian population'.

After another bomb attack in the centre of Lisburn the following December the compensation bill exceeded £2 million. During 1990 bombs containing 1,000 lb. or more of HME became the norm, causing massive damage to police stations and surrounding areas in Ballymena, County Antrim, and Loughgall, County Armagh. A proxy attack was mounted against RUC Rosslea County Fermanagh but the 3,500 lb.

device failed to function. The following year, in January 1991, the sheer destructiveness of incendiaries was again evident when a shopping centre at Sprucefield, ten miles from Belfast, was razed. The two-year-old centre, one of the biggest new commercial investments for years, symbolised the growing economic regeneration. A week later a newspaper reporter armed with a mocked-up incendiary toured twenty stores in central Belfast during an afternoon and found an alarming degree of complacency and inconsistency in security checks. One store had rigorous checks on its front door but none at a rear entrance, while in most of the others the checks were cursory.

A few months later the IRA changed the composition of its HME by adding icing sugar to the mix. The new ingredient, thought to mark a move away from other accelerants with carcinogenic properties potentially harmful to the bomb-makers, was first used in an elaborate ambush near the Spelga Dam in the Mourne Mountains at the beginning of May 1991. Every year, over the May bank holiday weekend, a car time-trial and hill-climb over the rugged mountain and forest track attracted a large crowd. Prior to the event, a team of police and soldiers checked the route and customarily used a sheep pen to lie up overnight. However, in line with the well-established procedure to avoid repeating routes and patterns, the team this time used an alternative spot in the woods nearby, a decision that saved their lives, for a 640 lb. bomb had been dug in underneath the pen and linked by command wire to a firing point 1,400 yards away. Accordingly the terrorists were forced to abandon their long-planned ambush. A few days after the motoring event, the Downtown Radio newsroom received an anonymous call saying that a bomb had been abandoned at the dam, which formed the reservoir for a high proportion of the water supply to Belfast. Given the remote nature of the area, the security forces were not going to rush in, so the area was placed out of bounds to patrols. This precaution was justified that evening when a forestry worker reported seeing two men, one clad in a boiler suit and gloves. Twenty-four hours after the first call, the radio station received another, this one pinpointing the location of the bomb to a sheep pen near the dam. Again caution was the watchword and it was another two days before a patrol went to scout the surrounding area and found the white twin-flex command wire snaking across the hillside into a stream which flowed close to the sheep pen.

Two days later, just before 7 a.m., WO1 KL Allen led a full EOD operation. After a stretch of public road was checked for devices, a pathway was cleared along a vehicle track close to the sheep pen and an incident control point was set up. From there, an Explosive Ordnance Reconnaissance search team and the ATO discovered the device buried eighteen inches down inside the pen. Step by step the plastic containers were uncovered, the command wire severed and the main charge isolated. In the final stage of the twelve-hour operation, the hillside firing point was cleared and the bell-push and a Tupperware box containing the firing mechanism were recovered.

From that summer on, exploiting the necessity for EOD teams to treat every incident as a live one, the IRA augmented bomb attacks with a series of disruption operations to undermine public and commercial confidence. The first operation began in mid-afternoon on 15 August 1991, when a 3 lb. high-explosive bomb exploded on a bus at Donegall Square East in Belfast as bomb-disposal officers were working to defuse it. The bus was gutted by fire. By the time of the evening rush hour, thousands of shop and office workers had been evacuated and other devices had caused the two motorways in and out of the city to be closed as well as the main cross-river bridges and other traffic arteries. The jams tailed back for miles and by 10 p.m. bomb-disposal officers had still not cleared all the devices, most of which turned out to be elaborate hoaxes. By the end of the Christmas shopping season, which accounted for nearly half the annual income of most traders, there had been twenty-four similarly costly days of disruption. December was also marked by the detonation of a 1,200 lb. device in Glengall Street, Belfast, which shattered the Grand Opera House and caused the cancellation of the Christmas pantomime. In other attacks, a vehicle bomb containing 2,000 lb. of explosive devastated the centre of Craigavon, wrecking a church, school and many houses, while the Law Courts in Belfast were hit yet again. That year the government had budgeted £20 million in compensation for damage caused by terrorism but the provisional sum was already estimated as at least twice that, so for the first time the British government announced that the cost would have to be borne within the existing Northern Ireland budget. Other programmes would therefore be cut to find the money.

Whether as a conscious gesture of defiance or not, the Belfast IRA responded on successive days early in January 1992 by setting off an 800 lb. bomb in Bedford Street and another of 500 lb. in High Street, causing further destruction to two commercial areas. Surveying the third wave of damage sustained by his Plaza Hotel in six weeks, Diljit Rana, one of the most active property developers in the regeneration of the city, said the bombings were 'undermining all that had been achieved in rebuilding

Belfast and future confidence'. There were now the first disturbing signs that after seven years of increasingly normal life, the people of Belfast were losing their legendary resilience. The Lord Mayor, Nigel Dodds, and other business leaders called angrily for far tighter security. 'There should be a ring of policemen around the city to protect it,' suggested one, wading through the rubble of his shop. Richard Needham, the entrepreneurially-minded economic minister at the Northern Ireland Office, refused to bow to the criticism or the IRA.

> Every tile that has been torn off, every window knocked out and every building that has been damaged will be repaired because the government is determined to maintain the revitalisation of the business and commercial life of the city. No matter how many times buildings are bombed we will rebuild them and replace them better than before. I understand the anger and fury of the business people. I share it but we must keep the city open. Do they want to go back to the dark days of the 1970s, close the city down, don't allow any traffic in and make the place a desert again?

They were bold words, for the bill for seven attacks in the city over the previous six weeks was provisionally calculated at £10 million. Other damaging attacks followed on targets including Lurgan, the RUC station in Donegall Pass, Belfast, and the city's Bedford Street; the main shopping street in Bangor; RUC Glengormley, where a 200 lb. vehicle bomb shattered many nearby houses, and Coleraine, where blast and fire damage resulted in 227 claims for compensation and a final payout amounting to over £10,500,000.

At 8.11 p.m. on 23 September 1992, as Captain Peter Smith was nearing the end of the first day of a four-month tour with the Belfast EOD detachment, the main police switchboard received the first of a series of telephoned warnings that a bomb had been abandoned in a lorry parked against the perimeter fence of the Forensic Science Laboratory at Newtownbreda in south Belfast. Smith and his unit sped to the location with the klaxons and blue lights on their two armoured Dodge vans wailing and flashing. They set up their incident control point eighty yards from the vehicle but after a frantic ten minutes the 3,300 lb. of HME detonated just as an armed Wheelbarrow was being trundled forward. The first casualty was the £50,000 robot, bits of which were found eighty yards away. Five of the escort and the six members of the EOD team crouched behind their protected vehicles as the blast rocked the area.

Debris punctured one vehicle's radiator and shattered its armoured windscreen. The bang was heard ten miles away and the soldiers closest by suffered deafness in both ears. The bomb totally devastated the main target, which had to relocate its laboratories and other facilities on a new site. Where the lorry had been standing in the road there was now a crater some forty by twenty feet wide and seven feet deep. Seven hundred houses, a church and other community facilities over a half-mile radius were damaged and water and electricity mains severed. Hundreds of people suffered shock, and when the final bill was totted up there were 851 claims for property damage and a payout totalling over £6,260,000.

With the terrorists apparently able to choose their targets and bomb them at will, the security presence on the streets was visibly stepped up and the police and Army redoubled their efforts to gather intelligence. Security gates were re-erected around many towns, sealing them to traffic at night for the first time in well over ten years, and pickets patrolled likely targets to intercept proxy bombs. Two twenty-four-hour check-points were set up to scrutinise all traffic passing along the Knock Road in east Belfast to protect the police headquarters, and stand-off areas and security zones were set up around other Army and police bases. However, as always the initiative rested with the terrorists and the security forces knew that as resources were deployed in strength to meet one type of threat they would switch targets or locations to bypass them. For instance, the larger than usual numbers of patrols on the streets and at checkpoints were highly vulnerable to attack by hit-and-run gunmen.

The IRA disrupted preChristmas activity again with twenty vehicles abandoned in Belfast at 6 p.m. on the Friday before, one near the BBC building in Ormeau Avenue which put local radio and television off the air for over an hour. The hard-pressed 321 EOD teams carried out a series of rapid controlled explosions to get the city moving again. Altogether there were 404 bomb and incendiary attacks during 1992 and the EOD teams answered 1,582 calls. The following year the onslaught continued with multi-million pound damage resulting from 1,000 lb. explosions in Bangor, Portadown, Magherafelt, Newtownards, Armagh and Belfast, with the Grand Opera House and the nearby headquarters of the Ulster Unionist party sustaining even more damage from a bomb planted in a builder's skip on a lorry to prevent the EOD team deploying Wheelbarrow to attack it. Twice in one day bombers evaded intense security to explode two devices, one 300 lb., the other 500 lb., seventeen hours apart in different parts of Belfast, but in August a 3,000 lb. vehicle bomb was abandoned outside Portadown because of security activity.

Notable developments during the year were the first use of wheelie bins as bomb containers and the appearance of improvised detonating cord. By the end of 1992 there had been a total of 302 explosions and incendiary attacks but the security forces had captured a massive 10.5 tons of HME, almost as much as the total for the previous two years.

The worst single month of violence since October 1976 began on the afternoon of 23 October 1992 when two IRA bombers planted a device in a busy fishmonger's on the Shankill Road, intended to kill the leaders of a Loyalist terror group, the Ulster Freedom Fighters, who frequented a room above the shop but were absent at the time. Ten people were killed and fifty-seven injured as the device went off without warning, the fatalities including one of the bombers. As Protestant fury boiled over, six Catholics were shot dead over the following week and in all twenty-seven people were murdered in one month. In September 1993 two ATOs had heart-stopping moments. On the 2nd, Captain Anthony McVey had to rescue civilians inside a cordoned area. He was manoeuvring Wheelbarrow outside the Court House in Armagh when he was told that a light had suddenly come on in one of the houses overlooking the scene, which should all have been empty. Then on 13 September Staff Sergeant Alan Joy was called to the Stormont Hotel car park in Belfast where the police had identified a suspect car after a telephone warning. He was within ten yards of the vehicle when an obviously intoxicated man emerged from the doorway of the supposedly evacuated hotel. Without hesitation, the ATO halted the Wheelbarrow, ran towards the man and grabbed him. The bomb went off seconds later when they were barely thirty yards away. The ATO, the man and other members of the security forces, who had also run to his aid, all suffered blast injuries. Both Joy and McVey were awarded the Queen's Gallantry Medal.

After the fall of the Berlin Wall, the intractability of the ongoing conflict in Northern Ireland was the despair of some Army officers. 'From our bases in Germany we can now drive peacefully all the way to Moscow,' said one border patrol-base commander. 'From here I can see the beautiful hills of Donegal only a few miles away but I cannot go and visit them.' During the period up to 1993, RUC stations and Army bases had come under consistent attack, especially the chain of four observation towers, seven hill-top observation posts and sixteen fortified patrol bases and checkpoints on the border. One of these bases, at Derryard on the Fermanagh–Monaghan border, had suffered an unprecedented frontal attack late on 13 December 1989, as darkness was closing in. Preparations for the engagement had begun over a week earlier when a high-sided quarry lorry was stolen at Mullingar in the Irish Republic and taken to a farmhouse near the checkpoint. A heavy wooden frame was fitted inside the rear bucket and filled with sand while three machine-gun mounts were welded onto the body. Bales of straw were piled up to give cover and a wall of sandbags was packed into the cab to help protect the driver.

The attack commenced just after 4.30 p.m. when the driver reversed into the bay of the checkpoint and sounded the horn. As soon as two soldiers from the King's Own Scottish Borderers emerged, gunmen in the back of the lorry opened fire and at least five hand grenades were thrown, fatally wounding one of the soldiers. Other soldiers gave covering fire as he was pulled inside one of the buildings. The lorry then drove out of the checkpoint and an Isuzu van carrying a 500 lb. bomb was driven in. A second soldier died when this bomb partially exploded and another in a sentry box was injured. All this time heavy fire was being exchanged between the outnumbered soldiers holding the post and up to twenty terrorists using a flamethrower and RPG7 rockets. Twenty minutes later, a foot patrol returned to the base and helped to drive the terrorists back towards the border, where they abandoned the quarry lorry with 500 lb. of unexploded HME on board. The gang got away, some with their weapons, in a tractor and other vehicles waiting over the border. Afterwards it was calculated that the terrorists had fired almost 3,000 shots during the engagement. Staff Sergeant P Grimsley, who carried out the EOD operation after the incident, concluded: 'This was a very well planned and executed attack which without intervention from the satellite patrol could have resulted in far more fatalities.'

On 24 October 1990 the vulnerability of the frontier checkpoints was exposed by another groundbreaking tactic when 'human bombs' were used to mount two simultaneous attacks. Just after midnight, sixty-seven-year-old James McEvoy, his wife and five children were asleep in their house, adjacent to their shop and petrol filling station at Rathfriland Road, Newry, when armed and masked men broke in. The family were abducted and held hostage in a house at Rathfriland, some twelve miles away. McEvoy was then blindfolded and taken away on his own in a car. After a time he was ordered out and, still blindfolded, forced into the driving seat of a yellow Toyota Hiace van between two of the terrorists. A short time later the van stopped, the blindfold was removed and the terrorists got out, ordering McEvoy to drive to the Romeo 15 checkpoint at Cloghogue on the main Belfast–Dublin road straight ahead. If he did not do so, they said, his two sons would be shot. It was just after 4 a.m.

when McEvoy approached the post from the south with the terrorists' unlit car following a short way behind. As instructed, he crossed the two traffic ramps before pulling the van sharply to the right across the road with its bonnet close to the door of the command post from where passing traffic was monitored. He shut off the engine and got out, running northwards for his life. Eight soldiers and a police officer were on guard duty and a further twenty-four soldiers and two police officers were asleep in a fortified accommodation block close by. The guards had been alerted by the approach of the van. Two soldiers broke cover, caught up with McEvoy and insisted he go back to move the van but he was paralysed with fear. One of the soldiers ran back towards the van, shouting a warning, but within seconds the device was detonated by the watching terrorists. The soldier near the van was killed, while yards away McEvoy and the other soldier were blown off their feet. Another sentry later described how he was tapping the registration number of the van into his computer to carry out a security check when there was 'a very bright, blue flash' followed by an explosion which shook the post to its foundations. The blast, later calculated to have been caused by 500 lb. of explosive in gas cylinders, structurally damaged houses over 250 yards away and a blew a six-foot deep crater in the road. The dead soldier, twenty-one-year-old Royal Irish Ranger John Smith, was posthumously awarded the Queen's Gallantry Medal for his efforts to raise the alarm. McEvoy, who suffered a broken leg, immediately after his ordeal sold his business and moved house but he never regained his health and died in hospital eight months later.

While Romeo 15 was being attacked, an episode of even greater callousness was taking place at the opposite end of the border, near Londonderry. The hostage in this case was Patsy Gillespie, a forty-two-year-old married man with three children, who worked in the canteen at the Army's Fort George base. He too was taken from his bed by armed men and driven away in his own car. It was the second time he had been abducted to plant a bomb. This time he was tied into the driver's seat of a van laden with explosives and ordered to drive it into the Coshquin checkpoint on the cross-border road leading to County Donegal. Terrorists following in Gillespie's car set off the device while their hostage was still strapped into the driving seat. The huge blast devastated the post, damaged houses over a wide radius and killed five members of the King's Regiment. A third attempt was made on an Army barracks, in Omagh, County Tyrone, with a van laden with explosives but they did not detonate and the hostage was able to free himself.

The use of 'human bombs' plumbed new depths of depravity on the part of the terrorists and Dr Edward Daly, the Catholic Bishop of Derry, said they had 'crossed a new threshold of evil'. As usual the IRA shrugged off the criticism and not long afterwards a hostage was again used to plant a bomb. On 25 November 1990, a heavy truck was driven into the Annaghmartin checkpoint on the Fermanagh border. The terrified driver, whose family were being held, had been told the bomb would go off in two minutes but he raised the alarm and soldiers took cover. As Staff Sergeant Aminul Islam and his team were flown south from Omagh by helicopter the operations room at the checkpoint reported a small explosion, so, despite the heavy rain and strong winds, the ATO and his men set to work as soon as they landed. Their remote vehicles failed and Islam was forced to make a number of manual approaches. He concluded that the device consisted of six booster charges wired to a much larger quantity of HME and that one had exploded without setting off the rest of the now highly unstable device. During further approaches he cut the booster links one by one, disconnected the timer and recovered the HME, which turned out to weigh almost 3,500 lb. His skill was recognised by the award of the Queen's Gallantry Medal but Islam believes the real hero was the driver. 'Despite fears for his family and no doubt himself, he warned the soldiers at the checkpoint and then waited until I arrived, when he patiently answered the myriad of questions I put to him and all before he was medically treated.' (In April 1997 Islam had to climb high up underneath an arch at Junction 9 on the M6 motorway in the west Midlands to deal with two IRA bombs, one of which had partly functioned, without his protective suit or remote equipment. He successfully neutralised both bombs and was awarded the George Medal for his remarkable fortitude and technical skill.)

Another attack, notable for the size of the explosion, took place on 31 May 1991. At 11.35 p.m. a man heard a heavy lorry being reversed into a lane beside his house at Glenanne, County Armagh. Watching from a darkened bedroom window he saw the lorry being driven across a field, knocking down a fence and heading for the heavily fortified UDR barracks on the southern outskirts of the small village. He also saw a Hiace van parked across the laneway and two masked men, one with a handgun, the other with a machine gun, standing beside it. As he watched, four more men got into the back of the van which quickly drove away. He had good reason to be alarmed, for as a lance-corporal in the Ulster Defence Regiment he was a constant terrorist target, but a more immediate worry was the safety of his barracks, so he telephoned the main operations room at Drumadd Barracks in Armagh to report what he had seen.

As he spoke, the now driverless Mercedes lorry was rolling slowly downhill towards the rear of Glenanne base. Once again the IRA had spotted a fatal weakness in military fortifications. The lorry easily traversed a line of concrete bollards and crashed through the perimeter fence. Inside the base there would normally only have been an eight-strong guard but that night there were forty people present, the others attending a function in the unit's social club. Alerted by a sentry even before the warning call came through from Armagh, two soldiers on their way to investigate the lorry were killed as it exploded in a ball of flame, digging a crater 200 feet deep and hurling debris and shrapnel as far as 300 yards. A third soldier perished when the guard room and part of the main building collapsed and a fierce fire started. All the other people on the premises were injured. Their cars outside were mangled and set ablaze. Nearby cows in the fields were killed and residents of the village were showered with glass and debris as windows were blown in and ceilings fell around them. The detonation of the 2,000 lb. of explosive was heard fifty miles away.

The Annaghmartin post was targeted again on 3 September 1991 when the IRA used hijacked vehicles to block roads south of the border. Armed terrorists then took over two homes overlooking the base, held the occupants including children hostage and brought in a tractor and silage trailer, loaded with explosive, which they intended to roll downhill towards the checkpoint. A local man was forced to drive the tractor into position but the overloaded vehicle slipped sideways off the track, heeled over and became bogged down in swampy ground. Soon afterwards another local man was held up and ordered to take his tractor to the spot but all efforts failed to tow the first one out and the crowd of about twenty men melted away across the border into the darkness.

Fearing a complex ambush the ATO, Staff Sergeant Q Bradshaw, let the trailer soak for some thirty hours before he moved in. After opening the tailgate with a controlled explosion he checked and removed fifteen 45-gallon oil drums, two smaller drums and eleven plastic sacks one by one, as well as a quantity of detonating cord, over nearly twelve hours. The explosive weighed almost 8,000 lb. making it the largest device ever used by the IRA. Three times more powerful than the largest conventional ordnance deployed by the UK armed forces, if it had worked as intended the post and the twenty soldiers inside would undoubtedly have been wiped out and the collateral damage would have stretched for a mile on both sides of the border.

Whatever justification there could be for hitting what terrorists described as legitimate or military targets, respect for hospitals was one of the basic conventions of conflict, yet the IRA chose to attack a hospital on the afternoon of Saturday 2 November 1991. From the early days of the Army's involvement in Northern Ireland, a wing of the Musgrave Park Hospital in Belfast had been screened off to provide safe accommodation for injured security-force personnel. The high-explosive bomb was placed after terrorists breached a steel security door in an underground tunnel leading from the civilian part of the hospital and it exploded without warning underneath a recreation room, causing the entire two-storey building to collapse and killing two soldiers. About the same time, police in the Irish Republic thwarted another evilly inventive effort to attack a border checkpoint. The plan was to drive an articulated lorry loaded with 3,000 lb. of explosive into the middle of the post between Strabane and Lifford, County Donegal. The driver would have operated a quick-release modification to detach the trailer without leaving the cab and driven off, uncoiling a length of chain from the cab to the trailer which would have triggered the explosion. The Garda found that heavy steel sheeting had been welded into the cab around the driving seat to protect the driver if the fleeing vehicle was fired on.

The defensive weaknesses exposed by this series of attacks were addressed in a £30 million project to redesign and strengthen the sixteen most vulnerable bases along the border. At the same time the opportunity was taken to increase levels of comfort and personal safety for the soldiers and reduce inconvenience to the community by speeding up traffic flow through the busiest checkpoints where between 3,000 and 10,000 vehicles crossed every day. The new patrol bases combined Roman military principles with the latest technology. They were built in the shape of a triangle so that sentries in two sixty-foot towers could observe the entire area. Moats were dug to prevent bombs being rolled against the boundary walls and other earth mounds were raised to deflect blast. The stand-off distance from a potential proxy bomb was increased by moving the operations blocks and living quarters well back from the roadside. The windowless, air-conditioned buildings, with double airlock doors at each end, were described as 'submarines' by their occupants. The improved blast walls and hardened roofs were designed to withstand even the largest mortar and roadside bombs.

To reduce the exposure of individual soldiers, traffic flow through the checkpoints was largely automated and conducted from a protected command point overlooking the transit area. As each vehicle approached, its number was read by a camera, projected on to a screen in the control room and verified by a central computer containing details of all Northern Ireland vehicles. After that, by means of remote-controlled television cameras and barriers, directional traffic lights or an intercom, vehicles could be waved through or directed into the search lay-by. At night vehicles were scrutinised by CCTV. The bases were equipped with other anti-terrorist measures. 'Shark's teeth', intended to shred vehicle tyres, could be bared at the touch of a button and hydraulic steel bollards could be raised or steel girders dropped across approach roads.

The new patrol bases were made as 'user-friendly' as possible with fortifications, moats and mounds landscaped and planted with flower beds, while the military green-and-grey concrete was relieved by the use of red brick and other building materials and paints. Orders were given to erect lighted trees at Christmas. Every detail was accounted for in the planning, to the extent that sentries no longer had to climb up and down sixty feet of ladders to relieve themselves – a flushing 'comfort pipe' was installed in each look-out. The building programme was hampered by IRA attacks on contractors and in the end 1,000 extra troops were brought in to guard convoys of construction vehicles. Most of the buildings and fences were prefabricated and had only to be assembled on site. Chinook helicopters were used to bring in items like armour-plated sentry boxes and lower them into position.

As ever the IRA terrorists were watching for ways to mount a deadly attack and soon succeeded. Romeo 15 at Cloghogue had been extensively reconfigured to prevent any repeat of the 1990 'human bomb' attack. Now traffic passing through on the main Dublin–Belfast road was channelled through search bays enclosed by blast walls. Sections of heavy concrete sewer pipe had been positioned so that soldiers could take cover and the replacement accommodation buildings were made from reinforced concrete slabs specially designed to provide blast and mortar protection for those inside. There was a helicopter landing pad near by and the whole compound was overlooked by a new 160-foot observation tower on top of Cloghogue mountain which afforded a view of the countryside for miles in every direction.

However, the IRA had spotted that the defences were principally geared to foiling an attack by road and that only a chainlink fence separated the rear of the post from the main north–south railway line. Just before midnight on 30 April 1992 four armed men wearing German army combat clothing and balaclavas arrived outside a newly built house a couple of miles away. The terrified occupants, a young couple who had returned from their honeymoon only forty-eight hours earlier, crouched in their upstairs bedroom as the men rang the doorbell, pounded on the windows and finally smashed through the glass front door with a plank. Once inside they asked for the keys of an Hitachi excavator parked outside the house where it was being used to dig drains. The young couple did not have the keys, or a telephone, so they were told to wait in their bedroom for at least ninety minutes. Soon they heard the excavator being started up and taken away.

Earlier that night, the thirty-eight Royal Fusiliers located in the post had been warned of a proxy bomb attack and a patrol had been put out overnight to monitor traffic approaching from the south. Just before 2 a.m. the officer in charge of the patrol was talking to the driver of a van when he heard a strange metallic noise. Looking to his left he saw a motor van travelling north on the railway line at about 10 mph. About 300 yards behind him, a sentry dug into a machine-gun emplacement in a clump of bushes between the road and the railway also heard the strange noise, 'like a car running on a flat tyre'. Moments later the driverless van passed close to his concealed position. The back doors were open and a length of cable was being paid out along the railway line behind it.

By now the strange noise and sightings had generated radio warnings from the advance lookout positions, so Fusilier Andrew Grundy, who was on sentry duty in the East Sangar, a six-sided armoured box on a ten-foot platform at the southern edge of the post beside the railway, was looking out for the van. He shouted a warning over the intercom but as he did so the van came to a stop and exploded with a bright flash. The sentry box was blown off its platform and inside the Fusilier died instantly from the effects of the huge blast, which severed the railway line leaving a crater thirty feet across. Elsewhere in the post, although some were blown off their feet, the remaining soldiers and police officers were protected from injury by the new fortifications. Thirty yards of fencing was torn away and some unprotected buildings, such as the laundry and kitchen, were demolished. Houses close to the post suffered a wave of blast damage. All that was eventually recovered of the bomb was a few strands of insulating tape. The next day an ATO pieced together the full story. The laundry van had been stolen in Dundalk on 14 April and its tyres removed so that it could run along the railway track on its metal rims. Shortly before the attack it had been taken to a railway crossing point two miles south of the target and lifted onto the tracks by the stolen excavator. Then, loaded with some 1,000 lb. of explosive and long coils of command wire, it was set in gear and sent driverless along the railway line.

Intermittent mortar attacks on security bases continued but one incident stands out because of the exceptional devotion to duty demonstrated by WO1 Barry Johnson, who was sent to deal with it. The London-born officer, aged thirty-seven, had completed his first EOD tour in Belfast in 1978. On 7 October 1989, with three weeks of his second tour remaining, he was sent to a hijacked vehicle carrying mortars aimed at a nearby security force base, which had been abandoned on a housing estate beside a hospital. The standard procedure would have been to deal with the six mortars by remotely disrupting the launch mechanism, but Johnson was concerned that the highly inaccurate mortars could endanger civilian lives if they were launched inadvertently. He therefore decided to lift the bombs from their firing tubes and dismantle them by hand. With the help of Corporal Melia, his assistant, he removed the firing tubes from the back of the vehicle and placed them on the ground, pointing away from the hospital.

As the next stage of the neutralisation was extremely perilous, Johnson sent his assistant back behind cover. Working alone in the dark and in bitterly cold drizzle, which made the handling of the metal shells even more hazardous, he carefully removed and neutralised five mortars. While he was working at the last one it exploded and he was thrown across the road by the force of the blast. Although in great pain he refused to be evacuated until he had briefed his Number Two on the precise details of the device so that the dismantling could be completed by a replacement operator. Melia, ignoring his own safety, had run to the aid of his Number One and administered first aid as he listened to Johnson's instructions. He was mentioned in dispatches for his 'prompt action and undoubted courage far beyond that expected of a soldier of his rank'. Johnson's injuries were so severe that he had to endure seven major operations over eleven weeks. He lost the sight of one eye and his vision in the other is permanently impaired but his courage and selflessness by remaining at the scene despite his grave injuries earned him the George Cross. He was the first bomb-disposal officer to receive it since George Styles in 1972. Shortly before the ceremony at Buckingham Palace on 11 December 1990, Johnson insisted:

> I was only doing my job. To be honest, at the time I was amazed to find I was still alive. Even to this day I find it hard to believe I survived. It is part of a soldier's instinct to hand over before leaving the scene of an incident. I was quite determined that nobody else should get hurt and that I should warn them of any dangers in the area.

There were further developments in the use of mortars in 1989. On 13 May, four were fired at the Glassdrumman observation post in south Armagh. Three exploded but the fourth warhead was recovered and proved to be yet another variant, the Mark 11. Thirty inches long and six wide, the cylindrical projectile was made from rolled steel, had a range up to 500 yards, weighed over 40 lb. and could carry 25 lb. of explosive. Two of them were combined with two more powerful Mark 12 warheads, the latter being used for the first time, in a two-phase attack on the police–Army post at Crossmaglen on 26 October 1989. The immediate target was the 'Borucki' sangar, the fortified ground-level observation post which stood in the village square close to the spot where Private James Borucki of the Parachute Regiment had been ambushed and killed on 8 August 1976. The terrorists intended the Mark 11s to tear a hole in the outer steel mesh of the sangar so that the more powerful Mark 12s would explode directly against the sangar wall.

The well-planned operation began just after breakfast-time when four armed and masked men took a local man hostage and stole his tractor. Elsewhere accomplices were already working to convert a silage trailer to launch the mortars. A hole was cut in one side, covered with polythene and then painted to camouflage the modification. In the rear of the vehicle, a base plate and frame holding the four mortars was welded into place and the firing mechanisms were connected and wired through to the cab of the tractor. With everything armed, the tractor was driven into the village just after noon and parked in the square with the mortars pointing directly at the sangar from behind the polythene. The tractor driver dismounted and went into the nearby gents from where he promptly disappeared. Just over ten minutes later the two Mark 11 mortars ripped through the flimsy polythene and exploded on impact with the mesh, tearing a hole as planned. Almost immediately the two heavier missiles followed but although they went off against the sangar, its steel and concrete shell remained intact and three members of the Royal Anglian Regiment inside suffered only shock.

The Mark 12, thirty inches long and five inches in diameter, was a cone-shaped projectile with tail fins and an impact fuse to detonate the 5 lb. explosive charge. One was recovered intact on 28 October 1990 by Captain Richard Maybery who found it aimed at Dungannon police station from the top of a stepladder through the window of a boiler house at South Tyrone Hospital. Unable to wear his EOD suit because of the confined space, the ATO dismantled the device, knowing that its impact fuse would set it off if it hit the ground. Recovering it was a great prize, allowing a technical assessment of the fusing mechanism and propulsion system. A more ambitious attack was launched on 2 August 1991 when three radio-controlled warheads were fired at a Puma helicopter disembarking troops in Newtownhamilton. The pilot immediately lifted off and three explosions were heard. Next day, during a search by EOR teams and an ATO, the sequence of events was pieced together. The firing point was at the rear of a garage in the town centre and the three shells had overshot the Army base by several hundred yards.

Another version of this mortar, the most ambitious to date and by far the largest, was already posing a potentially serious threat to security bases. The Mark 13 consisted of a forty-five-gallon oil drum containing a 350 lb. charge of HME and was designed to be fired over the wall of a security force base. It was first seen on 22 May 1990 after a planned attack on the RUC station at Dungannon was aborted when an off-duty policeman spotted it mounted on the back of a lorry. A similar operation at Omagh a few days later was equally unsuccessful. There, just before 11 p.m., a flatbed Renault van was driven into a yard at the rear of the police station and parked three yards from the perimeter fence by a man who then ran off. Within one minute the propellant exploded but it flung the main mortar only about three yards, well short of the station wall, and the main 100 lb. charge did not go off on impact. However, the danger posed by close-up attack with the weapon was not underestimated. 'The shape of things to come,' said the incident report.

Diesel tanks from lorries were used as projectiles in further Mark 13 attacks as the IRA made ever more determined efforts to inflict casualties and damage at police and Army installations. A Mark 14, first used on 31 May 1992 at Crossmaglen, utilised the top halves of two 25 lb. gas cylinders welded together with an array of tail fins and could hold nearly 50 lb. of HME. On 7 December 1992 came the first use of the Mark 15 'barrack-buster' mortar at RUC Ballygawley. It was made from a 75 lb. industrial-gas cylinder nearly two feet long and one foot wide and could propel a payload of 175 lb. over 100 yards. Another was used at RUC Clogher on 20 January. On 4 February 1993 at Crossmaglen the device was concealed in a hay bale and launched from the back of a tractor. Mark 15s were also welded into vans and other vehicles and driven close to bases to be detonated, as on 3 March 1993 when two were fired at Bessbrook police station, damaging it and 100 houses nearby. Five days later another claimed a life at Keady police station when it exploded inside the station fence while a civilian crane driver was swinging a portable building into position.

A series of hush-hush tests on a revolutionary new concept for blast-proof buildings was now under way on military ranges in Britain. Known as the 'Mark 15 Cube', it had an internal steel frame covered with prefabricated, layered panels of steel and concrete. The linking technique not only provided greater protection from blast but allowed the structure to absorb and distribute blast pressure with less likelihood of collapse. In order to improve interior working conditions window 'plugs' could be fitted to let in daylight in areas of less risk, with the option of going windowless if a threat developed. A series of vulnerable border stations were quickly rebuilt early in 1993 and over the following years fifteen more Mark 15 Cubes were made. A further IRA upgrade was revealed on 13 July 1993 when the Mark 16 mortar was first used at William Street, Londonderry. It was launched from a portable tube concealed in the bonnet of a car and the nose-cone of the foot-long projectile was designed to explode on impact, setting off a charge of up to 2 lb.

On 1 March 1991 the IRA had unveiled another deadly improvised weapon which would bring tough new countermeasures. Shortly before 9 p.m. two UDR Land Rovers halted at traffic lights on the Killylea Road, Armagh. There were four soldiers in each vehicle, a driver and passenger in the front and two standing in the rear, their heads and shoulders exposed above the roof of the vehicle. Suddenly a projectile, fired by command wire attached to a launcher concealed at the roadside, struck the rear left-hand side of the front vehicle and exploded. The driver and one of the top-cover sentries died instantly while the other two soldiers were badly injured. More fatalities followed. A police officer was killed the following September in Swatragh, County Londonderry, when one of the 5 lb. warheads hit his Land Rover and in November another soldier perished in an identical attack at Bellaghy.

The same year saw the introduction of the Mark 15 hand grenade or 'coffee-jar' bomb, which would figure in seventy-three incidents and cause two deaths, and the PRIG (Propelled Recoilless Improvised Grenade). This was perhaps the ultimate improvised weapon utilising, apart from the 1 lb. Semtex charge, a number of everyday components. The shoulder-fired launcher was made from a thirty-inch length of metal pipe with a wooden handgrip and electrical detonation pack. The projectile consisted of a food tin packed with the explosive. The recoilless effect was created by counter-balancing the tin with a similar weight, usually a couple of packs of biscuits. When it was fired the tin shot out of the front while the biscuits were ejected from the rear. Despite its basic components, this was a lethal weapon if it struck its target. Early in

January 1994 one bored a hole in a heavily armoured police Land Rover in Belfast. The three officers inside were injured but survived.

The lethality of the coffee-jar bomb had been demonstrated when it was first used. Every day at about 5.30 p.m. the dogs kennelled close to the perimeter wall of the North Howard Street Mill Army base on the Belfast 'peace line' were fed by their handlers. On 25 May 1991, as this ritual was taking place, a coffee-jar bomb was thrown over the wall and exploded as it hit the ground. One soldier was killed outright and another lost both legs and two fingers. On 5 June WO2 Duane Duffy, who had recently dealt with the first PRIG, was called to the Suffolk Road, Belfast where he found an unexploded coffee-jar device. Recognising the importance of recovering it intact, he opted for the hazardous route of dismantling it by hand. It consisted of a 2 lb. Semtex charge in a glass coffee jar which would be fired electronically once the impact fuse completed the circuit. For his bravery in this and 135 other tasks completed during his four-month tour, Duffy was awarded the George Medal.

A month or so later, on 25 June, a coffee-jar bomb was thrown at two Belfast policemen just yards from their police station in Queen Street. Surgeons worked for hours to save the leg of one of the injured officers and the blast caused extensive damage to cars parked along the street and the front of nearby buildings. On 15 August a twenty-three-year-old man was killed by a PRIG after he was mistaken for a soldier. Among thirty similar incidents in the three months after it was introduced there were several instances of civilians being injured, including children who picked up unexploded devices in the street. The threat posed by the weapon was so serious that the police and Army took the unusual step of warning that anyone using it could be shot dead.

A deadly adaptation of an American-made photo-flash slave unit worth £70 cost one police officer her life and maimed another at Merchant's Quay in Newry in April 1992. As their armoured police car came within range of the ambush point, a watching terrorist flashed the primary unit at the secondary unit, mounted on the sun visor of a parked car. This triggered the propulsion charge and launched a Mark 12 mortar rigged up in the boot. The shell exploded on impact with the police car, killing Constable Colleen McMurray. Constable Paul Slaine, who was travelling with her, lost both legs in the explosion. On 12 April 2000 he had the honour of receiving from the Queen the George Cross awarded to the RUC for its collective courage and sacrifice during the years of the Northern Ireland conflict.

The IRA in Newry had been working on the use of flash-initiated devices for some time. The first one encountered, on 31 March 1990, was incorporated in a booby-trapped bicycle left in the town centre. The ATO who neutralised a timer-power unit under the saddle and removed a quantity of Semtex from the cycle frame assumed that terrorists had intended to detonate it by radio control, but a police scenes of crime officer discovered that the bomb-maker had incorporated a flash-gun slave unit in the mudguard reflector. The same technique was used successfully in September 1991 to initiate an explosion at RUC Warrenpoint. At this time the IRA were also experimenting with infrared and radar devices to set off both vehicle bombs and mortars, but although ambushes were put in place, the organisation's growing sensitivity to unintended civilian killings forced them to pull back, for such devices, once planted, were largely outside the control of the attackers. An infra-red device could be set off by animals in a field or a farmer going about his work. In an urban environment the chances of indiscriminate detonation were even greater. Light-sensitive devices too could easily be set off at the wrong time, for example by the headlights of a passing car.

However, despite their new-found caution an array of proven and lethal weapons remained at the terrorists' disposal. The IRA's under-car booby-trap devices had often failed to operate but the weapon became progressively more sophisticated and reliable. In June 1992 they mounted a daring raid on a police car in the centre of Belfast. As the armoured Ford Sierra halted at the security checkpoint in High Street, a youth dashed from the pavement and placed a device on the roof. Within seconds, as he escaped into the crowds, the 2 lb. Semtex bomb went off, turning the vehicle into a fireball. The RUC officers had been warned to expect something of the sort after an informer had leaked details of a plan to attack an MP with just such a 'limpet weapon', so as soon as they heard the device being set on the roof they dived out of the car. This incident has gone down in the annals of the Troubles as a 'limpet mine' attack, with a strong magnet supposedly being used to clamp the bomb to the car roof. In fact the device was in a plastic cassette player, which minimised the shrapnel effect, and was merely set on the roof of the stationary car. The ATO concluded the intention was to kill the police officers in the car with the high explosive and reduce the possibility of injury to anyone standing nearby. As he reported, 'the policemen escaped almost certain death by their quick reactions.'

About 200 radio-controlled devices had now been used by the IRA, with inconsistent results. From a modest start with simple model-aircraft components, this strand of the campaign had quickly evolved to the point where state-of-the-art electronics were being used by both sides. It was not unknown for the Army to 'bug' arms caches in order to catch bombers red-handed. In February 1988, as the battle of wits intensified, terrorists used a combined command-wire and radio-control arrangement on a 200 lb. landmine planted at the Glassdrumman post in south Armagh. The theory was that the sixty yards of command wire would extend beyond the limits of the electronic safety bubble created by the portable electronic countermeasures kit – known as the 'green monkey' – carried by each patrol. Other explosions had been triggered by adapted walkie-talkie radios and other pieces of electronic equipment, many acquired legally and imported from the US and elsewhere. Captain Andrew Salmons was awarded the Queen's Gallantry Medal for disregarding his personal safety to dismantle a new type of radio-controlled device attached to a 550 lb. bomb on 16 September 1991. On 29 July 1992, in another operation 'fraught with danger', as his George Medal citation later stated, WO1 John Balding dismantled an infrared initiation device twelve feet up in a tree, linked to 450 lb. of HME buried near by. The clearance was further complicated by the presence of a 2 lb. Semtex self-destruct charge designed to go after the main bomb and destroy all evidence of the firing mechanism. This was one of the most secret and sensitive areas of the campaign with a constant battle for advantage being fought over hundreds of frequency bands on the airwaves.

Compared with the 1980s lull when the EOD teams were complaining about the lack of 'street heat', the early 1990s saw them once more at full stretch. Some of the operators and members of the twelve teams deployed during this period attended as many as 100 incidents during a tour. Acting Captain Christopher Hodder answered 110 calls from March to July 1987, of which twenty-six were to live explosions and fifteen to unexploded devices. Between August 1990 and the following January WO2 Kenneth Cross, working with the Bessbrook team who had christened themselves 'the bang gang', carried out fifty-two tasks including six complex clearances on the Belfast–Dublin railway line. From March to September 1991 WO2 Duane Duffy completed 135 tasks, fifteen of them dealing with live devices.

The ranks of the unsung heroes of 321 EOD include people like Lance-Corporal Jones, the driver and escort for the commanding officer of 321 in March 1985. During his two-year tour he constantly braved the high risk of attack as he drove his boss on a 55,000-mile gauntlet around some 600 EOD incidents. Another driver went out on seventy operations during a four-month tour and spent the rest of his time maintaining the section's ageing Humber vehicles to prevent them breaking down in an area where they might come under attack. WO Guy Crofts, one of the Royal Signals Bleeps, completed an unprecedented four-year tour with 321 EOD in 1986. He was awarded the MBE for his groundbreaking work in countering radio-controlled devices, once escaping death or serious injury helping to recover a new type of device intact. 'I think there have been about a thousand people who have served with the unit over the years and their heroics and dedication are every bit as much a part of the story of 321 EOD as that of the Number Ones,' says Major Ian Jones.

In 1987 it was calculated that every pound of explosive that went off caused £1,500 worth of damage. By that estimation the work of the EOD teams had already saved £250 million. In 1987 alone the IRA set off some 14,500 lb. of explosive and the security forces captured almost 10,000 lb. After that the annual total rose inexorably, year by year, to reach an all-time high in 1993 when a massive 35,000 lb. was detonated. From 1988 until 1993 a total of 161,600 lb. of home-made explosive was set off and 53,700 lb. captured. 1991 was the busiest year for the EOD teams since 1978, with 1,758 taskings, 230 explosions and 142 incendiary attacks.

It was therefore very much business as usual for the company when it notched up twenty-one years' continuous service in Northern Ireland on 9 November 1992. That morning, one of the teams was defusing a 100 lb. device in the New Lodge district of Belfast but the others were able to join past members – 'the old and bold' – at a commemorative function in Army headquarters at Lisburn. Among them were Barry Johnson GC and 'Lofty' Pattinson, the man who had done so much to make the Wheelbarrow the success it had become. Also present were some of the men who had been awarded the two George Crosses, sixteen OBEs, twenty-one MBEs, nineteen BEMs, thirty-three George Medals, sixty-five Queen's Gallantry Medals and well over 100 commendations and mentions in dispatches which gave 321 EOD the unrivalled distinction of having won more awards in peacetime than any other unit in the British Army.

During the day the unit received a large number of congratulatory messages. The Northern Ireland Secretary, Sir Patrick Mayhew, said their work over twenty-one years 'dealing with the devices with which terrorists seek to destroy lives and livelihoods . . . has undoubtedly saved many from the misery of unemployment, from the shock and trauma of destroyed homes and, most importantly of all, from shattered lives'. Lieutenant-General Sir John Wilsey, the GOC Northern Ireland, said:

'The contribution our bomb-disposal men have made to the safety of the public goes far beyond these shores. The skills and knowledge they have accumulated have been used to benefit people all over the world.' He pointed out that the work of the unit had not been without great sacrifice, twenty of its officers having lost their lives and another twenty-three having been injured while dealing with terrorist devices. The *Belfast Telegraph* reminded its readers that 'the unit is the most highly decorated in the Army but no amount of medals or citations can equal the thanks that the people of Northern Ireland owe to the bomb-disposal experts.'

This sentiment was followed up a couple of months later when the General Purposes and Finance Committee of Belfast City Council unanimously decided to award 321 the freedom of the city in recognition of the unit's extraordinary role in protecting life and property. Although the decision had to be formally ratified by the entire council, the committee believed that despite the presence of Sinn Fein councillors there would be sufficient support to approve it by the required two-thirds majority. When the matter came up during the meeting on 1 February 1993, the Sinn Fein councillors walked out of the council chamber. What the committee had not expected was that the Social Democratic and Labour Party councillors would join them, leaving just thirty-three councillors, one short of a sufficient majority. The proposal had to be dropped, causing an angry political fallout. Alban Maginness, the leader of the SDLP councillors, explained they had withdrawn to avoid the appearance of snubbing the unit.

> We have the greatest respect and admiration for the bravery of the bomb squad and acknowledge that they have done a tremendous amount of work for Belfast. But this was a highly political motion and we were not consulted about it beforehand. If we had been, we would have explained why it is impossible for the SDLP to support such a motion until there is political consensus in this society.

Their attitude was criticised by Tom Campbell, the Alliance party councillor who had proposed the honour. He accused the SDLP of administering 'a slap in the face for the brave men and women in the bomb squad who have worked hard and without fear or favour for the people of this city'. Sir Patrick Mayhew merely said it was 'a great pity that a very brave and admirable unit of the British Army has been embroiled in this particular controversy', but Peter Gurney, who had since won a bar to his George Medal for his work as an explosives officer with the London Metropolitan Police, said it would have been a 'tremendous honour' for 321 and he knew that members of the unit would feel hurt. 'The bomb squad does not ask what allegiances or political views a person has before defusing a device. Our only concern is to save lives,' he told the *Belfast Telegraph*. By way of consolation, the neighbouring Newtownabbey Council stepped in soon afterwards and awarded 321 EOD the freedom of its borough.

The shameful controversy in Belfast coincided with a more painful milestone in unit history, the loss of its cherished Royal Army Ordnance Corps cap badge. The change came about on 5 April 1993 when the corps was amalgamated with the Royal Corps of Transport, the Royal Pioneer Corps, the Army Catering Corps and the Postal and Courier Service of the Royal Engineers to form the 16,500-strong Royal Logistics Corps, whose role was summed up by a new motto: 'We sustain'. The change had no practical effect on the role or operation of 321 although its official designation was changed to 321 EOD Squadron, Royal Logistics Corps to bring it into line with corps nomenclature. Its close relationship with the 11 EOD Regiment and the other widely dispersed EOD formations in the Army continued as before.

On 30 March 1993 an EOD team was called out to a suspect device under a car outside a house at the Rathenraw estate in Antrim. For once, the team was not at its usual high degree of readiness that morning. The Number One, Staff Sergeant Colin Whitworth, was awaiting the arrival of his replacement from England before he drove to Armagh to take over another team temporarily. Twenty-seven-year-old Whitworth, whose six-month tour was nearing its end, was in good spirits because he had earlier opened a posting order confirming a coveted appointment to another specialised ammunition job. Then in quick succession came two telephone calls. The first was from the replacement ATO to say that his flight was delayed indefinitely. The other was the tasking message to go to Rathenraw. 'Like any ATO would, I quickly changed out of my civvies into my combats and we deployed.'

The suspicious device was underneath a silver-blue Ford Escort belonging to a man with Sinn Fein connections who had spotted it when he came out to take his children to school. By the time the two EOD Tacticas arrived about an hour later, the immediate area had been sealed off by local police and the team quickly set to work. Clad in his EOD suit, with thin rubber forensic gloves on his hands, Whitworth first sent Wheelbarrow up close to the car to take a look. 'We had received a warning fax a couple of days earlier about a new Loyalist under-car pipe-bomb device, largely made from plumbing components, and so that is what I was expecting to find, which I did.' Whitworth knew that a similar device had fallen off a car and injured a man who picked it up. Another had been spotted on a vehicle but had gone off when a Pigstick disrupter was fired at it, so Whitworth decided to tackle this example manually, as he recalls:

> The critical contact was that between a small pendulum which was designed to swing over when the car moved and set off the device by hitting two copper contacts. Something slim and rigid was needed to stop them making contact so I slipped in my Visa card which seemed the perfect thing and then taped it back to prevent it moving. I also noticed there was a pinhole for a safety device so I decided to get one. Bob's your uncle, the device is safe, I thought, as I walked back to the incident control point.
>
> I made another manual approach and this time inserted the pin, attached a hook and line and pulled the device off the car and clear of it by about six feet or so. Then I rolled and tumbled it a few times. Again I remember thinking to myself, well, that's the most dangerous part of the operation over.
>
> The next step was to X-ray the device to see precisely how it was put together and where the power source was. I was not concerned about a victim-operated mechanism, for the Loyalists had never taken on an ATO before.

At 11.24 a.m., having allowed the device to soak, he went forward again, removed the magnets which held it to the underside of the car and lifted it into position for the X-ray. It was then he noticed a battery soldered into the circuitry.

> It was a standard PP3 battery so I started to slice at the insulating tape to free it, thinking that would be the device neutralised, happy days, end of story. But then I felt the device getting hot in my left hand, not hot enough to drop, but heating up and then smoke came out. Just as I was moving to set it down gently, it suddenly exploded and threw me three or four yards onto my back.
>
> I could feel the fragmented bits of metal hitting my visor and the steel breastplate on my suit. It seemed like an age but then I stood up and looked around. The people at the incident control point didn't think

the device had functioned but they came running towards me. I didn't feel any pain but I wiped my right eye across the surface of the visor which was now rough and sharp with shards of metal and I cut it before I lifted the visor. It was then that I saw my left hand was gone. The nerve ends were wriggling around like little bits of spaghetti.

Then my guys started putting field dressings on it and I felt the pain, pain like I'd never felt in my life before. Unbelievable pain. I was taken to hospital in Ballymena, conscious, bleeding all the way. There was a great clump of field dressings on the arm. I knew the bomb suit had saved my life, prevented more injuries. I had the visor down and that helped. It's a bad habit but many operators, me included, often work with the visor up.

Once at the hospital the emergency team awaiting his arrival swung into action.

They were tremendous, superb. They offered to screen off my face but I declined and told them the hand was already gone, that I'd seen it. I don't think they believed me at first because of the big clump of dressings on my left arm but then I offered to sell them my golf clubs cheap.

David Gleadhill, the accident and emergency consultant who initially cared for Whitworth, was so impressed at the way he conducted himself in the hospital that soon afterwards he wrote to CATO:

Despite the nature of his very serious injury he maintained an equilibrium throughout his immediate care that I have rarely encountered. I fully appreciate that officers working in this field must be made of particularly 'stern stuff' but his mettle had a lasting impression on not only myself but all who work in this department. In view of the strength of personality shown by him at the critical time after this incident I cannot help but feel that his future will be favourable despite the obvious difficulties he will initially encounter.

The prognosis was entirely accurate in all respects. Whitworth refused to be invalided out of the Army and, moreover, worked his way back into his old job. How he did so is another tale of remarkable determination and achievement. The official investigation cleared him of all blame. The device was of unconventional design and construction and, it was concluded, had short-circuited during the neutralisation process and then gone off. 'Paramilitary devices are often as dangerous as those produced by cranks,' the official report noted. Whitworth was commended for having his visor down. The pockmarked suit with its shrapnel-peppered visor, which, undoubtedly saved his sight and protected him from far more serious injury if not death, is now exhibited at the training centre for bomb-disposal officers as a stark reminder of the value of wearing the garb at all times. 'Even when I was in the ambulance going to hospital,' Whitworth says, 'my only concern was "did I cock up". It's a professional thing really. We all think we are good operators. I thought I was a good operator and when I was later told that it was just bad luck, that the device was made in a Mickey-Mouse way, I was relieved.'

After four weeks' hospital treatment in Northern Ireland, he was moved to Woolwich where he was advised his discharge papers would soon be served. There followed what he calls 'a violent encounter' with the brigadier concerned, but the EOD establishment moved in and found him a job as Number Two at the Joint Services EOD operations room at Didcot.

> The trade and the regiment looked after me and kept me involved in bomb disposal. That meant a lot to me and kept me sane. I don't know what would have happened if I'd been discharged. I've never really been concerned about losing my hand. Even the loss of everything would have been nothing compared to losing my job. One door closed and thirty others opened for me. As operators we're almost prepared for something to happen to us. When I joined up, after choosing the ammunition trade, the old recruiting sergeant asked me if I had a full set of fingers and he told me I wouldn't have when I left the Army.

But Whitworth was not content to run a desk at Didcot and over the next few years, with the help of the prosthetic experts, he developed a set of special attachments to enable him to work as an operator again. He also made various adaptations so that he could carry the equipment with lanyards and clips. The only thing he could not manage was clipping lengths of insulating tape from a roll, so he carried a dispenser to peel them off with one hand. Such was his determination that he steadily worked his way up from staff sergeant to WO2, WO1 and finally captain. On the way he successfully completed the various standard and special courses to regain his EOD operator's licence and to serve again in

Northern Ireland. In 2004 he was temporarily assigned from his job as second-in-command of 321 to serve for a time in Iraq.

After the 1993 Shankill Road fish shop bombing an angry man had phoned a radio station and declared: 'The politicians fiddle while Belfast bleeds.' It was a point of view shared by many ordinary people who despaired that their political representatives appeared to preside passively over the endless death and destruction. What most of them did not know was that a remarkable process of secret negotiation, involving not only politicians but also the hitherto excluded terrorist groupings, was gathering pace.

Soon after the Enniskillen bombing in 1987 the SDLP leader John Hume had begun a series of talks with Gerry Adams. About the same time, a secret channel between a senior British intelligence official and the IRA was reopened for a parallel dialogue about bringing the conflict to an end. Meanwhile other intermediaries were talking to Loyalists. The dialogue was painfully slow and the great escalation of violence that accompanied it discouraged all but the most optimistic. In 1993, for instance, the IRA detonated over 32,000 lb. of explosive, half as much again as in 1992. By the summer, with an imminent ceasefire predicted, the IRA was determined to show it was not calling off its violence on account of any weakness or with any hint of surrender. So until the silence of the guns came into effect at midnight on 31 August there was no weakening of murderous intent on the part of the IRA. On the 29th a house was taken over near Pomeroy, County Tyrone, and a silver Renault car and a blue Ford Transit van were taken away. The thefts were not reported until after midnight, about the same time as passing motorists started reporting a blue Ford van abandoned three miles from Pomeroy. Just after 2.30 a.m. a Gazelle helicopter pilot reported the vehicle was parked on the right-hand side of the road, pointing towards the town with its headlights still on. Just after dawn, undercover officers drove past in an unmarked car. Although it was a highly dangerous mission, expert covert surveillance of potential bomb scenes could yield valuable intelligence or reveal a false alarm. In this case, the observers said they were sure there was a Mark 15 mortar in the back of the van.

Captain Chris Henson, who had been in Northern Ireland for two months, was the ATO on call that morning. Although this was his first EOD tour, he had previously served in Northern Ireland with the Royal Hampshires and as a second lieutenant had been part of the cover operation for Barry Johnson in Londonderry the night he earned his GC.

Henson and his team were on the road at 6.25 a.m. and took up position near the suspect mortar bomb an hour later. After making the usual checks he used a Wheelbarrow to break the front passenger window. When he approached he saw the firing mechanism lying in the front, linked by a series of dangling wires and detonating cords to the warhead, a Calor gas cylinder protruding from a steel launch tube on a sheet-metal base plate bolted to the floor of the van. Henson first ensured the mortar would not launch by cutting the wires to the firing packs, then opened the rear and side doors with Wheelbarrow, cut away more wiring and pulled out the firing pack to get at the mortar itself.

By now he was quite confident that terrorists had been forced to abort an attack on Pomeroy police station because the van, belonging to a builder and packed with paint tins, tools and other paraphernalia, had run out of fuel. 'We all knew the ceasefire was coming and this seemed to be intended for one last hit,' he recalls.

> But as I was unbolting the base plate from the plywood floor of the van, I suddenly noticed something that shouldn't be there. Instead of there being a propellant charge, all I could see was a timer-power unit with a red light winking at me so having found that, I went back to the control point pretty quickly and we decided to have a cup of tea and some lunch and wait to see what would happen.

After letting the device soak, Henson decided to attack the concealed booby-trap directly. He removed the detonators and disconnected the firing pack, which he found was linked to five fertiliser bags of HME and a two-gallon container of petrol to enhance the effect of the blast. This part of the device had been carefully constructed to operate once the ATO attempted to move the mortar launcher. 'This made it intensely personal. I thought, they're out to get an ATO, get me, with the ceasefire coming.' It was well after 7 p.m., nearly twelve hours since the start of the operation, before the clearance was complete. The 'barrack-buster' was found to contain 170 lb. of ANS with a 7 lb. HME propellant charge in addition to the 200 lb. of explosive in the fertiliser bags.

After their long day, there was still one more job for the team before they could get to bed. Not long before midnight, an explosion was reported at a restaurant at Coagh, County Tyrone. When they got there, they found that a blast incendiary had partially detonated but that the attached explosive and petrol had not ignited. These were the last significant clearances before the ceasefire.

When what the IRA called its 'cessation of military operations' came into effect, jubilant supporters all over Northern Ireland took to the streets in convoys of hooting cars and long congas of people, but the euphoria was punctured by still militant Loyalists who abducted and shot dead a Catholic workman. Over the next few weeks, likeminded Loyalists continued to provide work for the EOD teams. On 4 September, a car bomb outside the Sinn Fein office in Belfast was more damaging than anything Loyalists had used before and on 12 September three passengers were injured when only the detonators exploded in an attempted bombing on the Belfast–Dublin train. On 13 October 1994, however, the various Loyalist factions declared an open-ended ceasefire. After that, although the EOD teams got the respite they had long deserved, for a time there were regular call-outs to investigate reports of nocturnal explosions in rural areas and examine fresh holes in the ground. Everybody hoped that by disposing of their explosive stocks, as they seemed to be doing, the terrorists were signalling that after a quarter of a century the war was really over.

Chapter Fourteen

A Special Kind of Courage

It is not widely known that some of the world's most expert 'terrorists' are discreetly based in the English Midlands. There they monitor every terrorist organisation and incident and constantly devise and set up lethal attack and ambush scenarios. Their intentions are, however, entirely honourable for they are the handful of instructors at the world-renowned Felix Training Centre at Kineton in Warwickshire where bomb-disposal operators are trained, primarily for Northern Ireland. 'The aim is for complete reality,' says Lieutenant-Colonel Mike Dolamore, the commanding officer. 'We want the students to think they are on the streets of Belfast or on the border in south Armagh so that when they experience the real thing, it will be completely familiar to them.'

More recently, with the global war on terror and the campaigns in Afghanistan and Iraq, the centre's work has taken on an increasingly international dimension. At the end of 2004 there were seventy British bomb disposal experts, many of them Felix Centre graduates, stationed in Iraq. As evidenced by the group pictures, plaques and coats of arms which decorate the walls in the centre's main buildings, its graduates include soldiers and police officers from some 100 countries. 'Our doctrine and philosophy is now world-renowned and we cannot keep pace with the demand for places,' says Dolamore. So, around the clock and from around the world, the instructors are plugged into the international bomb intelligence network which disseminates detailed reports about technical and tactical innovations adopted by terrorists from about sixty countries. Whether it be a roadside bomb in Iraq, a complex ambush along the leafy lanes of South Armagh, a train bomb in Madrid, a nuisance bomber in Manhattan, a guerrilla in Kashmir or an embassy bomber in east Africa, details of the device and its delivery will be reported and analysed. The service is vital for bomb-disposal officers in every country, for it ensures that an explosives officer in Scotland Yard would recognise an Al Qaeda device previously used only in the Far East, or a Spanish operator would have some idea of how to tackle a vehicle bomb constructed and planted by ETA in line with know-how supplied by the IRA.

Nowhere are the reports more thoroughly analysed than at the Felix Centre, where the theory and practice of IEDD (Improvised Explosive Devices Disposal) is taught in depth. The instruction and rigorous training are designed to instil the necessary skills and confidence while weeding out individuals who are temperamentally unsuited for the task. According to a parliamentary answer in 2000, it typically costs £45,750 to train a sergeant, excluding his pay. Standards are ruthlessly maintained by the instructors, mostly decorated veterans of Northern Ireland and other conflicts. At the end of each training course, the student must complete three of four clearance tasks to pass. In the two years to 2001 a total of 108 out of 170 students passed, but the proportion varies from course to course. Borderline cases are never given the benefit of the doubt. An ill-prepared and unsuitable student could cause the deaths of others by mishandling an incident, or lose his or her own life. 'No matter how pressing the need for trained operators, the stringent standards are rigorously maintained and never compromised,' says Dolamore. Every year Kineton's in-house 'terrorist cell' sets up more than 1,000 'incidents' to test students' skill, patience and nerve. Every scenario is based on a permutation of real ones and they use working copies of IEDs but the devices contain bags of sand rather than doctored fertiliser and produce only a flash and a bang when set off. In all other respects the tests are as lifelike as possible, played out in real time, round the clock, in all weathers. However, well before they reach the Felix Centre, aspirant bomb-disposal officers must travel a long road.

Not surprisingly, no one, however brave, can just walk into a recruiting office and sign on. Indeed, while dealing with terrorist bombs is an important military skill, the Royal Logistics Corps and its predecessor body, the RAOC, have traditionally regarded the terrorist bomb-disposal task as a subsidiary skill to be acquired by an ATO (on a captain's salary, about £35,000) or an AT (typically a staff sergeant on £30,000), whose prime responsibility is the safe storage, transit and deployment of the ammunition and explosives required on the battlefield. There has always been stiff competition for the trade with a hundred applicants competing for the twenty or thirty posts that come up every year. 'The first step is having their head read,' says Rod 'Fluff' Roberts, the Testing and Validation Officer at the Army School of Ammunition. 'If we think they're temperamentally suited to the job, which is judged by their performance in psychometric tests, then they can move on to the next stage of the selection procedure. After achieving the basic ammunition qualifications their suitability to do the job and advance their careers mainly depends on their ability to pass the various IEDD courses.' Even then, they have to complete and pass regular refresher courses to keep their knowledge up to date. Again the standards are stringent and ruthlessly maintained. No matter how experienced an officer or how distinguished their record, they must pass three out of four tasks in a day. 'The quality of training may make the difference between life and death but students have, of course, the greatest of all motivation to keep on top of their profession – survival,' says former Lieutenant-Colonel Mackenzie-Orr.

There are two routes into what the Army calls the ammunition family. One is a sixteen-month course for officers, who become ATOs with the rank of captain. The second, for non-commissioned ranks, lasts twelve months and qualifies them as ATs, but here the division between officers and other ranks is not as rigid as in some arms of the service, and non-commissioned officers frequently gain promotion. The special stresses of the bomb-disposal profession further smudge the distinction. Although it is strictly inaccurate, leaders of bomb-disposal teams are widely known as ATOs, and particularly in Northern Ireland, where they live and work in such close proximity, a close bond of trust and intimacy develops and the formalities of rank are often replaced by nicknames and wicked humour.

To become an AT an applicant must demonstrate key skills and qualities, in particular the ability to grasp complex technical matters, assess facts and write them up clearly and accurately. The first stage of the training, the Class 2 course at Kineton, lasts for twenty weeks and three days. Students are taught the physical, chemical, and materials science aspects of ammunition and explosives and the principles and application of study, quality control and ammunition disposal. Most of this knowledge is acquired in classrooms but there is also considerable practical work in storage bunkers and on the ranges. The course includes five weeks' instruction at the Royal Military College of Science, first established at Shrivenham in 1946, which provides education in defence-related science and technology. Having passed the examinations and completed the practical tests the student qualifies as a Class 2 AT, judged competent to inspect, repair, test and modify all ammunition and explosives used by the British Army including guided missiles. At this stage the technician is mainly assigned routine technical work under the supervision of a Class 1 AT but may also be required to assist with inspecting ammunition stocks, disposing of stray ammunition and explosives and rendering IEDs safe. After an average of three years' experience the AT can take the nineteen-week Class 1 course aimed at consolidating previous training, updating the soldier on new equipment and increasing his or her capabilities, including planning and supervising the work of others.

The other way to become a commissioned ATO requires at least A levels in the sciences. The first part of the course, twenty-two weeks at Shrivenham, gives students a basic grounding in explosives and ammunition science. The syllabus includes extensive study, with lectures and practicals, of physics, chemistry, mathematics, ballistics, electronics and metallurgy. Time is also allocated to nuclear, biological and chemical weapon design, radiological and chemical protection systems and automatic data processing. At the end of this phase, each student is required to distil what has been learned into a project, write a report and give a presentation to an audience of officers and academics. For the second part of the course, students move to Kineton where over thirty-seven weeks they learn the theory and practice of ammunition design, surveillance, storage and movement and how to dispose of unserviceable ammunition by demolition, open burning, incineration and deflagration techniques, as well as to recognise and dispose of UXOs (Unexploded Explosive Ordnance) and biological and chemical munitions. The course also contains a module on Improvised Explosive Device Disposal.

Having attained the basic ammunition qualifications, ATs usually make the transition into bomb disposal by becoming Number Twos, graduating to Number One team leaders after a tour in Northern Ireland. However, commissioned ATOs and non-commissioned ATs can only become bomb-disposal officers through specialised courses such as that in Counter-Terrorist Bomb Disposal, or the similar NATO Joint Service IEDD course, both of which are conducted at Kineton. They must also pass the five-week Northern Ireland 'special-to-theatre' course before going to the province. Refresher and advanced courses give operators the expertise to handle biological, chemical and nuclear clearance incidents. Since 2003, students passing the Army's demanding Explosive Ordnance Disposal courses are also entitled to a National Vocational Qualification in Search and Munitions skills, allowing them to engage in similar work, including post-conflict mine clearance, after they leave the Army.

Established in 1941, the Defence Munitions Centre in Warwickshire expanded during the Second World War to 2,500 acres with ninety miles of railway track serving 252 munitions warehouses. Although scaled down considerably since then, it remains the Army's largest ammunition storage facility and while the two main storage areas are now serviced by road, twenty-five miles of railway survive, some of them used to store civilian rolling stock. The School of Ammunition moved there from Bramley in 1975 and trains about 1,000 students a year with alumni from sixty-seven countries. They learn conventional munitions disposal (CMD) and explosive ordnance disposal as well as the rudiments of Improvised Explosive Device Disposal (IEDD), but the specialised training is carried out in the Felix Centre.

Before the Northern Ireland conflict began in 1969, specialised EOD training was not given a high priority. Neutralising techniques had changed little since the end of the Second World War and devices were relatively crude and easily rendered safe. Bomb-disposal training was an add-on to the main ammunition instruction, with students sent to defuse boxes in dark corners of disused sheds at the 2,000-acre Central Ammunition Depot in Bramley. Major Martin Pope remembers that sometimes secondary devices would be planted in a pen of truculent goats just to make the exercise a little less straightforward. As the complexity of devices accelerated and the need for more focused training was recognised, a two-week course for those going to Northern Ireland was begun during 1971. Mike Coldrick recalls it was a pretty rudimentary preparation: 'We studied and constructed terrorist-type devices to be familiar with them and practised the evaluation of suspect bomb situations and devices, questioning witnesses and the like.' Some of the instruction took places in old huts, much of it outdoors in all weathers, just like the real thing.

When they got to Northern Ireland, in the early days, everybody spent a couple of days at Lisburn looking at dismantled devices, reading reports and intelligence summaries and going out on tasks as 'shadow' operators, observing at close quarters. This was also the first time many of them saw new equipment such as Wheelbarrow and Pigstick. 'The operational need on the ground was so urgent that none of it could be spared for training at Bramley so it was only when we got to Lisburn that we could see and try them,' recalls Dave Williams, who did the first of three tours in 1973. Colin Goodson remembers how traditional military relationships changed as the concept of the EOD team developed. 'We had all been good soldiers trained not to question but then we had to learn not to take anything for granted, to check everything out ourselves. A different sort of discipline developed. Warrant Officers and privates got on first name terms and "Sir" was not heard all that often after a time.'

More extensive training exercises were developed at the Fire Service Training College, Long Marston, an old tank and gunnery range at Melton Mowbray and Longmoor Camp in Hampshire. The IEDD Branch, as it was known, first moved to a complex of Nissen huts at Kineton, with its better facilities, in 1974. There the first dedicated Felix Centre was opened on 17 July 1980 by Lieutenant-General Sir Richard Lawson, then GOC Northern Ireland. Although the vast ranges at Kineton, the railway sidings and the enclosed rural area with its woods, meadows, streams, paths and roads provided an ideal training environment, facilities for instructors and trainers remained inadequate until the £6 million state-of-the-art Felix Centre was opened on 16 September 1992 by the Duke of Kent. Apart from the administrative centre, museum and lecture blocks, the centrepieces of the hundred-acre site are the five 'stands' where the scenarios are set.

As the principal focus of the Army's EOD effort has long been to combat the IRA threat, it is not surprising that the scenarios have a distinctive Irish flavour. There is a farm complex, a housing estate, a pub, a hotel and a railway and bus station, every bit as ramshackle as the real things, a car showroom with a forecourt packed with vehicles, and street furniture such as pillar boxes and lamp-posts which could contain bombs as they have done in the reality of Northern Ireland. (In 2004, work started on a sixth stand which can represent the Balkans or Iraq, where EOD personnel have most recently been required to use their skills.) Students are also set tasks in other parts of the complex. There could be a bomb alert on a train in the extensive railway sidings, a multiple landmine ambush in the heart of a wood, a booby-trapped vehicle in a cul-de-sac of houses or a culvert bomb under one of the roads criss-crossing the base. These tests are set up by the four 'terrorists', or exercise support staff as they are formally known, who comb EOD incident reports to plan their scenarios. They keep a little black book recording precisely which test incidents have been set for which students, so they never get the same one again during advanced or refresher training. The scenarios are updated every time a new device or tactic appears. Not surprisingly, the 'terrorists' have a standing arrangement with local scrapyards to ensure a regular supply of old cars for destruction.

Students have access to all the equipment and vehicles they would use in Northern Ireland. The curriculum provides for both individual and collective team training. Number One operators are put through their paces while Number Twos learn about the equipment and how to remotely drive the Wheelbarrow and fit and use its various attachments. Electronic countermeasures (ECM) training also takes place. (The only person missing is the driver/escort. Students are trained for driving EOD teams in Northern Ireland at the Defence School of Transport at Leconfield, Yorkshire.) As one graduate says:

> OK, there's no blood at Kineton and we use sand instead of ANFO but the pressure and the training is so realistic that no matter what you encounter in Northern Ireland itself, it's tolerable. At Kineton you put yourself under pressure because you want to succeed and do well and you're under constant observation by the instructors. You never experience that sort of pressure in real life. When you're in Armagh or somewhere it just seems surreal.

Fluff Roberts says:

> If they have come this far they are mentally able to do it and physically able to do it, so, in my mind, if they can cope with it here they can cope with it anywhere. The conditions are far more exacting than they would be in real life. The four jobs that they do here prior to going to Ireland are probably the four largest jobs they ever do because they're under assessment by their peer group. Self-imposed pressure is what they fail on. They put more pressure on themselves in trying to pass the necessary three tests than anything we can give them.

Since the early 1990s, the Northern Ireland EOD teams have deployed in a pair of purpose-built Alvis Tactica vehicles, designed and armoured for maximum protection from roadside bombings, snipers and angry crowds. They have four-wheel drive and run-flat tyres and can operate off road. At the scene of an incident they park to form a protected V with drop-down panels preventing explosive debris slithering underneath. The first vehicle carries two of the team and the Wheelbarrow and other equipment, while the second vehicle is taken up by the ECM kit and operator. The team is self-contained with mobile generator capacity and even limited catering facilities.

The most basic protective piece of equipment remains the EOD suit, which despite several improvements necessarily remains cumbersome and heavy to protect against blast, heat, pressure and fragmentation. Various modifications have been made to the helmet and some versions incorporate a blower to help prevent the visor misting up, a problem that persists to the irritation of operators. After two Kineton students noticed the high turnover of original helmet liners, their design for a washable insert was taken up and they were rewarded under an incentive scheme for the suggestion, which has saved an estimated £20,000 a year. In July 2002, as part of the process of constantly upgrading and improving EOD equipment, the Ministry of Defence gave a £650,000 development contract to NP Aerospace Ltd, Coventry, for a new 'Mark 5' suit. Although the result is some five pounds heavier, operators who have tried it say this disadvantage is more than compensated for by its stronger and more flexible body armour and improved ergonomic properties.

In the mid-1970s a rival for Wheelbarrow was developed at great cost and trialled in Northern Ireland in 1977. The Marauder had three separate sections of track on each side, providing a better capability to climb stairs than Wheelbarrow's single track. It was also better in a confined space because the body could rotate and pivot on the chassis. It had two independently controlled arms, one for disrupters, a shotgun or other tools, the other with a gripper hand which could open a car door with a key by remote control. From 4 May to 17 June 1977 the Belfast section deployed Marauder on 113 out of 220 tasks and Derrick Patrick says the machine did everything required of it. 'It was a brilliant design and a mechanical masterpiece.' However, he and the lieutenant-colonel tasked with its evaluation independently came to the same conclusion that it was too sophisticated and expensive.'We could have had four Wheelbarrows for the price of one Marauder,' Patrick says. It was sent back to Northern Ireland again in 1981 but, as one former ATO says, 'the computer and electronic technology of the day was not up to it so it was complicated and unreliable.' The technology and rights were eventually put to use in the nuclear industry. Much more successful was a mini-Wheelbarrow, called Buckeye by the army and Cyclops by its manufacturers, which could be operated by either radio or fibre-optic cable control. Its short tracks enabled it to climb stairs and it was small enough to run along the aisle of a train or aircraft to investigate under the seats and in other places inaccessible to the larger Wheelbarrow.

So by the mid-1990s Wheelbarrow was still the foundation of the diagnostic, disruption and dismantling process, dealing with seven out of every ten IED incidents. In Britain, the Mark 7s remained in service until 1984, some of them controlled by cable, others by radio. Operators liked it not least because of its reliability. The Mark 8 proved an equal stalwart until 1994 when a rolling two-year programme to refurbish and upgrade them to all to Mark 8b was completed. The commercial rights to

Wheelbarrow currently belong to Remotec Inc., a Tennessee subsidiary of the Los Angeles-based Northrop Grumman Corporation, which acquired them from Alvis plc in May 2000 for $2,200,000. The deal included the takeover of Alvis's Coventry production centre.

Soon afterwards the MOD established the first of two research projects to ensure the effectiveness and compatibility of future EOD equipment. One of the core tasks was to examine whether Wheelbarrow was capable of further development or if an entirely new breed of remote-control vehicle was needed. The research was influenced in part by the Chernobyl nuclear disaster in 1986 and by growing forecasts that terrorists may in the future resort to the use of 'dirty bombs', containing chemical or biological contaminants. It was decided that Wheelbarrow would be useless in such circumstances and that the future lay with vehicles sophisticated enough to steer and manoeuvre themselves. Such robots would be able to undertake clearance operations in areas contaminated by radiation and other harmful substances. A specification was drawn up for one of this new generation of remote-control vehicles, provisionally given the appellation 'Cutlass', and the ministry launched a competition to win an order for 150 vehicles and a fifteen-year maintenance and development contract worth up to £30 million.

The challenge was initially taken up by some twenty companies, finally whittled down to two British-led consortia. British Aerospace believes robots are set to play a major role in future military systems. Its future products, taking advantage of recent developments in robotics and artificial intelligence, will include autonomous land, sea, air and under-water robotic platforms capable of operating for extended periods without supervision and performing complex missions that currently require human intervention. The company says this promises unprece-dented capability for armed forces, allowing them to automate activities that are currently expensive, dangerous or simply mundane. For the purposes of developing the new EOD remote-control vehicle for Britain, BAe has combined its efforts with Remotec, which has already produced a vehicle called Andros which employs new wheel technology to climb stairs and operate across all terrains. The second consortium is that of Marshall Specialist Vehicles of Cambridge with a German partner, telerob Gesellschaft für Fernhantierungstechnik mbH, whose robotics experts originally developed a heavy manipulator vehicle to work in unfriendly environments such as nuclear power plants. It utilises a revolutionary master-slave manipulator system which can reproduce the movements of the human arm and lift over 200 lb. The system incorporates a unique sensitivity facility for the operator to tell just how much force he is exerting and is so precise that it can be used for remote welding and other intricate tasks. 'Although it can't fly or swim, it can do just about everything else,' says one of the development team. The company produces a range of EOD equipment including a tracked EOD vehicle which has already been on successful active service in Germany, the Middle East and parts of the former Soviet Union. Among its many innovative features is a seventy-two-fold zoom camera and an on-board diagnostic facility which enables the manufacturer to identify and correct systems failures online.

Both consortia delivered their prototype vehicles to Kineton for evaluation in the late summer of 2004 to be put through their paces in the Felix Centre, then pulled apart and subjected to structural tests. The final choice is to be made in 2005. One experienced EOD operator says, 'The idea is that the range of equipment on board the new robot will give the operator virtually the same capability as his eyes and his hands but from a totally safe distance.' The replacement vehicle will be equipped with a newly developed recoilless version of Pigstick to prevent its sensitive technology from being knocked out.

Most of the time the EOD teams in Northern Ireland operate by road with their Tacticas, but over the years their ability to deploy by air has been developed and streamlined. The first 'bomb buggy' was improvised by Staff Sergeant Roy Gutteridge and Sergeant John Burns, of the 3 Field Workshop REME, who spent six days stripping down a standard Land Rover. They discarded all but the most vital components, removed all unnecessary wiring, replaced the bonnet and other parts with lightweight aluminium and reduced the size of the radiator and fuel tank by half. The vehicle could now be airlifted near to bomb scenes in order to transport an EOD team or tow an equipment trailer closer to the site. Four years later it was followed by four 'Goblins', modified Berg-Trak Alpine buggies. In trials with a Lynx helicopter, it was found that a fully laden Goblin could be deployed at 90 knots, 125 per cent faster than a Wessex could carry the heavier vehicles then in service. Later a trailer, Blackboard, was developed to carry equipment including Wheelbarrow off-road.

Many companies sprang up to service the expanding market for countermeasures against the terrorist threat and a considerable number of Northern Ireland veterans enhanced their military pensions by becoming consultants. The traditional ATO toolbox was superseded by a newer version with a variety of basic tools made of non-magnetic alloy as well as rubber wedges, needles, wood blocks and all sorts of things that ATOs had used on the ground. Virtually every equipment shortcoming, whether basic or technical or even wishful, has been taken up and fulfilled. A portable battery-powered detector can reveal a command wire buried up to eighteen inches deep. Stethoscopes can now detect conventional and electronic timers through brickwork, wood and plastic. Other detector mechanisms, radar imaging and X-ray devices with digital technology give operators instant images and information about suspect objects, increasingly on a computer screen in the safety of an incident control point. Sophisticated sniffer devices can quickly determine if a suspect package is live. The days when an operator might have to whack a car window several times with the arm of a Wheelbarrow are long gone. Breaking and entering has been simplified by a device which fires ceramic particles. The basic hook and line, still one of the most fundamental and practical means of accessing devices, has been augmented by a range of rigging equipment with load-bearing tripods, pulleys, hooks and other implements. Everything is aimed at reducing the exposure of the operator to the live device.

The most critical weapon for this purpose remains Pigstick, with its power to prevent devices functioning. Variations have been developed and proven in action: Hotrod is effective against devices in containers, parcels or boxes while Needle was specifically developed to attack soft-skin parcels, letter bombs and incendiaries. Many subsidiary pieces of equipment can be deployed on Wheelbarrow with the Modular Weapon Mounting System. In 1981 an explosive extractor known as Paw Paw was developed to throw beer kegs, milk churns or other containers well clear of a car boot or interior, frustrating any booby-trap. The operator can then use Flatsword to slice them open from a distance.

Among the latest items, introduced in 2004, is a blast-proof blanket. The concept was investigated in the 1970s but never proved workable. However, soon after he became CATO in 2001 Lieutenant-Colonel Alex Boyd came up with a new approach: a blanket consisting of layered ballistic sheeting would absorb the blast and contain the fragmentation of a pipe bomb. After extensive trials and the addition of a perlite bag which often saw the test team showered with white powder, a viable 'mitigation blanket' was perfected and is now standard equipment in public-order situations. The epidemic of pipe bombs since 1993 prompted the development of another attachment for Wheelbarrow, this one designed to cut through metal plumbing components. Bomb-disposal teams have also been issued with the AW50F .5 bolt action rifle fitted with a powerful telescopic sight and a laser range-finder. Its tungsten-cored ammunition, designed to be used against bombs of 500 lb. or more, is powerful enough to pierce bomb casings to ignite the explosive and allow it to burn off harmlessly. All of these additions are in line with the early EOD philosophy that an operator should have a club in the bag for every situation encountered.

As terrorists, including the IRA, expanded their ability to detonate devices remotely using portable telephones and electronic pagers, countermeasures moved in step. EOD teams now have the capability not only to detect and jam radio-control devices but to 'harden' targets against attack by creating a protective electronic shield around them which prevents penetration by any signal that could set off a bomb. This facility is routinely used to protect the prime minister and other vulnerable figures and to prevent the targeting of soldiers participating in ceremonial duties in London as well as those on patrol in the still dangerous hot-spots in Northern Ireland.

Despite all the space-age technology and comprehensive training, one factor has remained constant through the travails of the Northern Ireland campaign. It still requires a special kind of courage to become a bomb-disposal officer, to gamble your life against the utter unpredictability of the improvised devices that terrorists continue to deploy. The unflinching stalwarts of the early days, men like Styles, Calladene, Crosby, Gaff, Mackenzie-Orr and their contemporaries, possessed it in abundance, but in the early horrors of the Northern Ireland conflict, when existing EOD know-how was virtually overpowered and the sheer courage of the operators was their most potent weapon, there was a fear that maybe unsuitable men were being sent out to face the bombs. One old-timer recalls: 'When Northern Ireland came along, we had lots of deaths compared to the small number of people involved and the question was asked was there some psychological flaw in these guys.'

At the outset, the risk factor for ATOs was truly alarming. Eight out of eighteen operators exposed at any one time were killed in the two years from January 1971, compared with 214 soldiers killed out of an average exposed strength of 14,619. In December 1972, after a series of incidents in which operators had been killed, ammunition specialists of all ranks undergoing two weeks' preliminary training for Northern Ireland were subjected to psychological aptitude tests for the first time. In the EOD report for the six months from October 1972, the Chief Inspector Land Services Ammunition said the tests were similar to those taken by members of the Special Forces and by Polaris (nuclear deterrent) submariners and are intended to assess a person's ability to withstand particular conditions of employment. Our object is to ensure that men who have not got the aptitude for EOD work are not placed at risk. The fact that a few men have been shown to be unsuited to this particular type of work does not imply that they are not perfectly capable in other fields and the test results will not interfere with their career prospects.

Managing the welfare of the men in the front line was an inexact process in the early days with urgent operational necessity overriding every other consideration. Hugh McCormack was sent in with just twenty-four hours' notice in 1972 after the deaths of operators Cracknell, Butcher and Calladene during the previous ten days. 'I had just completed the training course and gone to Germany for three weeks' leave when I got the call to be in Northern Ireland tomorrow.' He carried out almost 100 operations and was awarded the George Medal. One operator in Belfast returned to base after completing a gruelling series of tasks only to hear on a mess television that two of his closest colleagues had been killed in an explosion earlier in the day. There was no arrangement to let him know and nobody had made any effort to do so.

> That was a terrible blow. We are a small, interlocked extended family. We all know each other. We have been best men at each other's weddings. Our wives have been bridesmaids for other wives. We are godparents for each other's children. When we are told we are going to Northern Ireland, the wives rally round each other. When we are out there, they look out for each other. So, when one of us is killed, it is the loss of a family member.

Mike Coldrick believes that 'the people in the ivory tower didn't understand the intensity of the pressure':

> We were the victims of amateur psychology by our masters and commanders. Some guys were concerned that we hadn't been involved in the funerals of our colleagues that were killed. There was no feedback about how they came to be killed, no counselling in those days. The decision was taken they would not dwell on the gory business of who had been killed and how. Nothing should distract from the next device that came in. My feeling was that they were remiss in

not discussing the possibility of what might happen, what had
happened. That was a source of some resentment.

In those frantic early days, the operators had mainly to look out for each
other. Before the deaths of Cracknell and Butcher and the introduction of
the 'one-man risk' rule they tended to work in pairs. 'Some of it was
learning on the job, for the newcomers, but when there were two, the
other could restrain you from doing something perhaps foolish,' recalls
Coldrick. He remembers an incident when a captain lost his nerve. 'It was
at the Oldpark Road in Belfast and he went forward to look at what was
a pretty crude but simple Loyalist device in a gas bottle. But when he
came back he was sweaty and pallid. "What's wrong, Boss?" "I don't like
it," he said. "Would you like me to . . ." so I did.'

It was no wonder that some people broke. They were on duty for
twenty-four hours and supposedly on standby for the next twenty-four,
but some were being called to as many as twenty-five incidents a day.
Hugh McCormack remembers a colleague who would not shirk any work.
'He was going about with bags under his eyes, absolutely worn out, so we
got him moved to a quieter area for his own good to have a rest, but he
was only there two days when a two or three-day border clearance with
six devices came up.' He recalls another young officer coming in to start
a tour and being taken from incident to incident to familiarise him. 'He
knew all about it technically but he just couldn't bring himself to go
forward and deal with a device so he was sent back.' A small number of
people were indeed 'returned to unit', but the decisions were often hotly
disputed and in the early 321 logs notes of dissent are recorded by local
commanders who were overruled. Hugh McCormack, who returned as
CATO in 1993–4, says:

> People who did well at the school often didn't do so well on the ground.
> I remember one guy who was an absolute disaster at the school – three
> goes to pass his exams – who was only allowed to go to Northern
> Ireland with caveats but who did a brilliant job once he was there. He
> wouldn't be allowed to go now, of course, but I found that once it's for
> real, some guys just soak up the atmosphere and react to it whereas at
> the school, with the best will in the world, it's always slightly false.

The first psychometric tests were carried out in December 1972. For a
time, only 'doubtful' operators were screened but by early 1974, every
officer was tested. The process took place over two days. On the first, the

officer completed two written tests. The first, a clinical analysis questionaire, asked 144 questions designed to profile sixteen 'wellbeing factors' including hypochondria, depression, guilt, boredom, despression, paranoia or suicidal tendencies. The second test profiled 187 'Personality Factors'. Together, the psychiatrists said, they 'provided a comprehensive disclosure of an individual's psychological state: measures of sociability, intelligence, calmness, assertiveness, impulsiveness, conscientiousness, boldness, toughness of mind, practicality, shrewdness, self-assurance, self-sufficiency, attitude to discipline and contentment'. The following day, each candidate was interviewed privately for about forty minutes by a psychiatrist.

The early work was done personally by the Director of Army Psychiatry, Brigadier PD Wickenden, who used the findings to profile the 'ideal' EOD operator. He would be of at least bright intelligence, satisfied with his career, wholly identified with ammunition work, free from serious personal worries, in good physical and mental health, methodical and courageous, fairly adventuresome, thoughtful and decisive and free from group dependency. The ideal operator would also be socially at ease, have good impulse control and not suffer from nervousness or hypochondria, self-doubt, delinquent traits or perfectionism.

Old hands treated the tests with a certain degree of cynicism. 'There was such a pressing need for people to go to Ireland at the time, you were unlikely to be failed,' said one. Another felt it was all too obvious. 'I was invited to Bramley to talk to a nice man who sat me down and showed me several dozen pictures of people with dangerous jobs, firemen up ladders in flames, steel erectors walking along girders forty storeys up, and dangerous things, kids standing at an open electric fire, an electrical socket with nineteen plugs in it. I told him these were the dangerous things, not the jobs.' Asked how he came to that conclusion, he said it was because the firemen and the steel erectors were trained. 'We are trained and if you follow the rules our job is not dangerous.' In *Fetch Felix*, Derrick Patrick realls being asked 'such things as "What are your favourite colours?", "Do you like looking at railway lines disappearing into the distance?", "Do you enjoy sexual dreams?" As far as I am aware, the only thing psychometric testing does is to identify the clinically insane.'

Wickenden thought the candidate viewed his encounter with the psychiatrist rather like his encounter with a bomb:

> He is faced with an unfamiliar situation, is unsure what to expect, and
> must tread warily because if he gives the wrong impression it is not

unreasonable for him to suppose that the psychiatrist may blow up and wreck his career. I therefore expect people to be a little cautious, even slightly nervous, but I do get worried if a man enters, seats himself and fixes me with the terror-stricken gaze of a mouse about to be devoured by a snake.

I note the individual who is excessively restless but I also note, somewhat unfavourably, the person whose manner is offhand and careless or who seems brashly over self-confident. During the interview I pay as much attention to how a candidate answers my questions as to what he says. Handling an EOD situation calls for a precise and decisive personality, not someone who is vague, discursive and inconsistent. I like someone who has given thought to life, who has espoused some philosophical and ethical standards, and I regard with some misgivings the person who opportunistically seems to float through life never asking himself why be behaves in the way he does.

After this process, which also took into account service history and medical record, every operator was characterised either A (entirely satisfactory), B+ (satisfactory with minor reservations), B- (to be retested) or C (unsuitable because of either personality flaws or personal circumstances which might be temporary). The individuals were not told their grades, but some years later a survey was carried out to assess the effectiveness of the testing in weeding out people who might otherwise have been killed. Of seventy-two ATOs tested from 1980 to 1983, 40.3 per cent were classified A and 22.2 per cent B+. The B- grades made up 19.5 per cent and C eighteen per cent. Among ATs only 23.3 per cent made the top grade while 51.2 per cent were judged B+. The B- figure at 18.6 per cent was similar to that for officers but there were fewer C grades, just 6.9 per cent. Wickenden believed this showed that the screening had been successful, 'because although there are far fewer bomb incidents in Northern Ireland [in the early 1980s] than there used to be, the saving of life has been even more pronounced.'

A separate team from the Institute of Psychiatry tried to correlate the results of the psychological screening programme with the practical performance of operators as judged by individual end-of-tour reports and decorations for gallantry. They were unable to come to any clear conclusions except the finding that the characteristic of forthrightness or tough-mindedness in tests was associated with above-average reports. 'The examination of those who had been decorated revealed that they displayed a very significant lack of hypochondriacal traits. A low level of hypochondriasis is associated with physical courage, healthiness and a sense of wellbeing,' Wickenden wrote in a paper. He continued:

> My friends in the RAOC are sceptical about these results and feel that whether a man acquires a medal depends upon the chance of finding himself in a situation which might earn an award. However, statistical analysis is calculated to minimise the effect of chance circumstances, and the finding in the research was of a significant relationship between the ability to rise to a challenge and the absence of hypochondriacal neurotic features.

The brigadier himself concluded that while that psychological screening probably had some direct influence in reducing the casualty rate, the overall reasons for this success were complex.

> We know that all the operators were intelligent, experienced and well-trained. We know that the casualties included one major and four warrant officers. It is improbable that all five of these senior men, or even the others, would have been failed on our tests; had they been of such poor quality it is probable that they would have been spotted and rejected by their own organisation . . . It is difficult to escape the conclusion that perfectly normal, competent, well-trained, well-adjusted people are vulnerable to certain subtle and dangerous psychological tendencies when exposed repeatedly to the peculiar and isolated experience of leading a bomb disposal team. We must remember that a Number One EOD operator is a rare specialist who accepts a solitary position of absolute control when on the job.

So, just what sort of men fit the mould and what attracts them to the job? Paul Myring was signed into the Army in 1974 by his father, a recruiting officer, in a month when his figures were down. 'I joined the Royal Artillery and was sent to train at Woolwich but then the opportunity to become an AT was presented to me,' he says. 'It just seemed to happen. One minute I was a Gunner, the next I was at Kineton as an AT. In the end, my father and I did each other a favour. I helped his monthly figures and he got me a career.'

Phil Yeaman started his military career as an infantryman in the Black Watch and served several tours in Northern Ireland with the regiment before transferring to the RAOC. When he found himself back in Northern Ireland with 321, he had already learned many of the most important lessons. 'I was able to look after myself and I knew that you never ever went to look at a device just to look.' He says that an operator needs 'an analytical mind. You've got to be able to receive, digest and analyse information, then produce a response at the sweep of a finger. If you make the wrong call, there can be terrible consequences.'

Dave Williams, who completed three tours in Northern Ireland, wanted to be a vehicle mechanic when he joined up in 1962 but was steered toward becoming an AT. 'I told them I wanted a good job after serving nine years and they said the ammunition trade would get me a good job at ICI in my native Teesside, so I signed.' Forty years later he is one of the team of ex-Army bomb-disposal officers at Scotland Yard.

After seven years as a chef in civvy street, Brian Calder presented himself at his local recruitment office intent on joining the Scots Guards. Although there was no history of military service in his family, he had long wanted to be a soldier and decided to take the plunge 'after the Falklands war caught my imagination'. But he was directed away from the infantry towards a trade, and on the basis that 'driving trucks wasn't for me' he found his way to Kineton. Calder, an ebullient Scotsman, is remembered there for organising a boisterous weekend trip to Rome 'for a pizza', which has become so notorious that 'there are at least a hundred people who claim to have been on it.' After passing his AT training, including qualifying as a parachutist, he was sent to Northolt where he spent long periods on standby to deal with any terrorist threat. 'I didn't want a boring job and London was boring. I thought, why be in bomb disposal if you're never going to get called out?' So he applied for and passed the Northern Ireland course, serving in Omagh and later Antrim and Belfast. Despite his exuberant behaviour, which is not the norm among those in the job, Calder proved himself with two tours back-to-back in thirteen months. 'I was stressed to fuck but it's not the job that bothers me, it's the shite that goes with it.'

Ian Magee quit teaching and joined the Army as a young officer in 1990. The next year he passed out from Sandhurst as a second lieutenant in the Royal Corps of Transport and soon found himself posted to Bosnia as a troop commander running fuel and food convoys. The son of a policeman based at Newry in Northern Ireland, he had grown with the background of the constant bombings and shootings in the flashpoint border town, so he sought a transfer there and was accepted as a captain by the Royal Irish Regiment. However, before taking up the post, he was offered a place on the ATO course at Shrivenham. Having qualified and passed the subsequent bomb-disposal courses he was posted to Girdwood

Barracks in Belfast in 1997. Over the next two years, before leaving the Army and following his father and sister into the police in Northern Ireland, he did two six-month tours as a bomb-disposal officer as well as a number of short fill-in periods.

> I was just thrilled. I had hated working the computers and flying a desk, which was my first job at Didcot and when I passed the Northern Ireland course, where there is a higher failure rate than for Special Air Service selection, it was a fantastic feeling. Being an ATO is a complete ego trip, you're at 40,000 feet and climbing but you do fly by the seat of the pants and you live by the drills and standard operating procedures you have been taught. But it is a team effort and there is no deference so you should never be afraid to call back to headquarters for advice. I don't mind saying that every time, when I was suited up, before going down the road, I would stand by the wagon and say a prayer. 'Father, I don't speak to you very often but guide my mind and steady my hand.' Anybody who says they are not afraid is lying and should not be doing the job. It's the fear that keeps you going.

Another experienced officer, a past commander of 321, believes 'he who has no fear does not last long.' Dave Williams disagrees and says he never thinks of the danger:

> The psychological tests weed out the people with the wrong personality while the training weeds out those not skilled enough. After that we are not special people, we are products of a system and the training. We are trained to use the equipment, take the right precautions and interpret the training. When I am behind the visor I don't ask 'Is this really me in this suit and helmet?' I think 'What's the next move,' but none of us work the same, no one knows how anyone else works.

A captain who served in Belfast in the late 1980s says,

> I would much rather do my job than be in the infantry, patrolling twelve hours a day, every minute expecting to get shot or blown up. Because of my training I know what I'm going into. I work inside a cordon. There's a reduced chance of me being shot. They're the brave ones, not us.

Colin Goodson recalls the 'professional thrill' of going to Northern Ireland and 'doing the job for real. I never remember being bored, there were always tasks, something happening and when it wasn't busy you could watch the telly and have a doze.' The pressure during a four or six-month tour has always been unrelenting and most team members look forward to the five-day rest and recuperation break at the midpoint. For the single men, especially, this came to be something of a 'blowout' time and tales of spending as much as £500 on a bout of 'drinking, eating and sex' are not uncommon.

Bomb-disposal men try to shelter their nearest and dearest from the reality. One captain told his mother that the job entailed cutting a series of coloured wires in the right order. Others conceal altogether what they will be doing in Northern Ireland. Those who confess either ring home regularly to reassure their families or make themselves available by mobile for contact whenever it is safe to have the phone switched on. Superstitions abound, of course, and while some put their affairs in order before a tour, many prefer not to tempt Providence.

By long custom and practice in the super-macho military world, bomb-disposal work was for men not women, but as the role of women in society and business radically changed from the 1970s onwards, women in uniform pressed for a more substantial operational role. As their status in the armed forces began to change slowly to one of greater participation in many tasks, though not frontline combat, the all-male bastion of EOD appears to have been breached for the first time in September 1982, when twenty-six-year-old Corporal Pat Purcell volunteered for and outpaced some male colleagues to pass the RAF bomb-disposal course. It was another six years before the first female members of the Army matched her achievement: in August 1988 two Territorial Army lieutenants, Julie Owen, aged twenty-two, and Kate Boxell, twenty-three, serving with 33 EOD Regiment, the Royal Engineers, passed the selection tests and successfully completed the seven-week training course. But while the Army came to tolerate a wider role for women, there was still resistance in some quarters. In June 1991, RAF Sergeant Caroline Kelly applied for an IEDD course at Kineton. Despite top-level pressure from the RAF, the Army refused her a place, although two women from NATO armies were at that very time doing the same course and a Canadian woman had come top the previous year. At only four feet six inches tall, Kelly was all the more remarkable in her achievement because instructors had to pull her head through the EOD suit so she could see out. A year later the Women's Royal Army Corps was disbanded and its members dispersed into the ranks of other units, where many of the longstanding barriers against females taking certain support jobs were removed although the ban on them being trained for frontline combat remained. The way was thus cleared for a woman to become a bomb-disposal operator, and the first to pass the IEDD course was Jeannette Widger. However, the first woman operator to serve in Northern Ireland turned out to be a native.

Shirley Lyle was born at the height of the Troubles in June 1972 and grew up on the family farm, well away from the most disturbed areas and the fury of the bullets and the bombs. Like many families, hers led a normal life but the effects of the conflict still intruded. Family outings were limited to where it was safe to travel and everyday trips to school or the shops were interrupted by security checks and bomb scares. By the time she finished school and went to Queen's University, Belfast in 1990 to read chemistry, there was talk of peace in the air but the killings, shootings and bombings were still taking place and she frequently saw the 'bomb vehicles' rushing through the streets. She confesses to a fascination with them. 'I had a wee notion it was a job I would like to do but deep down I never really thought it was possible.' Instead she concentrated on her studies, graduated in chemistry and decided to stay on to complete a Master's.

'During this time I realised that life in a laboratory carrying out research was not for me and I decided to join the Army.' Lyle was already familiar with military life from her membership of the Officer Training Corps at university, and she gained a place at the Royal Military Academy, Sandhurst where since 1947 the British Army had trained its future officers. Since the Women's Royal Army Corps College at Bagshot closed in 1985 female officer cadets had been trained at Sandhurst and by the time she got there, in 1996, the training of male and female students had been fully integrated in what was called the Commissioning Course, introduced in 1992. Its aim was to develop qualities of leadership, character and intellect, turning out officers with the courage, willpower and temperament for decisive action in difficult and dangerous circumstances.

During her studies, Lyle opted to join the recently formed Royal Logistics Corps, and after passing out found herself posted to 2 Close Support Regiment, based at the former RAF airfield at Gutersloh in Germany, from where she ran convoys of fuel and heavy lift trucks to Poland and Bosnia. With her scientific training, she realised she was eligible to seek a place on the training course for ATOs, so she applied, was selected and qualified after six months. Another female officer had started the course but dropped out after a short time.

> This was because she did not like the attitude of some of the male
> officers on the course. I decided to carry on regardless but by the end
> of the long course, I was sick of the sight of the lads. There was just no
> way of getting away from the relentless male dominance in the Army.
> You're a female so you're never properly part of the group. In the end
> you tend to get fed up constantly having to prove yourself.

Now promoted captain, Lyle was deemed competent to manage and
handle the entire range of Army weaponry, ammunition and explosives
from the smallest bullets to the latest guided missiles, and to take
command of EOD teams as part of counter-terrorist operations in a low-
risk environment. She also successfully completed an additional three-
week joint services training course which qualified her to conduct IEDD
operations as a Number One on the British mainland. Although she was
then posted back to 6 Supply Regiment at Gutersloh, she applied for the
five-week Northern Ireland special-to-theatre course even though no
woman had ever passed it. She received a lot of support from Bruce
Martin, a senior AT, and Lieutenant-Colonel Rory Maxwell, the commanding officer of 921 EOD Squadron, who had both served in Northern
Ireland. They encouraged her to believe that she was fit, mature and
experienced enough to withstand the mental and physical rigours of
active service on her home turf and fulfil the 'wee notion' about
becoming a bomb-disposal officer that she had quietly nourished since
her university days. Although the prevailing wisdom was that women
should not become EOD operators, especially in Northern Ireland, she
reported to Kineton for the course with encouragement from her family
and friends and no lack of determination on her own part. 'I said to
myself, go for it.'

But her best was not good enough and, along with the majority of the
participants, she failed to make the grade. 'Looking back I was not ready,
not prepared enough, so much out of my league that I'm not surprised I
failed. But I did learn a lot from the instructors and felt I had earned
credibility with them.' It was made clear to her that they would indeed
have her back for another try at the course. So it was back to Gutersloh
for more training including early-morning running clad in the heavy EOD
suit and carrying two full jerry-cans of water to build up her strength.
'This was all in the sweltering German heat and as there was only one
small suit, I would often have to put on the helmet still filled with sweat
from the previous occupant.' She received further help from members of
921. Paul Grimsley, the second-in-command, tested her on render-safe

procedures for all sorts of incidents, written in blood from the hard-earned experience of those who had been there before. In July 2001, she was asked back to Kineton for a week-long filter course and after coming top in a series of aptitude tests she was offered another chance to qualify for service in Northern Ireland.

During the course Lyle read old EOD reports on how the most complex ambushes had been cleared and immersed herself in details of the whole range of terrorist devices. This time she succeeded and, moments after being told she had passed, was ordered to report to the 321 section based at Drumadd Barracks, Armagh, on 8 November 2001. It was a proud moment, although her pride in the achievement was in passing the course, not that she was the first woman to do so.

At home in Northern Ireland, her father and mother were also proud but concerned. They could imagine only too well the scale of the ordeal and the pressures she would now be facing. Unlike the families of EOD personnel in Britain, they were aware from local news that rarely a day passed without ATOs being involved in some sort of incident. Lyle herself remembers being 'chuffed to bits' and says there was 'too much happening for me to have time to worry'. The men under her command were not perturbed at having a woman boss and proudly stencilled the call-sign 'Pussycat' on the section's vehicles, the first time a female feline designation had ever been used.

Captain Tim Gould, whom she replaced, told her that most of the call-outs in Armagh were hoaxes or false alarms, but she felt 'street heat' early on, getting a fabled 'big live one' on her very first call-out. On the evening of Tuesday 20 November 2001, a police patrol halted a Vauxhall Astra car at Knappagh Road on the outskirts of Armagh. A man with known terrorist connections, dressed in a boiler suit and gloves, was arrested and the car was found to be a travelling bomb bound for the police station. Lyle and her team were tasked to clear the bomb and first travelled to the police station to be briefed. News of the arrest coup had spread quickly and senior police and Army figures had gathered to congratulate the undercover team involved. She found it difficult to convince them that a blonde girl with a distinctive Northern Ireland accent was a serious figure as an ATO, and had to be quite persistent to get the information she required.

Out at the scene, with Lyle formally in control, Wheelbarrow was deployed to take a close look at the car, but it overturned, forcing the team to deploy a back-up vehicle. Having established that the timer-power unit was on the front seat, and after allowing some soak time, she approached the car intending to sever some of the unit's wiring but judged it was too risky. Instead she opted to open the boot with a controlled explosion and sever the wires there before dealing with the main explosive charge. Both operations went according to plan and she turned her attention to dealing with the HME. Unusually, it was not in a container or a plastic bag but had simply been tipped in, so she began the gruelling task of scooping the mix from the boot and bagging it to be taken away for destruction. 'I was having to make manual approaches to the device, some nine or ten in all . . . My nose and eyes were running and the edge of the suit chafed my wrists and caused them to bleed. Inevitably the ammonium nitrate got onto the open wounds and they stung like mad.' To make things worse from her point of view, photographers and television cameraman spotted the bob of blonde hair under her helmet and concluded correctly that the ATO was female. 'I then had to put a binbag over the fallen Wheelbarrow to hide it from the cameras and go through this rigmarole of letting them take pictures of me checking the car while my boss, Major Jim Convery, the commander of 321 who was at the scene, was looking on. With him there I had to do everything by the book.' The only respite was the arrival of an undercover unit in plain clothes and an unmarked car. They were easily persuaded to go off and find a 'chippy' and bring back some warming food and drinks for the team.

Finally, after six long, cold hours, the demanding operation was over. Because of the recalcitrant Wheelbarrow it had not gone strictly according to the book, but the bomb, which was found to contain almost 200 lb. of explosive, had been prevented from reaching its target and was successfully neutralised without any injuries or damage. Thanks to Lyle's careful recovery of forensic evidence, the terrorist was eventually convicted. There was added significance in the fact that it was the first time a female ATO had cleared a major bomb in Northern Ireland. That night her mother saw the television pictures, instantly recognised the silhouette of the helmeted ATO and was quickly on the telephone to be reassured that 'Pussycat' was safe.

After almost six months in Armagh, Lyle returned to England for a time but came back in late July 2002 to work with another EOD team at Ebrington Barracks in Londonderry. On the morning of 2 August there was another 'big one' on her patch. She was aware of it before the official call-out for she was woken by police sirens as officers rushed to the scene, an explosion at a nearby Territorial Army camp. When she arrived she was told that a civilian workman had been injured in an explosion in a canteen hut and had been rushed to hospital. She wanted to find out as much as possible from the victim, who, she was advised, was talking to a police officer and would be able to answer her questions. A telephone link was patched through to the officer at the Altnagelvin Hospital but almost immediately the reply came back that the man had collapsed and died. 'That was terribly tragic and I realised I was now dealing with a murder scene and the most important thing was to work out what had happened and preserve any forensic evidence.'

There was no way in for the Wheelbarrow so, wearing the cumbersome EOD suit and kitted out with her tools and ECM box, Shirley went on the long walk. Her initial task was to ensure there were no secondary devices intended for herself or others, and that the first device posed no further threat. After that, her objective was to gather any evidence that could show how it had functioned and lead the police to the killers. 'It was a gruesome site. There was blood everywhere and once the bomb had gone off, the injured victim had left bloody hand marks on the wall as he frantically felt his way round looking for a way out.' After her careful examination of the scene and later consultation with the forensic scientists, she concluded the bomb had been concealed in a plastic box with an anti-lifting mechanism which had functioned when the victim, David Caldwell, himself a former soldier, had lifted or moved it. Although he had injuries to his arm, legs and abdomen, his death was attributable to a piece of flying shrapnel which hit him in the head. It was a grim job but one Lyle took in her stride because of the training.

Lyle left Northern Ireland in October 2002 and returned to study at Shrivenham, but five months later she was asked to go back, this time to Omagh where there was an unplanned vacancy because not enough operators had passed the most recent Northern Ireland course at Kineton. By now her parents had become used to her work and would occasionally visit her team location. 'Mum always brought chicken and buns to feed "the men" and Dad became pretty expert at manoeuvring the Wheelbarrow.' After three months Lyle deployed to a staff job in the RLC's ammunition organisation in Iraq before returning to another posting in Britain in 2004. In recognition of her achievement and unique place in the history of the EOD campaign in Northern Ireland, she was awarded the Queen's Commendation for Valuable Service in the Operational Honours List published in April 2003. The citation recorded that she had completed fifty-five EOD tasks involving deployment by road and air and rendered safe four improvised explosive devices, showing 'sound technical judgement and leadership under extreme pressure'. She was surprised at the accolade. 'I didn't realise it fully at the time but looking back, I know now that was the most amazing and interesting job I will ever do in my entire life.'

Another woman who was attracted into bomb disposal was Victoria Henson. She joined the Army after graduating in public relations from Leeds Metropolitan University. 'What I had studied seemed a bit shallow while the Army seemed one of those jobs where you could be outside a bit, there was old-fashioned leadership and traditional values of loyalty and that sort of thing.' She started at Sandhurst in January 1996 and opted to join the Royal Logistics Corps. 'We went on a two-day familiarisation visit to Deepcut where I saw the Wheelbarrow and bomb suit and said that's for me. I had no notion of it until I saw them and that was one of the reasons for joining the RLC because that is what I wanted to do. I wanted to be an ATO.' Henson completed the training courses and was posted to an element of 11 EOD Regiment at Shorncliffe, where the workload mainly consisted of old Second World War munitions. In August 2001 she decided to have a go at the Northern Ireland course.

> I learnt a lot in the five weeks but didn't do very well. I took on board the principles but didn't really apply them very well. You have to do four jobs and when the first has not gone well and you can't quite pinpoint why then the second one goes wrong, you think this is not going well at all. In the end, I failed three out of the four big style but, in due course, I was asked to pop back and did very much better. By the second go it was a totally different scenario.

Newly married to bomb-disposal officer Chris Henson, and just back from honeymoon, she sailed through the course and in February 2002 was posted to Lisburn. After a short induction period she spent two months of her first tour with the Holywood detachment and then over three months in Belfast at Girdwood. 'I did seventy-eight jobs altogether, the first one in Bangor recovering a captured weapon in a vehicle clearance. Belfast was unpredictable, more concerning and there was constant pressure to get off the ground as quickly as you could.' Like Shirley Lyle, she found a reluctance on the part of other soldiers and the police to recognise her as the ATO. 'They always assume that you're not the ATO and ask the corporal instead, but once word gets round there's a girl ATO, the police want you to be capable of dealing with an incident and they don't care if it's a man or a woman. They just want you to get on with it.'

After a break, Henson returned to Northern Ireland in September 2002, this time to serve with the Londonderry detachment. Her vehicle was petrol-bombed on the way back from one job, a commentary on just how far from tranquillity life still was in Northern Ireland. She left the Army in March 2003 to start a family. 'The first year we were married we had just a few weeks together and because we had the same job, we were never going to be together, working together.'

Looking back, she remembers the level of friendship and trust she felt in her team. 'I'm the ATO, Boss, not ma'am. In the same way wouldn't want to be treated differently, you don't treat them any differently. Then you all bond within a team.'

Chapter Fifteen
The Tightrope of Peace

In November 1996 321 EOD Squadron marked its twenty-fifth anniversary in Northern Ireland with a low-key function at Palace Barracks, Holywood. One of the guests of honour, Chief Constable of the RUC Sir Ronnie Flanagan, said the squadron had paid a horrendous price while saving countless lives and preventing the destruction of property on a vast scale. John Major, the prime minister, sent a congratulatory message expressing his admiration for the squadron's 'extraordinary skill, dedication and courage'. The people of Northern Ireland know the reality of their achievements, he added: 'countless lives and livelihoods saved; homes protected from devastation; and untold suffering prevented'. Noting that the unit had never been stronger than 100 even at the high points of the conflict, he concluded: 'The remarkable valour of those who have served with the squadron have made it the most decorated unit in the British Army for actions undertaken in peacetime. It is tragic that in saving and protecting others your small unit has suffered so many comrades killed and injured.' One of the 'old and bold' who vividly remembered the dangers of the early days remarked that without the loss of dozens of Wheelbarrows in action over the years, there would have been even more names on the roll of honour.

Over the years, when the public spotlight has fallen on the EOD role in Northern Ireland, it has been the CATO who speaks on behalf of the teams. Although figuring regularly in the television news, team members traditionally remain silent and anonymous beside their armoured Tacticas and the operator is concealed by the visor on his helmet when he breaks cover for the long walk. But there is another vital cog in the EOD machinery in Northern Ireland: the succession of majors who have followed the ill-fated Bernard Calladene in commanding 321. Consistently decorated for their work, they have been notable for supporting teams on the ground, encouraging operators in their first few days, giving a word of encouragement or advice during a complex clearance and ensuring that the teams and their equipment are always ready to meet a task. Most of the commanding officers served one or more tours in a team before assuming command, such as Major M Blatherwick, who was awarded the MBE in 1989 and the George Medal in 1991. Roger Davies was awarded the Queen's Gallantry Medal in 1992 and Major Ian Jones received the MBE in 1993 for 'commanding the teams with style, example and inspiration' during a period from 1992 which saw the introduction of infrared devices, flash-initiated weapons and more powerful mortars.

Four of the officers who have served as CATO started as operators and then commanded 321 before returning to the top job. The first was David Furness-Gibbon, a founder member of the shadow 321 unit back in 1968. As a major he commanded the company from March until November 1980, during which period the teams neutralised eighty-six out of 660 devices. The following year he was awarded the MBE and seven years later he returned as CATO. It was on his watch in July 1988 that Major John Howard lost his life, an event which, Furness-Gibbon said, knocked the teams sideways. The others were lieutenant-colonels JR Hawkins OBE, Alan Swindley MBE 1985 and OBE 1994 and Mark Wickham, who was awarded the QGM in 1980 and the MBE after his spell commanding 321 from January 1994 to March 1995. Then the teams were coming to terms with the changed conditions of the peace process, a factor which also dominated Wickham's tour as CATO in 2004.

Within the extended 321 fraternity the advent of peace, however fragile, and the prospect of a permanent scaling down of the Army's involvement in Northern Ireland focused renewed attention on the price that the squadron had paid in helping bring about the return of 'normality'. In January 2002 their sacrifice was given permanent recognition with the opening of the Felix Memorial Garden at the 321 headquarters at Thiepval Barracks. The military artist Kelvin Hunter was commissioned to paint a mural on one of the unit's buildings depicting a Belfast street scene with an EOD officer unobtrusively working at a bomb. The mural, inscribed with the words of John Bunyan, 'Who would true valour see, let him come hither', forms the backdrop for the garden where there is a marble memorial and an individual headstone for each of the fallen of 321. Their ranks, names, corps and dates of birth and death are engraved alongside a representation of Felix. The dedication and blessing of the garden was an emotional occasion for their families who were traced all over Britain by Captain Paul Snape and invited to the ceremony. Most had never been to Northern Ireland before and, in many cases, approached the trip with sorrow and trepidation. Some of those attending were there to pay tribute to fathers they scarcely remembered, who had died when they were infants. Their memories were too painful for the majority of relatives, but others wanted to know more about how and where their father or son or brother had died and the circumstances were sympathetically explained by their modern counterparts. Lieutenant-Colonel Alex Boyd, then CATO, said: 'The memorial garden provides a permanent focus for members of the Squadron but most importantly for the families of those who lost their lives. It gives us an opportunity to reflect on what our predecessors have done and to remember that it is through their sacrifice that we are here today.'

The roll of honour and pictures of the memorial garden have also been posted on the internet. There, Kaye Furminger, sister of Gunner Richard Furminger who was killed in 1979, recalls how her twenty-year-old brother had been 'recommended for his first stripe on his return from Ireland. Unfortunately this never happened, he just didn't make it back. It is something you never get over, the death of one so young. That's why the memorial garden is so important to me, because each time someone visits, looks at the headstones, they are remembering those poor souls who did not make it back.'

The period immediately after the 1994 ceasefires was the quietest since the beginning of the campaign. There were only two explosions recorded in 1995 and six the following year. The teams were called out 1,388 times in 1994 but only 263 times in 1995, making it the least busy year since 1970. However, the sincerity of the IRA was called into question after just two months when gunmen shot dead a postal worker who tried to prevent them robbing the sorting office in Newry. The killing was the first stage in a long period of ambiguity during which the IRA refused to state that its ceasefire was permanent or fully to decommission its remaining arsenal. Indeed, there was consistent evidence that the organisation was continuing to train its members, target victims, procure munitions, develop weaponry and engage in criminal activities. Such actions encouraged doubts among its political opponents, who were understandably in an unforgiving mood.

This distrust was exacerbated by the IRA's temporary 'return to war' without warning on 9 February 1996 with a bombing at Canary Wharf in the London Docklands which caused extensive property damage and killed two shopkeepers. The attack caused consternation in Northern Ireland, where in response to the ceasefire there had been a visible reduction in security precautions. Routine military patrolling in support of the police had been withdrawn in eight of the twelve police divisions and significantly scaled down elsewhere. The reduced threat meant that soldiers wore their regimental headdress rather than helmets and no longer put on camouflage cream when out on patrol. The strength of patrols had also been reduced from twelve soldiers to eight in Fermanagh and from twenty-four to twelve in south Armagh. The police had responded to the ceasefire by reducing sentry cover at stations, putting more saloon cars on the road and going out on the beat on foot, without the protection of armoured Land Rovers, heavy firearms or body armour. That Friday night EOD reinforcements were urgently summoned from Britain but in Northern Ireland an uneasy normality remained. Further attacks in Britain followed as political efforts were made to rekindle the peace process. The detonation of a 3,500 lb. vehicle bomb which injured 206 people in the centre of Manchester and devastated the city centre symbolised the gulf of distrust that had developed between the IRA and the British government.

Apart from an incident in February, when fifty-seven shots were fired into the home of a policeman at Moy, County Tyrone, Northern Ireland was largely exempt from the renewed violence until 13 July, when seventeen people were injured in an explosion at the Killyhevlin Hotel at Enniskillen. Worryingly, responsibility for the blast was attributed to a breakaway IRA faction disillusioned with the entire peace process. At the end of September 1996 an EOD team defused a 250 lb. bomb in a car abandoned in the centre of Belfast. This attack was claimed by a new body called the Continuity IRA, which announced it was opposed to the ceasefire strategy.

The mainstream IRA struck a serious blow at the Army in Northern Ireland when two vehicle bombs exploded inside Thiepval Barracks on 7 October causing over thirty casualties, many of them people fleeing the first explosion who were caught by the effect of the second. Among them was forty-three-year-old Warrant Officer James Bradwell, who was taken to the medical centre after being critically hurt in the first blast. He sustained further injuries when the second vehicle exploded and died two days later.

On 21 November, as internal Republican differences mounted, the Continuity IRA claimed responsibility for a 600 lb. car bomb defused by an ATO outside RUC Strand Road, Londonderry. A week later another EOD success prevented Drumadd Barracks, Armagh being devastated by a 1,000 lb. trailer bomb. At the end of the year the Irish police seized several significant batches of explosives and mortars and a number of attacks on border posts were aborted. The capture of incendiary devices in a sophisticated hide-out in a house in west Belfast foiled attacks on shops. After the comparative peace of 1995, the political deadlock was reflected in the fact that bombings increased to 125 in 1996 and the number of call-outs answered by 321 EOD also more than doubled, from 263 to 553, although these resulted in successful defusings and a haul of over two tons of explosive. During a pre-Christmas visit to Belfast, John Major said that Britain would not yield to the IRA even if the campaign lasted another fifty years.

Two bombs intended for security-force patrols were made safe at Belfast Castle over the New Year period. The terrorists said they had been abandoned because of security activity in the area. In January 1997, a 250 lb. bomb was neutralised at Cullyhanna and another of 1,000 lb. was defused near Strabane. However, the run of success ended tragically on 12 February when Lance-Bombardier Stephen Restorick, aged twenty-three, was shot dead by a sniper while conducting a vehicle check at Bessbrook. Soon afterwards, the IRA responded to the general election with a series of disruption operations, giving bomb warnings which halted the running of the Grand National and brought repeated chaos to railways, motorways and airports in Britain during the campaign. On 29 March an attack on the Army base at Ballykinler was foiled when a 1,000 lb. bomb was discovered and neutralised.

As expected, Tony Blair's new Labour party won the election in May. Underlining the priority he would give to settling the Northern Ireland problem, Blair's first trip outside London was to Belfast, where he set in motion efforts to restore the IRA ceasefire. The cold-blooded murder of two police officers on the street in Lurgan seemed set to derail them, but Blair persisted and on 20 July 1997 the ceasefire was restored, clearing the way for negotiations to begin.

Meanwhile there was growing evidence that while the IRA had not formally split, a significant dissident faction with the necessary know-how and access to weapons and explosives was intent on maintaining violence. They operated under two names – the Continuity IRA and the Real IRA. In July they were prevented from blowing up a hotel in County Fermanagh when an EOD team neutralised a 1,000 lb. device and a month later their efforts were frustrated again when the Garda Siochana uncovered a bomb factory and captured explosives. At Markethill in September they caused major damage with a 350 lb. van bomb aimed at the police station. A 500 lb. vehicle bomb was defused in Banbridge early in January but within days a 300 lb. device exploded at a nightclub in Enniskillen. On 20 February, a 500 lb. car bomb outside the police station at Moira, County Down caused widespread damage to houses and shops and three days later a 350 lb. bomb went off in the centre of Portadown. A 600 lb. bomb bound for Armagh was captured by the Garda on 3 March but a week later the terrorists changed tack and launched a mortar attack on the police station in the city. It failed to cause serious harm but the fact that the weapon was a previously unused version of the mortar, designated the Mark 17, indicated that the breakaway terrorists had inherited at least some of the IRA's capacity.

By this point the protracted political negotiations at Stormont, chaired by former US senator George Mitchell, had made far more progress than anyone had dreamed of and on Good Friday 1998 the Belfast Agreement was concluded between the British and Irish governments and local politicians, whose ranks included representatives of both Republican and Loyalist terrorist groupings. The terms of the deal transformed the political status of Northern Ireland more fundamentally than at any time since Partition with a range of provisions to meet the conflicting needs of the various parties. 'There was gain and pain for everyone,' one politician said.

Despite the resumption of the IRA ceasefire, decommissioning remained a massive sticking point. Republicans would not budge on the issue, while Unionists said there could be no place for Sinn Fein in the democratic process or institutions of government while they were backed by an armed force. When sustained pressure from all sides did force the IRA into a number of symbolic acts of decommissioning, it was always too little and too late for their critics and on all sides the issue significantly corroded faith in the Belfast Agreement, which had originally been endorsed by a large majority in simultaneous referenda on both sides of the border. Opposition to the Agreement grew to the point where the anti-Agreement Democratic Unionists, led by Ian Paisley, emerged as the majority voice after elections in November 2003.

The dissident Republicans were among the minority opposed to the deal and their intermittent attacks continued. A 600 lb. car bomb was defused in Lisburn, the police station at Belleek was mortared, and Armagh police station was again saved when an ATO neutralised a 750 lb. vehicle bomb. On 15 May yet another new mortar, the Mark 18, was unveiled in an attack on the border police station at Rosslea. A 200 lb. bomb planted at Newtownhamilton on 20 June injured five people and caused widespread damage. On 23 June, there was a particularly worrying development when a huge explosion at Drumintee, near Newry, was initiated by cellular phone. Although the technique had already been used by other terrorists, such as the Spanish group ETA, this was its first use by Republicans and the incident set off a massive reappraisal of electronic countermeasures capability. An attempt to mortar Newry police station on 21 July failed but bombers succeeded in detonating a 500 lb. car bomb in the centre of Banbridge on 1 August. It was a harbinger of much worse.

Two weeks later, on the afternoon of Saturday 15 August, a newsroom assistant at Ulster Television in Belfast received a telephone warning that a bomb had been planted in the Court House in Omagh. She immediately alerted the police and they quickly began clearing people away from the location the caller had stated. The car containing the 300 lb. bomb was, however, at the opposite end of the street and it went off without further warning in the midst of the fleeing crowd, killing twenty-nine people and two unborn babies and maiming or injuring another 360 victims. It was the largest death toll in a single incident in Northern Ireland throughout the entire Troubles and caused universal horror and condemnation from all sides, not least from Republican leaders such as Adams and McGuinness, who criticised it in unprecedented terms. Responsibility was admitted by the Real IRA, who also declared an end to their military operations.

The shock effect of the Omagh bombing reminded people of the violent nightmare they thought was over and angered hardline Loyalists, whose militancy had been on the rise for some time. Over the years Loyalist militants had played every bit as bloody a role in the conflict as Republicans, but the security forces had rarely been their primary target. Their main activity was sectarian attacks on Catholics with guns, knives and even meat cleavers. Their hatred was often given such distasteful expression as jeering at Catholics attending church services. On one notorious occasion, Loyalist activists even defecated on the altar of a Catholic church. 'ATD' ('Any Taig (Catholic) will do'), the slogan scrawled on walls in Loyalist heartlands, was sufficient proof of their unwillingness to distinguish between ordinary Catholics and Republican activists. The use of explosives was very much subsidiary to their customary reliance on doorstep assassinations or 'spray jobs'. However, Colin Whitworth's injury in 1993, the first serious harm inflicted on an ATO by Loyalists, highlighted the expansion in their explosives capability over the previous eighteen months. Army figures showed that the proportion of bombings carried out by Loyalists had more than doubled from eighteen to forty per cent in the period and their devices were becoming increasingly effective and more difficult to neutralise, not least, as the Whitworth incident demonstrated, because of their imperfections.

Loyalists had of course started the decades of bombing back in 1969 when they attacked Belfast's electricity and water systems in order to bring down Terence O'Neill. For years afterwards, however, the terms 'Prot job' or 'Loyalist bomb' had been synonymous with failure. Although they periodically carried out strikes on targets associated with Catholics, the most successful were simple arson attacks. From time to time they employed basic pipe bombs packed with gunpowder from fireworks, but these usually made more noise than they caused damage. Similarly, use was made of home-made explosive packed into gas cylinders and other containers but stories abounded of fuses going out before the mix ignited or of main charges failing to function. But one incident at North Queen Street, Belfast on 4 December 1971, demonstrated that these activities were not mere comic opera. That Saturday night, when a bomb was thrown into McGurk's Bar, sixteen people died including the owner's wife and daughter, the worst casualty toll attributable to a single Loyalist attack. The most ambitious and deadly bombing operation attributed to Loyalists was in Dublin and Monaghan on 17 May 1974, during the Ulster Workers' Council strike, with three car bombs in quick succession in Dublin during the evening rush hour and then another in Monaghan. All the vehicles had Northern Ireland registration plates and some had been stolen from Loyalist areas. Altogether thirty-three people died in the explosions and well over 150 were injured. The Loyalists' known lack of bombing expertise fuelled allegations, which still persist, that members of the security forces in Northern Ireland assisted in mounting the attacks, but no conclusive evidence has come to light.

Although the security forces were rarely the target of Loyalist terrorism, some became victims because of the indiscriminate nature of their bombs. One such was RUC Reserve Constable Mildred Harrison, who died on 16 March 1975 when a pipe bomb exploded on the window sill of a public house in Bangor. She was the first female police casualty of terrorism. Thereafter, the main Loyalist terror groups occasionally made use of commercial gelignite, such as Gelamex, obtained from sympathisers in Scotland. In 1976 an ATO found 12 lb. of it when he dismantled a device at a farmhouse in Aughnacloy. The Loyalists had their share of 'own goals', and attacks across the border were regularly frustrated when the bomb-layers were intercepted in transit or their devices discovered.

From 1985 onwards, when efforts to control contentious Orange parades began, street disorder escalated and the use of crude pipe bombs against the security forces resumed. By the mid-1990s the basic design consisted of readily available plumbing components packed with low explosive. When it detonated, the aluminium, copper, steel or cast-iron pipe provided a deadly shrapnel effect. As well as throwing these devices, with their fuses lit, at security forces in public-order situations, Loyalists began to use them with timers as under-car victim-operated devices. In September 1993 these were planted at the homes of several SDLP councillors in Belfast to express distaste for the peace talks which the party leader, John Hume, was conducting with the IRA. A month later, one was planted at the Sinn Fein office on the Falls Road. On 4 January 1994 two Irish Army bomb-disposal officers were injured in a postal sorting office when one of two Loyalist parcel bombs sent to Sinn Fein in Dublin partially functioned.

Francis Brown, a thirty-eight-year-old Catholic haulier, died on 11 March in a bomb attack that was unusually sophisticated for Loyalists. At 7.30 a.m. when he came out of his home to check his brother's lorry for oil and water he found a concrete breeze block against the front wheel of the vehicle. When he moved it, a 2 lb. bomb in the hollowed-out interior went off. Soon afterwards similar attacks set light to cars outside the homes of SDLP activists and on 23 March two workmen were the victims of a bomb which exploded on the window sill of a ground-floor room at Belfast City Hall normally occupied by Sinn Fein councillors. In September 1994, the main Sinn Fein office was damaged by a Loyalist car bomb which caused damage to surrounding property more characteristic of an IRA attack. A few days later only the detonator of a device planted on the Belfast–Dublin train exploded, preventing a far more serious incident. These incidents demonstrated major advances in Loyalist bomb-making capacity but because of technical limitations and a scarcity of high explosive the consequences were not as lethal as they could have been. Nevertheless, use was now being made of passive infra-red sensors to set off victim-operated devices, and an electronic pager and adapted parts from a remote-control car were used in two ventures into radio-controlled detonation. Loyalists had also learned to use mercury-tilt switches and even 'party poppers' to set off booby-traps. Efforts to emulate the damage caused by IRA vehicle-borne IEDs met with little success, however, when they could not perfect the technique of igniting inflammable gas vented from cylinders into a sealed car or van.

On 13 October, not long after the IRA, Loyalists too announced a

ceasefire but, as on the Republican side, violence continued intermittently. After the dispute over the 1994 Drumcree church parade, the
July period every year thereafter was marked by associated violence and
there were fatalities in a number of incidents involving explosives.
During the Saturday afternoon of 5 September 1997 a Loyalist crowd,
which at one point numbered 700, staged a demonstration in Portadown
town centre. Carrying placards proclaiming 'No Taigs Here', they jostled
and shouted abuse at Catholics. Shortly before 5 p.m. a Catholic-owned
business was gutted in a petrol-bomb attack and others were damaged by
thugs openly carrying baseball bats, chains and crowbars. The RUC
became engaged in a series of running battles as they tried to calm the
situation. During a confrontation at Corcrain Road, from the cover of the
protesters a small section of metal pipe packed with explosives,
ammunition and shotgun pellets was hurled towards a line of police
officers. It landed close to the feet of Constable Frank O'Reilly, who took
the full force of the blast. Some of the crowd cheered as the thirty-year-
old officer was taken to Craigavon Hospital, where it was discovered that
he had lost an eye and had shrapnel embedded in his skull. He was rushed
to the Royal Victoria Hospital in Belfast for specialist surgery but it was
unsuccessful and he died soon afterwards.

Against this uneasy background, Jim McDonald, the Independent
Assessor of Military Complaints, summed up the security forces'
dilemma in his 2000 annual report: 'To walk the tightrope of peace with
eyes on the future but being aware of the high level of threat still present
from terrorism is a difficult concept to get across to a population which,
on the whole, desires perfect peace.' The 1998 Omagh bombing had not
had the long-term chastening effect that might have been hoped for. EOD
taskings rose steadily from their 1995 low point to 553 in 1996 and 849 a
year later, with 767 in 1998 and 581 in 1999. Over the same period the
number of explosions increased from twenty-five in 1996 to ninety-three
a year later and 243 in 1998, with a fall again to 100 in 1999. Much of the
EOD workload that year was concentrated in the traditionally tense
month of July when one operator carried out fifty tasks in twelve days.

Dissident Republicans continued to wage war on security forces in both
Northern Ireland and Britain. In February 2000 industrial gas tanks
packed with explosives were placed against the gable end of an accommodation block inside the Army barracks at Ballykelly. If the device had
fully functioned, the thirty soldiers sleeping in the block would have
perished. The following September there was another near tragedy when
an 80 lb. device concealed at the Magilligan training centre only partially

exploded, injuring one soldier. A secondary device nearby was dismantled by an ATO. In November an RUC officer suffered serious abdominal injuries and the loss of a leg, finger and thumb when he moved a booby-trapped traffic cone outside the police station at Castlewellan. There were also significant successes. In March police intercepted a car with a 500 lb. bomb on board as it was being driven towards Belfast; in October a similar device in a horsebox was captured in the city, and in November a vehicle loaded with a 'barrack-buster' was halted close to the Fermanagh border. Not long before, Irish police had seized a vehicle carrying a 500 lb. bomb destined for Northern Ireland after a high-speed chase.

There was a similar pattern of attacks over the next couple of years, the vast majority either malfunctioning or disarmed through EOD intervention. There were two casualties. David Caldwell was killed in Londonderry in August 2002 in the incident attended by Shirley Lyle, and in February that year a forty-nine-year-old security guard at the Magilligan Army base lost both his arms and partial vision and suffered severe abdominal injuries when a booby-trapped military water bottle exploded by the perimeter fence.

In the early 1990s, for the first time Loyalists murdered or maimed more people than their Republican counterparts. Their activities were still heavily motivated by sectarian considerations, but rivals in their criminal interests, especially drugs and racketeering operations, increasingly came into their firing line. From an EOD perspective, however, the threat was on a significantly lower scale with the greatest danger arising from public-order clashes. In 2001, for instance, there were 236 incidents involving 309 pipe bombs, most attributable to Loyalists. A seventeen-year-old bomber died when a device exploded in his hand during sectarian rioting in north Belfast, and an eighteen-year-old Royal Welch Fusilier was seriously injured when Loyalists threw a pipe bomb during disturbances associated with disputed access for Catholic children to the Holy Cross School at Ardoyne. Mass murder was averted in August, however, when a Loyalist device in a car abandoned without warning among the crowds at the Auld Lammas Fair in Ballycastle failed to detonate. A tiny fragment of paint had prevented the timer from functioning.

After the dramatic reduction in the number of EOD taskings since 1995, call-outs had risen again to 704 in 2004. Nevertheless, the marked reduction in violence and the resulting decrease in the need to provide support for the police enabled the Army to make steady progress in returning to the pre-Troubles garrison of about 5,000 personnel accommodated in no more than twenty locations. Step by cautious step an open-border policy was implemented with the 291 recognised crossing points being progressively freed of checkpoints or obstructions. Permanent vehicle checkpoints and border patrol bases were then closed and demolished. Among the military landmarks removed were several which had figured repeatedly in the battle for supremacy between the bombers and the EOD experts: the Borucki sangar at Crossmaglen, demolished on 31 July 2001; the Cloghogue observation base south of Newry, closed and demolished in September 2001; the Magherafelt base, closed on 24 October 2001; the Glasdrumman observation tower, demolished in January 2002; the observation towers on Cloghogue Mountain and Tievecrom, removed in May 2003; and Ebrington Barracks, Londonderry, closed in December 2003 after 162 years as a military base. Since 1994 the Army has closed or demolished forty-eight of the 105 bases and installations it occupied at the time. Over the same period, the number of troops has been steadily reduced.

By the time of its 1994 ceasefire, in pursuit of its aim to drive the British Army out of Northern Ireland and unite the country, the IRA had succeeded in exploding 16,500 bombs and well over 2,000 incendiaries. The bombs ranged in size from a couple of ounces to some 8,000 lb. of commercial, military or home-made explosive, set off by seventeen marks of timer-power unit and commercial and improvised detonators and igniters traced back to manufacturers and suppliers in Britain, the United States and several other countries. The IRA had developed and deployed fifteen marks of hand grenade, sixteen versions of mortars and other deadly bombards, nail bombs, coffee-jar bombs, under-car booby-traps and anti-armour and home-made explosive projectiles. Fires caused by cassette, blast and chemical incendiaries had also caused massive damage to life and property. Everyday items such as books, cigarette packets, gas cylinders, video-recorder timers, parking-meter reminders, plumbing components, bell-pushes, clothes pegs, mousetraps, clocks and ball bearings had all been adapted or incorporated into IEDs. The human cost of this conflict was vast, with some 3,700 lives lost in Northern Ireland, the Irish Republic, the British mainland and elsewhere, including several European countries. Over the years a total of £659 million has been paid out to compensate for criminal injuries and £980 million for damage to property. It has been calculated by the Northern Ireland Affairs Committee of the House of Commons that for every £1 invested in their campaigns by terrorists on both sides, it cost the government £130 to counter and repair the damage. Thus the cost of terrorism to the public purse in 1993 alone was £2 billion.

Despite the demonstrable futility of the violence over three decades, there is still a blinkered minority who want to influence the affairs of Northern Ireland by violence. Three large stores were damaged by dissident Republican firebombers who carried out fifteen attacks over the Christmas period in 2004. Some of them are sincerely motivated by concepts of Republican or Loyalist patriotism but, as a consequence of the events of the last thirty years, the frontiers between terrorism and criminality have been blurred and many more are now simply in it for the money, finding the cloak of jingoism a convenient cover for their corruption. After the headquarters of a Belfast bank was relieved of £26,500,000 in a complex robbery a few days before Christmas 2004, the finger of suspicion was immediately pointed at the IRA.

While the rest of the British Army scales down its aid to the civil power, for 321 EOD Squadron there is no immediate prospect of an end to their commitment in Northern Ireland. The prognosis is that local political institutions at Stormont will be restored in time, but because of the inevitable fragility of the peace, EOD resources will have to be available as a deterrent and a precaution for a long time to come. So six teams remain in post with another two rear-based in Britain and ready to fly back at short notice. In the longer term the Army wants its peacetime garrison in Northern Ireland to blend into the background. Already, as part of that approach, under Operation Wedgwood the fleet of armoured EOD Tactica vehicles has been replaced by the white-painted, customised Leyland DAF lorries used by bomb-disposal teams elsewhere in the UK. 'The lorries, known as "Wedgies", are our contribution to normality,' says one ATO.

By 1984, 646 ATOs and ATs had served in Northern Ireland with 321. Twenty years later the total number was well over 1,000. The roll of honour to date numbers twenty and the latest record of gallantry is headed by two George Crosses, thirty-six George Medals, seventy-five Queen's Gallantry Medals, 117 mentions in dispatches, eighteen Queen's Commendations for Brave Conduct, eighteen OBEs, thirty-four MBEs, three British Empire Medals, one Military Service Medal, eleven Queen's Commendations for Valuable Service and nineteen GOC's commendations. In addition twenty-one officers were awarded either the MBE or BEM for gallantry before these categories were abolished in 1974.

The total overall number of taskings dealt with by 321 EOD has now reached 54,000, but the trend is firmly downwards. Despite the continued activities of dissident Republicans and Loyalist hardliners, many of the recent taskings have been precautionary, to deal with suspicious objects or postal packets. In July 2004 one call-out was of a type more often experienced in mainland Britain, when a teenager found a grenade on the beach at Warrenpoint and brought it home. An ATO was called, found it to be of Second World War vintage and took it away for disposal.

The expertise and courage of the men and women engaged in EOD work is being refocused as their role in Northern Ireland declines. The emerging threat, far more daunting than anything they have faced before, is from international suicidal terrorists using 'dirty' bombs – nuclear, biological or chemical. As new military doctrines of homeland security and national resilience are being drafted in the aftermath of the Cold War, the unprecedented attacks in the United States on 11 September 2001 and the campaign in Iraq, the frontiers of British Army's EOD task are rapidly expanding well beyond Northern Ireland.

Postscript

Tony Blair, the British prime minister, paid a personal tribute to the 'matchless bravery and dedication' of the ATOs of 321 EOD Squadron when he received a small delegation from the unit in the Cabinet Room at 10 Downing Street, London on the afternoon of 12 May 2005.

Escorted by Lieutenant General Sir Alistair Irwin KCB CBE, General Officer Commanding Northern Ireland 2000–3, who had just recently retired from the Army, the 321 team was led by Lieutenant-Colonel Mark Wickham, the Chief Ammunition Technical Officer, Major Gino Harris, the newly appointed Officer Commanding 321 Squadron, and Captain Colin Whitworth, who had just learned that after a recent tour as an EOD officer in Iraq his expertise and bravery were to be honoured by the US Army with the award of a Bronze Star. The fourth member of the party was Warrant Officer Two Marcus Dewstowe, who was clad in the heavy protective suit used during clearance operations. Also present were Mike and Sean Walsh, whose brother, Martin, was one of the twenty ATOs who had been murdered during the years of the Northern Ireland campaign.

As the prime minister, and his wife Cherie, questioned their guests closely for more than forty minutes, much longer than the time scheduled for the visit, the members of the team described their work and its unique challenges. Cherie Blair closely examined the heavy suit while the Walsh brothers spoke about the effect on families like their own and the impact of a death or injury. Directly opposite the prime minister, Colin Whitworth's prosthetic hand resting on the blotter pad normally used by a government minister further emphasised the great human cost exacted by ruthless terrorism.

Before they left the historic room from which British forces have been assigned to wars and other operations for generations, one of the prime minister's aides produced a letter of commendation which Blair signed and presented to Mark Wickham. It read:

Northern Ireland has made real progress towards a better and more peaceful future. But we should not forget the gallantry and dedication of the British Army Ammunition Technical Officers and their teams who have worked tirelessly for 35 years in service of the whole community in Northern Ireland. For more than three decades, an Explosive Ordnance Disposal team of 321 EOD Squadron, Royal Logistic Corps was called out on average every six hours to neutralise and make safe a suspect device in Northern Ireland. The men and women who answered each of those 54,000 calls did not ask who planted the bomb or mortar, or why. They simply – and deliberately – put themselves in harm's way to save lives and property. This selfless unflinching courage has not been without cost. Twenty members of the squadron have died tragically in the course of their work in Northern Ireland, their lives cut short by the bombs and improvised devices of faceless and brutal terrorists. Many others have been injured. More than 50 tons of explosive were used by terrorists in some 19,000 devices across Northern Ireland. Many of these were made safe by the bomb disposal operators. The death toll and devastation would undoubtedly have been much worse without the dedication and sacrifice of these courageous men and women. Such courage and commitment have earned members of 321 EOD Squadron RLC more honours and awards for bravery than any other Army unit in peacetime. The 'long walk' of the operator from the safety cordon to the device itself is an enduring image for us all, but the operator depends on the professionalism of the whole squadron at each and every incident. I pay heartfelt tribute to all personnel of 321 EOD Squadron RLC for their matchless bravery and dedication, especially those who so tragically died saving the lives of others. And I applaud the Squadron as it continues to carry out its dangerous task.

In the months after the visit, despite the consolidating peace process, the EOD teams in Northern Ireland continued to face regular call-outs to bomb alerts, but in line with the overall reduction in violence flowing from the 1994 terrorist ceasefires, the jobs were not as frequent or as demanding as those so regularly encountered at the height of the conflict. One month the teams responded to fewer than thirty alerts and most months the total was well under fifty. The terrible casualty toll from terrorism also appeared to be petering out for the police attributed only five of the twenty-six murders in Northern Ireland in 2005 to the security situation. There were also significantly fewer live or viable improvised explosive devices to be dealt with as bombings dropped from seventy-one to forty-eight in 2004–5, but there was an increase in the use of incendiary devices from three to twenty-nine. A major reduction in the amount of explosive material captured, from 92 kgs. to 26.5 kg., further reflected the more peaceful atmosphere that was attracting record numbers of tourists and visitors to Northern Ireland. Altogether the EOD teams answered 495 call-outs during 2005, the devices mostly planted by hardline and dissident elements of the Republican movement opposed to what they regarded as the 'surrender' of the peace process without the prospect of British withdrawal or the border being removed well into the foreseeable future. The potentially most serious attacks failed because the devices malfunctioned or the Operators managed to neutralise them. But there were still occasions when major casualties were only narrowly averted. On 2 May 2005, a live remote control device was discovered and defused at the 12-mile point on the route of the Belfast marathon. Security experts concluded that it was targeted at Hugh Orde, the chief constable, who was among the runners, but if it had been detonated anyone in its indiscriminate path would have been maimed or killed.

Even after 28 July 2005, when the IRA leadership at last moved from ceasefire posture and announced that it had formally ordered an end to the armed campaign and instructed its members to dump arms, a diehard element continued to pose a real threat. Over the next nine months there were further incidents where serious loss of life or limb was again only prevented by the action of an ATO or the malfunctioning of a device. An elaborately mounted attack on the City Hotel in Armagh on 11 January 2006 failed when an ATO carried out controlled explosions on a stolen car abandoned outside the building and rendered safe a gas cylinders device inside it. A month later in Belfast, a viable mortar was made safe after being found in a vehicle abandoned alongside the Antrim Road police base in the north of the city. The customary forensic and technical examinations after these incidents revealed worrying evidence that a new generation of bomb makers was being trained and experimenting to develop ever more lethal improvised explosive devices.

Over the same period, Loyalist terrorist explosive capacity remained crude but still potentially lethal with various versions of the pipe bomb being used for sectarian attacks. More notably, such bombs were used during inter-factional feuding which was less concerned with the patriotism in which the organisations insisted they were cloaked, and more to do with the defence of racketeering and criminal empires, including drug trafficking. There were instances when families asleep in their homes only avoided serious injury because the devices were discovered or failed to fully detonate. Loyalist violence, hitherto sectarian or internecine, assumed a cynical new twist with a growing number of violent attacks on people from ethnic minority communities who had settled in Northern Ireland in ever increasing numbers over recent years. Racial incidents, as the police categorised them, numbered 813 in 2004–5, a major escalation from the 226 recorded in 2002–3, and ATOs were called to deal with the blast and pipe bombs frequently used in such attacks.

This residual security threat, albeit at considerably reduced levels by the brutal standards of Northern Ireland, helped compound the lingering political distrust between the elected representatives which slowed to a crawling pace the political negotiations intended to revitalise and implement the 1998 Belfast Agreement. Nevertheless, the British government and the chief constable of the Police Service of Northern Ireland judged that it was prudent to go on dismantling the apparatus of conflict and continue to run down the levels of military aid to the civil power to pre-1969 levels.

Over the eleven-year period from the 1994 ceasefires until the IRA's 'dump arms' order, the Army force level had been reduced progressively from 14,000 to just over 10,000. Over the same period, sixty-six of the Army's 106 operational locations, which included hilltop observation posts along the South Armagh border, patrol bases and co-located deployments with the police, had been abandoned and closed down. A further stage of this 'normalisation' programme, published on 1 August 2005, pledged that by August 2007 Operation Banner – the military codename for the long-running Northern Ireland campaign – would have come to an end, and the Army would be off the streets and in peacetime mode with a garrison of up to 5,000 soldiers occupying no more than fourteen bases. Their primary role would be to train for the other early twenty-first-century global defence roles to which the Army had been committed. Thereafter, the only support routinely available to the police would be troops for public order duties, but only in extreme situations; a limited amount of helicopter hours to back up major operations; and the continued services of 321 EOD, who would remain in Northern Ireland in strength and readiness indefinitely to provide their special expertise to the police and the community.

With EOD Branch at Headquarters Northern Ireland in Lisburn among the detachments earmarked for withdrawal or shutdown, Lieutenant Colonel David Ockleton arrived in the summer of 2005 in the knowledge that his would be the last name engraved in gold paint on the roll of CATOs which dated back to the beginning of the conflict and Paul

Crosby's appointment in late 1971. Unlike his predecessors, whose operational priority had been to hone the cutting edge of the Improvised Explosive Device Disposal task, his primary role was to maintain the edge but reconfigure future capability, bedding down important changes to the way 321 Squadron was organised and would operate in tandem with the Police Service of Northern Ireland.

Although its members regularly interchanged with the other Squadrons of 11 EOD Regiment, the Army's specialist unit responsible for counter-terrorist bomb disposal and the safety of military ammunition and explosives worldwide, 321 EOD had traditionally operated at arms-length from it. No more. From 2007, it was to come under direct regimental control and would be tasked from the Joint Services EOD Operations Centre at Didcot in Oxfordshire. The Northern Ireland police, like their counterparts elsewhere in the UK, would request assistance from there when it was required. Up to 100 EOD personnel – teams and their back-up – would remain dispersed in Northern Ireland serving rotating two-year tours, with married soldiers being accompanied by their families.

321 EOD would still be fully equipped to deal with the likely requirements of countering terrorist devices in Northern Ireland. In 2006, for instance, they took delivery of six of the new Balter air-portable, all-terrain vehicles designed to convey a fully equipped EOD team across country at speeds of up to 30 mph. They were also issued with the latest model of EOD suit, a vast improvement on earlier versions because the protective layers of Kevlar had been given flexibility without losing any of their protective power. As a result, the Operator could easily put on the suit without the assistance of a team member and, thanks to a new overlapping elbow section, enjoy greater freedom of movement while working at a device. It was therefore much easier to crouch down to place equipment. 'It's so good, I can even hold and drink a cup of coffee without taking it off,' one Operator reported. For the first time, NBC suits and other specially developed equipment were issued to the Northern Ireland teams: for henceforth they were also to take on the additional responsibility of dealing with Chemical, Biological, Radiological or Nuclear weapons, a task already allocated to the mainland based EOD teams as ever more ominous warnings of extremist plans to use 'dirty devices' continued to dominate counter-terrorist planning not only in Britain but internationally.

11 EOD Regiment is, in fact, at the international forefront of this work which is directed from its Didcot headquarters. David Ockleton believes that the bomb disposal trade failed sufficiently to absorb the lessons of

the EOD task in Hong Kong and Cyprus and apply them to Northern Ireland when the trouble there first flared up. 'We are not making that mistake again. The lessons of the Northern Ireland campaign, hard-learned at great cost, have been applied so that we can maintain our capability and expertise in dealing expeditiously with any further problems there. They are also being built on and applied to the assessment we make of the threats worldwide and what additional expertise we have to develop to counter them successfully and maintain our world-leading role in EOD,' he says.

As a result, Didcot has become the operational nerve centre of a national and international shield against the most dangerous excesses of indiscriminate terrorism, and the 500-strong regiment is equipped to carry out its mission throughout Britain, at British Forces bases in Germany, and on all deployed and expeditionary operations worldwide.

As 321 EOD is deployed in Northern Ireland, EOD cover for Scotland, North Wales and the north of England is provided by 521 EOD Squadron which has detachments based at Edinburgh, Catterick and Chester. 621 Squadron, with teams based at Shorncliffe, Colchester, Aldershot and Northolt protects the south-east of England and East Anglia, while south-west and central England and South Wales are the responsibility of 721 Squadron which deploys teams from Nottingham, Ashchurch and Tidworth. The teams have at their disposal a fleet of Vauxhall Omega Command Vehicles, whose police-trained drivers can convey Operators and Royal Signals 'Bleeps' to an incident scene at speeds of up to 150 mph. The Metropolitan Police are the only force to maintain their own bomb disposal capability but 621 EOD Squadron is geared to providing back-up in the city when necessary, and there is a cadre of Bleeps who are specially trained to navigate the London traffic on Honda motorcycles to support them. There are further highly trained and versatile teams at Didcot and in Germany, who can be deployed at short notice anywhere in the world that a requirement develops. The lessons of terrorism worldwide have been analysed and applied to ensure that British interests can be effectively protected anywhere in the world. The internationally renowned Felix Centre at Kineton, where these officers and teams are trained, remains another important centre for ensuring the effectiveness of the bomb disposal shield.

This expertise and machinery, extensively strengthened after the 9/11 New York and Washington attacks in 2001, was given its first real test on 7 July 2005 when four suicide bombers detonated devices on London's public transport system, causing fifty-four deaths and injuring hundreds of passengers and passers-by, many of them very seriously. EOD teams were rushed into London to support the police units, and others played a critical part in the follow-up investigation over succeeding days as the steps of the bombers were retraced to Luton and a series of houses and flats in West Yorkshire, where explosive material and bomb-making equipment was rendered safe. The EOD teams were called into action again on 21 July when another series of attacks was attempted but this time the would-be bombers were foiled and police made several arrests after hot pursuit operations throughout London.

However, as a result of these incidents, which surpassed even the worst toll of death and destruction ever inflicted on the British mainland by IRA terrorists, the security services believe similar incidents in the future are inevitable. In consequence, the entire national emergency response facility, including the EOD teams, remains almost constantly on a high level of alert.

Beyond Britain, other members of the EOD family, deployed from Didcot, continue on front-line active service with the Army in the battlegrounds of Afghanistan and Iraq. The EOD task there is of compelling magnitude with suicide bombers often claiming between fifty and 200 lives a day, despite the most determined efforts of US Army EOD teams equipped with state-of-the-art, high technology equipment. The combat troops are also in great danger from remotely detonated roadside bombs as they move about the country, and such ambushes have claimed many US and British military lives and limbs. The Pentagon calculates that two-thirds of the 17,000 soldiers wounded in Operation Iraqi Freedom have been the victims of improvised explosive devices. Likewise, of the more than one hundred British soldiers killed while serving in Iraq, many have perished in incidents where improvised explosive devices have been targeted against them.

British EOD experts, trained at the Felix Centre and operationally proved in Northern Ireland, have been drafted in to assist and advise the US forces in developing more effective patrolling and detection techniques against the bombs. The devices are large but crudely constructed by IRA standards, often consisting of explosive packed into vintage artillery shells or bomb cases, originally designed to be dropped from aircraft, remotely detonated from afar. It has inevitably proved to be a perilous mission for the British teams. On 31 March 2003, Staff Sergeant Chris Muir, aged thirty-two, was killed during an explosive ordnance disposal operation in southern Iraq. Based at the Army School of Ammunition, Kineton, where he was an instructor, Staff Sergeant Muir had recently been selected for promotion to Warrant Officer. He is survived by his son, Ben, and his wife, Gillian, who said:

> Chris was the sort of person that could light up a room just by being in it. He had a fantastic sense of humour and always tried to see the funny side, no matter what the situation. I know that Chris was very proud to wear the badge of an Ammunition Technician, and I take small comfort from the knowledge that he died doing the job that he loved. He has left me and our families with the most fantastic of memories, the greatest one being our son, Ben, who can grow up knowing that his father was a good, honest, hardworking soldier, who died trying to do the right thing.

Since then three more 11 EOD soldiers have sustained serious injuries in similar incidents in Iraq and paid a heavy physical price. In 2005, an EOD team driver and the 'Bleep' each lost their two legs when a roadside bomb exploded as they were moving north towards the outskirts of Baghdad with a battle group led by the Black Watch. Later Captain Pete Norton, forty-three, lost an arm and a leg when a terrorist device exploded close to where he was working in Baghdad in July 2005.

Their plight inspired their closest colleagues to engage in an almighty surge of sympathetic generosity to raise funds for their long-term rehabilitation. At 321 headquarters in Lisburn, where the pain of the casualties was most understood, an auction of football and Northern Ireland campaign memorabilia raised an astonishing £18,000. Six months later, in December, 156 Army colleagues from all over Britain took part in a 'longest walk' exercise at Kineton. Clad in the full 40 kg. EOD suit, pairs of participants walked as many laps as possible within an hour around an internal circuit, passing a baton to those next in line as they completed their stint. In all the walkers covered an extraordinary 201 miles over twenty-six hours and raised a hefty £26,500 for the cause. Twenty took part in a similar 'longest walk' out in Iraq where another generous sum resulted. Among the most assiduous fund raisers have been the Walsh brothers, whose own outstanding generosity has helped swell the rehabilitation fund to almost £60,000. At the height of the bidding at the Lisburn function one senior man who had just returned unscathed from a tour in Iraq oberved that: 'Despite all our training and skills, we live with the constant fact that what happened to Pete and the others could as easily have happened to any one of us whether in Northern Ireland, Afghanistan, Iraq or a back street in Leeds. There but for the grace of God,' he said, as he shrugged and turned away.

Bibliography

Barzilay, David, *The British Army in Ulster*, volumes 1–4 (Century Services Ltd, Belfast, 1973–81)

Birchall, Peter, *The Longest Walk* (Arms and Armour Press, London, 1997)

Gurney, Peter, *Braver Men Walk Away* (Harper Collins, London, 1993)

Macdonald, P. G., *Stopping the Clock* (Robert Hale Ltd, London, 1977)

Patrick, Lieutenant-Colonel Derrick, *Fetch Felix* (Hamish Hamilton, London, 1981)

Phelps, Major-General L. T. H., *A History of the Royal Army Ordnance Corps 1945–1982* (Trustees of the RAOC, 1991)

Styles, Lieutenant-Colonel George, GC, *Bombs Have No Pity* (William Luscombe Publisher Ltd, London, 1975)

Wakeling, Lieutenant-Colonel E. E., *A Short History of Royal Engineer Bomb Disposal* (B. D. Publishing, Bourne End, Buckinghamshire, 1997)

Index